Stanford Studies in Jewish History and Culture
Edited by David Biale and Sarah Abrevaya Stein

It Could Lead to Dancing

IT COULD
LEAD
TO DANCING

Mixed-Sex Dancing and Jewish Modernity

Sonia Gollance

STANFORD UNIVERSITY PRESS
Stanford, California

STANFORD UNIVERSITY PRESS
Stanford, California

Printed in the United States of America on acid-free, archival-quality paper

Library of Congress Cataloging-in-Publication Data
Names: Gollance, Sonia, author.
Title: It could lead to dancing : mixed-sex dancing and Jewish modernity /
  Sonia Gollance.
Other titles: Stanford studies in Jewish history and culture.
Description: Stanford, California : Stanford University Press, 2021. |
  Series: Stanford studies in Jewish history and culture | Includes
  bibliographical references and index. |
Identifiers: LCCN 2020035318 (print) | LCCN 2020035319 (ebook) |
  ISBN 9781503613492 (cloth) | ISBN 9781503627802 (ebook)
Subjects: LCSH: Dance in literature. | German fiction—History and
  criticism. | Yiddish fiction—History and criticism. | Jewish dance in
  literature. | Jews in literature. | Sex role in literature. | Jews—Social life
  and customs. | Jews—Cultural assimilation—History.
Classification: LCC PN3352.D36 G65 2021 (print) | LCC PN3352.D36
  (ebook) | DDC 809/.933579—dc23
LC record available at https://lccn.loc.gov/2020035318
LC ebook record available at https://lccn.loc.gov/2020035319

Cover photo: Postcard of Yiddish theater actors N. Kompaneyets and A.
Poliakov dancing a tango.

Cover design: Rob Ehle

Typeset by Kevin Barrett Kane in 10.25/15 Caslon

In loving memory of my uncles,
DR. PETER G. SHIFRIN *z"l*
and
RICHARD M. GOLLANCE *z"l*

"Leybke, my love, no good will come of it,

Your stubbornness will make me throw a fit.

You must learn to dance, I swear it to you,

Or else, today you and I are through—

You can be what you are:

A Zionist who spars,

A Bundist, it isn't a crime.

All those "ists" now for some time,

Even the pious ones,

Dance tango and Charleston."

Mordechai Gebirtig, "Kum, Leybke, tantsn"
(Come Leybke, Let's Dance)
Translated by Sonia Gollance[1]

TABLE OF CONTENTS

ACKNOWLEDGMENTS

This is a book about mobility: of dancing bodies, shifting social expectations, and migration from towns to cities and across national borders. It is perhaps fitting that I wrote most of it during a period of my life when I was almost constantly in motion. Large portions of the manuscript were written and revised on intercity trains across Europe, Israel, and the United States. During the five most intensive years of research and writing, I essentially moved internationally an average of more than once a year and was the fortunate recipient of home hospitality from friends, family, and friends-of-friends more often than I can count. This path was not one I could have anticipated, nor one I would recommend lightly. While my trajectory was in many ways determined by the reality of an interdisciplinary academic career in the humanities, I have found that my circuitous journey, my access to international archives, and the many experiences I accumulated along the way have enriched my project immeasurably.

In contrast to my physical whereabouts, my research trajectory has, in certain respects, been very linear. I first became interested in the role of gender in modern Jewish literature as an undergraduate at the University of Chicago. My thinking on this topic was influenced by a seminar taught by Jan Schwarz, whose constructive criticism helped me to become a better writer. The year I spent as a Fulbright Scholar at Heinrich-Heine-Universität Düsseldorf, supervised by Marion Aptroot, had the unintended consequence of making me more aware of nineteenth-century German Jewry. It was during this time that I attended my first dance workshop at Yiddish Summer Weimar and began to consider the actual presence of mixed-sex dancing in Jewish culture. Both Jan and Marion invited me to workshop parts of my manuscript in Lund and Düsseldorf, respectively, in 2018, which helped me to refine ideas that had just started percolating when I was their student.

My *Doktormütter*, Kathryn Hellerstein and Catriona MacLeod, helped me develop my project in its early stages and hone my skills as a writer. Faculty, fellows, graduate students, and staff at the University of Pennsylvania provided support in large and small ways. Colleagues at my fellowships in Jerusalem, Vienna, and New York gave me a rich intellectual community. Eric Jarosinski encouraged me to write about dance in a term paper, and Marion Kant guided me into the field once I did. Louise Hecht suggested the opening to Chapter 4; she and Dieter J. Hecht put several crucial texts on my radar and took me to a Viennese ball when I needed it the most. Laura Levitt and Beth S. Wenger separately asked the question that led to Chapter 2. Marsha Rozenblit and Kerry Wallach weighed in on a slew of research and professional questions. My work would not have been possible without the contributions of Petra Ernst z"l and Jonathan M. Hess z"l, two scholars of middlebrow German Jewish literature whose academic research was equaled by their incredible generosity.

The two years I spent as a Moritz Stern Fellow in Modern Jewish Studies at Lichtenberg-Kolleg—the Göttingen Institute for Advanced Study in the Humanities and Social Sciences at the Georg-August-Universität Göttingen—provided me with the time, space, flexibility, and resources I needed to write my book manuscript. I am grateful to my colleagues and the LiKo staff for creating such a collegial environment. Special thanks to my first book support group—Madeleine Elfenbein, Rachel Koroloff, and Defne Over—and to Bob Moore for his careful reading of my book proposal. I am indebted to Martin van Gelderen, Pavel Khazanov, and Nava Streiter for their participation in an elaborate international heist involving the Vatican Post.

My colleagues at The Ohio State University welcomed me with open arms. I would like to thank the College of Arts and Sciences and the Melton Center for Jewish Studies for book subventions, which were supported by my chairs, Robert C. Holub and Tamar Rudavsky. Paul Reitter read over my entire manuscript and helped me think about the bigger picture. Matthew H. Birkhold, Naomi Brenner, Angela Brintlinger, Elizabeth Dillenburg, Robin Judd, Merrill Kaplan, and Hannah Kosstrin provided various types of assistance with the final manuscript, from photos of sources to advice about intellectual property. I have shared several primary texts from this book with students in my classes, which has pushed me to articulate the continued relevance of these works.

My writing group—Christine Kenison, Annegret Oehme, and Jamele Watkins—commented rigorously on several sections of the book. Elissa Bemporad read my first chapter and backed me in various ways even after the Paula Hyman Mentoring Program ended. Jonathan Skolnik invited me to give a talk at the University of Massachusetts-Amherst and assisted me through the publication process. Joel Berkowitz, Debra Caplan, and Nick Underwood introduced me to the pleasures of academic collaboration and read sections of my manuscript. Karen Eliot, Deborah Holmes, Emily Sigalow, Lisa Silverman, and Katrin Wittler weighed in on drafts of articles that became part of this project. I am grateful to the colleagues who have read portions of this book and offered invaluable feedback: Rachel Adelstein, Ayelet Brinn, Glenn Dynner, Rachel B. Gross, Vardit Lightstone, Claire Taylor Jones, Alex Moshkin, Emily Winerock, and Sarah Zarrow. Jessica Kirzane read my entire manuscript despite unexpectedly running an at-home daycare during a pandemic. Within approximately one hour of my arrival at the 2019 Association for Jewish Studies conference, Josh Lambert and Naomi Seidman both revealed to me that they had refereed my book. Their incisive comments improved the manuscript.

My work has been enriched by conversations with colleagues, including Walter Zev Feldman, Jill Gellerman, Vivian Liska, Elizabeth Loentz, Diana Matut, Paul Mendes-Flohr, Avia Moore, Benjamin Nathans, Anita Norich, Simon Richter, Meri-Jane Rochelson, Sven-Erik Rose, Lucia Ruprecht, Anthony Mordechai Tzvi Russell, Andreas Schmitges, Dani Schrire, Michael Silber, Eliyahu Stern, Steven Lee Weintraub, and Daniel Wildmann. I have received assistance with translation and language questions from Natalia Aleksiun, Benjy Fox-Rosen, Avi Garelick, Motl Gordon, Seth

Hoff, Jordan Katz, Mitia Khramtsov, David Schlitt, and Wojciech Tworek. Individuals who suggested texts to me or helped me interpret them include Jesse Abelman, Allan Amanik, Federico Dal Bo, Karen Goodman, Daniel Kennedy, Karen Levit, Sharon Liberman Mintz, William Zev Prahl, Eli Rosenblatt, David G. Roskies, Yael Sela, Avinoam J. Stillman, Shayna Weiss, Joanna Wharton, and Helen Winkler. Binyomin Ginzberg, Natan M. Meir, Caraid O'Brien, and Lea Schäfer shared their unpublished work with me. Evan Torner encouraged me to think about game studies. Meira Wolkenfeld guided me through rabbinic writings about dance. Anastasiya Astapova, Alena Liaszkiewicz, and Dmitri Zisl Slepovitch provided information about *igrishches*. Michael Alpert generously shared his expertise on east European dance culture, including translating entries from a Belarusian ethnographic study. My Yiddish dance community, and the broader klezmer music scene, have nurtured the more hands-on aspects of my project and given me the opportunity to speak about my work at venues such as KlezKanada and Yiddish New York.

My research was made possible by grants and fellowships from the Association for Jewish Studies, the Center for Jewish History, an Ernst Mach Grant from the Österreichischer Austauschdienst, the Franz Rosenzweig Minerva Research Center, the Hadassah-Brandeis Institute, and the YIVO Institute for Jewish Research. I am grateful to the librarians, archivists, and staff at the following: Bayerische Staatsbibliothek München, Center for Jewish History, Dance Library of Israel, Derra de Moroda Dance Archives, Deutsches Tanzarchiv Köln, Bibliothek des Jüdischen Museums Wien, Library of Congress, National Library of Israel, New York Public Library, Niedersächsische Staats- und Universitätsbibliothek Göttingen, The Ohio State University Libraries, Österreichische Nationalbibliothek, Rijksmuseum, University of Pennsylvania Libraries, University of Toronto Libraries, Wienbibliothek im Rathaus, and Yiddish Book Center. Special thanks to Irina Dannenberg, Victoria Khodorkovsky, Tyi-Kimya Marx, Eddy Portnoy, Amanda (Miryem-Khaye) Seigel, Sophia Shoulson, Ilya Slavutskiy, and Elissa Sperling. Although I largely wrote this book during a period in which I could travel regularly between various archives and libraries, I completed my final revisions during the COVID-19 pandemic, at a time when most research institutions were closed. Joseph Galron-Goldschläger found digital versions of texts I needed and answered bibliographic questions. David Mazower, who shares my enthusiasm for Yiddish ephemera, went to great lengths to help me acquire scans of several images for this book.

I would like to thank Margo Irvin and the production team at Stanford University Press, especially Stephanie Adams, Cindy Lim, Emily E. Smith, and copyeditor Jennifer Gordon. Thanks to David Biale and Sarah Abrevaya Stein for believing in this project. The Association for Jewish Studies has fostered my work in many ways over the years. I was honored to receive a Cashmere Subvention Grant from the AJS Women's Caucus.

My friendships both in- and outside the academy have sustained me. The Bielers (who share my fondness for Marcus Lehmann), Costas, Marissa Elgrissy, Artem Gurvich, the Isaacsons, Kalins, Moriah Levin and Rachel Garland, the Liskas, Moras, Moskovicses, Hannah Myers, the Schleys, Sperlings, Martin Stechauner, Judy Sweet, the von Tiedemanns, and others have shared their homes and libraries with me on my travels. Vardit Lightstone, Nava Streiter, and Faygle Train have offered cheeky yet astute support. Ross Doppelt first told me the joke that opens the introduction. Molly Sinderbrand and Jonathan Gerstenhaber made the last week of writing the final manuscript a joy. I wrote sections of this book while staying with my extended family: the Bar-Els, Gottliebs, Levinsons, Shifrins, Smoliars, and Barbara Shifrin Hass z"l, as well as with my *Gasteltern*, the Spieckers. An itinerant academic life can be both the best and worst of times; Carolyn, Philip, and Melissa Gollance have supported me through both.

Peter G. Shifrin z"l, whose life story resembled that of many of the Yiddish writers I discuss, suggested that I learn his first language and in doing so changed my life. Richard M. Gollance z"l, a creator of popular entertainment and an activist who challenged social mores, was one of the biggest champions of my unconventional life choices. My conversations with each of them on topics such as immigration and assimilation deeply influenced my research interests and life trajectory. This book is dedicated, with love, to them.

Portions of Chapters 2 and 4 were published previously in "'Spaß mit der schönen Jüdin'. Mixed Space and Dancing in Karl Emil Franzos's *Judith*

Trachtenberg," *Austrian Studies* 24 (2016): 65–78. Chapter 6 was derived in part from "'A *Valtz* from the Land of *Valtzes*!'": Dance as a Form of Americanization in Abraham Cahan's Fiction," *Dance Chronicle* 41, no. 3 (2018): 393–417, available online: https://doi.org/10.1080/01472526.2018.1518077. I thank the Modern Humanities Research Association and Taylor & Francis for permission to reproduce this material.

THE SPACE OF THE DANCE FLOOR

A YOUNG MAN who is engaged to be married goes to his rabbi to learn about marital intimacy. Red-faced with embarrassment, he listens as the rabbi instructs him in how to properly perform the *mitzvah* (commandment) of sexual intercourse with his wife. Finally, the rabbi asks the young man if he has any questions. Stammering, the young man asks if it is permissible to perform the *mitzvah* with the man on top. "Certainly, my son," the rabbi reassures him. "This is a classic way of fulfilling the mitzvah." The young man relaxes slightly and, although still blushing, continues with a second question. "What about with the woman on top?" Again, the rabbi reassures him: "Also perfectly acceptable. Some people even prefer it. May you be fruitful and multiply!" The young man relaxes even more and begins to get more creative. He suggests several additional variations, and the rabbi enthusiastically approves of each one. Finally, with scarcely a trace of embarrassment, the young man asks if the mitzvah can be performed standing up. "Absolutely not!" the rabbi bellows. "It could lead to mixed dancing."[1]

When I told people that I was writing a book about Jewish mixed-sex dancing, they frequently recalled this classic joke. Mixed-sex dancing—whether bourgeois ballroom dances or risqué tangos—is frequently associated with sexual behavior.[2] Indeed, the absurdity of the joke's punchline is based on the assumption that mixed-sex dancing functions as a kind of foreplay. This concern that mixed-sex dancing could lead dancers to commit sexual transgressions is not unique to Jewish culture—other religious leaders have condemned this popular practice,[3] and indeed, there are also non-Jewish variants of the same joke.[4] Partner dancing is an intimate physical act that demands that partners engage with each other as individuals—and yet, unlike sexual intercourse, it is commonly performed in front of spectators and may quickly become normalized. While authorities can claim ignorance about illicit sexual behavior in the private sphere, transgressive dancing is often viewed as a public provocation that requires a response. Prohibitions on mixed-sex dancing reflect concerns that this behavior could ultimately lead to the private flouting of additional, more explicitly sexual taboos, especially premarital sex, adultery, or marriages between partners from different social groups.

Yet mixed-sex dancing represents more than simply unbridled sexuality. In contemporary American Jewish communities, the joke's punchline has become a favorite way of talking about cultural mixing and modernization. Although the joke mocks the logic behind rabbinic prohibitions, particularly the principle of "building a fence around the Torah" (according to which, guidelines about religious practice should be made more stringent to prevent any possible transgression of Jewish law), it is popular among religiously engaged Jews who use the punchline to signal their awareness of communal norms.[5] As satirical Orthodox blogger Heshy Fried observes, "Whenever something is banned or restricted in the frum [Orthodox] community, people like to jokingly say that it could lead to mixed dancing."[6] Jokes about mixed-sex dancing are an effective tool for poking fun at communal restrictions and for showing awareness of a social taboo. Even so, contemporary Jewish communal politics only partially explain the joke's appeal. For over two centuries, dancing has represented a range of cultural practices that traditional Jewish authorities regard as foreign, threatening, or too modern.

This book deals with literary and historical materials from a period—roughly 1780 to 1940—when social dancing was one of the most universally popular mixed-sex leisure activities. It was an era during which Jews and their neighbors grappled with the social changes wrought by modernity—including the Enlightenment, secularization, debates about Jewish emancipation, urbanization, migration, war, and shifting ideas about women's place in society.[7] Scandalous partner dances, like the waltz in the early nineteenth century, challenged notions of proper intimacy for couples on the dance floor. For many Jews, especially those who no longer felt as strictly bound by traditional religious law, mixed-sex dancing was an enjoyable marker of acculturation and a preferred way to meet potential romantic partners without the involvement of parents or a matchmaker. At a time when most European Jews faced legal barriers to full integration, an invitation to a non-Jewish ball offered the seductive possibility of social acceptance—at least for one night.

The appeal of dance was nearly universal, in life and in the literary imagination. Dancing took place in a variety of venues, from working-class taverns to elite balls. It was performed at rural Galician weddings, in Nuremberg dance academies, and in New York dance halls. Patriots danced to celebrate their monarch's birthday,[8] while radicals attended Yom Kippur balls.[9] Salon hostess Fanny von Arnstein (1758–1818) and anarchist Emma Goldman (1869–1940) both attended balls. Austrian Jewish writer Arthur Schnitzler (1862–1931) viewed dancing as part of being a member of the Viennese bourgeoisie, whereas Yiddish writer and journalist Abraham Cahan (1860–1951) identified dancing with his participation in radical politics in Vilna. Yiddish writer Israel Joshua Singer (1893–1944) recalled how his grandfather, a rabbi, put a stop to mixed-sex dancing at a lower-class wedding, while German Jewish writer Fanny Lewald (1811–1889) associated dancing with proper courtship.[10] German Jewish philosopher Solomon Maimon (1753–1800) deployed a masquerade ball as an extended metaphor for philosophy.[11] German Jewish writer Berthold Auerbach (1812–1882) compared most conversations with women to leading a dance partner, since "you keep her in rhythm and under your authority."[12] Yiddish writer Hersh Dovid Nomberg (1876–1927) was famous for tangoing with married women at the *Fareyn fun yidishe literatn un zhurnalistn in Varshe* (Association of Jewish Writers and Journalists in Warsaw, 13 Tłomackie Street).[13] Social dancing was everywhere, and collectively writers described encounters on the dance floor in all the genres in which they wrote: novels, novellas, memoirs, short stories, plays, feuilletons, poetry, and more.

The mixed-sex dance floor came into prominence as a Jewish space in a context of shifting gender expectations. One important feature of Jewish modernity was the phenomenon of individuals exchanging homosocial spaces

FIGURE 1. "On Olympus." Hersh Dovid Nomberg tangos at Tłomackie 13, observed by writers such as Johann Wolfgang von Goethe, Heinrich Heine, Homer, Maimonides, and William Shakespeare.

I L. Peretz (looking down from Olympus): What kind of literature is this?

Sholem Aleichem (gasping): No! That's "Jewish Culture" they're creating!

Source: Khayim Goldberg, *A bisl rekhiles: vegn shrayber, kintsler un shimi-tentser* [A Little Gossip: About Writers, Artists, and Shimmy Dancers] (Warsaw: I. Hendler, 1923), 3. Courtesy of the Yiddish Book Center.

for heterosocial spaces.[14] Where once men and women studied, worked, prayed, and socialized in separate groups, young people increasingly mingled with members of the opposite sex in salons, cafés, political organizations, universities, and dance halls.[15] Memoir accounts note the traditional expectation that men and women live separate lives and give dancing as an example of an officially forbidden activity. Writing in the early 1940s, Zionist feminist Puah Rakovsky, who was born in Bialystock in 1865, recalls, "Fifty or sixty years ago, Jewish girls from pious houses didn't know anything about flirting, didn't sit in coffee houses with suitors, didn't go to dance classes. . . . A girl was only allowed to talk with boys who were close relatives, and even then they could converse only in the presence of her parents."[16] Mixed-sex dancing became a metaphor for changing gender norms in Jewish communities during the modern era.[17] In literary texts, the dance floor was the most thrilling setting for young people to explore their newfound freedoms with the opposite sex.

The long nineteenth century witnessed the rise of the German *Bildungsbürgertum* (educated middle class), a group that Karin Wurst closely identifies with leisure and entertainment culture, material consumption, the pursuit of pleasure, and the love match.[18] Bourgeois leisure activities were a way of displaying refinement and good taste, qualities that Jewish members of the Bildungsbürgertum demonstrated through their participation in social dance.[19] Yet pastimes such as attending balls, visiting spas, and reading middlebrow fiction also brought pleasure.[20] Anthropologist Victor Turner describes modern leisure culture as a form of "*play*" that can be used to support or subvert existing power structures,[21] as is frequently corroborated by literary dance scenes. However, Turner leans heavily on Max Weber's theorization of the Protestant work ethic and does not directly address the way in which, for Jews, bourgeois leisure culture was imbued with aspirational qualities. There was perhaps no more aspirational Jewish social space than the dance floor, particularly as it was represented in literature.

Since social dance is a leisure activity that involves complex rules regulating interactions between multiple participants in a defined space, it can be useful to consider the dance floor using theoretical models that are more commonly applied to the study of games. Indeed, balls often coincide with carnival, and young people in the nineteenth century amused themselves throughout the year playing dancing games like the German cotillion.[22] In the context of melodramatic literary texts, dance scenes serve a function similar to what Clifford Geertz describes as "deep play"—an activity in which a particular community has deep emotional investment because the dynamics of the game mirror existing social tensions.[23] Readers may have come to expect transgressive, high-risk dance scenes, which heightened the drama of a work and their own enjoyment of it.

Mixed-sex dancing does not only illustrate new norms and aspirations for gender mixing; it also articulates new models for ideal masculinity toward which elements of the Jewish community were beginning to aspire. Literary fiction about mixed-sex dancing from the nineteenth and early twentieth centuries frequently subverts the traditional idea that a Talmud scholar is the ideal Jewish husband. While scholars adhered to male-dominated religious institutions and mastered Talmudic precedent set by male rabbinic authorities, modern Jewish literature questioned the advisability of this kind of sex segregation.[24] These texts introduced heteronormative courtship spaces, like the dance floor, in which women were essential. This book builds upon recent studies of Jewish private life that focus on the role of romantic love and shows how the dance floor played a pivotal role in changing expectations of courtship.[25] Male prowess on the dance floor was determined in large part on the basis of gallantry, stamina, and giving women pleasure by deftly leading them through the dance figures. While women had specific and often constrained roles in both traditionally Jewish and more acculturated milieux, at social dances women could at least be visible, take up space, and expect to receive certain tokens of chivalry. The texts I analyze throughout this book reveal the tensions between the gender-segregated spaces of traditional Jewish culture (including separate-sex dance spaces) and the shocking intimacy of the mixed-sex dance floor.

While dancing was nearly ubiquitous, dance descriptions do not appear equally in all literature from this period. The scenes I analyze come predominantly from texts that analyze the dilemmas of modern Jewry in a critical, yet entertaining, way and engage directly with questions of gender. In short, they are often—but not exclusively—works of middlebrow literature. Mixed-sex dancing features most notably in works about society, corporeality, and the development of family relationships—although social dance (like the novel itself) demands attention to the individual.[26] The bodies described in these texts are rarely martial bodies in the service of the nation or empire, but instead the softer, more vulnerable bodies of the bourgeoisie, lovers, and young people struggling to make sense of society and their own heated emotions. Celebrated modernists who write about the alienation of the modern condition do not play a significant role here, although it is worth pointing out that even Franz Kafka includes a frenzied dance scene in his 1922 novel *Das Schloß* (*The Castle*).[27] Novels and novellas are particularly well represented among the texts I analyze in depth, which is not surprising: Not only are the dance scenes longer and more developed, but the novel is a genre that is particularly identified with romantic feelings.[28] Yet unlike canonical European marriage plots, or many of the Jewish novels Naomi Seidman discusses in her recent study *The Marriage Plot*, most of the texts I analyze could be described as failed marriage plots. They end in tragedy because authors could not imagine a happy synthesis between the bourgeois marriage plot and the novel of emancipation in a world where Jews still struggled to achieve social integration.

German and Yiddish writers provide crucial insights into depictions of Jewish mixed-sex dancing. On one hand, they offer two disparate trajectories of acculturation. While academic and popular accounts of Jewish modernization often emphasize the centrality of the bourgeois German Jewish experience, Yiddish is frequently identified with the concerns of the east European Jewish masses. Despite these differences, German- and Yiddish-speaking Jews were frequently in dialogue with one another. They typically lived in relatively close proximity, their languages were mutually comprehensible (in speech if not in writing), and their literatures often depicted some of the same traditional Jewish communities in Habsburg Galicia. Yet although German and Yiddish literary texts provide an important point of comparison in narrating Ashkenazic experiences of modernity, they were not unique in depicting Jewish social dance.[29] I will also address examples from British, American, Hebrew, and Danish literature.

Throughout this study, I refer to authors and texts using designations such as "German," "Yiddish," "American Yiddish," "American Jewish," and "German Jewish." These terms can be slippery, since they do not map out neatly onto national boundaries and often refer to individuals who

negotiated hybrid identities.[30] Moreover, an author's choice to include or
exclude Jewish themes does not necessarily indicate his or her own religious
or ethnic affiliation. When I refer to texts and authors as "German" or "Yiddish," it refers broadly to the language in which the author wrote the text,
rather than to the national or religious affiliation of the author. I sometimes
find it helpful to use the more specific term "American Yiddish" when referring to writers who published Yiddish literature in America, regardless of
where these authors were born or their texts take place. In most cases, the
American Yiddish writers I discuss first achieved literary fame in the United
States, even though they were born in Europe. I typically refer to authors
who built their Yiddish literary careers in Europe as "Yiddish writers," unless I provide a more specific regional designation, such as "Polish Yiddish
writer." These writers lived in (and often moved between) different empires
and nation-states, whose borders changed over the course of the nineteenth
and twentieth centuries. Many Yiddish writers also published in other languages, including Hebrew and Russian. Finally, the term "German Jewish"
refers to the cultural milieu of German-speaking Jews in the German states,
German empire, Germany, and Habsburg empire, as well as scholarship that
investigates the Jewish contexts of German (and to a certain extent Austrian
or Habsburg) literature, culture, and history. In some cases, I refer to "German Jewish literature," by which I mean German-language works that have
Jewish themes and were typically written by a Jewish writer or published for
a Jewish audience.

For the purposes of this book, mixed-sex dancing refers to occasions in
which men and women interact with each other on the dance floor. Most
authors do not distinguish between biological sex and gender identity in
their texts. I have chosen to use the term "mixed-sex dancing" instead of
"mixed-gender dancing," since the few texts that do note gender ambiguity
ultimately stress the physical bodies of their characters.[31] While mixed-sex
dancing typically involves couple dances where partners touch each other,
sometimes glances can be exchanged in ways that flout propriety even when
dancers do not physically touch.[32] Additionally, writers sometimes describe
scenes in which a character dances with a proxy while actually thinking
about or making eye contact with another person with whom the character
is not actually able to dance. Thus, a dance between a man and a woman may

sometimes convey more information about a relationship between two men.[33] By that same token, in a gender-segregated setting, a woman may dance with the sister of the man she wishes were her dance partner.[34] My choice of the term "mixed-sex dancing" rather than the commonly used "mixed dancing" emphasizes a concern with men and women dancing together in couples. Nonetheless, dancers from different classes or religions frequently interact while dancing, thus creating additional layers of social mixing. Indeed, in many cases mixed-sex dancing was tacitly accepted unless dancers also transgressed other social taboos.

The dances described in my corpus are usually social or folk dances. In cases such as the Bohemian peasant dance in Leopold Kompert's *Die Kinder des Randars* (The Randar's Children), folk dances could underscore emerging nationalism.[35] In other instances, such as Zionist balls, social events might have explicitly political connotations. While the structure[36] of individual dances can elucidate the way in which characters engage physically with their dance partners, often writers do not provide specific details about the dance steps beyond the name of the dance or a general description of how characters interact with one another. Even when Yiddish writers do identify particular dances in their texts, translators sometimes opt to replace a dance that readers might not recognize with a better-known dance; thus a hopke or pas d'espagne sometimes becomes a polka. While I generally use published English translations when available, in such instances I provide modified language in brackets or use my own translation and refer to the alternate translation in the notes.

Many of the German-language texts I discuss are *Ghettogeschichten* (ghetto tales), a nineteenth- and early twentieth-century genre of regional fiction that describes traditional Jewish life in central and eastern Europe.[37] Ghetto tales were aimed at Jewish and non-Jewish readers, although even the Jewish readers were German-speakers who were typically more acculturated, more educated in secular topics, and from further west than the Yiddish-speakers depicted in these texts. Many of the Yiddish texts I discuss describe traditional Jewish life in *shtetlekh* (the plural of *shtetl*), eastern European towns with a significant but not exclusively Jewish population. Writers of shtetl tales targeted a Jewish audience that often had, like the writers themselves, been born in these communities and sometimes still lived there.[38] Yet whether urban or rural, rustic or refined, dance scenes helped writers convey the impact of modern life on intimate personal relationships.

Dance is an ephemeral art form, which resists being captured in the written word. As Lucia Ruprecht observes, studies of dance in literature confront the "fundamental remoteness between dance as one of the most physical and literature as one of the most abstracted of arts."[39]

Although dance is difficult to convey through text, it is a frequent literary theme. According to one guide to literary symbols, dances are "often occasions for courtship, for coming of age, and for significant discoveries, especially for the heroine" in modern novels.[40] In works of fiction, such as the Jewish literature I analyze in this book, well-placed dance scenes convey local color, emotional tension, and ways for characters to relate to one another without words. Dance scenes move the plot forward in important ways; they frequently appear at pivotal moments and serve as catalysts for changed social interaction between characters. The "deep play" of dancing is associated not only with the disruption of normal matchmaking practices, but even with violence, divorce, and suicide, as in at least one variant of the German folk ballad "Die Jüdintochter" (The Jewish Daughter).[41] The act of dancing increases the dramatic stakes and creates a space in which it is possible to display emotions and attractions that might otherwise remain hidden.

In literary texts, social dance becomes a metaphor for how characters navigate their social landscape. Since partner dances involve music, physical contact, and the potential for intimate conversation, the dance floor frequently becomes a heady, passionate space in which emotions are excited and ordinary rules of etiquette or proper gender and class relations fall away. This heightened emotional landscape resembles Turner's characterization of *spontaneous communitas*.[42] At the same time, certain rules and formations are maintained, and those who stumble or do not perform well may feel compelled to marshal other forms of authority in order to regain their social position after the dancing stops. Numerous writers portrayed dance both as a pivotal moment for plot development and as a lens for observing insider and outsider status.

My analysis of the motif of mixed-sex dancing in modern Jewish literature draws from recent literary dance studies scholarship. More than simply noting the presence of dance scenes in literary texts, literary dance studies considers the ways dance scenes contribute to the texture of literary plots, character development, and social commentary. This research direction is particularly prevalent in the field of English literature and includes discussions of dances in Jane Austen's novels. I have paid specific attention to methodologies that interrogate the relationships between dance figures, literary plot structures, and contemporaneous cultural developments.[43] At the same time, especially since literary dance studies has tended not to address works with Jewish themes,[44] I have also relied upon ethnographic and social history studies that explain the dance cultures that would have been familiar to the authors I discuss.[45] Literary dance scenes can flesh out our understanding of Jewish dance practice and its cultural context[46]—yet fiction can also display the way historical figures thought about dancing. Nineteenth-century writers incorporated numerous references to dance in their works, in large part because their readers were accustomed to interpreting the nuances of the dance floor. Dancing was, therefore, a daily life practice and a favorite metaphor for authors.

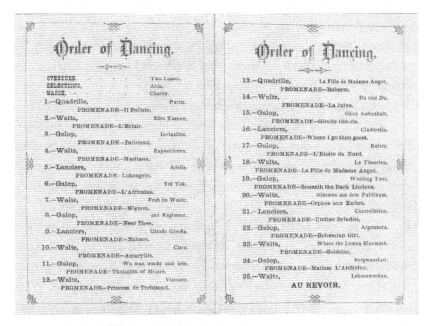

FIGURE 2. Dance card from the Hebrew Charity Ball at the Academy of Music. New York, February 16, 1875.

Source: Courtesy of The Hyman Bogomolny Grinstein Collection on the Early Jews of New York of Yeshiva University Museum.

The dance floor is a liminal space that eludes all kinds of boundaries.[47] It has generally escaped the notice of spatial theorists,[48] perhaps because, by the late twentieth century, social dance was no longer a universal activity in the way it once was.[49] Even literary dance studies scholars tend not to demarcate the dance floor in spatial terms. Yet, like Johan Huizinga's characterization of the "magic circle" in which a game takes place, the social dance floor is a unique space with its own rules.[50] By "rules" I do not simply refer to etiquette but also to the ways that dancers and spectators interact in order to define the space itself. The nature of this space, and the types of events at which dancing occurs, lead dancers to perceive the dance floor as a space of fantasy and desire. Revealingly, Emma Bovary in Gustave Flaubert's *Madame Bovary* is "seduced" by an elite ball long before she commits adultery—and, like so many fictional dancers, experiences a tragic outcome because she does not limit her flirtations to the dance floor. When socially marginalized characters attend such events, they experience a harsh contrast between the emotions they feel on the dance floor—inspired by the seeming permissibility of this space—and their actual social possibilities. Jewish mixed-sex dancing is thus not only a story of changing Jewish social mores, but also a case study for the importance of the dance floor space as reflected in the experience of a heterogeneous, diasporic minority group.

Unlike many other spaces, a dance floor is created through action: Virtually any space can become a dance floor, as long as people are dancing.[51] While some spaces may be reserved for dancing, it is questionable whether certain spaces remain dance floors once the dancing stops. Dance floors transcend social boundaries: A corner in a humble saloon can become a dance floor just as readily as a room in an elegant wedding hall. As a result, dancing often involves ephemeral gestures in a temporary space. Dance floors also involve certain expectations about participation. Social dancing, as the name implies, is generally a public, communal activity. Dance floors generally involve at least two dancers, who may or may not dance with each other. What is more, there is also often a presumption of spectatorship. At the same time that people are dancing, individuals on the edges of the dance floor watch the dancers and interpret or even judge the social signals they are sending. In a particularly famous example, Mrs. Bennet in Jane Austen's *Pride and Prejudice* keeps careful track of her daughters' dance partners, since these pairings help determine their marital prospects. Similarly, ball guests in Sophie von La Roche's eighteenth-century German novel *Geschichte des Fräuleins von Sternheim* (*The History of Lady Sophia Sternheim*) falsely assume that the protagonist is having an affair with a prince when they both show up at a masquerade ball wearing matching Spanish costumes.[52] Nonetheless, in contrast to a raised theater stage, there is often no clear physical separation between dancers and spectators, and individuals might switch roles over the course of an event. While French poet Paul Valéry claims the dancing body appears to be unaware of its surroundings, the social dancing body is caught in a dynamic interplay between dancer, dance partner, other dancing couples, and those witnessing the events on the dance floor.[53] Participants cannot escape the social aspects of the dance floor, with the accompanying demands of gender and class expectations. Nevertheless, they often view the dance floor as a utopian space.

Dances and balls appear throughout literature as places for young people to meet, flirt, and form relationships, as any reader of *Romeo and Juliet*, *War and Peace*, or *Pride and Prejudice* can attest. It is no accident that, in one of the most famous cases of star-crossed love in the German canon, Johann Wolfgang von Goethe's *Die Leiden des jungen Werthers* (*The Sorrows of Young Werther*), Werther meets Lotte on his way to a country dance and assumes their shared waltz is a sign that they would be an emotionally compatible couple, since he is the only young man who has mastered this new, fast-paced dance style. A dance allows young people to explore mixed-sex sociability in an environment enhanced by music, alcohol, and fine clothes. Dance scenes help characters negotiate religious, class, and national boundaries—often in a transgressive fashion, since the dance floor is a space where individuals can engage with people who are not regarded as acceptable matrimonial partners. At the same time, social dances are often carefully choreographed, socially stratified affairs that reaffirm the dancers' conformity to social norms. Dance scenes are thus a way for writers to criticize societal expectations about courtship and partner choice while simultaneously entertaining their readers.

While many of these social functions exist at Jewish dances, dance carries a special symbolic significance in traditional Jewish culture. Dance is an important vehicle of acculturation and cultural transfer, especially since traditional Jewish law prohibits men and women from dancing together. On one hand, the ability to dance well could both help fulfill the commandment of making a bride happy at her wedding[54] and enable an individual to demonstrate good breeding and proper management of the body, a token of acculturation into European society. On the other hand, one faces the risk of dancing too close, too fast, too passionately, or with the wrong person. While even traditional communities have varied interpretations of the prohibition on mixed-sex dancing, in literature such boundaries are frequently transgressed. Dancing or listening to dance music could inspire flirtation and present a challenge to the practice of arranged marriages. Even when Jews adapt aristocratic social dances for their own weddings and parties, rather than participating in non-Jewish balls, the act of dancing can have destabilizing consequences.[55] Dance gives expression to unruly desires in a deceptively permissive space, yet when the dancing stops, the dominant social structures remain enforced, and characters who do not adapt their passions often suffer a tragic fate. As such, dance becomes a tool for narrating Jewish social inclusion and exclusion.

This book is divided into two parts. Part one (Chapters 1 and 2) examines mixed-sex dancing from a cultural-historical perspective and demonstrates the importance of mixed-sex dancing for Jewish acculturation into European society. Chapter 1 gives an overview of the Jewish prohibition on mixed-sex dancing, examines the discourse about mixed-sex dancing since the Enlightenment, and explains how mixed-sex dancing became an important metaphor for the Jewish process of acculturation. Chapter 2 investigates how central and eastern European Jewish youth learned how to dance, especially social dances that could be performed in a mixed-sex context. Dance lessons not only trained young people in proper physical deportment, but they also guided them through gender, social, and class expectations, including those related to more tender emotions.

Part two (Chapters 3 through 6) focuses on four types of dance spaces and examines the role they played in literary texts. It interrogates the ways in which the tavern, ballroom, wedding, and dance hall each offered distinct options for social encounters and partner dances. At the same time, the contexts of each of these spaces allow writers to bring different social concerns to the fore. The chapters in part two are roughly chronological, beginning in Chapter 3 with works that depict the Habsburg and Russian empires in the nineteenth century, and concluding with the discussion in Chapter 6 of texts about New York at the turn of the century through World War II. These chapters also map out the life cycle of the dancers themselves: Chapter 3 concerns the leisure activities of rural tavernkeepers' children, Chapter 4 analyzes balls in the context of courtship, Chapter 5 is focused on wedding dancing, and Chapter 6 delves into married life and whether it is appropriate for a married man to visit a dancing academy. In all of these spaces, dance scenes enable authors to convey information about social norms and attitudes toward romantic love.

In the joke that opened this introduction, a rabbi warns against behavior that could lead to mixed-sex dancing. For historical rabbis, the threatening catalyst was nothing short of modernity itself. In prohibitions since the Enlightenment, communal authorities raised grave concerns about the risks of men and women interacting socially with one another on the dance floor. The threat of influences from outside the Jewish community could be even more pressing than sexual matters—especially when it came to issues such as assimilation, conversion, or intermarriage.[56] The cultural practices that lead to mixed-sex dancing, in life and in literature, had both real and imagined consequences for the consolidation of modern Jewish identity.

CHAPTER 1

THE CHOREOGRAPHY OF ACCULTURATION

WHEN SATAN VISITS A POLISH TOWN, he convinces the Jews to hold a masquerade ball. Yet in Yiddish writer Israel Joshua Singer's 1930 feuilleton "Ofitsirn tantsn mit yidishe meydlekh af a yidishn bal un in shtetl iz khoyshekh" (Officers Dance with Jewish girls at a Jewish Ball, and All Hell Breaks Loose in Town), the agent of disorder could just as easily be modernity.[1] Singer describes how the *yetser hore* (evil inclination, in this context another name for Satan) struggles at first to find a way to tempt the local Jews into sin, since the young men have already left for foreign shores in search of economic opportunity.[2] This obstacle is not insurmountable, however: The town has many Christian men, and they are also capable of sinning with Jewish women. The yetser hore cleverly persuades the Jewish community that they should open a newfangled hospital and raise money for it in the modern way: by hosting a charity masquerade ball.[3] Because the Jewish community is poor, they will have to invite local officers. These men are only too happy to dance with dark-eyed Jewish beauties.

Despite the concerns of some community elders, formal Polish-language invitations are sent out, and a merry blurring of social boundaries ensues. The Jewish women dress as shepherdesses and peasant girls, Christian officers disguise themselves as Hasidim in beards and *payes* (sidelocks), and the military orchestra plays Hasidic melodies and folksy hopkes all night long.

The ball raises money for a hospital and medical instruments—and Jewish women soon start converting to Christianity in order to marry their dancing partners. While Singer slyly blames Satan for the chaos in the community, he and many other writers found mixed-sex dancing to be a useful metaphor for Jewish modernity. The trope of Jewish mixed-sex dancing appears throughout modern literature, and German and Yiddish texts provide crucial insights into this phenomenon. Although largely written for urban bourgeois audiences, on the one hand, and working-class Jews from traditional backgrounds on the other, both literatures broadly consider the possibilities and risks of acculturation, often depicting the same Habsburg Jewish communities.

Between the late eighteenth and early twentieth centuries, a shift appears to have taken place in attitudes toward mixed-sex dancing. Jewish engagement in transgressive dancing was not new: Rabbis had been prohibiting the practice, and Jewish communities had been finding ways around the restrictions, for centuries.[4] Yet while earlier Jewish writings on the topic tended to emphasize the threat of sexual impropriety *within* a Jewish community context, starting around 1780 there was a greater concern—particularly in literary fiction—with the relationship between improper dancing and the violation of religious or class boundaries.[5] In short, improper dancing was understood to reveal the influence of values from *outside* the traditional community, and such behavior demanded a fitting response. Modernity offered Jews new social possibilities outside of their religious communities, and these options for social mobility were quite literally embodied on the dance floor.

Dance became an important metaphor for the process of acculturation in literary texts, coinciding with three historical phenomena: greater Jewish integration in non-Jewish society, the evolving concept of companionate marriage,[6] and the increased popularity of intimate partner dances across social classes. Dances such as the waltz[7] involved significant physical contact and provided opportunities for dance partners to individualize their interaction on the dance floor rather than relying on the directives of a dance master.[8] In his 1917 *Sittenreinheit: Ein Mahnwort an Israels Söhne und Töchter, Väter und Mütter* (Moral Purity: A Warning for Israel's Sons and Daughters, Fathers and Mothers), German Orthodox Rabbi Salomon Carlebach (1845–1919) declared, "Admittedly our holy scripture tells of dances [Tänzen und Reigen]. But I hardly believe that the Israelite maidens had dance lessons [Tanzunterricht], and surely they did not spin in circles entwined in the arms of youths or perform charming polonaises."[9] As Carlebach suggested, the dance floor presented a distinctly modern source of temptation and a threat to traditional boundaries in Jewish communities. According to Hungarian historian and Reform Rabbi Leopold Löw (1811–1875), "Within Germany, the home of Jewish reform, the first real stirring of opposition to the established authorities did not concern the school or the synagogue or any communal institution at all, but rather the dance hall [Tanzsaal]."[10]

Dance halls and ballrooms were contested sites in texts from the *Haskalah* (Jewish Enlightenment; Yiddish: *Haskole*) and the decades that followed.[11] Rabbis and lay writers used these spaces to stage the drama of changing Jewish social norms. It is telling that a pornographic Hebrew poem by Judah Leib Ben-Ze'ev (1764–1811) "describes in great detail an act of sexual intercourse between his male narrator and a woman whom he 'picks up' at a ball."[12] The idea that the ballroom challenged traditional Jewish values is echoed in the work of Rabbi Samson Raphael Hirsch (1808–1888), the founder of neo-Orthodoxy, when he includes balls in his list of bourgeois leisure spaces where "the sons and daughters of the new age" might consider "the old Judaism" to be "in the way" and "completely out of place."[13]

This is not to suggest that understandings of Jewish law had changed. Rabbinic authorities continued to prohibit mixed-sex dancing, often referring to some of the same issues of sexual misconduct. Yet the contexts in which such prohibitions were written had shifted, as these very condemnations reflect. One example is the phenomenon of rabbis seeking the help of secular authorities to prevent Jews from engaging in mixed-sex dancing, particularly when they might be dancing in Christian social settings. Since non-Jewish authorities would not necessarily be convinced by the dictates of Jewish law, rabbis found it useful to invoke secular reasons for preventing transgressive behavior. Such rhetoric drew upon the modern language of citizenship to argue that the kind of person who violates religious precepts would also be inclined to flout secular laws.

In the period following the Enlightenment, religious communities were forever changed by the growth of secularism, and Jewish communities in particular grappled with acculturation, religious reform, and political emancipation.

FIGURE 3. "Gemaskerd bal bij Joods Poerimfeest" [Masked Ball at Jewish Purim Celebration]. Caspar Jacobsz. Philips, after Pieter Wagenaar (II), 1780. Courtesy of the Rijksmuseum, Amsterdam.

Historian Jacob Katz observes that until the last third of the eighteenth century, "Jews were always recognizable as a clearly defined social unit, distinctly set apart from the community at large in whose midst they had settled. Their religious traditions with the attendant institutions, rites, and symbolic expressions created for the adherent an exclusive sphere."[14] Yet when European Jews went from being a tolerated and socially segregated group (with its own particular religious practice and ethnic culture) to gaining citizenship, their sense of self-identity also shifted. "In the second or third generation at the latest, these new citizens became extensively adjusted to the customs of their respective bourgeois societies, thus creating a new type: the German, French, or English Jew."[15] Even within a Jewish communal context, interpretations of Jewish law did not necessarily carry the same force as in previous generations, and it was necessary for authorities to appeal to such concerns as Jewish continuity, anti-semitism, the family, and bourgeois propriety. Writers of Jewish popular fiction, whether they were religiously inclined or staunchly secular, portrayed mixed-sex dancing as a threat to the social order.

FIGURE 4. "The Hebrew Purim Ball at the Academy of Music, March 14."

Source: *Frank Leslie's Illustrated Newspaper*, April 1, 1865, p. 21. Courtesy of the Prints & Photographs Division, Library of Congress, LC-USZ62-75130.

It is no coincidence that anxiety about mixed-sex dancing coincided with the period of Jewish acculturation and emancipation, since social dancing was arguably the most popular (and intimate) mixed-sex leisure activity. It was, moreover, an important way for young people to display their adherence to the rules of fashion and etiquette while seeking out a marriage partner. Mixed-sex dancing was, in short, a pivotal way for both sexes, in different ways, to show their commitment to modern social norms and to display this commitment in a heterosocial setting within the context of courtship. The stakes were, therefore, potentially quite high—for the community, the family, and the individual him- or herself. Gustav Freytag's best-selling 1855 German novel *Soll und Haben* (*Debit and Credit*) states the importance of appropriate dance pairings in characteristically unsubtle terms: "[I]t begins with dancing, it ends with a wedding."[16]

Writers often negotiated the thorny process of Jewish cultural engagement by putting Jews on the dance floor—and describing what happens when they encounter an unsuitable dance partner. Yet the tales of these Jewish dancers often end tragically precisely because authors could not envision a successful resolution for them. Jewish women were particularly vulnerable to ill-fated love affairs, since an advantageous marriage was their main form of social mobility in the literary imagination.[17] The fatal mismatch between the utopian fantasy suggested by the dance floor and a society that was unprepared to deal with a mésalliance meant that Jewish dancers could not find a proper place for themselves. As a result, the delights of the dance floor often led to tragic consequences.

In literature, the dance floor is a microcosm of Jewish integration into broader society, whether in Europe or in the United States.[18] Dance scenes convey the appeal of a mixed-sex leisure pursuit in a seemingly permissive setting, yet also reveal the limited options for actual social mobility. Despite these overall patterns, individual scenes vary in terms of social context, type of dance, amount of description, and precise nature of engagement with non-Jewish culture. While I typically use the neutral term "acculturation," since it expresses a form of cultural integration that does not exclude affiliations with a Jewish community or institutions, in the context of certain literary texts it might also be appropriate to use terms such as "assimilation" or, conversely, "dissimulation" to characterize the specific ways in which characters affiliate with or reject certain types of cultural engagement.[19] Nonetheless, all three terms point to the question of how and where boundaries should be drawn between religious groups and cultural practices. In literary plots, dance scenes take place at the fracture points between these identities, and they embody the problems of modern Jews, in a manner that was designed to appeal to readers.

The Jewish Taboo of Mixed-Sex Dancing

When rabbinic authorities invoke biblical prohibitions to forbid mixed-sex dancing, they are usually concerned with sexual impropriety. According to a 1923 study of the prohibition on mixed-sex dancing, published in a German Orthodox Jewish journal, "Dances in the Bible were performed primarily to please and honor others; as a result individual sensuality did not really show to advantage. Modern dances are exclusively for one's own delight, thus they have more to do with sensuality."[20] Although mixed-sex dancing is not specifically prohibited in the Bible, scholars of Jewish legal texts cite regulations that can be understood to prevent mixed-sex dancing (other than between a husband and wife when she was not considered ritually impure). They are typically concerned with the prohibition on lewdness (Leviticus 19:29), the possibility of a man coveting another man's wife (Exodus 20:14), or the prospect of a man touching (and therefore risking sexual contact with) a woman who is in a state of *niddah*, ritual impurity (Leviticus 18:19). Sometimes precedents of separate-sex dancing might be invoked, such as Miriam dancing with the Israelite women after the parting of the Red Sea (Exodus 15:20) and Michal watching King David's victory dance from a window (2 Samuel 6:16), since they suggest separate-sex dancing was the norm.[21]

There may be a further precedent for separate-sex dancing in the Talmud. According to the Tosefta (T. Sukkah 4:1) and later in the Babylonian Talmud (B. Sukkah 51b), in order to avoid frivolous behavior, men and women should be kept separate during Simhat Beit Hashoevah (the Ceremony of Drawing the Water), an ancient Sukkot celebration at the Temple in Jerusalem that included dancing.[22] According to Feigue Berman, "This separation culminated in total segregation that extended to weddings and funerals."[23] By restricting the interactions between men and women on festive occasions, rabbinic authorities hoped to shield their communities from the threat of sexual temptation. Yet other Talmudic sources could be more ambiguous, particularly with regard to the commandment that wedding guests dance before a bride to bring her joy. In the fourth century, Rabbi Aha was questioned by his colleagues about his practice of dancing with a bride on his shoulders (B. Ketubot 17a).[24] He claimed that, for him, the bride's legs were like beams of wood, but he did not recommend this style of dancing for men who might react differently to such close proximity to a woman's body.

In the ensuing centuries, Jewish communal authorities continued to condemn the practice of mixed-sex dancing in frequently colorful terms. Historian Leopold Zunz (1794–1886), founder of the *Wissenschaft des Judentums* (Science of Judaism) movement, recounts that Jewish men and women were kept strictly separated in medieval Ashkenaz, in a manner he claims would be completely foreign to his nineteenth-century readers: "[I]t was invariably frowned upon and often forbidden for young men to dance with young women."[25] Rabbi Meir of Rottenberg (ca. 1215–1293) refers to a specific ban on men and women dancing together in the late medieval book of legal rulings *Kol Bo*.[26] A fifteenth-century manuscript by Rabbi Yohanan Luria of Alsace scolds men who embrace women, including married women, with their bare hands and dance with them while singing and drinking.[27] Although there were Jewish dance masters in Renaissance Italy—and some rabbis waived restrictions on mixed-sex dancing at weddings and during the holiday of Purim—this permissive environment seems to have been an unusual situation that was largely limited to the fifteenth century.[28] By 1610, the Mantua Jewish community forbade Jewish men and women from dancing together, except for the ritual mitsve tants (dance that fulfills the commandment of entertaining a bride at her wedding).[29] Rabbi Binyamin Ze'ev ben Matityahu (who lived in Greece in the first half of the sixteenth century) advised excommunication for married couples who switched partners while dancing.[30] He asserted that it is improper for a married woman to dance with anyone other than her husband, not only out of respect for biblical prohibitions, but also out of concern that a man might inappropriately grab or fondle a married woman.[31] As this prohibition suggests, mixed-sex dancing is often forbidden because it is taken as a license for sexual misbehavior, understood as a type of foreplay, or even seen as a metaphor for sexual intercourse.

The anonymous late medieval *Sefer ha-Kanah*, a kabbalistic text, further illuminates concern with the potential for dance to corrupt married women. Stating that mixed-sex dancing (literally, dances with women) is forbidden, the text proclaims that women who participate in mixed-sex dancing are suspected of having forbidden sexual relations. Even if they later have marital relations, they will still think back on their dance partners: "And so when there is a dance of men and women who are married, and the women have intercourse with their husbands, their thoughts will not part [from dancing] even at the time of intercourse, because they remember their dance partner's movements."[32] The text makes an explicit connection between dancing and the sex act and further elaborates upon this connection by detailing the twenty-six sins that result from mixed-sex dance—including pressing bodies against each other while dancing, suggestively holding hands, kissing, fondling, intercourse, coveting a neighbor's wife, desecrating the Sabbath, and forbidden or adulterous relations. While these various transgressions might not all carry equal weight or apply in every instance, the cumulative list represents a damning condemnation of mixed-sex dancing, focused primarily on sexual transgressions.

Both Jewish and Christian authorities issued restrictions on Jewish dancing in the early modern period. Christian authorities regulated Jewish celebrations, which was part of an effort to control Jewish use of public space and to enforce Jewish recognizability in an age of sumptuary laws. As seen in *Judenordnungen* (regulations on the Jews) issued between 1547 and 1613, Jews in Alsace faced notable restrictions on dancing at their weddings.[33] A 1658 version of this regulation states that Jewish weddings could not be held publicly in the streets where ordinary Christians could see them, or on Friday or Sunday, and that public dancing by Jews or dances by Jews with Christians (*Juden mit Christenpersonen*) were subject to punishment.[34] Similar regulations were made in the first two decades of the eighteenth century in Strasbourg, Vienna, and Rome.[35] In a police account of an unauthorized Purim ball held on April 24, 1799, in the Bohemian town of Kasejovice on Good Friday, Jews who were involved in the ball were punished with fines, physical blows, or detention, depending on their social class, and the police commissioner was reprimanded.[36] While in this situation a rabbi was put under house arrest, in other cases Jewish religious leaders may not have objected to restrictions on dancing that maintained their power in the community.

In his 1707 Yiddish-language moral tract *Simkhes hanefesh* (Delight of the Soul), Elhanan Hendel Kirchhan criticizes the "mischief" of sending children to study in a dance school.[37] More imposingly, in 1726 the Jewish community of Hamburg and Altona forbid youths, maidens, and servants of both sexes from studying dance with a dance master; such transgressions were to be punished with a fine of thirty reichsthaler and the threat of banishment.[38] Nonetheless, in his account of eighteenth-century German Jewish customs, Protestant theologian Johann Christoph Georg Bodenschatz (1717–1797) noted that he saw Jews dancing at a wedding "in the French and German manner, like Christians."[39] While Jewish leaders continued to reprimand participation in fashionable dancing, particularly when men and women danced together, their ability to enforce such prohibitions diminished in the early modern era.

More recently, the renowned Polish Rabbi Yisrael Meir Kagan (also known as Chofetz Chaim, 1838–1933) detailed the transgressive nature of mixed-sex dancing in his *Mishnah Berurah* commentary to the legal codex

Shulhan Arukh. Improper dancing leads to prostitution, masturbation, and punishment in *gehenem* (hell). It is the responsibility of rabbis to forbid it, since regardless of what simple people may believe, there is no difference in degree in transgressions, even when women are unmarried: "[T]here is no bigger fence to safeguard against nakedness [ervah] than the annulment of dances [rikudin u-meholot] of men and women together, regardless of whether they are married or single, as there is no degree in lewdness, and it leads to nakedness [ervah] and moreover it makes people accustomed to transgressions."[40] Kagan claimed that mixed-sex dancing is the gateway to other licentious behavior and should be avoided in order to prevent these other sins. His list of multiple prohibitions on mixed-sex dancing suggested that Jews did not reliably follow the bans on dancing that were proscribed by their religious leaders. The historical record contains many examples of prohibitions, implying that Jews frequently broke the rules.

Despite such prohibitions, even traditional European Jewish communities often had complicated notions about what constituted mixed-sex dancing and what amount of contact was appropriate between the sexes. Some sources point to the ubiquity of *tantshoyzer* (dance halls) in medieval Jewish communities, although it is unclear whether they were actually sites for mixed-sex dancing or simply a term for a community building used as a wedding hall.[41] Walter Zev Feldman distinguishes between European couple dances and traditional Ashkenazic dances for mixed pairs "without prolonged and intimate physical contact" like the sher or patsh tants that may not have been viewed as problematic, especially prior to the second half of the nineteenth century.[42] Zvi Friedhaber suggests that most east European Jews in the sixteenth and seventeenth centuries did not refrain from direct contact during mixed-sex dancing, leading to rabbinic warnings.[43] In western Europe, a tradition developed of wrapping a bride's hand with a cloth (such as a glove or part of her skirt) to avoid direct physical contact with men. In eastern Europe, a handkerchief (called a *fatshayle* or *tikhl*) was the preferred form of separation.[44] The resulting dance—where men (and famously Hasidic rebbes) danced with a bride with the aid of a separating handkerchief—was known as the mitsve tants or even the kosher tants.[45] In Hasidic religious thought, this dance was imbued with spiritual qualities rather than erotic potential.[46] Nonetheless, in his novel of Hasidic life in

Poland, *Pshiskhe un Kotsk* (*A Fire Burns in Kotsk*), Menashe Unger describes how wedding guests prevent a young groom from dancing with his bride any longer than the minimum required by custom "so that he might not, God forbid, dance too much with the bride and have improper thoughts."[47]

Eighteenth- and nineteenth-century memoirs recount both traditional separate-sex dancing and Jewish versions of European social dances, including quadrilles, lancers, and waltzes.[48] While in many cases these social dances were performed by groups of young women, some of these dances were danced by men and women together.[49] Feldman classifies such dances as the cosmopolitan repertoire.[50]

In many instances Jews integrated social dances into their own communal contexts, yet they also danced in non-Jewish milieux. Such acts presented a greater challenge to the social order, in part because Christian establishments were outside the purview of Jewish communal leaders. As a result, rabbis might feel compelled to seek out the assistance of state authorities to bring an end to such transgressive behavior. Rabbi Yedidia Weil of Karlsruhe wrote to his local government to request help in forbidding Jews from attending dances and masquerades. In a document from February 22, 1786, he explained why Jewish youth should be punished for immoral behavior if they attend balls and masquerades: It was already forbidden by the community; only the kind of Jew who wished to consume unkosher products would attend such events in a mask; most masquerade clothing was made of a combination of linen and wool (*shatnez*) that was forbidden by Jewish law; there was a tendency to engage in cross-dressing in violation of a biblical commandment; and it was forbidden for men to dance with women.[51] While most of Weil's grounds for his prohibition are based on scripture, his list also suggests a specific concern with Jews interacting with Christians by attending non-Jewish functions in disguise (so that they can eat forbidden food) and frequenting non-Jewish tailors (who would make masquerade clothing that was not designed according to the dictates of Jewish law). What is more, although Weil cites scripture to explain why these actions are against Jewish customs, he requests governmental assistance in order to restore respect for the Jewish court, rather than for divine law. While transgressive dancing violates traditional Jewish law, it is primarily treated as an offense against the community's ability to regulate morality.

Weil was not the only Jewish leader to petition the state for support in upholding Jewish morality. On August 3, 1827, the chief rabbi of Warsaw, Shlomo Zalman Lipschitz (also called Chemdas Shlomo) decided to put an end to the debauched behavior of the Jewish youth, who were taking advantage of the warm weather to go carousing in Christian gardens, where the community beadles had no authority.[52] According to a later report about this incident, "The 'immoral' people did as they wished, boys danced with girls [*getantst bokhurim mit meydlekh*], they drank and spent money on the Jewish Sabbath and holidays."[53] Lipschitz went to the municipal authorities to request military support for the beadles in eradicating such improper conduct, claiming that a person who engaged in such practices could not be a good, loyal citizen. His request was granted. As a result of these (sometimes violent) measures, Jews were largely confined to the Jewish quarter.

Yet by 1833, Warsaw Jews were audaciously engaging in questionable leisuretime pursuits—including dancing—in both summer and winter.[54] Because the chain of command had shifted since the Polish revolt, this time the Congregational Board (Dozór Bóżniczy) went to the police commissioner to request that the beadles be granted the authority to compel violators of Jewish law to appear in the police commissioner's administrative office.[55] The request was granted, reestablishing the power of community authorities through cooperation with state forces. Jewish communal leaders and state authorities shared a common interest in keeping the Jewish youth pious, decorous, and restricted to the Jewish quarter. While Jewish leaders may have professed the importance of religious law to the Jewish masses, they petitioned state authorities using the language of good citizenship, obedience to authority, and general morality. Such cooperation displays changing power structures in the modern nation-state, since in the early modern period restrictions on the size and prominence of Jewish weddings also interfered with the traditional celebrations of pious Jews.

While most of the texts discussed in this section depict the concerns of communal leaders—and defiance by Jewish dancers—mixed-sex dancing was also an important symbol for modern writers and their urban audiences. Even the claim by Yiddish writer Mendele Moykher-Sforim (pseudonym for Sholem Yankev Abramovitsh, 1835–1917), while listing European romantic tropes that were missing from Jewish literature, that "we couldn't dance quadrilles with females at balls," points to the association between social dances and pleasure reading.[56] Acculturated Jews, many of whom participated in social dances themselves, were aware of the significance of dance in both a traditional Jewish and refined European context. By gesturing to traditional prohibitions on mixed-sex dance and alluding to the appeal of the ballroom, writers of fiction with Jewish themes could titillate their audiences while addressing the clash between tradition and modernization in critical terms. These writers represented a diversity of viewpoints, as well as languages. Some opposed dancing on religious grounds, others welcomed it as a sign of education and modernization, and still others found dance to be a convenient narrative device for expressing more ambivalent views about society. Yet despite their differences of perspective, these writers all used the controversial practice of mixed-sex dancing to embody the central conflicts of their literary texts and to depict the consequences of the changing times.

Mixed-Sex Dancing and German Jewish Literature

Dancing is one way of determining the precise limits of Jewish integration into German and Austrian society. An 1876 report in the *Breslauer Morgenzeitung* (Breslau Morning Paper) on the annual ball of a local chamber of commerce is revealing: "Our Christian and Jewish merchants have marketed [*marchandiert*], discounted [*discontiert*], dined [*diniert*], and supped [*soupiert*] together. They've even intermarried [*spousiert*], but they never dance [*getanzt*] with one another. Is this not highly remarkable?"[57] The use of verbs derived from French, in contrast with the Germanic *getanzt*, suggests that the merchants are willing to engage in all kinds of sophisticated activities yet are somehow unwilling to engage in a partnership on the dance floor. While there are numerous examples of instances in which Jews and Christians did in fact dance together, this newspaper report underscores the significance of the dance floor in negotiating a Jewish place in society.

In their memoirs and journals, upwardly mobile German-speaking Jews note the importance of dancing for recreation and meeting suitably cultured spouses. Prominent German and Austrian Jews wrote about their love of dancing, an activity that helped them reaffirm their social position. Fanny Lewald declares her passion for salon sociability and dancing, describing such activities as "distraction, refreshment, an actual need for me and a means to be happy with myself."[58] As a child, Berlin salonière Henriette Herz (1764–1847) took particular pleasure in weddings, since "there was always dancing, and usually I could not fall asleep the night before in anticipation of these pleasures."[59] Yet her ambivalent account of a ball her parents threw on the occasion of her 1779 marriage to Marcus Herz, a physician twice her age, suggests that dance is one indication of Jews acculturating at different rates: Marcus does not dance, which means his young bride opened the ball by dancing a minuet with her father.[60] A century later, German-speaking Jewish men had caught up in terms of ballroom activities: Arthur Schnitzler's youthful diaries from Vienna recount his exploits with a woman of his class, including various courtship activities that take place on the dance floor: conversation, kissing, love declarations, and passing flirtatious notes.[61]

Leisure activities, including dancing, played an important role in the creation of companionate marriages. This social reality was even more true in the case of romance between Jews and Christians, since, in a society that strongly discouraged individuals from marrying outside of their religious confession, couples who did not share the same background conducted their courtships outside the traditional matchmaking channels. Dance serves as an unacknowledged leitmotif in Kerstin Meiring's chapter on first encounters in her study of mixed marriages in Germany from 1840 through 1933. Meiring notes that acculturated Jews in imperial Germany tended to socialize largely with other Jewish families, giving the illustrative example of Dora H.'s diary from Mannheim (May 1890–September 1892), where non-Jewish visitors to the family home were so infrequent that the young girl found it necessary to note such occurrences.[62] Interestingly, one of these rare guests was "her dance partner at a carnival ball, 'a frightfully noble Christian,' whom her Aunt Lilly brought with her," which indicated that *even though* a Christian guest was noteworthy, such a visitor could be brought by a relative and was seen as a permissible (if imposing) dance partner for an impressionable young girl.[63] Meiring's study of marriage patterns does not focus on dance yet mentions it repeatedly, including in examples that refer more explicitly to marriage.[64] Indeed, a study of boundary-crossing marriage patterns and romantic encounters that take place outside of conventional matchmaking norms cannot help *but* feature the dance floor as a key site of encounter in nineteenth- and early twentieth-century German Jewish society. The connection between dance and modern courtship becomes even more clear in literary texts.

Austrian writer Leopold von Sacher-Masoch, a Catholic nobleman, explicitly identifies mixed-sex dancing with changes to Jewish social norms as a result of acculturation. In his 1891 short story "Wie Slobe ihre Schwester verheiratet" ("How Slobe Gets Her Sister Married"), Sacher-Masoch describes how Danish Jews shift away from formally arranged marriages. He underscores this social change with the motif of mixed-sex dancing at a wedding ball. Young people dance in mixed-sex couples while elderly men dance with one another: "Grandfather Ohrenstein and Grandfather Jadassohn at last grew cheerful, and since in their time only men could dance with men and women with women, the two old men danced together amidst unanimous shouts of joy."[65] While the older generation is most comfortable performing separate-sex dancing and accustomed to relying on matchmakers, the younger generation embraces mixed-sex dancing and forgoes the professional matchmaker. Nonetheless, both generations are able to celebrate together in the same ballroom space, and the grandfathers marvel at the changes rather than objecting to the new ways. In the image illustrating this scene, the two older men appear to dance the same European social dance as the mixed-sex couple, a choice that suggests the dancers' movements are aligned, even if their dance partnerships are different. Although Sacher-Masoch's sentimental story may be colored by his philosemitism, Jewish writers also used the dance floor to depict the transformation of Jewish society.

In Austrian Jewish writer Karl Emil Franzos's 1877 novella *Esterka Regina*, from his first collection of tales about his hometown of Czortków in Galicia (here called Barnow), a wealthy acculturated widow named Frau Sprinze Klein hosts a party with mixed-sex dancing. This style of dance challenges Jewish cultural norms and represents the latest example of Frau Sprinze's love of progress: "[T]he dancing at her daughter's wedding would not be in the 'Jewish manner'—men with men, women with women—but instead in the 'Christian fashion': the gentlemen with the ladies."[66] Mixed-sex dancing exists in a nebulous realm between competing notions of sanctioned and forbidden, which sets the stage for a tragic romance between a local young woman Rachel Welt and an assimilated medical student Adolf (born Aaron) Leiblinger. The novella explicitly codes mixed-sex dancing as Christian, and

FIGURE 5. Mixed- and separate-sex wedding dancing in Leopold von Sacher-Masoch's "Wie Slobe ihre Schwester verheiratet." Illustration by Alphonse Levy.

Source: Leopold von Sacher-Masoch, *Jüdisches Leben in Wort und Bild* [Jewish Life in Words and Pictures] (Mannheim: J. Bensheimer, 1891), 103. Courtesy of the Bayerische Staatsbibliothek München, 4 Jud. 54 L-1, Bildnr. 165, urn:nbn:de:bvb:12-bsb00073771-2.

thus foreign, yet Frau Sprinze considers it appropriate for a Jewish wedding. Her more traditional guests, such as Rachel, do not shun the festivities, although Frau Sprinze finds it necessary to invite two visiting medical students from Vienna because otherwise the young women would lack dancing partners. Even the language Franzos uses suggests that mixed-sex dancing has the potential to elevate the participants and heighten the festive mood; the men (*Männer*) and women (*Weiber*) become gentlemen (*Herren*) and ladies (*Damen*). Mixed-sex dancing is presented as a logistical challenge, since few Jewish men are trained in it, rather than as a moral quandary. It thus serves as a convenient plot device for Franzos to thrust a dashing medical student and pious young woman into the same physical space, while also underscoring the cultural choices they must navigate as they begin their ill-fated romance.

One of the striking features of German-language dance scenes involving Jewish mixed-sex dancing is the frequency with which Jews and Christians dance together. Clementine Krämer's 1918 serialized novel *Der Weg des jungen Hermann Kahn* (The Path of Young Hermann Kahn) depicts political and social barriers to Jewish social integration. The experience of Hermann's cousin-once-removed Aunt Elise reveals the pitfalls of a woman trying to integrate too quickly by marrying outside of her community. Aunt Elise is described as a red-haired beauty who speaks flawless German and rejects her Jewish suitors. She is much more intrigued by the attentions of a non-Jewish French "nobleman" she meets at a dance at a local spa: "[W]hen Aunt Elise went, on Sundays, with the other Jewish girls to the spa to dance, he danced with her the whole evening" despite his heart condition.[67] Aunt Elise runs off to Paris with her suitor, and her traditionally observant family in Germany mourns her as if she had died. Ultimately, Krämer questions whether Aunt Elise's encounter on the dance floor lived up to its romantic promise. Literary texts frequently suggest that an alluring Jewish woman is vulnerable to the attentions of Christian suitors, but she may not end up any happier than would a less attractive Jewish woman.

As shown by these examples, German-language dance scenes negotiate between Jewish urban and rural life. Some texts focus on the acculturated social milieu of German Jewish readers and the urban centers in which the authors lived as adults. For instance, the Jewish protagonist Martha Wolg in Gertrud Kolmar's (pseudonym for Gertrud Käthe Chodziesner) novel

Die Jüdische Mutter (*A Jewish Mother from Berlin*) visits an interwar Berlin dance hall and receives an invitation to dance from someone whom she thinks is a woman, only to find out (after she explains that she does not dance with women) that she is in fact speaking to a man in drag.[68] Martha's intensely negative reaction shows how an author uses a dance space (in this case, strikingly, a queer one) to show a Jewish character's discomfort in an urban environment. In contrast, ghetto tales depict the lives of traditional, rural Jews, yet remain conscious of the contexts that were familiar for their urban readers. Authors frequently gloss Yiddish terms, depict socially liberal characters, and describe small families that would have been more typical for bourgeois urbanites than for pious small-town Jews.

Furthermore, writers build upon the narrative expectations of their readers and use dances that may not have actually reflected the normal reality of their characters. In a depiction of a Purim bacchanalia in Sacher-Masoch's 1882 novella *Der Judenraphael* (The Raphael of the Jews), Hasidic Jews dress as King Solomon and his harem, a narrative choice that says more about the reading preferences of the novella's audience than it does about the actual Purim festivities of Polish Hasidim. Writers of German fiction about Jewish topics grapple with issues of acculturation and modernization in Germany and Austria, even when they portray Yiddish-speaking Jews. For this reason, it makes particular sense to place these works in conversation with Yiddish texts. Both German and Yiddish literature often depicted Galician Jews, yet Yiddish writers wrote with the assumption that their readers knew the vernacular language, folkways, and dance practices of their characters.

Mixed-Sex Dancing in Yiddish Literature

Far from being taken for granted, as one of numerous social practices adopted in the course of acculturation, mixed-sex dancing was a token of modernization in Yiddish literature. Naomi Seidman argues that courtship, specifically attention to the sexual compatibility of the two potential spouses, was a revolutionary step in Ashkenazic culture. As she explains, matchmakers were so focused on the suitability of the two families, rather than the connection between the bridal couple as individuals, that Yiddish folklore and literature include several notable examples of matchmakers who accidentally broker matches between two young people of the same sex: "Traditional [Jewish] heteronormativity . . . invests gender difference with so little individual, sexual, psychological, spiritual, dialectical, or romantic meaning that it comes close to treating all candidates for marriage, of whatever sex (although not all families), as essentially interchangeable."[69] In sharp distinction, the act of dancing as a couple in the context of courtship puts physical performance and compatibility at the center of marriage negotiations. Social dances, by their nature, invite young people to consider their dance partners as individuals whose physical compatibility and adherence to social graces are a necessary prerequisite to a successful marriage.

Memoirs describe mixed-sex dancing as a sign of social change.[70] In his memoirs of his Polish Hasidic upbringing between 1894 and 1905, *Fun a velt vos iz nishto mer* (*From a World That Is No More*), Israel Joshua Singer suggests that dance is a threat to the normal social order. He describes how his grandfather, a prominent *mitnagdic* (opponent of Hasidism; Yiddish: *misnagdic*) rabbi, cracks down on mixed-sex dancing (*shatnez-tents*) at a lower-class wedding.[71] The use of the term for a forbidden combination of wool and linen, shatnez, underscores the transgressiveness of men and women dancing together. Later in the memoir, young Israel Joshua witnesses the "sophisticated merrymaking" of wedding guests from Leszno, which has a wealthy and more acculturated community: After "the proper and simple people of Leoncin had dispersed, they doused the lights and paired off for dancing polkas and waltzes. . . . [W]e watched couples kiss, embrace, mock the other guests, and offer all kinds of obscene observations about the bride and groom."[72] Mixed-sex dancing may start out as bawdy lower-class entertainment, but it becomes identified with the way more modern Jews flout the traditional rules.

Frequently social change occurred in the context of Jewish urbanization. In his memoirs, Abraham Cahan describes the radical circle of his youth in late nineteenth-century Vilna, and he recounts how he learned to dance a quadrille and lancers on Saturday afternoons in the same alley where he discussed intellectual ideas with his friends during the week.[73] Dance was the physical embodiment of Cahan's radical education program, a sign of Jewish modernization and the political ideas that ultimately led him to flee to the United States. Cahan suggests that pairings on the dance floor lead to couplings of a more intimate nature. While the Jewish radicals practiced the social pleasantries of European courtship with other men's sweethearts, women who did not have protectors were fair game for "amusing hours of the sort one does not write about."[74] Dancing provides a gateway into more serious flirtations and more intimate interactions between men and women.

Young city-dwellers introduced new forms of dance on their visits to their families in traditional villages. One particularly illustrative account can be found in Moyshe-Leyzer Mintz's memoirs, which were published in the *Pinkes Khmielnik* (Community Records of Chmielnik, Poland). Mintz recalls a clash between musicians and wedding guests in a community where the rabbi had asked the local *marshalik* (wedding jester, another term for *badkhn*) and musicians to promise that they would "never play at a wedding where boys and maidens dance together."[75] The status quo was maintained until a wedding in 1895, when the bridegroom's brother Shmuel decides to show off that he is a "real sport" with a big city salary.[76] He pays the musicians an entire ruble—which the musicians' leader inserts into a locked tin can—to play a complicated dance for eight couples.[77] The musicians begin to play in a separate room from the dancers, so at first they fail to notice the forbidden mixed-sex dancing. When the musicians discover that men and women are dancing together, they stop playing immediately but are unable to refund the ruble because the key to the tin can is kept in the marshalik's home. Eventually Shmuel breaks a fiddle over the head of the musician who first reported the transgressive dancing, and the wedding guests beat up the teeto-taling musicians. The consequences of mixed-sex dancing in the memoir are obvious—the episode is literally titled "Di tseshterte khasene" ("The Ruined Wedding"). Literary accounts share similar concerns with the influence of urban values, yet they tend to focus more attention on the emotions of Jewish dancers.

In Yehoshue Perle's largely autobiographical 1935 novel *Yidn fun a gants yor* (*Everyday Jews*), two of the narrator's half-siblings (his father's daughter Ite and his mother's son Yoyne) come home for Passover, bringing with them the cultural norms they experienced in Warsaw and Łódź. Although Ite is initially bothered by Yoyne's rudeness to her father, she reconsiders her opinion of him when they dance together.

> "Do you know how to dance [konen zi tantsn]?" he once asked Ite, showing off his lone gold tooth.

"Why shouldn't I?" Ite smiled down into her double chin.

"Well, let's see what you know." Yoyne held out his hand to her.

Ite said nothing, and Yoyne asked no more questions. Silently, lips pursed, he put his arms, bent at the elbow, around Ite's ample waist. He twirled her around the room several times, whistling all the while to set the beat, and although Ite carried a few extra pounds on her, Yoyne nevertheless said that when she danced, she was light as a feather.[78]

Yoyne addresses Ite in a Germanicized Yiddish, which—like the social dancing itself—is a sign of his metropolitan pretensions. In the same way that Yoyne treats most people in an arrogant manner, he takes hold of his stepsister's body without waiting for her to formally accept his teasing invitation to dance. Yoyne's flirtatious questioning of Ite's competence, and assessment of her skill, turns the entire dance scene into a test of Ite's physical abilities, rather than an opportunity for her to decide Yoyne's compatibility as a partner. Soon after this encounter, Yoyne and Ite begin a short-lived sexual affair, which takes place, awkwardly, in the family's one-room house. Perle implies that Yoyne's urban swagger on the dance floor distracted Ite from her very real concerns about her stepbrother's brash personality, which might have otherwise prevented her from entering into a more physically intimate relationship with him.

While Yoyne and Ite's flirtation takes place informally and in private, mixed-sex dancing at weddings represents a public transgression that is much harder to ignore. In Joseph Opatoshu's 1924 short story "A khasene" (A Wedding), the presence of more than twenty non-Jewish Russian officers at a Hasidic wedding is one of several controversial signs of change, such as the fact that the local klezmer musicians have been replaced by a military orchestra that cannot properly execute a *krekhts* musical ornament. The uniformed officers waltz with young women while waiting for the *badekns* (ritual veiling of the bride), and the mothers of the bride and groom pretend not to notice "how the officers took the bride dancing in turn."[79] Yet the groom refuses to simply accept officers taking liberties with his bride: When the famous badkhn Moyshe Kozak invites the officers to kiss her according to what he claims is a Russian custom, the young man does not permit it. Ultimately the tense situation is resolved with a gallant compromise: The officers line up to kiss the blushing bride on her hand. Opatoshu's story draws a connection between mixed-sex dancing and greater opportunities for physical, even sexual, contact.

Dancing was often a sign of changing relationships between Jews and Christians. In Isaac Bashevis Singer's novel *Der hoyf* (*The Manor*), the first half of a two-book family saga set between the 1863 Polish uprising and the end of the nineteenth century, Polish Countess Helena attends a Jewish wedding and dances with Miriam Lieba, a young Jewish woman who speaks Polish. Helena's willingness to participate in Jewish wedding dancing is remarkable:[80] "When the band struck up and the girls paired off with each other for dancing, Helena, requesting a mazurka from the musicians, threw a coin onto the drum as was the custom, bowed like a gallant before Miriam Lieba, and asked her to dance."[81] For Jewish wedding guests, Helena and Miriam Lieba's dance is striking, but not transgressive, since both dancers are women. Onlookers laugh and clap at the spectacle of a Polish countess following the norms of Jewish separate-sex wedding dancing, and they seem not to consider that this cultural mixing could go in both directions.

Yet even this seemingly innocent dance has devastating consequences for Miriam Lieba. Through her new friendship with Helena, cemented by a Polish social dance at a Jewish wedding, Miriam Lieba has a second momentous encounter that further challenges normal relations between Jews and Polish nobility: She meets the countess' dissolute brother Lucian. Lucian informs Miriam Lieba, in their very first conversation, just how extraordinary he finds Helena's attendance at a Jewish wedding: "Times are changing then. Not so long ago, that would have been impossible. My father always felt sympathy for the Jews, but other landowners ridiculed them, even set their dogs on them. At balls, the court Jew was forced to disguise himself as a bear to entertain the guests."[82] Where once Polish noblemen forced Jews to participate in humiliating dances, now it is possible for a Polish noblewoman to dance with a Jewish woman and invite her to visit her home.

Ultimately, Lucian pushes Miriam Lieba's unusual closeness with the Polish aristocracy one step further, since, at the dramatic conclusion of the first part of the novel, he invites Miriam Lieba to elope with him, and she agrees. Yet as dashing as she considers Lucian, he turns out to be an irresponsible and unfaithful husband. Although Miriam Lieba may have thought that her well-intentioned dance with Helena was a sign of mutual respect and admiration, her sad fate reveals the limitations of her encounter with the Polish nobility, a sign of how vulnerable Singer considered even acculturated Polish Jews.

Singer, who described the precarity of Jewish–Christian relations in nineteenth-century Poland, wrote in the 1950s with full knowledge of the Holocaust. Yet he was not unique in using dance scenes to criticize social relationships. As demonstrated by German and Yiddish texts from and about the period between the Enlightenment and World War II, dance was a leading metaphor for courtship, itself a leading metaphor for modernity in Jewish literature. In the chapters that follow, this study presents a variety of texts in different linguistic and geographic contexts, each introducing dance as a way of representing and negotiating the consequential shifts in Jewish societies in the nineteenth and twentieth centuries.

————

In her study of Jewish romance literature, Naomi Seidman distinguishes between the "thick Jewish context" of the Hebrew and Yiddish literature that she draws upon to develop her paradigm and the "pathologizing lens of Central European sexual stigmatization" that falls outside her research scope.[83] Although Seidman's use of source material is ultimately more diverse than this comparison might suggest, it points to the way German Jewish and Yiddish texts have frequently been understood to inhabit very different contexts. The contributions of the German Jewish intellectual elite—and their often-complicated relationships with their Jewish identities—have justifiably received a great deal of scholarly attention. Yet when we take a step back and consider middlebrow genres such as regional fiction, the dividing lines between Yiddish and German literature become less obvious and more interesting. Dance scenes in German Jewish and Yiddish literature reflect concerns both with social mixing and changes to cultural norms. Works of regional fiction frequently depict small-town or village life in Polish lands, yet memoirs and works in other genres reflect trajectories of urbanization that can follow similar patterns regardless of language, especially when Jews who grew up speaking Yiddish in eastern Europe ultimately decided to write in German. Nonetheless, there are some notable differences between German and Yiddish literary texts that are worth exploring.

First of all, the German texts I discuss were primarily written in the second half of the nineteenth century, whereas the Yiddish texts tend to come from the first half of the twentieth century. This timing reflects Jewish acculturation trends in the German states and the Habsburg empire, on the one hand, and the great wave of eastern European Jewish immigration to America at the turn of the twentieth century, on the other. Many of the Yiddish texts I discuss were written in the United States (even if they were set in Europe), and their authors often first achieved literary renown after arriving in New York.

Similarly, while writers such as Sacher-Masoch, Franzos, and American Yiddish modernist Fradel Shtok all depict their native region, the Habsburg territory of Galicia, they differ greatly in terms of language, tone, style, and political and aesthetic concerns. Some of the factors that distinguish these authors include the era in which they were writing; their relationship to a Jewish community; their audience; whether they lived in a European or an American metropolis; and their attitudes toward gender. Although I take these nuances into account in my longer literary analysis sections, ultimately I focus on the literary possibilities offered by different types of dance space. While I have found that there are more ball scenes in German than in Yiddish and that New York immigrant dance halls feature more prominently in Yiddish than in German, the tavern, ballroom, wedding, and dance hall each offer a different set of social relationships to negotiate. Not surprisingly, references to each type of dance floor, and the environment it creates, can be found in multiple languages.

German and Yiddish texts also tend to diverge with regard to audience. Where the authors of regional fiction tend to describe the small towns of their youth, only the Yiddish writers could assume that their readership would be familiar with the language and traditional culture they depicted. Readers of Yiddish fiction were generally no more than a generation removed from traditional Jewish life, which meant that Yiddish writers did not need to explain Jewish rituals. Yiddish writers wrote for a largely Jewish audience, and most of the authors I reference were committed to developing and raising the status of Yiddish literature. In part for this reason, the Yiddish texts I discuss tend to be considered more highbrow than the German texts, even though Yiddish and German writers were similarly devoted to questions of gender and patterns of modernization.

German writers, in comparison, often explained Jewish rituals and termi-
nology, since many of their non-Jewish or acculturated readers would have
been unfamiliar with them. By the nineteenth century, German literature
was already on a fairly strong footing, and the German writers I discuss were
frequently more concerned with raising the status of Jews—or persuading
them to follow a particular approach to modernity—than with aesthetic
innovations. Literary fiction about emancipation has sometimes been dispar-
aged as *Tendenzliteratur* (tendentious literature), although recent scholarship
has recognized the importance of popular texts for German Jewish self-
conceptualization.[84] In comparison to Yiddish writers, German-language
writers were more likely to present Jewish protagonists in a flattering light, to
incorporate characters who fit certain stereotypes (such as the exotic Jewish
woman or the physically awkward Jewish man), and to educate their audiences about the evils of antisemitism. While it is true that some stylistic
differences can also be attributed to the writer's era or geographic context,
Yiddish writers seem to have had more freedom to depict Jewish antiheroes,
since their texts were designed for an audience of insiders.

Finally, German and Yiddish texts differ with regard to the kinds of
transgressions they tend to depict on the dance floor. German-language fiction is particularly concerned with Jews and Christians dancing together.
Writers deployed plot elements that were designed to excite readers and
incite them to consider the feasibility of Jewish integration into European
society. The dance scenes in Yiddish texts, in contrast, most typically transgress class differences. In comparison to the largely bourgeois readership of
Jews and non-Jews for ghetto fiction, Yiddish readers tended to share a Jewish working-class background and were often engaged in left wing politics.
Moreover, male American Yiddish writers often used dance scenes to inject
physicality into their works, such as through the motif of a married man who
dances with a seductive woman to whom he is not married. Yiddish literature probes issues of class boundaries and challenges the traditional scholarly
masculine ideal.

Mixed-sex dancing was an important metaphor for modernization that
enabled Jews to test the limits of their social inclusion and display their
participation in non-Jewish culture. Dancing reveals the way that acculturation becomes embodied—in different, gendered ways—for Jewish men and

women. As will be seen in the following chapter, dance lessons were a way for young people to learn gender-specific physical expectations at a young age, as well as a crucial location for transmitting ideas of social class and proper deportment.

CHAPTER 2

HOW JEWS LEARNED TO DANCE

IN BERTHOLD AUERBACH'S 1839 historical novel *Dichter und Kaufmann* (*Poet and Merchant*), Enlightenment poet Ephraim Moses Kuh (1731–1790) attends a lavish masquerade ball.[1] Although Kuh received a traditional Jewish upbringing in Breslau, he now has the opportunity to blend in with the German aristocracy. He wears a Spanish costume, uses an assumed name, and gains the admiration of his hostess, Countess Aurora. Yet despite this apparent social success, Kuh feels ill at ease. His discomfort at the ball is underscored by the fact that he is unable to participate in one of the chief amusements of a masquerade: social dancing. Auerbach asks rhetorically, "[W]here should he have learned to dance?"[2] It is a question this chapter seeks to answer. Although social dancing was not typically part of a traditional Jewish man's education, there were more opportunities than Auerbach implies for Jewish young men (and certainly young women) to learn social dancing. As Kuh's ballroom escapades make clear, dance lessons were a prerequisite for participation in European sociability in a period when not knowing how to dance was a serious lapse. Alongside instruction in choreography, dance lessons conveyed social refinement, proper deportment, readiness for romantic love, class status, and gender roles. This training prepared young Jews to negotiate complex social situations in their adult lives.

Dance lessons gave young people an opportunity to experiment with romantic sentiments. In Karl Emil Franzos's 1875 novella *Die braune Rosa* (Brown Rose), the (presumably non-Jewish) narrator claims he first experienced love later than his friends, because he did not attend dance lessons in his fifth year of Gymnasium. In his words, "[T]he course in heartache coincides with the dance course [Tanzcursus]."[3] As seen in Franzos's novella, literary and memoir accounts acknowledge that dance lessons taught more than simply choreography. They were, as Kerstin Meiring notes, "a decisive initiation rite in the lives of adolescents."[4] In describing her social life as a bourgeois Jewish teenager in 1920s Berlin, Eleanor Alexander recounts, "We had dancing lessons conducted by the most attractive Mrs. Bernstein in private homes where you met boys for the first time. This was followed later on by dinner dances, very popular then, held at homes too."[5] As is clear from the Gymnasium and home settings in which they often took place, dance lessons were an opportunity for young people to experience mixed-sex sociability in a familiar and well-supervised environment.

In addition to instruction in more tender emotions, dance lessons transmitted ideas about gender roles and physical deportment.[6] Marion Kaplan notes that, among bourgeois Jews in imperial Germany, "Rigid dance rules regulated the young women's every movement and demanded their passivity."[7] Memoirist Olly Schwarz recalls how strict notions of ballroom etiquette and female behavior paradoxically prevented her from finding a romantic partner during her youth in 1880s Prague: "It was hard to find out if these young people had another side to them besides dancing, bowing, and flirting. If I ever introduced a slightly more serious topic, I was almost always confronted with a dismissal."[8] Although Schwarz ultimately resisted these expectations of female passivity, other historical and fictional dancers suffered repercussions for transgressing gender norms on the dance floor. In one literary example that reveals the way dance classes helped solidify social expectations about gender performance, the eponymous (presumably Christian) protagonist of Thomas Mann's 1903 novella *Tonio Kröger* is ostracized after he accidentally participates in a women's dance figure while dancing a quadrille at a dance lesson.[9] The kind of humiliation Tonio experiences was a serious concern for Jewish dancers, whose successes and failures on the dance floor were closely linked to their social identity.

Training in dance was also highly connected to class expectations, especially since dance lessons were themselves an indication of status and wealth. It is telling that, in Israel Joshua Singer's 1936 novel *Di brider Ashkenazi* (*The Brothers Ashkenazi*), set in Łódź, when German textile manufacturer Heinz Huntze becomes wealthy, his children urge him to learn social graces and insist upon holding balls.[10] He resents the fact that his Jewish business rival, Maximilian Flederbaum, has mastered the art of social dance, despite also coming from a humble background.[11] Participation in dance lessons was curated according to social status. The bourgeois Protestant hero of Gustav Freytag's *Soll und Haben* (*Debit and Credit*), Anton Wohlfahrt, is only invited to participate in aristocratic dance lessons after a friend, Fritz von Fink, misleads the hostess into thinking Wohlfahrt is the illegitimate son of a nobleman; upon discovering this subterfuge, Wohlfahrt feels honor-bound to leave the class.[12] Freytag makes stark distinctions between social groups in his novel, and it would have been unthinkable for his Jewish characters to participate in elite dance lessons, although in reality some Jews did learn to dance alongside Christians. Social status was a crucial element in participation in dance lessons, especially due to the close association between dancing and courtship.

Appropriate dance partners were tacitly presumed to be suitable marriage partners. As Kaplan notes, "Afternoon dance lessons provided an occasion for meeting potential marriage partners. Indeed, as a result of parental efforts to encourage endogamy, Jewish adolescents may have attended lessons organized specifically for Jews relatively more than their non-Jewish peers attended similar functions."[13] In his memoirs of his bourgeois Jewish childhood in Habsburg Ostrau (now Ostrava, Czech Republic), Joseph Wechsberg (1907–1983) recounts attending dance lessons with Gerda, the daughter of a doctor who had once been his mother's suitor: "We had great fun when we went to Herr Exner's dancing school together and our mothers were present. Once we even pretended to be in love, for their benefit (or irritation)."[14] Wechsberg's account suggests that even children recognized the connection between dancing and romantic love.

Dance lessons taught young people the physical and emotional roles that they were expected to perform as adults. The contexts for these roles differed depending on the gender of the dancers, whether they were in a traditionally pious or acculturated environment, and whether participants in dance lessons were all Jewish or ethnically mixed.[15] This chapter endeavors to answer the questions of where, when, and what European Jews learned to dance, and how such lessons exposed young people to romantic feelings that would not have been fostered in traditional Jewish society. By negotiating class and gender expectations on the dance floor, young people trained for the social roles they would be expected to perform and began, from a young age, to negotiate the tricky balancing act of acculturation.

Mastering the Art of the Dance

In a traditional Jewish context, where gender segregation was the norm, dance lessons facilitated proper separate-sex participation in community celebrations. There are more sources about how Jewish girls learned social dances, which is likely a reflection of the way, in such communities, women's dance repertoire involved more set and partner dances than did men's.[16] Indeed, women had greater access to cosmopolitan culture more broadly.[17] Furthermore, writers of literary fiction may have emphasized women's dance instruction out of a fascination with their bodies and romantic choices. Outside of a traditional milieu, acculturated and upwardly mobile Jews valued dance lessons because they allowed young people to engage with socially advantageous contacts. In this sense, dance lessons rehearsed the importance of balls for courtship. As this chapter demonstrates, young people learned how to conduct themselves on the dance floor and practiced appropriate behavior with their dancing partners well before they began seeking out marriage partners.

The topic of Jewish social dance education has received little attention, particularly in a pious central or eastern European context. While the Jewish dance masters of the Italian Renaissance are relatively well documented, individuals such as Guglielmo Ebreo of Pesaro are best known for the way they choreographed the movements of Italian courtiers, rather than for any teaching they did within a Jewish community.[18] Less is known about European Jewish dance masters in the modern era, although scholars such as Walter Salmen have collected scattered references to Jewish dance instructors who worked between the late sixteenth and mid-nineteenth centuries.[19] Paradoxically, Jewish dance masters taught grace and deportment to Christian students in a context in which Jews contended with grotesque stereotypes.[20] For this reason, dance instructors may not have been eager to identify themselves as Jewish. Even when dance teachers advertised in the German Jewish press, their religious background was not necessarily obvious from their names or advertisements, such as in the case of ballet master Max Feretty, who taught a dance and deportment course in 1902 at the Frankfurt Jewish girl's school.[21] On the other hand, *Tanzmeisterin* (female dance master) Trude Strauß, who appeared repeatedly in the German Jewish press in the 1930s, taught classes for children and adults and was involved in dance performances with Jewish themes.[22] She participated in a 1931 Purim celebration and in a 1934 dance evening organized by the *Gesellschaft für jüdische Volksbildung* (Society for Jewish National Education).

Dance masters advertised their skills by publishing dance manuals, yet it is unclear if any of these dance manuals were written by Jewish instructors. Although several Yiddish-language etiquette guides discuss ballroom etiquette,[23] there are no extant dance manuals in Yiddish, and dance manuals in other languages appear not to have been written with Jewish audiences in mind. Acculturated Jews may well have consulted dance manuals, but they would have been able to read these guides in other languages and, moreover, may have considered a specifically Jewish dance manual too parochial. Even German-language dance manuals that depict national dances do not describe Jewish folk dances; when they do refer to "Jewish" dances, it is in the context of biblical dances.[24] Memoirs and literary dance scenes, among other sources, suggest that acculturated German-speaking Jews performed popular social dances,[25] whereas ethnographic studies of eastern European Jews describe a combination of traditional, cosmopolitan, and regional dances in rural communities.[26] Nonetheless, in the absence of a tailored guide, the precise contours of acculturation in European Jewish dance practice remain murky. Such a lack points to the tricky situation the authors and readers of these dance scenes confronted: striving to perform (and even taking pleasure from) refined dance choreography in hopes of fitting into a society that did not necessarily accept or acknowledge them. The tension between dance manuals (or the absence thereof) and Jewish dancers reflects nothing less than the overall problems of modernization and emancipation, here refracted through the prism of mixed-sex leisure culture.

The exact choreography, repertoire, and identity of the dance instructors are often difficult to ascertain, whereas the implications of Jewish social dance are much easier to define. When Jews participated in dance lessons, they explicitly refuted notions that their bodies were incapable of executing proper physical comportment. Such attitudes toward Jewish bodies were clearly gendered. While Jewish men were frequently portrayed as slender, pale, effeminate,[27] grotesquely misshapen, and bent over Talmud volumes, young Jewish women were, at least in the nineteenth century, typically represented as beautiful and exotic.[28] The implications for the dance floor were clear: In literary texts, it is often assumed that Jewish women can dance, whereas Jewish men are unable to perform these steps.[29]

Not surprisingly, these portrayals of Jewish bodies carried sexual expectations: Young Jewish women were portrayed as romantic, demure, and sexually available, whereas Jewish men were unable to satisfy women by properly partnering with them, whether on the dance floor or (implicitly) in bed. Such attitudes were more prevalent in nineteenth-century German literature than in Yiddish literature. Although *maskilim* (proponents of the Haskalah) often incorporated some of these same stereotypes about Jewish men into their writings, they also often included positive male models who broke the traditional mold.[30] Modern Yiddish writers, especially in America, also challenged notions of Jewish masculinity by presenting more physically robust, nimble characters.[31] In depicting these Jewish character types, authors conveyed their anxieties about social dance, which did not always coincide with the concerns of Christian writers.

The Dangers of Dance in German Dance Manuals and Etiquette Guides

Jewish community leaders and writers of fiction with Jewish themes often had complicated feelings about mixed-sex dancing. Such apprehensions were not unique to Jews. Christian theologians warned about the risks of intimate dancing.[32] The rise of couple dances, such as the waltz and polka, was cause for concern about female sexuality and health.[33] German-language dancing manuals and etiquette guides written from a non-Jewish perspective also portrayed the dance floor as a fraught space. Yet their concerns were typically of a different nature than those of Jewish authorities. Since dance manuals doubled as a form of advertisement for the dancing masters who wrote them, the manuals cautioned of the dangers of not knowing the correct etiquette or dance steps. Proper attendance at dance lessons, or purchase of the book, would help rectify such deficiencies and give a dancer the proper cultural cachet on the marriage market: "[I]n many cases a good waltz carries more weight with the ballroom ladies than—a *Dr. cum laude*."[34] Women might find a few minutes of well-executed intimate dancing more compelling than a prestigious degree—and, by implication, the financial means or social position necessary to acquire one.

Other guides stressed concern for the well-being of female dancers. Physical exertion on the dance floor was an exhilarating aspect of courtship that, moralists warned, could pose a threat to the physical health of refined young women. One 1834 encyclopedia cautioned about the dangerous physical toll of dancing, warm air, and ill-timed consumption of heating and cooling drinks: "[I]t is no surprise that pulmonary consumption and spitting up blood are frequent consequences of dancing."[35] Writing in a similar, yet more dramatic, tone in 1820, L. Laenger cautions young ladies to pay heed to their physical health on the dance floor, warning against the hazards of so much strenuous activity: "I experienced the tragic case of a healthy, well-educated girl of 17 years who danced at a ball at 8 pm and was carried home dead at 2 am, because, while standing next to an open window after the dance, she drank a glass of almond milk, suddenly collapsed, and lay dead."[36] The plot of the Romantic ballet *Giselle* demonstrates that concerns with female fragility on the dance floor were also reflected in high culture, since the heroine dies prematurely while dancing—after other characters warn her to stop this exhausting activity.[37] Worries about the health of young women were compounded when it came to dancing in situations that threatened a young woman's virtue.

Even though dance manuals provided scrupulous advice about ballroom etiquette, moral guides warned against ethical lapses on the dance floor. In the story "Der erste Schritt: Eine Betrachtung nebst beigefügter Erzählung" (The First Step: A Contemplation Along with Enclosed Narrative), part of a polemical 1832 collection of stories and verse decrying the dangers of dancing, a fictional pastor declares that relationships that begin on the dance floor are almost never happy, since "a good man would rather seek out his wife in the church than on the dance floor; a maiden only binds an honest, upright youth to her through her quiet, domestic workings, her bashful, veiled tenderness, her demure, chaste, modest nature."[38] The text makes clear: While a man may enjoy wildly spinning his partner during a social dance, he will eventually seek out a more modest and retiring woman to marry.

Despite indication that dancing was, in fact, an acceptable form of courtship in working-class and elite circles alike, dancing could also be the locus of anxiety about unchecked female sexuality. In the context of German Jewish literature, a warning that a man would prefer to marry a woman he meets in church rather than one he encounters on the dance floor had particularly serious implications for Jewish women, who were unlikely to meet potential suitors in church. Describing how she was courted by Leopold Bock, a Protestant theology student, around 1828, Fanny Lewald recounts a similar dynamic: "I was geared to external success and had a burning desire for an exciting life in the world; a ball with wonderful dancers was much more on my mind than the quiet life of a remote parsonage. . . . He deplored my passion for dancing, because he did not like to dance."[39] While Lewald does not explicitly identify her passionate qualities with her Jewish upbringing, nor claim that Bock's more dour disposition was related to his religious faith, literary texts frequently portray ardent Jewish women with nimble feet. The trope of the exotic *schöne Jüdin* (beautiful Jewess) reveals the limits of Jewish women's social mobility in nineteenth-century literature. While these women may be vulnerable to disrespectful treatment, writers are far less concerned with their physical health and ability to dance properly than with how they encounter a clash of social identities on the dance floor.[40]

German-language dancing manuals and etiquette guides express apprehension about the risks of dancing, yet they tend not to address the threat of transgressing social boundaries. Dancing partners are generally assumed to be of a similar class, and religious differences are not addressed, since in a well-ordered ballroom all of the unmarried guests would be more or less appropriate marriage partners. Instead, these guides worry more generally about delicate female health and about proper etiquette and sexual morality. By and large, they seem to assume that the status quo will not be challenged through dance, even though German literature was full of momentous—and even transgressive—dance scenes.[41] In literary texts about dancing Jews, however, the dance floor is the site that reveals challenges to the social order: Ultimately, it is impossible for even the most idealistic dancers to overcome the social world around them.

Gendered Expectations for Jewish Bodies

Social dance was a pastime, social marker, and art form. In the words of dance master Rudolph Voss, "A beautiful posture of the body, as well as lovely movements of the same, should be given expression in dance."[42] Franz Wesner notes similarly in his dance manual, "One must pay attention to the posture of the body while standing, walking, and sitting, since nothing clothes a person more unpleasantly than a crooked-back posture, a careless walk, and sitting awry."[43] It was precisely this issue of upright posture and body deportment that made dance a complicated issue for Jews in the era of emancipation, since many Europeans (including European Jews) believed Jewish men lacked proper grace and physical carriage.[44] Reformers, German nationalists, and Zionists all claimed that Jewish men had spent too much time hunched over their Talmud volumes in crowded, unhealthy Jewish quarters. Since the discourse around Jewish physical deportment typically concerned masculine fitness, scholars have tended to focus on traditionally male activities (such as gymnastics, dueling, and military service) in the creation of the "New Jew."[45] Yet the mixed-sex space of the dance floor was also an important place for physical encounters that crossed social boundaries.

Social dance was an important form of masculine performance and a token of changing social mores in nineteenth- and twentieth-century literature. In contrast to other venues for demonstrating masculine physicality, such as military service, social dance required that men prove themselves—not merely to other men but also to women. As was the case with genteel salon culture, engagement with social dance was a sign of how becoming modern was characterized by participation in mixed-sex leisure culture.[46] Yet unlike the rarefied social circles of the most celebrated salons, social dance was popular across class boundaries. In literature, the dance floor permitted Jewish men to demonstrate their ability to become heads of family through physical dexterity, proper use of etiquette, and fluency in the language of love.[47] Dancing was a crucial way for men to prove their physical suitability when pursuing marriage partners or socializing at community celebrations, at a time when Jews were shifting away from arranged marriages toward companionate marriage. Proper performance on the dance floor demanded acculturation in a heterosexual context based on gallantry, flirtation, and notions of romantic love. Social dance was thus further removed from the traditional study house than the homosocial spaces of the dueling society or gymnastics club. In sharp contrast to these other spheres of male achievement, masculinity on the dance floor was defined in relation to women, and it was attained by complementing them aesthetically and giving them pleasure.

Writers in the long nineteenth century demonstrate a commingled fascination with and anxiety about Jewish men's ability to dance.[48] These concerns are closely identified with notions of courtship and romantic love, as well as with worries about Jewish men's suitability as lovers or marriage partners. While traditional Jewish society privileged male religious scholarship over physical strength or military service, in Jewish literature since the Enlightenment, young women tended to look more fondly on a beau with a secular education and physical abilities, both traits that often implied skill as a dancer. Yet dancing could also be a fraught activity for Jewish men—especially if they did not have a hardy constitution.

In Austrian Jewish writer Vicki Baum's 1924 short story "Der Knabe und die Tänzerin" (The Boy and the Dancer), the touring Australian dancer Iszaïl seeks a perfect male specimen to assist her in her sword dance. The youth she finally selects is sixteen-year-old Raffael Levy, a Sephardic Jew.[49] Since he grew up in a "ghetto," he is nonetheless identified with two elements that were often associated with Ashkenazim: effeminacy and degenerate traditional communities. The narration makes it clear that Iszaïl chooses him for his exotic good looks, rather than for any previous dance training. Baum contrasts Raffael's physical beauty and Iszaïl's orientalist performance with the young man's home in a dirty Jewish quarter, his sickly brother, and his father's chronic cough. Yet even though Iszaïl claims Raffael has a body "like a God" and takes him not merely as an assistant but also as a lover, Baum does not describe the adolescent's hard muscles or robust strength but rather the "tears in his eyes," how his fingers and hands "trembled," and how his lips "quivered in doubt."[50] The *femme fatale* dancer might think Raffael has the ideal male form, yet his fear, willingness to forget his family, and ultimate sacrifice of his life for Iszaïl prove he does not embody the conventional masculine attributes of aggression or dominance. Baum's story helps demonstrate the pervasiveness of stereotypes about Jewish men's physical vulnerability, since even a Jewish writer depicting a sympathetic and physically attractive Jewish man cannot imagine a happy ending for him. In fact, his tragic outcome is in certain respects similar to the fates of dancing Jewish women.

While the dance floor was one proving ground among several available to Jewish men, it played a unique role for Jewish women in the context of courtship and marriage. Although scholars have shown that, in reality, Jewish women had several options for social mobility in the nineteenth century,[51] marriage remained the preferred strategy in literary representations by Jewish and Christian authors alike. Marriage plots entertained the readers of the popular German Jewish weekly *Allgemeine Zeitung des Judentums* (Universal Journal of Jewry) and became one of the hallmarks of modern Jewish literature.[52] As famously shown in the Yiddish canon by Sholem Aleichem's (pseudonym for Shalom Rabinovitz) *Tevye der milkhiger* (*Tevye the Dairyman*, 1894–1914), a sheltered Jewish daughter's choice of suitor is a key way for an author to show the incursion of modern society into the domestic sphere.[53]

To put it bluntly, acculturated men could demand respect and display masculinity through professional success or physical prowess in the military, gymnasium, dueling club, or dance floor; women used their bodies to entice a suitable man to marry them and enhance their status. It is through such a choice, to the extent a Jewish daughter had one, that female characters could change their prospects and even bring modernization and secularization into the home. A woman's ability to choose her own marriage partner was an important theme for writers who sought to depict, and decry, the constrained social position of Jewish women in traditional communities. It is precisely because Jewish women had fewer opportunities for social mobility and acculturation outside of their choice of partner that marriage plots took on a crucial importance. These narratives often concern a sheltered daughter's love match with a suitor deemed inappropriate by her family, and the dance floor was a key location for their daring first encounter. Since the dance floor was one of the main social opportunities for young people to flirt and interact physically without the consent of their parents or a matchmaker, dancing plays a vital role in texts where characters choose their own romantic partners.

More socially constrained than their brothers, Jewish women nonetheless had several key advantages when it came to engaging with European non-Jewish culture, including dance. Traditional Jewish communities prized religious scholarship as the epitome of male accomplishments; boys who were well-off or gifted enough to receive a yeshiva education learned Talmud rather than German literary classics. In their biographical writings, male maskilim often describe rebellious activities like learning to read Russian, studying Hebrew grammar, or writing literature. Well-to-do girls, on the other hand, had more opportunity to learn modern languages and read fiction, which created a gulf between accomplished young ladies and the religious men their parents wanted them to marry.[54] A young woman was free to read cosmopolitan or romantic fiction, unless it interfered with an appropriate marriage and children in due course. In addition to this historical reality, Jewish women had a particular affinity for culture (and Christian men) in the European literary imagination. In nineteenth-century fiction, Jewish women are typically beautiful, graceful, feminine, and vulnerable. While it was often claimed that Jewish men needed to improve their physical constitutions, Jewish women were viewed as already available for Christian appraisal and delectation, including on the dance floor.

Jewish women encountered specific physical expectations and options for agency. Literary characters, such as Jessica in William Shakespeare's *Merchant of Venice* and Rebecca of York in Sir Walter Scott's *Ivanhoe*, are two of the most famous examples of a sexualized stereotype labeled variously as the beautiful Jewess, *belle juive*, ghetto rose, or schöne Jüdin.[55] Such a view was reinforced in German literature by texts such as Karl Gutzkow's *Wally, die Zweiflerin* (Wally, the Doubter, 1835) and Franz Grillparzer's *Die Jüdin von Toledo* (The Jewess of Toledo, 1851/1872).[56] In fact, a hopeful Christian suitor in George Eliot's 1876 novel *Daniel Deronda* assumes that the Jewish woman he adores will convert and marry him because, "[W]ho ever heard in tale or history that a woman's love went in the track of her race and religion? Moslem and Jewish damsels were always attracted towards Christians."[57]

Appearing throughout European literature, the beautiful Jewess was highly feminine in her oriental good looks, demure sexuality, and options for agency: chastity, suicide, or romantic love, typically with a Christian man.[58]

In fact, the wide-reaching popularity of Salomon Hermann Mosenthal's 1849 melodrama *Deborah* in its various incarnations demonstrates that audiences flocked to see as many of these outcomes as possible.[59] Yiddish writers tended not to orientalize their female characters—male writers were much more inclined to portray young Jewish women as innocent maidens or sensual *femme fatales*—yet these character types are similarly static and defined in relation to male desire.[60] It is the less respectable women, such as the unruly wife Rivke in Dovid Pinski's play *Yankl der Shmid* (Yankl the Blacksmith, 1906) or the medieval acrobat Rozlayn in Joseph Opatoshu's *A tog in regnsburg* (*A Day in Regensburg*, 1955), who are most likely to engage with men on the dance floor. While modern readers may bristle at the limited choices for female characters, liberal writers deployed the positive stereotype of the beautiful Jewess to advocate for social reform.

In this context, a Jewish woman's ability to dance was an attribute that enhanced her exotic appeal. The narrator of German writer Wilhelm Raabe's novella *Holunderblüte* (*Elderflowers*, 1865) is a physician who recalls his youthful infatuation with a beautiful Jewish woman, Jemima Löw, during his days as a medical student in Prague. Jemima is more a pastiche of stereotypical feminine traits than a fully realized character; the narrator claims that all of Shakespeare's heroines can be found in equal measure in "this uneducated Jewish girl" who had never heard of the Bard.[61] Not only does capricious and melancholy Jemima embody Shakespeare's female characters, she also feels a strong identification with Mahalath, the last Jew to be buried in the Jewish cemetery in the Prague ghetto. Jemima, like Mahalath, is a dancer who suffers from a weak heart. Jemima insists, passionately, that Mahalath died because of her weak heart and not as a result of her tragic love affair with a Christian man. She is convinced that she, too, will die of her heart condition and the stultified living environment of the ghetto.

Raabe's portrayal of the doomed Jewish dancing girl poignantly contrasts the vitality of dance with the finality of death, a juxtaposition underscored in the novella's frame narrative when the doctor narrator visits the home of a young (presumably Christian) woman who died of a fever shortly after attending a ball. Raabe thus provides tragic account of interethnic romance that justifies the hero's inaction,[62] while also echoing the concerns of dance manuals about the physical dangers of dancing for sheltered (Christian) women. Raabe's unrelenting association of Jemima with death questions the very possibility of Jewish cultural development or future. The authors I discuss in this chapter tend to have less fatalistic views about possible outcomes for Jewish dancers, especially since they frequently portray dance in the context of courtship.

Dance Lessons in a Traditional Jewish Context

Traditionally pious central and eastern European Jews likely taught their children to dance at home beginning at a young age. As is typical with folk transmission in general and folk dance in particular, there are few records of how dancing was passed from one generation to the next. In Shimen Beker-man's 1914 Yiddish novella *Der tants klas: A zeltener roman vos di lezer velin zayn hekhst tsu friden* (The Dance Class: A Singular Romance Which Will Greatly Please the Reader), a Jewish father refers nostalgically to the old days, when girls would learn to dance at home, after dinner, on the Sabbath and holidays.[63] Presumably children watched adults dancing before they joined in themselves. Bella Chagall, who was born in Vitebsk in 1895, mentions watching Simhat Torah (Yiddish: *Simkhes Toyre*) holiday dancing as a child.[64] Yiddish writer Avrom Reyzen suggests in his 1912 short story "Di vos tantsn nit" (Those Who Do Not Dance) that people may have drawn a distinction between skills passively learned from participating in wedding celebrations and formal training through dance lessons.[65] Although the protagonist was pulled into the wedding dancing during his childhood, he later claims that he cannot dance, which has a negative impact on his ability to court women once he arrives in the United States.

In addition to observing their elders, young people taught one another how to dance informally. Some sources refer to dances on Saturdays, presumably since Sabbath afternoons were an opportunity for leisure time, even though dancing was more logistically complicated on a day when Jews were forbidden to play musical instruments.[66] While Christian musicians were sometimes hired for *zmires* parties (during which a bride and her friends danced on the Friday night before her wedding),[67] participants in informal dances accompanied themselves by singing. In Leopold Kompert's German-language novella *Die Jahrzeit* (The Yortsayt; Yiddish for the anniversary of a death), which is set in rural Bohemia, a charismatic Hungarian man leads dancing for other young Jews on Saturday afternoons.[68]

Families with more financial resources (and perhaps more of a reformist inclination) arranged dancing instruction for their children. In his memoirs from Kamenetz in Grodno (now Belarus), Yekhezkel Kotik (1847–1921) recounts how children in his family learned to dance in preparation for family weddings. Although Kotik identifies his father's Hasidic lifestyle with frequent (male) dancing, he says that watching the dance lessons was a particularly favorite pastime for his mitnagdic grandfather: "If a wedding was in the offing within the family, the dancing lessons started three months in advance."[69] Kotik does not specify the types of dances he learned, or whether he learned to dance alongside his female cousins. Since the dance lessons seem to have been organized by Kotik's grandfather, and they lasted for three months, it is possible that Kotik learned elaborate set dances, like quadrilles and lancers, although such dances were most commonly performed by girls and women in traditional Jewish communities.

In his ethnographic study of the traditional Jewish school system, Yekhiel Shtern notes that girls in the *meydl-kheyder* (girl's primary school) reenacted weddings as a game, including popular social dances for couples or squares of couples.[70] On average, these girls were between seven and thirteen years old.[71] Young women also performed these dances as part of actual wedding celebrations. When describing a zmires party in honor of her sister's 1848 wedding, memoirist Pauline Wengeroff (1833–1916) remarks that some of the young women performed the role of the "cavaliers," due to "our religious upbringing forbidding dancing with men."[72] Wengeroff implies that dancers knew that partner dances were originally designed for a mixed-sex context, even though they typically modified the dance pairings to adhere to a community religious standard. This practice may help explain why writers assumed Jewish women would have the skills to perform mixed-sex social dances, even though their communities generally discouraged men and women from dancing together.

Eastern European Jewish Dance Classes

As Jews became more acculturated and urban, they also learned mixed-sex social dances.[73] Yiddish modernist writers wrote about shtetl Jews who fantasize about learning to dance. In her short story "A tants" ("A Dance"), Fradel Shtok notes that her protagonist Meyer, a free-thinker from Galicia,

once dreamed of taking dancing lessons.[74] Similarly, Celia Dropkin's character Gysia in "Di tentserin" ("The Dancer"), a young married woman in a
Polish shtetl, wants to dance but "she knew that to become a dancer you had
to study." [75] She begins to fantasize that, instead of following her husband
to the United States, she would leave her baby with her parents and "run
off to Warsaw and enroll in dance school. She would pay for these lessons
with the money her husband sent her for the fare to America."[76] While it is
unclear whether Gysia wanted to study social or modern dance, both Shtok
and Dropkin's protagonists associate dance lessons with escape from their
social circumstances. Likewise, in Chaim Grade's short story "Es hot zikh
ongehoybn" ("It Has Begun") about revolutionary Russia, a Jewish character
says that his son claimed dance lessons are the only way "to liberate yourself
from all sorrows," yet, unfortunately for him, these bourgeois social dances
have fallen out of favor, and girls only want to dance folk dances with Red
officers.[77] While neither Meyer nor Gysia are able to realize their dreams of
dancing lessons, more urban and affluent eastern European Jews took social
dancing lessons, in a way similar to their bourgeois Christian neighbors or to
upwardly mobile German Jews.[78]

Popular literature in Yiddish suggests that parents and moralists were
anxious about the kinds of potential marital partners young people would
encounter at dancing classes, as can be seen in Bekerman's *Der tants klas*. The
protagonist Celia is a modern young woman who wants to go to dancing
classes, a sign of changing social norms. Not only does Celia want to spend
money on questionable leisure culture,[79] she has already informed the dancing
master that she will be taking these lessons, without first asking her parents.
As she explains to them, all of her friends are attending classes at Wald-
mann's Dancing School: "These days every servant girl can go dancing but
I'm not allowed! Very nice of you! What's going to happen when I need to go
to a wedding?"[80] As this quote reveals, Bekerman is very concerned with the
question of whether dance classes are suitable entertainment for bourgeois
women.[81] At first Celia's father Borukh forbids her to attend these lessons,
since he fears dancing lessons are not an appropriate activity for someone
of his daughter's class and respectability. He bemoans the fact that young
people want to participate in mixed-sex dancing with skirt-chasers: "No
good can come from such classes, which were only designed for libertines

and idlers," since "certainly the sort of things happen that one doesn't talk about."[82] Borukh worries that the men who attend dancing schools might expect that dancing will lead to other forms of physical intimacy.

While Celia emphasizes the importance of dancing for keeping up with her friends and celebrating weddings, Borukh assumes dance leads to flirtation and seduction. Although his wife tries to reason with him that times are changing, Borukh only relents when a family friend tells him that she is also sending her own daughter to the dancing school, like other members of their social circle. Yet Borukh is correct about the connection between dance classes and romance: Celia meets a young man named Avrom at her first dance class, and he walks her home. Soon he walks her home every evening, and she stops dancing with other young men. Eventually Avrom proposes, and Celia delightedly accepts, even though her parents are unaware of her budding romance. Much to Celia's dismay, when her parents learn of her relationship with a man from the dancing school, they forbid her from contacting him and demand she discontinue dance lessons.

Ultimately, Borukh discovers Avrom's virtues through another channel, and Bekerman implies that dancing lessons are a reasonable courtship option for respectable young women. Avrom saves Borukh and Celia from a burning building at risk to his own life, and the story ends happily with Celia and Avrom's marriage. While changing times demand that young people have new ways to meet and court one another, the rather-contrived ending suggests that the author still hopes children would seek out their parents' approval. Naomi Seidman argues that Jewish marriage plots focus on the emotional relationship between a prospective father-in-law and son-in-law, and indeed it is not enough that Avrom pleases Celia on the dance floor and in conversation on their walks: Ultimately, he must also "court" her father.[83] Bekerman's story of romantic love and bourgeois entertainment refers to changing times but ultimately does not question parental authority, social respectability, or the end goal of marriage. While Celia has the good fortune to meet a virtuous young man, there is little about the unsupervised dance school that would ensure the social suitability of the man in whom she quickly became enamored. Even her friend Annette, who initially championed Celia's participation in dancing, is surprised that a young woman would keep a courtship secret from her parents. Instead, Bekerman seems to recommend that parents communicate with their daughters as they pursue appropriate bourgeois refinements on the dance floor.

While Bekerman shows how a romance begun on the dance floor can end in a respectable marriage, Polish Yiddish writer Khayim-Avrom Yakhnuk views dancing as a morally questionable practice that wastes working women's time. Yakhnuk harshly criticizes dance classes in his polemical 1905 story *Tants-klassin, oder di frehlikhe yugend: A kritishe ertsehlung fun yudishen lebin* (Dance Classes, or Happy Youth: A Critical Tale of Jewish Life), which depicts the miserable fate of a young woman who regularly abandons her husband and young child to attend dancing lessons (much as Gysia longed to do in Dropkin's "Di tentserin"). Yakhnuk disputes notions that dance is a sign of education and cultivation, instead portraying dance as laughable and, moreover, as an activity that distracts young women from learning the skills they need to run a proper household—which, in his view, is what working-class women should be doing once they come home in the evenings. He gives the example of a man whose wife knows no better than to put salt in his coffee.[84] More erudite readers may have understood this comical household mishap in sexual terms, as a reference to the Talmudic metaphor of an adulterous wife "spoiling" her husband's dish, which medieval commentator Rashi identifies with oversalting food.[85] Yakhnuk questions the utility of dancing classes for courtship purposes, since he suggests dancing interferes with a woman's ability to be a good housekeeper and faithful wife.

Yakhnuk criticizes the morality of women who participate in dancing lessons and casts doubt on the kinds of relationships into which they enter. Some women meet "cavaliers" at their dance lessons, swear eternal devotion, get engaged, "and very quickly there's a wedding and really soon, a month or two later, there's a circumcision."[86] The kind of woman who goes to dancing lessons, according to Yakhnuk, is the kind of woman who has a baby a month or two after her wedding. What is more, according to the broader plot arc of *Tants-klassin*, a woman who goes to dance classes before she gets married (even if she tells her prospective husband she is pious) will not stop after the wedding, but will instead leave her hardworking husband with all the household and childcare duties. She will get her comeuppance, though, after her husband works himself to death, since she will be left responsible for all of the same obligations he was, yet without the income a man could earn. Yakhnuk gestures toward the sexual morality of traditional prohibitions against mixed-sex dancing, but he also pays close attention to issues of time and marital divisions of labor, particularly in a working-class context.

Yiddish texts about dance lessons in Europe are concerned primarily with ideas of freedom, respectability, and sexual morality. Characters view dance lessons as a form of escape, either from a restrictive home environment or from family responsibilities. They may also welcome flirtation, which is a reason why some writers and characters express serious concerns with the sexual potential of the dance floor. Dancing is a way of meeting potential marriage partners, but narrators question whether it is possible to ensure that partnerships formed on the dance floor will be appropriate. In some situations, young women learn to dance as part of a bourgeois education, but they may experience a disconnect between their refined course of study and the traditional religious educations of the young men they are still expected to marry. This gender divide is also an important issue in German texts about dance classes, which emphasize the way that dance lessons expose young people to humiliation.

German Jewish Dance Classes

In comparison with Yiddish works of popular fiction, which stress the sexual implications of dance lessons, German texts about Jewish life emphasize the potential for embarrassing oneself.[87] The stakes of such embarrassment were higher when Jews and Christians learned to dance together, especially since dancing could be associated with social mobility. Marion Kaplan describes dance classes as "a prime symbol of bourgeois aspirations . . . [that] reinforced class distinctions and allowed some social movement within the urban bourgeoisie."[88] She adds that, by 1900, "[M]any of these dance classes provided a forum for young people to meet potential spouses from the same or 'better' backgrounds."[89] She cites memoirist Philipp Lowenfeld from Munich, who claimed that wealthier Jews sent their sons to dancing lessons that were also attended by Christians, whereas the children of ordinary Jewish businesspeople took dance lessons with other middle-class Jews. Writing about her mother's bourgeois upbringing in Nuremberg around 1900, memoirist Stephanie Orfali claims that dance lessons (*Tanzstunde*) were the means by which young women were presented to society: "This custom was more widely adhered to in our Jewish society than in society at large. Only a few of the Christian girls in our school attended a Tanzstunde, while most of the Jewish girls were invited as partners before the end of their 10th year of school."[90] Social dance was an important marker of social class and venue for impressing the opposite sex. Jewish writers and memoirists were concerned with the dance floor as a site for negotiating social inclusion.

The right sort of dancing lessons could be a status symbol, like the ones that Henriette Herz took as a girl with a French dancing master.[91] In 1820s Königsburg, Fanny Lewald attended dance lessons once a week in the home of the prominent Jewish Oppenheim family, along with five of the Oppenheim daughters and two young women from a Protestant academic family, the Kählers.[92] Alongside the dancing lessons, she and the other young people used to attend small soirées where they performed *tableaux vivants* and participated in other party games.[93] The fact that Lewald, the Oppenheims, and the Kählers took these lessons together suggests that they believed themselves to be of a roughly comparable class background. At the conclusion of the dancing lessons, the Kählers hosted a party, where Lewald met her first suitor, Leopold Bock, a relative of the hosts. Although this party did not include dancing, because the Kählers did not actually permit this activity in their home, the dancing lessons were indirectly responsible for Lewald's love affair with a Christian man. Both the dance lessons themselves and the associated social events facilitated types of social interaction that might not have otherwise occurred.

In his remarkable English-language diary of his leisure activities in 1830s Dresden, Louis Lesser, a Jewish bank clerk, recounts studying social dance with several dance masters, although he does not specify the religious background of his teachers or the composition of the classes. Initially Lesser practiced with his male friends to learn the steps, and the first time he has a mixed-sex dance lesson he complains, "[W]e were not glad, being not yet far advanced."[94] Lesser would have preferred to hone his skills before dancing with female partners. His diary suggests, and literary sources confirm, that for upwardly mobile Jewish men, the ability to conform to gender conventions on the dance floor was a particularly fraught sign of masculinity.

In a diary account describing a dancing lesson in 1904 Breslau, Adolf Riesenfeld similarly recalls how the "gentlemen" had dance instruction for several hours before being joined by the "ladies." Participants were described as students and young businesspeople, "almost all from Jewish middle class 'good families.'"[95] The dance lesson was carefully organized to give the young men an opportunity to master the steps, guarantee that enough men were invited so that young women would always have a partner, and ensure proper chaperonage. All of these measures were designed to allow participants to properly perform this bourgeois leisure activity with maximum comfort. Orfali also notes that when dance classes started in the fall, young men and women learned simple steps separately "so that the clumsy ones would not be embarrassed."[96] As dancers became more advanced, they danced in couples accompanied by a musical trio (and chaperones).

In literature, particularly in situations where Jews and Christians dance together, dance lessons are often a more complicated social space. Significantly, in Franzos's 1891 novel *Judith Trachtenberg*, which is set in Galicia and addresses the difficulty of Jewish acculturation in the Habsburg empire, the Trachtenberg siblings attend dancing lessons in the home of an aristocratic non-Jewish neighbor.[97] While the protagonist Judith feels affirmed in this cultured milieu, where she wins admiration for her beauty (and presumed sexual availability), her brother Rafael is derided for his Semitic appearance by his Christian dance partners until he refuses to participate in the dance lessons anymore. Franzos deftly uses a dance class to reveal the different ways in which his male and female Jewish characters are treated by their Christian social interlocutors.

Although Jewish women are typically depicted as graceful dancers, whether at balls or rural weddings, the few instances I have found of physically awkward Jewish women take place in the context of German literary depictions of dancing lessons. Even the title of Mosenthal's sentimental 1878 short story "Schlemilchen," about the Jewish community of his native Kassel, is a reminder of a young woman's inability to master activities like dancing. Poor but sympathetic orphan Emilchen is nicknamed "Schlemilchen" in a play on the Yiddish word *schlemiel* (incompetent person) on account of her clumsiness. When, at age sixteen, Emilchen attends dancing lessons, the other female students are afraid she will step heavily on their toes. Only the dancing master invites her to dance, "with quiet resignation."[98] While it is unclear whether any non-Jews participate in the lessons, Emilchen's social exclusion is clearly the result of her lack of grace rather than her Jewish identity.

Ludwig Jacobowski takes an entirely different tone in his 1892 *Werther der Jude* (Werther the Jew), a tendentious novel about the impossibility of Jewish integration into German society that refers in its title to Goethe's *Die Leiden des jungen Werthers* (*The Sorrows of Young Werther*).[99] Fräulein Rosalie attends a dancing class for students in a small German town, and her social exclusion is the obvious result of antisemitism. Even years after this incident (which took place in the sixth class of Gymnasium), her former classmates recall her lack of taste, "long nose," "specifically Semitic appearance," "flamboyant clothing," and "dreadful jewelry"—all characteristics of the stereotype of the crassly striving Jewish woman, which by the twentieth century was more prevalent than the beautiful Jewess trope.[100]

In one particularly distressing incident, Grete Berger, the most popular girl in the class, cruelly ignores Rosalie's greeting: "The Jewess was embarrassed; ugly glances from all sides; and then the entire bevy of girls laughed out loud at her standing there pale as death."[101] The novel's protagonist, Leo Wolff, resents the fact that Rosalie inadvertently forces him to think about his own Jewish background. Although he would rather chat blithely with Grete and dance with her, Leo feels compelled to defend Rosalie—even though he, too, finds it difficult to stomach the presence of "the daughter of an odious Jewish shopkeeper."[102] Jacobowski shows, rather heavy-handedly, how an acculturated Jew such as Leo feels trapped between his desire for social mobility and the reality of both external and internalized antisemitism in the 1890s. Dance lessons are a particularly effective device for making Leo's social predicament clear, as well as for showing how, by the turn of the century, Jewish women were often depicted using the same palette of ugly, grasping tropes as Jewish men.

Literary and autobiographical texts refer to the different kinds of dance instruction available to young people. The type of lesson was chosen based on the most appropriate social, regional, or class context—informal modeling at home, practice with peers, or formal lessons with a dance master, either at home or at a dance school. Young men and women faced different social

expectations about what and how they would perform, which were closely
identified with gender expectations more broadly. In Auerbach's *Dichter und
Kaufmann*, the poet Kuh had no opportunity to learn to dance, whereas his
sister Veilchen has a disturbing dream where she dances with her fiancé in
a field.[103] Unlike her brother, she is able to at least imagine her own dancing
body. Although in a few German literary instances Jewish women are unable
to perform properly in dancing lessons, in most cases a Jewish woman's ability to dance was an attribute that enhanced her exotic appeal.

In *Die braune Rosa*, Franzos describes how young people go through the
heady emotions of falling in love as they practice the figures of a quadrille.
Once the dance is over, this first experience of love is also forgotten. While
dance lessons prepare young people for romantic love and adult courtship,
ultimately they are just a preparatory exercise. Although authors often invoke
their feelings about romantic love and acculturation when they are discussing dancing lessons, the consequences of encounters at dancing lessons tend
to be less significant than in other dance spaces—especially when the same
characters later attend balls or weddings.[104] Young people are more likely to
fall in love with their dancing partners at balls than with their classmates
at dance lessons—although characters are more likely to engage in serious
flirtation if, as in Bekerman's *Der tants klas*, they are already of a marriageable
age. Memoirists like Orfali often recall their first love affairs at dance lessons
with particular fondness:

> [A] young man named Karl Blumenthal, a serious fellow who wanted to
> be a rabbi, asked me to join him in the Tanzstunde. . . . Karl and I remained
> inseparable friends through the year of the Tanzstunde and the parties that
> followed until we found out that the bond between us was infatuation, not
> love.[105]

While young people learned many important emotional, physical, and social
lessons on the dance floor, they might still feel like these exercises were a
kind of a game. As Orfali wryly notes: "He fell violently in love with me, and
I fell as violently in love with love."[106]

In the following chapters, we will delve deeper into specific dance venues
and the expectations, types of encounter, and styles of dance associated with
them. This survey begins—and thus our account continues—with a dance

space that was closely connected with the question of the type of modeling and education received by Jewish children. The Jewish-run tavern was a family business, which meant that the tavernkeeper's children often witnessed dancing as the workspace intruded into the domestic sphere. In this rural setting, Jewish youth learned to dance from their peasant neighbors. As we will see, this social contact and the porousness of boundaries between groups was a source of great concern for German and Yiddish writers alike.

CHAPTER 3

THE TAVERN

Jewish Participation in Rural Leisure Culture

IN HIS MEMOIRS of Jewish life in Lithuania, writer and cultural activist Hirsz Abramowicz (1881–1960) recounts a "typical innkeeper's tale," which at first glance seems as if it should be far from typical.[1] A rabbi, who has been collecting donations of food and money throughout the countryside, arrives at an inn where the local peasants are having a party called a *grishke* (from the Russian *igrishche*, or games), which may coincide with a holiday celebration. Soon after, other Jews enter the inn and are confronted with a shocking sight: The rabbi is dancing a hopke with a Christian woman. The rabbi greets the newcomers, and one of them asks: "But Rabbi, . . . is it proper for a rabbi to be dancing, and with a Christian [shikse] at that?"[2] The rabbi explains that his behavior comes with the occupation. Or, as Abramowicz clarifies, "[B]eing on the road and imbibing a little gives one license to do things at an inn that one would never do under other circumstances."[3] While Abramowicz's anecdote concerns an inn, taverns were similarly liminal spaces, especially since they welcomed drinking and dancing, and also often included guest houses.[4] As we will see in Leopold Kompert's novella *Die Kinder des Randars* (The Randar's Children) and Leon Kobrin's novella *Yankl Boyle*, Jewish tavernkeepers and their families faced the daily temptation of rural amusements such as igrishches.

Rural inns and taverns were sites that blurred boundaries between different groups of people—especially since alcohol was frequently involved. Although rabbinic legal thought created restrictions designed to prevent Jews and Christians from carousing or engaging in sexual relations with one another, even rabbis might find Slavic peasant culture to be irresistible.[5] Glenn Dynner notes that maskil Avraham Ber Gottlober and latter-day mitnaged Ephraim Deinard, criticized Hasidic religious leaders for performing Polish folk dances at their weddings; for touching brides with a bare hand; and for enjoying lowbrow Slavic amusements that mitnagdim considered more appropriate for peasants carousing in a tavern.[6] This was a context in which eastern European Jews looked down upon non-Jewish peasants as dangerous and base.[7] If even rabbis could not withstand the allure of peasant dancing, then tavernkeepers and their children had little hope of maintaining a distance from the customers they served. Mixed dancing in taverns—whether between men and women, Jews and Christians, or rich and poor—was the ultimate symbol of boundary transgression.

Jewish Tavernkeeping and Peasant Dancing

For centuries, most ordinary central and eastern European Jews lived in towns and villages, often running taverns at the local nobleman's behest.[8] In many cases there were few Jewish families in these rural communities, which could make it difficult for tavernkeeping families to give their children a Jewish education.[9] Numerous writers—including Sholem Aleichem, Hayim Nahman Bialik, Abraham Cahan, and S. An-sky (pseudonym for Shloyme Zaynvl Rapoport)—were the children of tavernkeepers and grew up in close proximity to their parents' places of business, especially since taverns were frequently extensions of the family's living quarters.[10] There was little separation between the private, domestic sphere and the tavern, where the parents catered to a peasant clientele and the demands of the local nobility. While the tavern was a space that ensured the family's livelihood, it also exposed the tavernkeeper's children to the thrill of peasant dancing.[11] Rural Jewish families struggled, at least in literature, with passing on Jewish knowledge and customs to children who may have found the pastimes of their neighbors more compelling. Mixed-sex dancing exemplified the transgressive intimacy of ethnic mixing in rural communities.

The Jewish-run tavern was a common institution in central and eastern European literature and culture.[12] As Ellie R. Schainker notes, taverns
were "an iconic fixture of the political economy of Jewish Eastern Europe
where Jews were overwhelmingly middle class since they made a living not as
peasants or nobility but rather as commercial agents engaged in petty trades,
shop- or tavern keeping, craft making, and money lending."[13] The tavern
was a mixed space, where Jewish tavernkeepers and their families encountered both the nobility and the peasantry. As Dynner demonstrates, Jews
were blamed for encouraging drunkenness in the peasantry at the same time
nobles kept leasing taverns to them because Jews were believed (not always
accurately) to be sober proprietors who knew how to extract money from
their customers without imbibing the goods themselves.[14] In his 1934 Yiddish novel *Der tilim-yid* (*Salvation*), Sholem Asch describes the difficulty a
tavernkeeping family faces in dealing with both peasant and noble customers:
Drunken peasants are overly familiar with the tavernkeeper's pretty daughter
Reisel, whereas visiting noblemen demand the family's Sabbath dinner, attempt to assault Reisel, and threaten her parents and husband at gunpoint.[15]
Not only was the tavern a place of altered consciousness, between sobriety
and drunkenness, it was also an establishment where different classes came
into contact, for better or worse.

Jewish tavernkeepers served as arendators (*randars* in Yiddish, *arendarzy*
in Polish), lease-holders on a village tavern or brandy distillery belonging
to a nobleman.[16] M.J. Rosman observes that taverns were important local
institutions that allowed locals and visitors to mix socially: "People gathered
on Sunday afternoons and in the evenings to drink, swap tales, sing folk
songs and enjoy each other's company; weddings and other celebrations were
catered there."[17] Taverns were also a place where visitors could assess their
new locale: "The quickest way to take the measure of a town or village was
to visit its tavern and traveling merchants, beggars and thieves all made it
their headquarters."[18] The tavern was full of temptation, moral quandary, and
boundary-crossing. In literature it is described, not surprisingly, as a challenging place to raise Jewish children.

In literary texts and memoirs, a Jewish tavernkeeper often epitomized the
simple, rural Jew. Living among peasants, apart from a Jewish community
or sources of Jewish learning, the tavernkeeper typically lacked a thorough

Jewish education. Yiddish writer Yehiel Yeshia Trunk (1887–1961) describes the limits of his tavernkeeper uncle's knowledge of Jewish ritual: "He was illiterate, could not tell a cross from an aleph, and could just barely manage to say the Hebrew benediction on bread."[19] A tavernkeeper might be described as physically robust or uncouth, in contrast to the scholarly Jewish male ideal. Trunk describes his Uncle Mordekhai-Ber and Aunt Genendl as "a personification of sex."[20] In her memoirs, Hinde Bergner (1870–1942) describes her paternal grandfather Moyshe (who runs an inn and, at least at one point, a tavern) in a manner consistent with other Jewish tavernkeepers: "Grandfather Moyshe was a show-off and a very healthy one at that. He had wide shoulders, big conspicuous hands, and a festive face [simkhes-toyre-ponem]."[21] Austrian Jewish writer Joseph Roth compares a Galician tavernkeeper in his 1932 novel *Radetzkymarsch* (*The Radetzky March*) to "a mountain in human guise."[22] In *Di brider Ashkenazi* (*The Brothers Ashkenazi*), Israel Joshua Singer represents Mendel Flederbaum, a tavernkeeper's son from Wulka (near Łódź), in markedly corporeal terms: "a powerful, lusty youth wearing metal-reinforced heels on his heavy boots and carrying a stick with which to beat off gentile dogs and shepherds who combined to harass any passing Jew."[23] Not surprisingly, Flederbaum proves to be an excellent dancer.[24] Women who worked in taverns were also described as brash and flirtatious, such as Hinde the barmaid in Fradel Shtok's 1919 Yiddish short story "Mandeln" (Almonds), who dances around her male customers to maintain control over her own space.[25] A tavernkeeper's frequent proximity to alcohol and dance meant he and his family were often associated with licentiousness and ribaldry.

Indeed, when Jews visited taverns, it was a sign that they were on the margins of respectability.[26] A Jew who goes to a tavern might find himself coerced into eating unkosher food, at least in the world of Leopold von Sacher-Masoch's 1882 novella *Der Judenraphael* (The Raphael of the Jews). Although the antisemitic artist Plutin Samojlenko and his friends enjoy playing mean-spirited pranks on the local Jews, Sacher-Masoch implies that the fiddler Abraham Tabak does not mind when they force him to consume forbidden food and wine at gunpoint.[27] Indeed, the incident is the start of their unlikely friendship. While Sacher-Masoch did not always share the same cultural concerns as his Jewish contemporaries—and has been accused of having a primarily aesthetic interest in Jewish life—he was not alone in portraying the tavern as a space in which normal social rules became muddled.

Even a Jewish-run tavern could be a morally ambiguous place for Jews to meet. In Dovid Pinski's 1906 Yiddish play *Yankl der shmid* (Yankl the Blacksmith), Yankl, a wagon driver's son who is known to enjoy alcohol and women at Khayke's tavern, tries to court Tamara, a young woman from a rabbinic family. Her uncle calls Yankl an "oysvurf" (scoundrel) and questions whether he can even be considered a Jew.[28] Although Yankl is charming and good-looking, his rowdy ways render him a dubious marital prospect; yet ultimately his ability to provide financially for the orphaned Tamara and his promise that he has given up the tavern overcome her family's objections to his social status and reputed intemperance.[29]

In his 1912 Yiddish novella *A roman fun a ferd-ganef* (*Romance of a Horse Thief*), Joseph Opatoshu depicts a seedy Polish tavern where Zanvl the horse thief goes to recuperate with his underworld friends after a successful smuggling venture. This scene serves a pivotal role in the novella, since it shows that Zanvl cannot escape his unscrupulous connections, even though he is in love with Rachel, a respectable Hasidic woman. In this context, tavern dancing underscores the full extent of the social gulf between the two lovers. Opatoshu emphasizes Zanvl's dubious milieu by describing Christian peasants who dance together in close proximity to the Jewish criminals: "The boy was half drunk, his eyes glazed and his hair disheveled. He held the girl very tightly, lifted her into the air and grunted loudly as they danced."[30] These nameless dancers project an air of drunkenness, coarseness, and physical intimacy between the sexes—all of which would undoubtedly be looked down upon by Rachel's family.

Yet while Hasidim might dismiss such dancing as irrelevant non-Jewish entertainment, the fact that the Jewish tavern guests also engage in mixed-sex dancing is much more problematic. Zanvl is reluctant to tell his friends about his new romance, which leads to complications when his former lover, Manke the tavern maid, "pulled Zanvl up by the hands and drew him into the waltz."[31] Although Zanvl eventually changes his mind and stops dancing, Opatoshu makes it clear that the tavern is not a location that inspires emotional fidelity. Zanvl's friend Gradul proceeds to dance a lively mazurka with Manke, even though he is newly married. Indeed, Opatoshu suggests that Manke deliberately dances in a way that will exhibit her legs for Zanvl's (and the reader's) delectation: "When it came time for her to stomp her foot and bang her heel, she turned her leg in such a way that the dress flew up and her legs looked out temptingly from beneath her striped stockings."[32] The tavern is a space that blurs social boundaries between ethnic groups, couples, and men and women. Ultimately it is a site that pulls Zanvl, despite his best intentions, back into the underworld.

Dancing often characterized the licentious behavior of rural taverns——especially mixed-sex dance. Trunk makes this association particularly clear in the case of his uncle, a lusty man whose sexual appetites lead him to constantly impregnate his wife and publicly pinch her rear end. Uncle Mordekhai-Ber also feels compelled to dance with local peasant girls (referred to in the text as *shikses*, a derogatory term). When his niece (Trunk's mother, daughter of a wealthy farmer) marries the scion of a prominent rabbinic dynasty, Mordekhai-Ber wants to engage in mixed-sex dancing, yet he feels it would be inappropriate to do so in his new silk finery, since this is the attire of a pious Jew. For a long time he tries to control these impulses:

> His eyes under the velvet skullcap bulged like a wolf's as they wandered over to the young Gentile girls dancing [vos hobn zikh tantsndik gedreyt] in bright Łowicz dresses and harkening to the lively music of the band. The feet of Uncle Mordekhai-Ber twitched, and he was in a mood to snag a girl and dance off with her as was his wont at the annual market in Osmolin, but he was spooked by the shining black silk coat he was wearing, and his nose still held the forbidding fragrance of the heavy coats and fur hats of the rabbis who had sat solemnly around the tables. And besides, he was scared to dance with a peasant woman at this moment in front of Grandfather Borukh as though it was just any market day![33]

Mordekhai-Ber struggles to behave properly in front of the illustrious guests from the groom's side, yet he is ultimately unable to resist the temptation of mixed-sex dancing. Used to living amongst and carousing with peasants, Mordekhai-Ber cannot help but join in the dancing, although he tacitly acknowledges the incompatibility of peasant dancing with Hasidic weddings by removing his Jewish wedding finery: "He hastily tore off the silk coat and tossed it to pregnant Aunt Genendl. . . . He rubbed his hands gleefully after the peasant fashion and grabbed a girl from among the dancing peasant couples and jolted with her into the circle [karahod]."[34] Mordekhai-Ber's behavior confirms the extent to which mixed-sex dancing is seen as behavior that belongs in a tavern or a marketplace, rather than at a respectable wedding.

Mordekhai-Ber struggles with his desire to—and, indeed, his typical practice of—dance. Trunk details his uncle's difficulties as a way of showing the way his mother's rural but prosperous family is far removed from his father's illustrious one, and he underscores the ways in which his mother was unprepared for her new status as the bride of a prominent rabbi's grandson. Yet if it is a challenge for his mother, how much the more so for her cousins, who are raised by such improper parents? Indeed, the issue of children is an important one in literary representations of taverns. A tavernkeeper's family might be the only Jewish family in a rural area, which meant it could be a challenge to provide children with a Jewish education or to prevent them from being influenced by the peasant culture around them. While it was possible to hire a tutor to teach them, children often considered a lone Hebrew instructor to be less compelling than the playmates, nature, tavern, and customs of the surrounding area. Additionally, it was a greater priority to teach boys about religious texts than girls, which meant young women might be even more influenced by the surrounding area.[35] The tavern was a space that ensured the family's livelihood, yet it was also one in which the tavernkeeper's children confronted the temptation of peasant dancing. Rural Jewish families struggled, at least in literature, with passing on Jewish knowledge and customs to children who may have found the pastimes of their neighbors more compelling.[36]

In literary texts, children do not need to personally participate in tavern dancing for it to exercise a destructive influence. Such is the case in Yiddish writer I. L. Peretz's 1904 short story "Aropgelozte oygn" ("Downcast Eyes"). Yekhiel Mikhl, an innkeeper who runs a tavern near Prague, is troubled by his daughter Malke's fascination with the tavern, since she "could not be torn from the tavern, especially at night, when the music played and there was dancing. She would sit there night after night feasting her eyes on the young male peasants as they flirted with the peasant girls and danced in a dizzying circle, singing to make the tavern resound and tremble."[37] While Yekhiel Mikhl and his wife view tavernkeeping as an occupation that allows them to support themselves and dower their daughters, Malke is obsessed with the worldly aspects of their profession. Even more ominously, when the young lord, the son of Yekhiel Mikhl's noble patron, catches sight of her one day in the tavern, he makes Yekhiel Mikhl an offer to "buy" his daughter, in exchange for a rent-free lease on the tavern for the rest of his life. The nobleman's offer to trade the tavern for Malke's virginity underscores the morally problematic nature of parenting as a tavernkeeper. Although Yekhiel Mikhl marries his daughter off in order to prevent her from entering into such an illicit relationship, she has already become infatuated with the young nobleman.[38]

Malke retreats into a dream world; her outward appearance was "as polished, sculpted, and pure as the finest crystal," but "inside lay the tavern with its singing and dancing and merrymaking."[39] Unbeknownst to her parents or even her husband, she fantasizes about the young nobleman who wanted to take her as his mistress:

> No sooner did she close her eyes, be it in the synagogue near the grating, or at the end of the Sabbath during the prayer "God of Abraham," or during the blessing of the Sabbath candles, then the passion in the blood erupted within her, and she danced—may God forgive her—with the young master in the middle of a circle in the tavern after the harvest.[40]

Malke imagines the forbidden physical pleasure of mixed-sex dancing in the familiar context of her parents' tavern. Her fantasy is deeply transgressive, yet there is also a logical path from the circumstances of her upbringing to her fantasies as an adult woman. Even when tavernkeepers are devout Jews who try doggedly to adhere to the requirements of their faith in a rural setting, writers suggest that the nature of their occupation risks their children's Jewish identities and even their life and happiness. As will be further elaborated through the examples of *Die Kinder des Randars* and *Yankl Boyle*, this predicament can be characterized by the issue of Jewish participation in peasant dancing.

"Where Is the Fatherland of the Jews?": *Die Kinder des Randars*

At a critical point midway through Kompert's 1848 German-language novella *Die Kinder des Randars*, the protagonist, a Jewish Gymnasium student and tavernkeeper's son named Moritz, visits a Bohemian peasant wedding with his Catholic classmate Honza. Moritz's landlord, a pious Jew, hears about the young man's exploits and writes a letter to Moritz's parents: "Do you know what your darling Moritz undertook? On the holy *yontef* [holiday], he went into town with his *khaver* (pal) Honza and there he danced and drank and eat. And with whom did he dance and drink? With peasant maids and boys, God have mercy!"[41] Most scholars who discuss *Die Kinder des Randars* or the scene of Moritz's transgression focus on the fact that the young man consumes unkosher food.[42] Here we consider the first offense on the list: dancing. More specifically, Moritz dances with a Bohemian peasant woman, as part of an attempt to prove to Honza that he can be a "Hussite," a paragon of Bohemian masculinity. In doing so, Moritz violates both communal boundaries and the traditional Jewish prohibition on mixed-sex dancing.

Dance scenes reveal changing social values and challenge the fabric of the Jewish family in Kompert's novella. Not only do these dance scenes explicitly depict men and women dancing together, but they also trespass religious norms. In *Die Kinder des Randars*, dance scenes occur when Jews and Bohemian peasants meet, and they coincide with moments when Honza persuades Moritz and his sister Hannele to commit acts that violate the values of their parents.[43] Transgressive dancing intensifies the emotional stakes, psychological drama, and moral dilemma in a way that is simultaneously entertaining for readers. By using mixed-sex dancing to underscore rebellion, rather than merely focusing on Moritz's acculturation, Kompert reveals the way each sibling's flirtation with Bohemian culture reflects gendered social and educational norms and underscores the centrality of the individual, as opposed to the community, in modernization.[44] That is to say, Kompert's novella depicts the way individual choices on or around the dance floor contribute to the breakdown of the traditional Jewish family.

Leopold Kompert (1822–1886) was born in Münchengrätz in Bohemia (today Mnichovo Hradiště, Czech Republic) and moved to Vienna in 1839. He came to prominence for his many German-language narratives of traditional Jewish life in Bohemia and Moravia, including two novels and five volumes of ghetto tales.[45] Jonathan Hess notes that such stories about traditional Jewish life were "the most prevalent form of literature produced and consumed by German Jews in the nineteenth century" and credits Kompert with popularizing the genre.[46] *Die Kinder des Randars* is one of Kompert's best-known works[47] and his first extended story, which was published in his debut collection *Aus dem Ghetto* (Out of the Ghetto). *Die Kinder des Randars* explores the temptation of non-Jewish culture. It draws unsettling conclusions about the future of Jewish communal life and the feasibility of negotiating between worlds.

The novella centers upon the sole Jewish family in a Bohemian village—the randar (arendator) Rebb Schmul; his wife, the randarin Rachel; and their two surviving children, Hannele and Moschele (later called Moritz). At the story's beginning, Rebb Schmul is a prosperous and respected man. He enjoys the special patronage of the count from whom he leases the tavern, due to the nobleman's lingering affection for Rachel, who was a beautiful woman in her youth. Rebb Schmul is friendly with his fellow villagers, the Bohemian peasants who patronize his tavern. What is more, Jewish beggars travel for miles to stay with him and enjoy his hospitality. Moschele grows particularly close to one of these guests, a proto-Zionist named Mendel Wilna who has abandoned his family to raise money for the cause of rebuilding Jerusalem. Rachel enlists the help of both Mendel Wilna and the count to convince Rebb Schmul to send Moschele to Gymnasium, even though such studies were unusual for a Jew at the time. She is eager for him to take advantage of this opportunity for social mobility and even changes her son's Jewish-sounding name to Moritz to aid in this endeavor. Hannele, meanwhile, remains in the village and works in the tavern.

Moritz excels in school and successfully negotiates the unfamiliar, sometimes hostile environment, yet his greatest challenge comes much closer to home. Honza is Moritz's only ally and greatest rival at school. Moritz and Honza grew up together in their village, Honza and his father drink at Rebb Schmul's tavern, and Honza is Hannele's best friend. Honza embodies Bohemian culture in the novella and tempts both siblings to rebel against their family and community. Honza convinces Moritz to join him at a peasant wedding, for which Moritz receives community censure and his mother's disapproval. Then Honza's father, who has a tendency to drink away his money, sets fire to the randar's barn, which lands the peasant in jail, devastates Rebb Schmul economically, and leads to the illness which costs Rachel her life. Honza wants to become a priest but cannot afford to do so, until Hannele lends him money she steals from her father and dying mother. After his return, Honza tries to persuade Hannele to convert to Christianity.

Since Hannele loves Honza and dreads the idea of an arranged marriage, she sneaks out of the family home in order to convert. In a dramatic confrontation, Moritz persuades Hannele to return home, but her decisions cost her her father (who dies shortly after), Honza's love, and any chance for marriage within the Jewish community. At the story's end, Moritz works as a doctor in the Jewish quarter and cares for his unmarried sister.

Dance reveals the influence and appeal of Czech culture in the novella, since it is a cultural practice and leisure pursuit that facilitates boundary-crossing, physical contact, and potential romance, all while transgressing Jewish cultural norms. In addition, Czech nationalists specifically cite the importance of dance in Bohemian folk culture. In his monumental 1836 history of Bohemia, published in German as *Geschichte von Böhmen* (History of Bohemia), historian František Palacký discusses the praiseworthy attributes of the old Bohemians and notes their "love of song, music, and dance."[48] Similarly, Albert Waldau argues in his 1859 *Böhmische Nationaltänze* (Bohemian National Dances) that Slavs particularly revere dance and that, even among the Slavs, Bohemians dance the most. At every social occasion, "there must be singing, rejoicing, and dancing."[49] Scholars attest to the rich variety of Bohemian folk dances, including the Husitská, a warlike dance performed by the late medieval Hussites, which has since been forgotten to history.[50] The most famous Bohemian dance is the polka, which achieved widespread fame as a ballroom dance.

In *Die Kinder des Randars*, dance scenes depict moments of tension, regardless of the cultural and religious background of the dancers. The fact that Kompert portrays a Jewish wedding,[51] a Bohemian peasant wedding, and tavern dancing as potentially catastrophic underscores Kompert's inability to envision a happy resolution for his characters. Nonetheless, Kompert focuses particular attention on dance scenes that occur when Jews and Christians meet in mixed spaces, such as the tavern.

Kompert describes the tavern as a place of mingling and even tolerance, yet dancing reveals the limits of religious coexistence in the village. The randarin Rachel's attitude toward dance exposes her dismissive opinion of her peasant customers, even though she depends upon their consumption of alcohol for her family's livelihood. Kompert notes, "When there was dancing in the tavern on Sundays, the children were never allowed to join."[52] The children are required to stay out of the way, as the peasants get "schicker" (drunk), a Yiddish word that Kompert defines as "trunken" in the text.[53] Moritz's mother tells him he does not need to see it, and Jews, moreover, are not designed to get drunk like peasants. Not surprisingly, Kompert includes Honza in this scene, as one of the peasants who consumes alcohol and engages in behavior that would be inappropriate for a Jew such as Moritz. By putting his archetypical Bohemian character in the tavern, Kompert underscores Rachel's distinction between Bohemian drunkenness and Jewish sobriety. Ultimately, however, the borders between Jewish and Bohemian behavior become blurred, and the parents cannot keep the children away from the dancing.

Kompert differentiates between how Honza tempts each of the siblings with Bohemian culture and reveals how both Moritz and Hannele rebel against Jewish communal norms. Moritz faces a choice between his Jewish upbringing, the German culture he encounters in school, and Czech nationalism. Hannele is tempted by Czech culture and the allure of romance. Kompert thus articulates two different, gendered paths for Jews to engage with Bohemian identity, which he presents in two key dance scenes: when Moritz joins Honza at a peasant wedding to prove his Bohemian masculinity and as a backdrop when Hannele leaves her dying mother to give Honza money so he can train to be a priest. Where Moritz's dancing is publicly undertaken, quickly regretted, and soon censured by the community, Hannele's action is covert and part of a long-term, unnoticed shift in her alliances, which continues to escalate. Significantly, Moritz's transgression occurs when he leaves home and encounters nationalist ideology at school, whereas Hannele opposes the norms of her family precisely because she was left uneducated and vulnerable to seduction at home.

In the chapter entitled, "Where Is the Fatherland of the Jews?" Honza advocates Bohemian independence and glorifies the Hussites. The Hussites were followers of late medieval Bohemian priest and Christian religious reformer Jan Hus. By the nineteenth century, both Protestants and Catholics characterized the Hussites as Bohemian freedom fighters and as symbols of national identity. Such ideas are more challenging for Moritz than the Christian prayer he encounters daily at school and which he already knows how to negotiate, by saying the *Shema* prayer to himself. As a Jew, Kompert explains, Moritz cannot fully grasp the essence of Bohemian religious and doctrinal conflicts, but he intuitively understands a struggle for freedom and independence because it reminds him of Jewish history and yearning for Jerusalem. Christian prayer and doctrine do not tempt Moritz, but he identifies with a liberal fight for freedom.

Moritz's perspective both reflects Kompert's liberal views and challenges the ideas of Moritz's friends and family. Jewish elders in the novella consider the concept of Bohemia to be yet another notion that is of little relevance for Jews, other than as a geographic designation that helps Jewish travelers find the tavern or as a political entity that treats Jews better than in Russian Poland. Honza, on the other hand, dismisses Moritz's claim about similarities between Bohemian and Jewish history completely. When Moritz tries to compare the Jewish Maccabees to the Bohemian Hussites, Honza claims that the Maccabees are long dead, whereas Hussites still live in anyone who speaks Czech. Moritz promises to be a Hussite but rightly wonders if Jewish identity has a place in Honza's Bohemian nationalism.

Honza's vision of Jewish inclusion in Bohemian culture demands complete assimilation. Whether or not Honza is aware of how Rachel dismissively refers to tavern customers as drunken non-Jews, he considers Jewish dietary laws and separation to be (or at least to be interpretable as) a mockery of Bohemian culture. When Moritz hears music from a peasant wedding and says he would like to see the festivities, Honza claims that the revelers will think Moritz is insulting them. Although Moritz denies this, Honza says that if they invite him to eat and he refuses to eat unkosher food, "aren't you laughing at them?"[54] Honza challenges Moritz, mockingly calling him a handsome Hussite, and Moritz impulsively tells Honza to come along as he proves that he belongs. He will show that he is a true Bohemian, which means embracing the legacy of a Christian religious sect. According to Honza's worldview, the main non-Jewish perspective in the novella, a Jew such as Moritz can join in Bohemian national identity, but at the cost of his own language, culture, and ritual practice.

Although Moritz flirts with this vision, like Hannele later on, he ultimately rejects a national identity that forces him to break completely with the Jewish community. For one night, however, Moritz tries to prove that he is a Hussite and joins in the festivities:

[Moritz] sprang forth, Honza following after him. Breathlessly they came
down the mountain and went into the village.

The resounding trumpets guided them to the wedding hall. Honza immediately threw himself into the middle of the turmoil on the dance floor, as
if he were a local. He seized a pretty lass and began a folk dance [volksthüm-
lichen Tanz] with her, stamping his feet and whooping for joy. Moritz stood
off to the side and watched. "Follow me, don't be shy." Moritz's head spun,
his feet began to turn on their own accord and before he knew what he was
doing, he was in the middle of the dancing and joined in the rejoicing and
cheering, holding a bony maid by the hand.[55]

Kompert's description emphasizes the ecstasy of this moment, while nonetheless acknowledging Moritz's outsider status. Although Moritz initially
makes the decision to join the festivities, spurred by Honza's cynicism and
the sound of the music, Honza is the first to actually participate in the dancing, and he still needs to encourage Moritz to copy him. Honza dances a
folk dance, grabs an attractive dance partner, and acts as if he belongs on the
dance floor. Even though Moritz executes the dance steps without needing
to even think about it, he must content himself with a bony maid instead of
a pretty lass. A more desirable partner, Kompert suggests, might be unwilling
to dance with a Jew. Even in the moment in which Moritz tries hardest to
show that he is Bohemian, Kompert's description questions how fully Bohemian a Jew can be. Such a question is emphasized by the fact that Honza
enjoys a feeling of shared companionship with Moritz throughout the wedding, whereas the randar's son soon recovers from his excesses of Bohemian
nationalism and regrets his actions.

Kompert focuses on the relationship between Moritz and Honza and on
the stakes of their shared participation in this Bohemian marriage celebration. Even the women with whom they dance are simply tools that the two
men use for their bonding, although Honza dances with a more decorative
partner. Mixed-sex dancing is an important symbol of boundary-crossing
and cultural difference, but the real mixed partnership on the dance floor is
between the randar's son and the future priest. One can even say that Moritz,
like his sister Hannele later on, is considering a metaphoric "marriage" with
Honza. Kompert does not imply that the two friends and sometime rivals

share romantic feelings (unlike Hannele and Honza, who also cannot marry), yet Moritz contemplates his participation in the Bohemian culture that Honza represents and a permanent solidarity with his childhood companion, all with the backdrop of a wedding.

Indeed, scholars such as Yaron Peleg acknowledge a homosocial and even homoerotic strain in nineteenth-century European nationalist discourse. Peleg considers homoeroticism, like nationalist ideology, to be a form of exaggerated masculinity, as exemplified by eighteenth-century classicist and art historian Johann Winckelmann, who inspired German interest in Greek imagery and body culture.[56] Honza and Moritz attempt to solidify their bond through shared physical activity and identification with national heroes. Moritz's reference to the Maccabees prefigures early twentieth-century Zionist rhetoric, which encouraged European Jews to seek out models in ancient, warlike Jewish men.[57] United in their identification with the Hussites, Moritz and Honza share a liberating, libidinal moment of masculine solidarity, which uses women's dancing bodies as props to convey a sense of community between men. Like the young lass, Moritz follows Honza in the dance, even though the two men mask the closeness of their interaction by use of female dance partners. The stakes of such a choice are apparent when members of the Jewish community hear about Moritz's participation in the revelry. They report the transgression to Moritz's landlord, who sends a reproving letter to the young man's parents, which Rachel receives and hides from her pious husband. While a dance might initially appear to be mere amusement, here it has very serious consequences. On her deathbed, Rachel tells Moritz that the letter broke her heart.

Hannele does not have a similar opportunity to hear her mother's last wishes and remarks. Rachel's sudden turn for the worse coincides with a parish fair, and the peasants insist on dancing in the tavern, despite the randar's attempts to stop the disturbance of his beloved wife's final hours. Hannele must tend to the guests, including wild Pawel, a man who physically assaulted her father in his own tavern when he tried to stop the dancing. The boisterous revelry creates sharp divisions between Jews and Bohemian peasants and reminds readers of how Rebb Schmul and his wife, once respected members of the village, have shrunk in influence and become marginal within their own home. Yet it is precisely in this context, under the cover of Pawel's rowdy dancing, that Hannele furtively helps Honza and further undermines the Jewish family. As is the case throughout the novella, Hannele's work in the tavern, and her family's benign neglect because she is female, give her greater freedom to spend time with Honza and greater vulnerability to his persuasions.

Where Moritz's one moment of transgression receives an immediate reprimand, nobody notices the gradual process by which Honza seduces Hannele away from the beliefs of her family over more than a decade. There is a stark contrast between the way Rebb Schmul questions whether Moritz can remain a good Jew while studying in Gymnasium and his utter disregard for Hannele's temptation at home. Moritz is surprised to hear his sister sing a plaintive Bohemian love song, but he does not grasp the deeper implications of her fondness for Bohemian culture and expression of romantic longing. What is more, the moment Moritz goes to school, Hannele's formal education ceases, since her parents no longer arrange for a tutor in Jewish subjects. Rachel does not object if her daughter (but not her son) receives practical training in the family business instead. This parental choice unintentionally makes Hannele vulnerable to Honza's advances, since she lacks sufficient religious or secular training to counter his theological arguments and, moreover, works in the tavern, where he can visit her without suspicion. Tragically, Honza is the only person who takes the trouble to actually teach or discuss ideas with Hannele. Despite the young peasant's frequent dismissal of Jewish concepts he does not understand or Jews who displease him, Honza and Hannele's affection for each other transcends religious boundaries.

The peasant festivities disguise the moment when Hannele brings Honza the twenty guilder he needs to study in seminary for two years, money that she takes from her family's income on this particularly profitable day. She thus prioritizes a Christian man's aspirations to become a priest over the financial well-being of her own family, giving a small fortune to the son of the man responsible for the family's financially precarious situation and her mother's fatal illness. Indeed, when Honza asks if Hannele's father knows about the money, she screams and runs back to the house, only to find that her conversation with Honza has cost her the last opportunity to speak with her dying mother and receive her blessing. Although Kompert does not reveal Hannele's inner thoughts at the time, she later tells Honza that giving him the money was "my great sin," since her mother died at the same moment.[58]

Hannele's covert action undermines her loyalty to her family, which is mirrored by disorder on the dance floor when she meets with Honza. "Hannele used a moment when the tavern had become tumultuous. Drunken Pawel had snatched the dance partner of another man, who refused to give her up. The result was one of those typical brawls, which were well known on the premises."[59] Although Hannele's transgression is much less public than her brother's involvement in the Bohemian wedding, and indeed never becomes known, they both take place in the context of Bohemian dancing. Furthermore, precise dance figure at the moment of her rebellious act mimics the social configuration between the three young people in the novel. Pawel, like Moritz and Honza at the wedding, has the opportunity to test out his prowess on the dance floor and negotiate his relationship to other men through his handling of a female partner's body. Pawel's very action—the attempt to take a woman away from her dance partner—underscores the stakes of Honza's request to Hannele. Honza asks Hannele to support him (in this case financially) at the expense of her family, an action he repeats (with graver consequences) when he returns from seminary and tries to convince her to convert. Indeed, he uses her remorse for her transgression that night as an argument in favor of baptism, since he reframes her deed as an act of Christian charity and suggests that conversion will give her absolution from her feelings of filial guilt. Pawel's wild actions on the dance floor are not merely a backdrop and a cover for Hannele's furtive actions in the garden, but they also reiterate them.

In this sense, the tavern dancing continues the pattern of substitution that took place in the wedding dancing. There Moritz and Honza "danced" together, using their female partners as surrogates. In this later scene, Pawel, his rival, and their dance partner stand in for the three young people. Moritz, who has just promised his dying mother to remain a Jew, will no longer indulge in peasant revelry. Instead, he guards his sister and seeks to prevent her from partaking permanently in the world he tested out so briefly. To put it in stark terms, Pawel's dance acts out the figure of the forthcoming struggle between Honza and Moritz for Hannele's soul. Honza, like Pawel, seeks to wrest a young woman from her "proper" place. Yet even though Moritz succeeds in preventing Hannele from leaving her community, it is a bitter triumph that costs Hannele her remaining parent and the chance of a good marriage. The fact that Honza's stand-in Pawel is the only dancer in the tavern with a name and a personality hints that the forces of order and the Jewish family might be fighting a losing battle. While the Hussites may be remembered in the hearts of Czech-speakers, rural Jews, Kompert warns, may soon be forgotten.

Dance is a leitmotif in Kompert's novel, a reoccurring theme that manifests the physical temptation of Bohemian peasant life. The randar and his wife initially shield their children from boisterous peasant dancing, yet they are ultimately unable to protect their children from the seductive physicality of Gentile culture—which they themselves invite into the family tavern. Kompert inserts dance at key narrative moments. Each sibling's crucial act of transgression takes place against the backdrop of peasant dancing. Moreover, the way both siblings interact with Honza is reminiscent of a dance figure. Honza "dances" with each of the siblings, pushing each one to challenge traditional restraints. To take the metaphor further, although Honza is conscious of the differences between his two dance "partners" and modifies his behavior depending on whether he engages with the educated brother or innocently doting sister, the steps he performs follow a similar pattern as he encourages the siblings to see his worldview and comply with his wishes.

Jonathan Hess rightly notes the novella's ambivalence and the fact that Moritz does not follow Kompert's path to Vienna, but instead remains in the Bohemian ghetto.[60] Moritz and Hannele remain isolated and unmarried at the novel's end; the chain of Jewish tradition ends with this generation. Moritz, a doctor, devotes himself to healing the bodies and souls of ghetto Jews, including his sister. The children of the randar do not have children of their own. Kompert's Jewish family is fractured, broken, and unsustainable, even though the randar's son has become a doctor. Yet, Kompert suggests, both the path of assimilation that Honza advocates and Mendel Wilna's dreams of Jerusalem are no real alternative for Bohemian Jews. Where is the fatherland of the Jews? Kompert never fully answers the question. Only when there is an answer, he suggests, will Jews be able to find a home for themselves on the dance floor.

"A Tremendous Dancer": *Yankl Boyle*

In *Die Kinder des Randars*, Moritz is instructed to stand quietly during the Christian prayers in Gymnasium and think of something that will bring him closer to God.[61] The *Shema* declaration of faith that Moritz says to himself is also an important sign of Jewish identity in Leon Kobrin's 1898 Yiddish novella *Yankl Boyle*. Yet where Moritz chooses to recite the Shema with full awareness of the Hebrew words and what they mean, Yankl cannot even remember the words to the prayer, a failure that shows how difficult it can be for a tavernkeeper's son to attain the most basic Jewish socialization. He views the Shema as a Jewish equivalent of crossing himself and tries to use it as a good luck charm to ward off his guilt-filled visions of his dead father.[62] Yankl is a fisherman[63] who has grown up among Russian peasants and feels most culturally identified with them. He nonetheless refuses to convert to Christianity, even though it means losing the woman he loves, and, ultimately, his own life. Throughout the novella, Kobrin stresses Yankl's ability to perform peasant dances, in sharp contrast to his utter failure to master basic Jewish liturgy or even properly pronounce his native Yiddish.

Yankl's predicament comes into particular focus when he attends an *igrishche* (peasant celebration involving dancing, carnivalesque elements, and games) with his sweetheart Natasha, who is not Jewish.[64] They had initially attended a fair in the village, yet Yankl's fellow fisherman Zalmen hassled the couple. He jealously predicted that Yankl would convert to Christianity and marry Natasha, an outcome that Yankl refuses to consider. He and Natasha go to the peasant dance instead, where they are less likely to face harassment, yet Yankl remains haunted by Zalmen's words and a vision of his deceased father: "An hour before, he would have thrown himself into the dancing crowd with such fire that they would all know how he, Yankl, can dance."[65] Yankl wishes that, like his neighbors, he could cross himself to ward off his disturbing vision. Yet while Christians can seek comfort in this gesture, a Jew must content himself with words—and words are not Yankl's forte. He tries to remember the Shema, yet to his shame he cannot remember even this fundamental prayer. He resolves to go home and be a proper Jew, like his father would have wished, but the dancing continues and Yankl cannot resist. He throws himself into the center of the circle and demonstrates his prowess on the dance floor, an act that exemplifies Yankl's inability to resist forbidden passion.

Born in Russia, Leon Kobrin (1872–1946) wrote stories, novels, and approximately twenty plays in Yiddish.[66] He immigrated to the United States when he was in his early twenties and supported his family by working in a laundry while getting his start as a writer.[67] His novella *Yankl Boyle* "established him as a major young writer."[68] Like many of his other works, it combines realism and melodrama. According to one obituary, Kobrin's protagonist Yankl "became one of the favorite characters of Jewish literature."[69] In 1908, Kobrin published a dramatic adaptation of the novella *Yankl Boyle*, which is also called *Der dorfsyung* (The Village Youth), translated as *The Child of Nature*.[70] To the extent Kobrin is known today, it is primarily as a dramatist. Although the theatrical adaptation[71] of *Yankl Boyle* has maintained greater popularity, his breakthrough novella received particular attention in its day. Prolific translator Isaac Goldberg wrote a letter to Kobrin on March 20, 1917, in which he stated that he was interested in "stirring up an interest in New York's Yiddish writers" and thought "your 'Yankel Boile'—in its story form, together with some of your other tales, might make a good venture."[72]

Kobrin depicts his character Yankl using some of the same tropes about rural life that Kompert employs in *Die Kinder des Randars*: the position of a Jewish tavernkeeper's family in a rural area, dancing that transgresses social boundaries, and the seeming impossibility of resolving conflicts between Jewish and peasant culture. Yet, at the same time, Kobrin's work has a very different tone, in large part because he conveys a strikingly different image of Jewish masculinity. Commenting in 1927 on the emergence of the *molodyets* (fine youth, a Russian loan word) figure in Yiddish theater, A. Mukdoyni writes:

> In the early days of Jewish operetta the dancing comedian was always a *shlimazl* with *payes* and a long *kapote*. Then a new type of Jewish lad appeared in the Russian-Jewish milieu. . . . An agile dancer, with a quick tongue, he will beat up anyone who insults him; he will fight for a girl, for the revolution, for a comrade. He is not comical. He is not a *yold* [fool] like the bourgeois sons and daughters. He is full of joy.[73]

Mukdoyni's description of the molodyets, a figure shaped by radical politics and Russian culture, explicitly contrasts traditional and more modern forms of dancing. The molodyets, like the Zionist "New Jew," is a nimble dancer who is comfortable with his body and sexuality.[74] He marks an explicit break with the comically pathetic Jewish dancer in his traditional garb, as well as with the bourgeoisie—incidentally two of the main Jewish male types in German-language literary texts about Jews by authors such as Kompert. By the turn of the twentieth century, Yiddish authors, in America and in European cities,

incorporated vigorous Jewish dancer types akin to the Yiddish theater characters and Zionists. As is not so surprising for a tavernkeeper's son, Yankl
Boyle embodies the robust dancing Jew. Yet, contrary to Mukdoyni's classification, Yankl's joy does not last. Torn between his Jewish identity and his
attachment to peasant culture, Yankl's passion for the dance floor and for
Natasha ultimately lead him to suicide.[75]

Yankl is the only son of Nokhem, the Jewish tavernkeeper in the village
of Kholm (now in Belarus). The closest *minyen* (prayer quorum of ten Jewish
men) is in a village over five kilometers away. Yankl grows up in close contact
with his Christian neighbors: "Yankl was born a Jew, but from his education,
his character, even his language, he was a Russian peasant."[76] Kobrin makes
it clear that Yankl's socialization is a result of his upbringing and his father's
occupation in a village that does not have a Jewish community. While boys
typically started *kheyder* (primary school) at age three, Yankl does not have
access to Jewish educational institutions. Until the age of seven, he is allowed
to run free with the peasant children, although his father warns him of divine
punishment if he eats their unkosher food.[77] When he is seven, his father
hires a tutor to give him a Jewish education. Kobrin implies that Nokhem
is not educated enough to teach his son, beyond his grim pronouncements
about the consequences of impious behavior. When Yankl asks him why the
God who makes Jews act differently from their neighbors is so bad (*shle-
kht*), Nokhem's response is to yell at him.[78] Writing for an audience of fellow
Yiddish-speaking Jews, Kobrin (unlike Kompert) feels no compunction to
defend Jewish religious beliefs, and characters such as Nokhem and Yankl
maintain their Jewish identities out of superstition, a sense of obligation, or
self-respect, rather than spiritual or intellectual conviction.

Yankl resents being forced to study when his friends can continue to play
outside in nature, and he decides to get rid of his tutor. At night he shoves
the sleeping young man off the oven (on top of which they both sleep) onto
his mother's side of the mattress on the floor below. By the time a new tutor
comes, it is too late: Yankl speaks like a peasant. While it may seem im-
probable that Yankl would speak Yiddish with a strikingly different accent
when he lives at home with his parents, Yankl's linguistic difficulties likely
resonated with Kobrin's immigrant audience in New York, who may have
regarded their children's Americanized Yiddish with ambivalence.[79] Yankl's

mother despairs that her son studies Torah like a Christian, and Nokhem's best efforts to coach Yankl in correct Hebrew pronunciation fail.[80] By the age of thirteen, he can barely manage the Hebrew prayers from a prayer book. Since Yankl is now considered an adult, and responsible for his own sins, Nokhem no longer forces him to study. He finds it embarrassing to take his son to the city, since people crowd around to hear Yankl's rustic speech. Nokhem's primary concern is that Yankl learn to properly recite the *Kaddish* memorial prayer after his death so that he will be spared hellfire, but he does not otherwise concern himself with his son's moral and spiritual development.

Yankl has not outgrown his love of rural amusements, although instead of climbing trees like he did in childhood, he now attends the festive village igrishches. Kobrin describes how, on Sundays and holidays, the unmarried peasant men and women gather together and dance to the accompaniment of local musicians.[81] Yankl is the best dancer in the village: "None of the peasants could kick their legs as high as Yankele, none of them was as eager to strike his rear on the ground as Yankele."[82] He dances kamarinskaias (*kamarinskes* in Yiddish) and hopkes until he drips with sweat.

As perhaps most famously rendered in composer Mikhail Glinka's 1848 "Kamarinskaia," an orchestral piece based on Russian folk melodies, the kamarinskaia is "a *naïgrish*, a dance to an ostinato melody that is repeated for as long as the dancers can keep it up."[83] This popular Russian folk dance, which was widespread among various ethnic groups in the Russian empire, involves stepping from heel to toe, with hands on the hips or spread to the sides, as well as squatting, jumping, leg extensions, and other acrobatic movements. It originated as a peasant dance, generally performed by men, but also developed women's, couple's, and group variants and was even danced at balls in the eighteenth and nineteenth centuries. In his novel *Selo Stepanchikovo i ego obitateli* (*The Village of Stepanchikovo and Its Inhabitants*), Fyodor Dostoyevsky describes a kamarinskaia performance with similar energy to Yankl's own dances: "[H]e whooped, shouted, laughed and clapped his hands; he danced as if impelled from within by an intangible force over which he had no control as he stamped his heels and strained to catch up with the ever-increasing tempo of the infectious tune."[84] This kind of dance demands great stamina and endurance. In contrast to German-language depictions of Jewish men

יאַנקעל בוילע (ד. קעסלער) : איך
טאַנץ! העי, מוזיקאַנטען, לעבעדיגער,
זשיווע י! העי־האָפ ! האָפ !

FIGURE 6. Caricature of actor David Kessler as Yankl Boyle in a typical pose, from a satirical New York Yiddish journal.

Yankl Boyle (D. Kessler): I'm dancing! Hey, musicians, make it livelier, *zhivey* [Russian: hurry up]! Hey-hop! Hop!

Source: *Der groyse kundes* [The Big Stick], December 8, 1916, p. 5. Courtesy of the Yiddish Book Center.

who have difficulty performing physically, Yankl is a better dancer than the Christian peasants.[85] Yankl's corporeality wins him praise from his neighbors, but it also leads him to tragedy.

The peasant women desire Yankl, for reasons Kobrin obligingly lists for his readers. First of all, Yankl can dance. Second, he is a very healthy young man. Third, unlike the other "cavaliers," he dresses like a nobleman. Natasha particularly appreciates Yankl for his dancing ability: "In her eyes, he was a suitable beau [kavalier] with every virtue: handsome, healthy, well-dressed, and a tremendous dancer."[86] Peasant women admire Yankl for his appearance and physicality, rather than for the attributes preferred by traditional Jews: refinement and scholarly erudition. While Yankl's relatives despair of his finding a suitable match with a Jewish woman on account of his rustic ways,[87] he fits in so well with the peasants that his religious confession does not seem to be much of an obstacle to them—although, of course, they would prefer that he convert to Christianity. While they are very aware he is a Jew, "The girls were so accustomed to Yankl that this race question never occurred to them."[88]

In striking contrast to Kompert's novella, antisemitism plays little role in *Yankl Boyle*.[89] The peasants are friendlier to Yankl when they think he may convert, and they see no reason why he would not wish to do so, but in general they seem to accept him.[90] At the same time, Jews speak dismissively of Christians, especially Christian women.[91] In a particularly troubling scene, the head fisherman, Reb Hersh Ber, tries to deflect Zalmen's jealousy of Yankl by groping Natasha himself. When she screams indignantly, Zalmen claims this is proof that Yankl's attentions have gone too far, since previously she did not object to such treatment. It is difficult to imagine Reb Hersh Ber looking for his "missing" tobacco pouch in a Jewish woman's bosom—in part because the novella includes almost no Jewish women, other than Yankl's mother, who dies early in the text. While Kobrin's description of tolerant peasants and defensive Jews might reflect his experience of rural relations in the late nineteenth century, it seems more probable that his portrayal was filtered through nostalgia or responded to American Jewish anxieties about the ease of assimilation into American culture. Indeed, Kobrin relies on stereotypical notions of peasants' earthy passion and openheartedness.[92]

Although Kobrin's plot hinges on the controversial topics of illicit sex and suicide, he avoids depicting the acts themselves. Other than a few passionate embraces, Kobrin's most explicit rendering of Yankl's physical prowess and unity with peasant culture occurs when he dances at an igrishche. As in *Die Kinder des Randars*, a Jewish man participates in peasant dancing in a manner that has both homosocial and heterosexual implications. Rather than dancing with a woman to show his connection to another man (as in Kompert's novella), Yankl dances with a man to impress a woman. With the crowd's encouragement, and in full view of Natasha, Yankl displays his masculine robustness by engaging in a public dance competition with another young man:

> Yankl began to move his shoulders, threw his head back, took hold of his right side and started dancing, first slowly, slowly and to one side. Soon though he went wild. . . . He shouted: hop, hop, hop! to the beat of the musicians, and he began to thrust his legs behind, throwing his backside to the ground, his legs beneath him, leaping up again and striking one bootleg against the other . . .[93]

The two men dance opposite each other, energized by the rivalry. In fact, sometimes the friendly dance competition veers closer to a brawl. Yankl mocks the other man by dancing facing away from him and, when they get close together, gives him a push with his behind. When the other dancer shouts to Yankl to stop and tries to grab his hand, he does not hear him and continues dancing, which leads them to blows, until Natasha throws herself between the two combatants and stops the fight. As this scene shows, Yankl displays the kind of physical performance that would make him a suitable match according to peasant courtship customs. Indeed, his sometimes comic antics might suggest an awareness of his spectators, showing that (unlike Moritz) Yankl feels he is part of a peasant community. Even Natasha finds a way to publicly show that she is partial to him. All that needs to be done, Natasha and the other peasants assume, is to fix the technicality of Yankl's religious confession.

Yankl's dancing reveals how, as a result of his father's occupation, he is much more adept at peasant masculinity than at Jewish ritual performance. At the same time, his father's expectations prevent him from embracing the culture in which he feels more at home, especially since he swore to Nokhem on his deathbed that he would remain a Jew. The fact that, for reasons that are not fully explained, Yankl never has the opportunity to take on his father's occupation further demonstrates that his upbringing has left him without a solid grounding.[94] Caught up in his own desires, he seems strangely unable, at least initially, to recognize how his behavior goes against the logic of both of the social worlds he inhabits, until it is pointed out to him by Zalmen and Natasha. Perhaps this outsider status is in part artificial: It seems difficult to imagine that Yankl's relatives cannot conceive of a Jewish woman from a similar rural background who might be able to share a life with him. Indeed, in Kobrin's play with the same title, Yankl is expected to marry his cousin.

Yet in the novella, for dramatic if not logical reasons, he is left in a terrible bind. Despite his most pious intentions, Yankl is unable to control his feelings for Natasha. Tragically, he combines superb physical performance with equally impressive failures in terms of his Jewish learning and emotional maturity. Even after his brutal initial rejection of Natasha (once she tells him she wants to marry him and reveals she is pregnant) and a period of increased religious observance, he again has intercourse with her when she seeks him out in the woods. Rather than admit to the strength of his feelings for the vulnerable mother of his unborn child, Yankl feels miserable that even his repentance and decision to follow a Jewish way of life cannot safeguard him from what he perceives as sinning with Natasha.

Yankl has committed his body physically to peasant culture, both in terms of the dancing that Kobrin describes and the sexual act that the author merely implies. Yet because he is unwilling to take the final step of baptizing his body, Yankl feels he must sacrifice his wayward body otherwise—ironically also through water, by drowning. Indeed, in the novella's dramatic final scene, as Yankl and the other fishman are out on the water during a thunderstorm, Kobrin returns to several motifs from the igrishche. Yankl reads the Shema in an effort to calm himself, and he has another terrifying vision of his dead father. Instead of throwing himself into a crowd of fellow dancers, Yankl performs an even more desperate and final act: He first tosses the paddles overboard (putting both himself and his boatmates at risk of drowning) and then throws himself into the water. While Yankl dances in a lively fashion, his physical escapades ultimately push him toward a watery end.

Both Kompert and Kobrin's works of fiction depict the temptation of rural leisure culture and the problem of how Jewish tavernkeepers should raise their children. Both male and female children struggle to negotiate competing values, educational expectations, and gender roles, at times finding it impossible to completely reconcile a Jewish and a rural identity. These stories help show how dancing took place among peasants—the sort of lower class, rural populations that might get less attention in other studies of modern leisure culture. Yet at the same time, writers such as Kompert and Kobrin addressed largely urban audiences, who might share similar concerns with how their children received a Jewish education and who their playmates were. The authors include details that would be familiar to their readers: Rebb Schmul and Rachel have only two children, which seems more typical for a bourgeois Viennese family than a rural Bohemian one, and Yankl speaks Yiddish with a peasant accent, which may reflect the way Kobrin's readers struggled with their children's Americanization. A story set in a European village might, on one hand, be a way for authors and readers to think nostalgically about their childhoods. It was also, however, a way for them to consider some of their own concerns about childrearing in a way that was displaced from the immediate reality of their own lives.

Literary fiction about tavernkeepers depicts a wide range of opportunities for dancing in rural areas: tavern gatherings, holiday celebrations, weddings, and market days. As exemplified by the igrishche, dancing was often a part of courtship. The next chapter demonstrates that there was also a close connection between dancing and courtship in urban, upwardly mobile circles. While rural Jews such as Yankl learned peasant dancing from their playmates while growing up, bourgeois Jews endeavored to master the more elaborate rules of ballroom etiquette. Yet despite their marked class and educational differences, Jews who attended balls might, like Moritz and Yankl, need to contend with being Jewish in a space with very few other Jewish dancers.

CHAPTER 4

THE BALLROOM

Questions of Admission and Exclusion

THE 1814–15 Congress of Vienna was the biggest party Europe had ever seen, and a Jewish woman, Baroness Fanny von Arnstein, was one of its most celebrated hostesses. In between political negotiations to redraw the map of Europe after the upheaval of Napoleonic conquest, delegates to the "dancing Congress" attended lavish balls, sophisticated salon gatherings, and raucous sleigh parties. According to historian Salo Baron, the Congress resembled "an uninterrupted dance."[1] Arnstein was renowned for her nightly gatherings and Tuesday salons, complete with music and dancing,[2] which were especially popular with diplomats from her native Prussia. She and her husband Nathan also hosted balls. For one particularly lavish event, they rented out the public ballroom *Zur Mehlgrube* in order to accommodate, in the words of memoirist Count Auguste de la Garde, the "most distinguished society of Vienna . . . all the influential people of the Congress, all foreigners of rank, all heads of the princely houses . . . only the sovereigns were missing."[3] The Arnsteins' social success marked the triumph of Vienna's upper bourgeoisie in the Napoleonic era.[4]

Yet the couple's public participation in these events also meant that they could be exposed to ridicule if they did not conform to proper ballroom etiquette. Count de la Garde describes an unfortunate incident in which the Arnsteins' daughter, Henriette von Pereira, was waltzing at a ball during the

Congress when she got caught in her gown and fell to the ground, taking her dancing partner rolling across the floor with her.[5] As the baptized daughter of a prominent, titled banker, Pereira was likely protected from the worst social consequences of her humiliating accident. Even her parents, who did not convert, belonged to a rarefied Jewish elite that enjoyed privileges that were unthinkable for their coreligionists across Europe. Arnstein sympathized with Jewish community representatives who had come to the Congress to lobby for civil rights;[6] but, at the same time, her privileged status meant that she was able to engage socially with the Christian nobility in ways that were unthinkable for all but the most elite Jews. In fact, the frequent association between the Congress of Vienna and balls is also apt in terms of conceptualizing class divides within the Jewish community, since balls helped formalize social hierarchies.

In memoirs and literary fiction, the ballroom was a particularly fraught space of encounter for Jews. This was true whether balls were majority Christian or Jewish. Indeed, balls were the primary location for Jewish and non-Jewish elites to dance together. It is no surprise that in Isaak Euchel's 1793 Yiddish play *Reb Henoch, oder: Woß tut me damit* (Reb Henoch, or, What Can Be Done with It?), Prussian officer Lieutenant Horn chooses a masquerade ball for an assignation with his married Jewish love interest, Elisabeth.[7] Their meeting is particularly transgressive since the ball is held on a Friday night, when Elisabeth's family is observing the Sabbath. European literary texts portray the ballroom as a site for testing Jewish admission to elite pastimes and present the ball as a window into Jewish cultural aspirations. Balls were, after all, venues where young people sought out socially appropriate future spouses. It was therefore incumbent upon dancers to exhibit grace and decorum, act according to gender-specific rules of etiquette, and associate with dance partners who could help them achieve or maintain their desired station in life.[8] Ball scenes show the limits of Jewish acculturation, because Jewish characters often do not get included as equals.

This chapter is concerned with two types of ballroom space: elite non-Jewish balls to which only select Jews were invited, and Jewish balls, which might also include a few Christian guests. Writers use both types of ball scene to depict issues of inclusion and exclusion. In either case, men sometimes impose their dominance over women and other men through displays of force, such as an insulting kiss in Karl Emil Franzos's *Judith Trachtenberg*, a text that will be discussed in greater detail in this chapter. When writers depict non-Jewish balls with only one or very few Jewish guests, they reveal the costs of this kind of social breakthrough for Jewish dancers. Their invitations might be precarious or conditional. They could face rude comments. Christian men might view Jewish women with particular sexual interest, which could verge into disrespect. Jewish ball guests were in a vulnerable situation, yet they were expected to be grateful for having been included.

Although Jews were in the majority at their own balls, guests still had to contend with a social hierarchy. Indeed, Jews often recapitulated the social expectations of non-Jewish balls at their own events. Ball scenes reveal tensions in the Jewish community, most commonly with regard to wealth, politics, or religious practice. When Christian men visit Jewish balls, Jewish women might deem them more attractive partners than Jewish men, as will be seen in the example of Clementine Krämer's *Der Weg des jungen Hermann Kahn* (The Path of Young Hermann Kahn). Not surprisingly, authors frequently use the ballroom in aborted or tragic marriage plots.

Non-Jewish Balls

Admission to balls was an important marker of Jewish social status. The way Jewish guests were treated at these social events demonstrated their degree of inclusion. More than any other dance space, the ballroom was a site where Jews sought to prove that they belonged in refined society. Writing about the Oppenheim banking family, the most prominent Jewish family in Königsberg in the mid-1820s, Fanny Lewald notes that the Christian mercantile elite tended to keep apart from the Oppenheims, and all Jews, because of antisemitism: "Only to the balls of the young Christian merchants and the other balls given collectively by the merchant aristocracy, the officials, and the nobility were the Oppenheims and one or two other rich Jewish families invited."[9] Although the Oppenheims had amassed great wealth, the fact that they were refused admission to the most elite balls shows the limits of their social integration.

Even when Jews did receive coveted invitations, there was no guarantee that they would not be insulted—especially, in literature, if this insult helped a writer with character development. In Anglo-Irish author Maria

Edgeworth's 1817 philosemitic novel *Harrington*, villainous Lord Mowbray meets Berenice Montenero at an officer's ball in Gibraltar where the
men draw lots for partners. Lord Mowbray's English officer friend picks
Berenice's name but rejects her, and Lord Mowbray dances with Berenice
instead, much to his delight: "The lady with the foreign-sounding name was
a Jewess, the handsomest, most graceful, the most agreeable woman in the
room. [Lord Mowbray] was, he said, the envy of every man, and especially of
his poor friend, who too late repented his rash renunciation of his ticket."[10]
While Berenice's first dancing partner objects to her Spanish name, rather
than to her religious background, Lord Mowbray's triumphant account of
the incident also points to assumptions that Jewish women were exotic and
sexually available.

Nineteenth-century Jewish women were particularly vulnerable to sexualized slights in the ballroom. In German Jewish writer Rahel Meyer's 1853
novel *Zwei Schwestern* (Two Sisters), Betty Lichtenfeld's family receives an
exclusive invitation to a ball in the prince's honor: "[I]t was decided, for the
first time, to also recognize Jews as fellow citizens, and to invite two of the
most respected and distinguished families."[11] When other guests are hostile
to Betty, she interprets it as a particularly painful form of anti-Jewish prejudice. Initially she is the only young woman without a dancing partner, and
she complains, "I had already endured some indignities as a result of the
prejudice that prevailed in my native city, but never before had I been condemned to the Tantalus torment of only being allowed to watch a dance."[12]
Betty feels acutely aware of her restricted social position as a Jewish woman
when she is deprived of the opportunity to dance, yet she ultimately experiences an even greater challenge when she meets an appealing Christian
nobleman at the ball. In a context in which a Jewish woman feels snubbed by
other ballroom guests, the attentions of a sympathetic Christian man can be
irresistible. Unlike many other flirtations in fictional ballrooms, this encounter leads to a loving marriage, yet Betty's feelings of guilt for having betrayed
her parents by converting can only be resolved by her death in childbirth.

Jewish women were not the only ones who risked social discomfort in
the ballroom. Meir Aron Goldschmidt's 1845 novel *En Jøde* (*A Jew*) uses a
ball to reveal a Jewish man's limited opportunities for social mobility. Originally written in Danish, the novel was popular internationally, appearing in

English in 1852 and in German in 1856. The protagonist Bendixen, a medical student, learns to dance at school, but he is almost denied admission to
his first ball on account of his Jewish background. Just moments after complaining about the scarcity of male dancing partners, Louise, the daughter
of the family hosting the ball (and sister of one of Bendixen's friends), asks
dismissively, "Is the Jew included?"[13] Her mother says that he can also be removed from the list. Louise is later mortified to find out Bendixen overheard
her remarks. Goldschmidt depicts ballroom sociability as an entry ticket to
Christian society while, at the same time, demonstrating the precarious position of even those Jews who are allowed into this social milieu.[14]

   Although many of the writers discussed here were acculturated and more
or less secular, German Orthodox Rabbi Marcus Lehmann's 1868 novella
Elvire, serialized in *Der Israelit* (The Israelite), the Orthodox journal he edited, explicitly discusses the role of dance in Jewish debates about German
culture.[15] *Elvire* is a didactic work that is narrated by a fictional rabbi who
warns against intermarriage, reading romances, and mixed-sex dancing.[16]
Lehmann takes care to connect the dance floor with contemporary political
concerns, particularly those related to liberalism and emancipation. He frequently interrupts his narrative with accounts of the rise and fall of the 1848
revolutions, events that provide an important backdrop for the motivations of
his characters. Lehmann sets the conflict between German culture and Jewish traditions in sharp relief when the family of Jewish banker Adolph Metz
receives an invitation to a noble ball. Adolph views the ball as an opportunity
to integrate into German society, since for once members of the bourgeoisie,
including Jews, are invited. As he remarks to his friend, the narrator, "Who
would have imagined it within a year—a Jew at a court festival!"[17] Much like
Betty's family in *Zwei Schwestern*, Adolph allows his naive hopes for social
acceptance to blind him to the threat posed by ballroom dancing.

   His rabbi friend does not share in Adolph's excitement about the ball.
He points out that mixed-sex dancing violates Jewish law and discourages
Adolph from attending the festive event. Even if the banker feels he must
attend, the rabbi warns him not to bring his impressionable young daughter
Elvire. As the rabbi explains, dramatically: "You know what I think of balls
in general. You know that I consider dance to be one of the most dangerous
and altogether reprehensible delights for the senses, and that this opinion is

not merely my own personal one, but rather one that is deeply grounded in Judaism."[18] Indeed, the rabbi's concerns about dancing reflect centuries of rabbinic condemnations of mixed-sex dancing.

Yet unlike many of these rabbinic prohibitions, *Elvire* does not simply warn against transgressive dancing. Instead, Lehmann writes a debate between his characters about whether Jews should be allowed to participate in mixed-sex dancing. Adolph fires back with an argument that might have been compelling for the German Jewish bourgeoisie: "In the Bible and the Talmud, dancing is often mentioned at joyous occasions."[19] Although Adolph's defense of dancing has a scriptural basis, his rabbi quickly refutes him. He points out that there is no biblical precedent for men and women dancing together. "The maidens of Israel performed dances, but not in the company of youths; the men danced before the holy Ark, but not with other men's wives."[20] The rabbi clearly states the forbidden nature of mixed-sex dancing at a ball. He challenges the notions of those who, like Jewish reformers, might choose to selectively interpret biblical texts to allow all kinds of dancing.

At the same time, the rabbi does not refer to the specific biblical prohibitions that are used to forbid mixed-sex dancing, even though such laws might convince an observant Jew like Adolph. Instead, Lehmann frames the debate around the question of acculturation, which is a sign of how even warnings against mixed-sex dancing changed in the modern era. Adolph accuses the rabbi of sounding antiquated and oriental, whereas the rabbi claims that the biblical Book of Esther provides a warning against the dangers of Jews attending non-Jewish court functions, claiming that all the misfortunes the Jews suffer in that account are a direct result of their participation in a Persian court feast. The rabbi seems most concerned with the possibility of intermarriage. His arguments would not necessarily prevent Jews from dancing with each other at their own social clubs. Yet Adolph is not convinced by the rabbi's justification that the near genocide of Jews in the Book of Esther was caused by Jews and Persians carousing together. He cannot bear to deprive his daughter of the pleasures of the ball.

Ultimately the events of the ball transpire as the rabbi suggests. Elvire's beauty and simple yet tasteful attire attract the attention of Dr. Wetting, a Christian lawyer who claims to be a proponent of emancipation and was once a frequent guest at the Metz's until he paid entirely too much attention to fifteen-year-old Elvire and was banned from their home. In the environment of the ballroom, full of music and expensive perfume, Wetting is able to gaze at Elvire, pay her compliments, and dance with her. Although Elvire feels flustered by Wetting's seductive words and wants to go home, she is trapped at the ball (and in Wetting's dangerous company) because her parents are too distracted to notice: Adolph plays cards with the local prince and Frau Metz chats with a countess. The Metz parents are so busy cavorting with the Christian nobility that they forget to look after their daughter's welfare. Although Elvire is initially shy, Wetting slowly reveals to her over the course of several dances that he would like to marry her in a civil ceremony. Indeed, since these dances involve close contact over several repeated intervals, Wetting has a particularly good opportunity to persuade a sheltered young woman to accept his controversial proposal. By the time the ball ends, after midnight, and Wetting escorts Elvire to her carriage, she suggests he discuss marriage with her father. Crucially, it is the space of the ballroom, with its social sanction and opportunity for intermingling of the sexes over the period of several hours, which enables the fateful courtship to transpire. Elvire is only thrust back into Wetting's vicinity because her parents did not adhere to the advice of their rabbi.

In *Elvire*, Lehmann presents a strong moral lesson with just enough titillation to keep his readers interested. Although he ultimately finds a way to end his story happily, with Elvire's eventual decision to leave Wetting and return to the Jewish community, other writers, such as Franzos, imagined tragic fates for Jewish women who attend balls.

"Fun with the Pretty Jewess":
Judith Trachtenberg

Charming and graceful steps, an elastic gait, levity, and obvious pleasure—according to the 1889 dance manual *Die Tanzkunst und die Tänze* (The Art of Dance and Dances)—these are some of the attributes of the quadrille, an elegant social dance.[21] These same qualities of grace and enjoyment in dance can be seen in Judith, the protagonist of Franzos's 1891 novel, *Judith Trachtenberg*.[22] Her love of social dances, as well as her fair hair, distinguish Judith from the other inhabitants of her city's Jewish quarter (referred to as the ghetto) and set her apart as a liminal figure in aristocratic Polish salon culture. Her beauty wins her admirers, but her Jewish identity makes her vulnerable. In this Galician setting, Franzos explores the aristocratic ballroom as a space that invites dancers to cross social boundaries, leading to tragic consequences.

Franzos (1847/48–1904) was born in Galicia to an assimilated, bourgeois family; later he moved to Vienna and then Berlin. He became one of the best-known writers of ghetto fiction and an "early master of the ethnographic novella."[23] Most of Franzos's oeuvre describes Jewish life in Galicia, often in sharply critical terms. His early works regard traditional Jewish communities as fanatical and blame them for failing to modernize—especially in stories about doomed interethnic relationships, which hold Jews responsible for the tragic outcome.[24] Yet by 1890, Franzos faced an increasingly antisemitic climate in Germany and a diminished market for his ghetto tales, a situation that affected him deeply.[25] Although *Judith Trachtenberg* is a work of historical fiction that is set in Galicia, Franzos's depiction of Polish antisemitism in his novel also reflects his disillusionment with the possibility of full Jewish participation in German and Austrian culture.

Judith Trachtenberg is melodramatic, readily invokes stereotypes, and, like many of Franzos's other ghetto tales, is blatantly didactic. It depicts the tragic love affair of a Jewish woman and a Polish nobleman she encounters at a ball. Dance plays an instrumental role in developing the transgressive romance plot and articulating the tricky balancing act of acculturation. Descriptions of dance crystallize the theme of boundary-crossing in *Judith Trachtenberg*. Several illustrative uses of dance in the book's first chapter underscore significant questions about Jewish inclusion in Galicia and prepare a foundation for the interfaith relationship that dominates the novel. Franzos uses dance to show the varied approaches his characters take as they negotiate between Jewish and Christian culture and identity.

Judith's father, Nathaniel Trachtenberg, is a central European Moses Mendelssohn figure, albeit one who is less resilient than the philosopher when his worldview is challenged. Even the name Nathaniel reminds a savvy reader of the hero of Gotthold Ephraim Lessing's Enlightenment play *Nathan der Weise* (*Nathan the Wise*), a character inspired by Mendelssohn. Nathaniel attempts to participate in Christian society as an observant Jew, with dubious success. While the elder Trachtenberg can balance, at least temporarily, between these worlds, this tenuous equilibrium proves impossible for his children. Tragically, Judith and Raphael's failure to find a path of moderation leads to Nathaniel's death of a heart attack when Judith is abducted by her Polish lover.

At the novel's opening, Nathaniel insists that his children engage in traditional Jewish learning with a Hebrew tutor, as well as studying modern European subjects, including social dancing. These dance classes in the home of Nathaniel's friend District Commissioner von Wroblewski reveal the Trachtenberg children's differing attitudes toward acculturation and show how they challenge their father's enlightened Judaism. Rafael decides after a dance lesson that he will no longer take part in Christian society, in part because he is tired of mistreatment by his dance partners on account of his Jewish appearance. Judith, in contrast, is admired for her fair features (which Franzos deems atypical for a Jewish woman) and Christian men take as an invitation for dalliance: "[T]hey cherished hopes for the Jewess that they would never have presumed for girls of their own social circle."[26] Judith naively overlooks these schemes and much prefers social dancing to Jewish learning. It is unclear whether the differing attitudes of the siblings are determined entirely by Christian reactions to their physical attributes or also by personal taste and inclination. In any case, both Trachtenbergs strive to satisfy their father while inwardly disapproving of one half of their educational curriculum.

Although Judith receives compliments from her Christian dance partners, she is not accepted as an equal. This lack of respect is particularly noticeable when Judith is invited at very short notice to the ball given by the Wroblewski family to welcome Count Agenor Baranowski, the new lord. Even though the ball will take place in the building in which Judith lives, she was not initially invited, nor were any other Jews. Since Judith is beautiful, wealthy, educated, and the daughter of the host's friend and landlord, the only possible reason for her exclusion is the fact that she is Jewish. At the same time, the Wroblewskis count on Judith as a reliable last-minute guest and expect her to be grateful for the honor, despite the insulting circumstances. She is neither someone who can be included on the initial guest list, nor someone who is inconceivable as a guest. Judith's position is unclear, and thus risky. She is not accorded the respect that would provide her with safety in a social situation, yet she is awarded too many compliments for her to comprehend her precarious position.

While Judith naively delights in these social activities, her brother Rafael worries about his sister's happiness and reputation. Rafael tells Judith that she is only desired at the ball because the Christian men like her appearance. Astonished that Judith has not noticed the way she is treated, he warns her, "Did it really never occur to you that these lordlings treat you differently than their Christian dancing partners. . . . They like to have their fun with the beautiful Jewess! Guard your soul, sister, protect your honor; you would not be the first."[27] Judith refuses to believe his accusations. In fact, the argument convinces Judith to attend the ball.

While Rafael's words prove to be well intended and, according to the novel's logic, correct, they also deny the possibility of female agency. All the actors in his account here are men. While Rafael can aspire to a publicly prominent role within the Jewish community—as a learned professional, wealthy businessman, or head of a household—Judith has fewer opportunities. For her, Christian society offers freedoms, such as mixed-sex dancing, which would not be possible within the Jewish community in Galicia. Even her father's aspirations for her, that she become the wife of an enlightened German Jew, give her only a limited degree of choice over her life. Judith savors the exciting literary and cultural possibilities that she experiences in the Wroblewski salon. She cannot bear to imagine that, as Franzos soon proves to his readers, the pleasures she encounters in this environment are actually an extended degradation and a plot to exploit her sexually. The stakes of Judith's decision of whether to attend the ball and participate in mixed-sex dancing are nothing less than a choice between submission to one of the roles constructed for her by the men in her family and testing out her autonomy with Christian men. If she accepts Rafael's account, she will have no choice but to limit herself to the confines of traditional Jewish life that even her father finds stifling. While Judith is unwilling to consider this possibility, her brother's words introduce the reader to the prospect of an interfaith romance by suggesting that motivation for such a dalliance exists. Ironically, Rafael's warning sets the plot in motion for Judith to come into close quarters with Agenor Baranowski. Even though she initially planned to stay at home with her brother, their dispute leads her to the ball, with fateful consequences.

When Judith arrives late, Frau von Wroblewska assigns her an unsatisfying partner and suggests that she would have gained a more favorable one if she had arrived earlier. The young man she is to dance with, Wladko Wolczinski, is a boorish and clumsy nobleman. While Frau von Wroblewska tries to mask the social hierarchy, Wladko reads his pairing with a Jew as a social snub and reacts accordingly. Rather than express resentment toward his hosts, Wladko directs a chilly demeanor to Judith. Although Judith initially attributes Wladko's coldness to a financial dispute between their fathers, she wonders if Rafael's concerns may have a basis in fact. Her misgivings are proven correct when Wladko aims an antisemitic barb at her father. Wladko's refusal even to look at Judith as they dance foreshadows his hostile words. The argument quickly escalates and gains the attention of neighboring couples, which only makes it more severe.

The quarrel probably would not have occurred or become so heated if Wladko and Judith had not been required to dance together. Wladko preferred to ignore Judith rather than speak with or bait her, and Judith similarly had little grounds for talking to him. Even after they partner for the quadrille, it takes time for Wladko's resentment to build. He initially remains silent and refuses to acknowledge Judith. Yet the dance requires them to remain in close quarters for a specific amount of time and provides opportunities for conversation. Wladko is thus able to embroil Judith in an argument that quickly becomes inflammatory. Interestingly, even though quadrilles involve a variety of dance figures, including those where dance partners switch temporarily, Franzos focuses on interactions between the couple, although he hints at the presence of other couples. Since quadrilles are danced in squares of four couples, the neighboring couples soon become aware of the argument, and Wladko feels social pressure to put Judith in her place, not only literally but also figuratively. The fact that the quarrel gains the attention of the other guests allows the entire affair to escalate from verbal barbs to a sexualized insult and potential duel.

Until this point, Judith has been unwilling to believe Rafael's warning. She lets Frau von Wroblewska lull her into a positive vision of her social milieu. She would rather believe that individuals such as Wladko are resentful on account of specific grievances, rather than harbor the possibility that her friends and admirers do not respect her because she is Jewish. When Wladko insults her, Judith does not act as if she is in a potentially hostile space. She spiritedly and forcefully defends her father, and by extension Jews, even though she does not identify with many aspects of Jewish culture. While Judith may want to believe that Wladko is a single rude guest, the public response to their argument challenges her optimism.

A drunken prior encourages Wladko to kiss the "beautiful Jewess" rather than argue with her.[28] Since they are already in intimate quarters as dancing partners, and Wladko has thus already been given social approval to handle her body in polite ways, it is not a great conceptual leap for the young man to escalate their physical contact. Although Judith trembles with rage or fear, the young man kisses her neck. Nearby guests laugh with approval, while it is clear that Judith feels violated: "In an instant he had wrapped his arms around her trembling form and kissed her on the neck. The bold deed earned laughter and applause."[29] Wladko is able to build an alliance with nearby dancers through his brazen conduct, while excluding Judith and making her into a sexual object. He shows mastery over her body, reminding her of her subordinate position as a Jewish woman. Whereas Judith's last rejoinder in her argument with Wladko received a few laughs, his obvious violation of her autonomy meets with boisterous approval.

By attending a ball, without an escort, at which she is the only Jewish guest, Judith enters an intermediary space that facilitates unwanted physical contact. If she had followed the path of most women in the Jewish quarter, she would not have had the opportunity to dance with Christian noblemen. She would have danced in a Jewish setting, in all likelihood apart from men or separated from direct physical contact by a handkerchief. The logical leap between a dance and a kiss is, intentionally, not as easy to traverse when partners do not touch hands. It would have been more difficult for Wladko to kiss Judith and handle her body if he were not already leading her around the dance floor. Likewise, even if Judith had danced with a man in a Jewish milieu, her father's status as a leader of the community would have rendered her immune to crude insult. Judith's honor was only insulted after Wladko had already spoken libelously of her father. Franzos exploits social boundaries and conventions on the dance floor to escalate the insults and sexual tension until they precipitate Judith's fateful encounter with Agenor.

While Judith did not invite untoward conduct by her own behavior, her mere presence at the ball inspires both Polish aristocrats and Jewish villagers to judge her actions and character negatively. Members of the Jewish community take a particularly harsh attitude when they note that scandalous things happen "when a Jewish girl, shamelessly exposed, goes among Christians and dances with men."[30] Their accusatory words emphasize the transgressive nature of the ball and the way Judith's attendance crosses social boundaries. The attitude of Wladko and the prior toward Judith reveal the sexualized role young men at the ball imagine for her. Although Judith eschews Christian society after this incident, she is later lured back to the salon as part of Herr von Wroblewski's plot to win her for Agenor. Wladko's kiss thus foreshadows the graver liberties Agenor takes with Judith's body and autonomy.

As lord and guest of honor, Agenor immediately defends Judith. He chastises Wladko, authoritatively escorts Judith home from the ball, leaves her at her doorstep with a deep bow, and later prepares to fight Wladko in a duel. He treats the young woman publicly with the respect her other associates have been lacking, even though they are socially inferior to him. Ultimately, however, Agenor's honorable treatment of Judith leads her to even greater suffering. Since Judith is Jewish, his behavior appears highly irregular. Her father takes pains to avoid a duel, as the ghetto inhabitants might face severe repercussions if a nobleman should lose his life to preserve the reputation of a Jewish woman. While Judith and others repeatedly ask Agenor if he would have gone to this trouble for a less attractive Jewish woman, the nobleman insists that he is no friend of the Jews and that he would uphold the honor of any female guest. The fact that he is infatuated with Judith, he privately claims to Herr von Wroblewski, plays no role in the matter.

Agenor's defense of Judith at the ball and immediately thereafter makes their romantic relationship not only possible, but almost inevitable. Agenor reveals a destructive sense of honor that will later cause him to deceive and make miserable the woman he loves. His chivalry puts him in greater contact with Judith, both as defender of her virtue and because his behavior leads him to admit that he bears amorous feelings toward the young woman. Ironically, Agenor's gallant actions lead him to mistreat Judith in a far more enduring manner than Wladko. He desires to make her his mistress but feels he cannot make her his wife. Since Judith will only consent to a marriage and Agenor is unwilling to lose her, Herr von Wroblewski suggests abduction, fake conversion, and sham marriage. Judith is thus deprived of family, marital status, chastity, and her own religion—a situation that ultimately leads to her death by suicide. Even the seemingly positive resolution of the incident at the ball points to a tragic conclusion.

The dance motif allows Franzos to explore Judith's precarious social position as a Jewish woman. Judith's participation in social dancing characterizes her relationships with four men who represent four different approaches to the place of Jews in Galicia, almost as if she were "dancing" with each of them in turn in the course of a quadrille: her father Nathaniel, her brother Rafael, Wladko, and Agenor. Structurally, Judith's tragedy can thus be compared to a failed quadrille. In this courtly dance, it is necessary for a dance master to dictate the formations performed by all four of the couples, creating an external power dynamic where rules are imposed on a group. In *Judith Trachtenberg*, Franzos takes on the role of the dance master, both by directing his characters according to didactic aims and in his use of specific dance figures to add aesthetic force. Through her interactions with each of the four men, Judith learns a bitter lesson, and Franzos demonstrates the limited options for a Jewish woman to experience social mobility or control her fate.

Judith is repeatedly passed between male interlocutors under the direction of the "dance master" Franzos—led, as it were, from one dance partner to another. The compromise of a civil marriage and baptized children ultimately leaves her dissatisfied. Both her father's precarious cultural balancing act and her brother's ethnocentrist worldview give her little room for autonomous expression, yet Wladko's overt anti-Jewish prejudice and Agenor's spineless attraction exploit her very real social vulnerability. Anna-Dorothea Ludewig observes that Judith is a passive figure whose actions are determined by the men around her, until her death by suicide leads to her burial with a tombstone that acknowledges her as a countess and as a Jew, a morbid model of successful integration.[31] In a milieu in which a woman's agency is determined, as in a social dance, by a male partner, her lack of a decisive and compatible counterpart leaves her without a proper place. *Judith Trachtenberg* reveals the social and political limitations that make full Jewish emancipation impossible.

Judith's death underscores the fact that, despite the social importance of marriage and Franzos's commitment to German culture, there is no satisfactory way of pairing her off. There is no successful trajectory between the bourgeois marriage plot, in which a heroine achieves social mobility through marriage, and the emancipation plot, which advocates social acceptance for Jews because an unproblematic marriage between a Jew and a Christian is unthinkable. Austrian political culture and German society have not progressed to the point that Jews like Judith—or Franzos—can live as free and equal imperial citizens. If Judith's four "dancing partners"—her father, her brother, Wladko, and Agenor—represent four different approaches to the "Jewish Question" in Galicia, then she herself stands for all four of the female dancers needed to complete the quadrille. This role gives her, despite her status as the title figure of the novel, a certain vagueness or lack of specificity that invites the reader to consider how she embodies the circumstances of Jewish women in Galicia.

Franzos uses social dance to make a broader point about how Habsburg society has failed Jews in general, and Jewish women in particular. His depiction of Judith as typically feminine and as a stereotypical beautiful Jewess helps him fit her into the existing social system and available plot structures, revealing the flaws in how the system treats Jews. As the only prominent Jewish woman in the story, Judith represents an alluring and nonthreatening cliché that Franzos exploits to convey his political message. Not only does Judith take the women's part in her dance with Wladko; when Franzos "leads" with his political agenda, Judith follows, until she commits a dramatic suicide at precisely the moment when it seemed as if her wishes had finally been fulfilled. Her strong will and pretty sentiment serve merely as ornamental expression to enhance the narrative that Franzos forcefully directs. Judith's role at the Wroblewski's ball and her "dancing" with other characters throughout the novel establish her complicated, and ultimately tragic, social status as a Jewish woman.

Jewish Balls

One way for Jews to avoid Judith's tragic fate was to keep away from Christian balls in favor of their own social gatherings. Indeed, Dresden diarist Louis Lesser recounts the balls he attended at his Jewish social club, the Union, including a Saturday night ball in 1835 to honor the king's birthday.[32]

Participants in Jewish balls tended to share a similar acculturated bourgeois Jewish background, which meant that parents who wanted their children to find partners who shared a common class and religious background were less likely to object to their children becoming romantically involved with their dance partners. As a result, authors tend not to discuss the taboo on mixed-sex dancing in the context of Jewish balls. At the same time, such events reveal divisions within the community and the way that Christian guests further destabilize these dynamics. Issues such as wealth, degree of acculturation, marital status, and political affiliation could create social tensions that reverberate onto the dance floor. Scenes at both Jewish and non-Jewish balls show that individual dancers are unable to fully overcome existing hierarchies. While Jewish dancers who attend non-Jewish balls often experience a momentous encounter with a dance partner they naively hope will become a viable spouse, Jewish dancers at Jewish balls frequently confront the reality that dancing to music ultimately will not change their personal circumstances.

In his 1892 bestselling novel *Children of the Ghetto: A Study of a Peculiar People*, Anglo-Jewish writer Israel Zangwill depicts dancing as an important marker in his comparison of "ghetto" and modern Anglo-Jewish life in the London slums of Whitechapel. He describes a Purim ball at a Jewish social club, which is attended by upwardly mobile Jews. In this light-hearted setting, young people dance, flirt, consume cakes and lemonade, and show off their finest clothing. The acculturated dancers at Zangwill's Purim ball are perfectly capable of performing the dance choreography:

> It was a merry party, almost like a family gathering, not merely because most of the dancers knew one another, but because "all Israel are brothers"—and sisters. They danced very buoyantly, not boisterously; the square dances symmetrically executed, every performer knowing his part; the waltzing full of rhythmic grace.[33]

Zangwill invokes a Jewish doctrine about brotherhood to show how this Jewish environment is characterized by close-knit relations between participants and physical harmony on the dance floor.

Zangwill's addition of the word "sisters" to his citation of Jewish communal feeling emphasizes the importance of mixed-sex sociability in modern Jewish culture. Free mixing of the sexes is an important part of this heady

FIGURE 7. Upwardly-mobile Jews at a ball in a cartoon from a Viennese satirical newspaper.

Daughter: Mama! That's the fifth dance partner I had to reject. Why don't you let me dance with anyone?

Mama: You should only dance with aristocrats from birth.

Daughter: Then I'll certainly sit here the entire night. Last year you let me dance with everyone. Mama [in Yiddish-inflected German]: Last year your tate [papa] was not yet a knight of the Iron Crown.

Source: *Figaro: humoristisches Wochenblatt* [Figaro: Humorous Weekly], August 9th, 1879, p. 6. Courtesy of ANNO: Historische Zeitungen und Zeitschriften, Österreichische Nationalbibliothek.

new milieu at the Club, where women are awarded a social freedom than was unthinkable in a traditional Jewish context. In sharp distinction, Zangwill's description of traditionally religious Jews makes clear the tensions between a masculine brotherhood and the perceived dangers of female sexuality on the dance floor. He narrates: "[T]he 'Sons of the Covenant' sent no representatives to the club balls, wotting neither of waltzes or of dress-coats, and preferring death to the embrace of a strange dancing woman."[34] Zangwill acknowledges the presence of desire at the Purim ball, yet in contrast to the more traditional "Sons of the Covenant," Zangwill supports the brokerage of companionate marriages on the dance floor.

Zangwill treats conversations and discreet forays into physical contact on the dance floor as a much more modern form of courtship than arranged marriages. He provides an even sharper contrast with one of the ways of getting married under Jewish law: A man can "acquire" a wife simply by putting a ring on a woman's finger and saying the appropriate Hebrew phrase of acquisition and consecration in front of witnesses.[35] This ritual features prominently in the novel, since Sam Levine accidentally marries Hannah Jacobs, a rabbi's daughter, without her consent as part of a thoughtless joke that has unexpected legal consequences. During the Purim ball, Hannah converses flirtatiously with another young man, even though she is technically still married to Sam. While initially Hannah refuses to dance with David Brandon, telling him she is a married woman, by the end of the chapter she reveals that she is soon to be divorced. Despite her initial reservations about David, she comes to acknowledge their philosophical compatibility, since David shares her desire to maintain a Jewish but non-Orthodox home. At the close of the chapter, after a buildup of several pages, Hannah finally consents to dance with David: "She put her hand lightly on his shoulder, he encircled her waist with his arm and they surrendered themselves to the intoxication of the slow, voluptuous music."[36] This sensual description of physical contact during a dance, accompanied by music, is the culmination of verbal exchange at the sidelines of the dance floor throughout the chapter. Indeed, Hannah and David would not have been introduced by a matchmaker, since David is a *cohen* (from a priestly lineage) and forbidden to marry a divorcée—a fact that later has dire consequences for their engagement. Zangwill uses the dance scene to reveal the close relationship between modern romantic notions of emotional suitability, Jewish acculturation, and physical compatibility on the dance floor.

Dancing is similarly illustrative of Jewish social stratification in another late nineteenth-century Anglo-Jewish novel: Amy Levy's 1888 *Reuben Sachs*.[37] Yet unlike Zangwill's glowing description of the Club, Levy uses a dance hosted by a Jewish family to depict Jewish social pretensions and materialism. The hosts of this ball, the Leuniger family, are very conscious of the fact that holding a dance can add to their social status. They take pains to invite Christian guests and resist including Jews who do not add to their notion of prestige. Levy describes interactions between potential dance partners in coldly commercial terms; a beautiful and high-spirited young woman who is known to have a generous dowry "goes down" as a tremendous social success.[38] Marriageable young men are conscious of being a scarce resource and "were aggressively conscious of commanding the market."[39] Nonetheless, dancing retains some measure of romantic choice: As Levy notes, "[A] great fortune . . . though it always brings proposals of marriage, does not invariably bring invitations to dance."[40] Indeed, men still dance with women whom they would not consider marrying.

Levy uses the ball to heighten the romance between Reuben Sachs and his cousins' poor relation, Judith Quixano, a beautiful Sephardic woman. Judith eagerly anticipates Reuben's attendance at the ball, since it was "in the crowded solitude of ball-rooms that they had hitherto found their best opportunity" for flirtation.[41] Levy was acutely aware that a sheltered young woman might find the ballroom overwhelming, as she notes in an 1886 *Jewish Chronicle* article about the social limitations faced by middle-class Jewish women: "Carefully excluded, with almost Eastern jealousy, from every-day intercourse with men and youths of her own age, she is plunged all at once—a half-fledged, often half-chaperoned creature—into the 'vortex' of a middle-class ball-room, and is there expected to find her own level."[42] A ballroom is a space that, by design, allows for more relaxed mixing of the sexes, and young couples can flirt without their families interfering on financial grounds. When Reuben arrives to the ball late, he observes Judith in close conversation with another admirer (a Christian man who plans on converting to Judaism), and he becomes jealous. Reuben performs a rather shocking breach of ballroom etiquette: He takes her full dance card and tears it into pieces.[43]

While most dancers are focused on wealth and social prestige, Reuben allows his romantic feelings to dictate his actions. By destroying the dance card, he symbolically makes Judith off-limits for other men, even though he has not proposed to her. Reuben has either decided to sabotage her marital prospects or chosen to disregard his own material aspirations by prioritizing his feelings for Judith over economic considerations. In either case, Reuben's reckless romantic encounter with Judith completely contradicts the Leunigers' aspirations for their ball. Levy portrays the ball as a symbol of crass materialism and shows how her characters transgress ballroom etiquette in their attempt to challenge broader social expectations. Yet this idealistic moment does not last. Reuben's romantic gesture proves to be his last attempt to court Judith: Later in the evening, he finds out that a seat in Parliament is suddenly available, and he chooses to prioritize his political career over his personal feelings (leaving Judith to marry her other admirer). Levy uses the ball as the emotional high point of her novel and as a way of interrogating the habits of her Jewish characters as they struggle to achieve social mobility. Yet ball scenes were not simply a feature of nineteenth-century sociability; they could also help crystallize the dizzying atmosphere of interwar Europe.

In contrast to the Leunigers' socially ambitious ball, the masquerade in Isaac Bashevis Singer's 1950 family epic *Di familye Mushkat* (*The Family Moskat*) is a chaotic affair that nonetheless reveals the continued importance of money in the ballroom. All of Jewish Warsaw seems to be in attendance, and characters find and lose one another as they share gossip, discuss politics, and try to escape their dismal economic situation. The experience of one married couple is particularly illustrative of the way Singer uses the fantasy of the ballroom to emphasize a harsh reality. Hadassah is excited to go to the ball, and her husband Asa Heshel reluctantly gives in to her demand that they attend, despite his concerns about the expense. At first, their preparations for the ball transform them and transport them out of their grim everyday lives: "Some of the gentile tenants of the building, riding down with them in the elevator, gaped at these elegant Jews who, for all their eternal complaining that the last bite of bread was being taxed out of their mouths, could still manage to go to balls."[44] Yet Hadassah soon becomes disillusioned by the teeming, disorienting party, where women repair broken finery, and men dance while disguised variously as European military officers and religious Jews. Although the evening was supposed to give her pleasure, it simply underscores her marital troubles; Asa Heshel quickly disappears in the crowd and avoids finding Hadassah because, "What would be the point of dragging around with his own wife?"[45] Instead, he flirts with a younger woman, and they later have an affair. Characters spend money they cannot afford in order to attend the ball, but they cannot escape class and gender hierarchies. The fact that balls are associated with fantasy and desire can make these reminders of the status quo even more painful. Indeed, balls can also reveal tensions about Jewish politics and male identity.

"The King and Queen at the Head":
Der Weg des jungen Hermann Kahn

Men and women had separate, and clearly delineated, roles in the ball-room. Men were expected to pay attention to their female dance partners without making untoward advances. At the same time, women had the right to refuse a dance or to favor one man over another. Jewish men might feel particularly sensitive about rejected dance invitations if these slights reminded them of barriers they faced to successful integration. Such is the case in Clementine Sophie Krämer's (née Cahnmann, 1873–1942) short novel *Der Weg des jungen Hermann Kahn*, which was serialized in 1918 in the *Allgemeine Zeitung des Judentums*.[46] Krämer was born in Rheinsbischofsheim in Baden, Germany. She moved to Munich after her marriage, where she became active as a feminist and pacifist. Krämer wrote prolifically in a variety of genres, and she published in both the Jewish and general German press.[47] Despite her attempts to emigrate, Krämer was unable to leave Nazi Germany before the outbreak of World War II, and she died of dysentery in Theresienstadt. Her serialized novels about Jewish topics reveal the way that acculturated Jewish men and women negotiate German society—and dance floors.

In the novel, Jewish medical student Hermann Kahn attends a Heidelberg Zionist ball, where the Jewish woman in whom he is smitten rebuffs him. Although Hermann is fascinated by ardently Zionist student Salomea Fingerhut, his commitment to living in Germany is a point of contention for such a politically active woman. Her sudden dismissal becomes even more complete when she instead decides to dance with Hermann's Christian friend, Lieutenant Horst Bäumke—even though she had previously urged Hermann to consider "the race" before rejecting Jewish nationalism.[48] The Zionist ball is thus a location where flirtation and romantic rivalry reveal tensions between German Jewish identity, Zionism, and assimilation. Salomea stars in the ball's opening pageant, which allows her to display her ardent Zionism and depict herself as a paragon of Jewish nationalist femininity. Yet, at the same time, Salomea dances with a Christian lieutenant instead of one of her Jewish admirers, which leads Hermann to question her true commitment to the Zionist cause.

Jewish organizations hosted balls for philanthropic purposes and to celebrate particular occasions, including Purim. In this context it is hardly surprising that Zionist groups also held balls.[49] Starting in the late nineteenth century, Zionist organizations in cities across Europe hosted holiday balls, which often celebrated the holidays of Hanukkah and Purim.[50] Yet Zionist balls presented a particular paradox, because they supported Jewish nationalism through a form of leisure culture that was unabashedly European and bourgeois—despite the socialist and agricultural leanings of Zionist youth organizations like *Hashomer Hatzair* (The Young Guard). During the 1920s and 30s, public Purim balls in Tel Aviv—often complete with costumed processions and the election of a Queen Esther—were designed to showcase the new Hebrew culture. Dancer and painter Baruch Agadati (1895–1975) organized lavish Purim balls, beginning with a 1921 costume ball for 500 elite guests who paid for their tickets. According to Hizky Shoham, "In a way, this celebrity event—the first of its kind in Tel Aviv—returned the balls' genre from the community event to the premodern aristocratic format."[51]

In writing about the 1937 National Dance Competition in Tel Aviv, Nina S. Spiegel explains that members of the *yishuv* (body of Jewish residents in Mandate Palestine) faced several contradictions in their quest to create a Hebrew theatrical dance form. They aspired to a style that was artistic according to European views: "choreographed, skillfully executed, evocative of European modern dance conventions during this period" and at the same time "authentically Middle Eastern, Jewish, evocative of biblical times or of their new life in Palestine."[52] Although folk dances did not have the prestige of modern theatrical dance, the circular hora was ubiquitous at Zionist gatherings, where mixed-sex groups of young people performed a dance that, by the founding of the state of Israel in 1948, "had become a quintessential marker of a new Jewish society."[53] The new Hebrew body culture was defined according to European values and notions of Jewish authenticity, yet the European social dances that Jews had (in many cases) only recently embraced were not given the same weight as modern dance, folk dance, or even ballet. In this context, Zionist balls were a way for Jews in the diaspora to show their support for the idea of a Jewish state, yet they did so using a style of dance that may have seemed incongruous to *halutzim* (pioneers) in the yishuv.

Krämer's depiction of the ball's opening pageant emphasizes monarchy, hierarchy, and ordered pairs—concepts that, as Shoham observed, seem far removed from the values of the yishuv. The pageant portrays the story of the meeting of King Solomon and the Queen of Sheba. Not surprisingly, Salomea plays the famous queen, a wise and prosperous monarch in the biblical account who helped Solomon prove his magnificence, yet who was later identified with the demon Lilith in postbiblical writings and depicted as a threatening dancer in Ashkenazic folklore.[54] The reenactment is proceeded by a prologue in verse that narrates the sad history of Jewish exile since the time of Solomon, saying that the diaspora Jew "lives in dark shadows."[55] Yet although these words demean European Jewish life, the royal couple leads a procession in a polonaise and waltz, two dances that were derived from central European folk dances and were frequently performed at noble balls:

> [T]the procession moved through the hall. The king and the queen at the head, followed by the entire court, appropriately organized in pairs. The onlookers . . . joined in the polonaise. And then the music changed to a waltz, and the couples swayed and spun around. The king and queen at the head.[56]

Krämer's repetition of the phrase "the king and queen at the head" underscores the preeminence of the two dancers who were selected as the royal couple. They have been chosen as paradigms of Zionist ideals and thus lead the other guests around in a grand march comprised of a line of couples.

None of the novel's characters object to being part of a royal "court"; indeed, most German Jews (especially when the story was published, in the last months of World War I) could only partake in court pageantry at a Jewish ball, if at all. In a certain sense, this spectacular ball opening—complete with verse, masquerade, and procession—resembles German early modern court entertainments. Claudia Schnitzer notes in her study of such festivities that even costumed amusements functioned to formalize each person's position in the court hierarchy.[57] Salomea's Zionism is not merely a Jewish form of European nationalism; it is a Jewish appropriation of European displays of kingship, used in service of an anticipated Jewish nation-state.

As the waltz ends, Krämer wryly comments about how the "royal personages" mix with the "common people."[58] The very first commoner she mentions is Hermann, who rushes over to Salomea. Much to his surprise, since they had previously been friendly, Salomea treats him disdainfully as if she were actually a queen. When he eagerly asks her for the next dance, she scolds him haughtily and says rather petulantly, "You threw that opportunity away eight days ago. . . . Next time you should wake up earlier, Herr Kahn!"[59] Hermann persists by asking her to partner him for the first française, another European ballroom dance. Salomea taunts him by brandishing her full dance card, "entirely inscribed with names and student circles," which suggests that she may have let young men reserve dances with her before the pageant even began.[60] Although Salomea has the right to decide with whom she will spend her time and which admirers she will permit to handle her body, the way she treats Hermann is deliberately hurtful: "'If a dance gets squeezed in,' she made herself gracious, 'then—maybe.'"[61] Earlier Salomea chided Hermann for his lack of Zionist enthusiasm, and she now punishes him for his lack of political ardor (or, as Hermann suspects, for neglecting her by recently visiting his mother in his native village) by refusing to dance with him.

Hermann's humiliation soon turns into jealousy. On a whim, because the ball invitation particularly encouraged male guests to attend, he invited his friend Bäumke, in part to see how the Christian officer would respond to Zionist politics. Unfortunately, however, by taking Bäumke with him, he has unwittingly brought along a romantic rival. When Bäumke approaches Salomea and gallantly asks to be introduced to the "queen," she "raised her eyes in surprise and did not attempt in the slightest to disguise how pleased she was by the young officer."[62] Bäumke treats Salomea with grandiose respect, allowing her to continue her fantasy of being royalty. Yet Salomea's interest in her new admirer defies the rules of etiquette. When Hermann later sees her clinging to Bäumke's arm for the française, she explains that she "shifted" her promised dance partner to dance with Bäumke instead.[63] Her condescending description of her slighted dance partner as a "kleines Jüngelchen" (small little boy) emphasizes Bäumke's strong military stature, as she praises him at the expense of yet another Jewish man.[64] Salomea's political conviction seems to wither in the face of Bäumke's good looks, since the Christian officer has no particular interest in the Zionist cause. Either Salomea is willing to make exceptions to her beliefs for particularly appealing men, or her Zionism is a thinly veiled European nationalism that considers a non-Jewish officer as compelling as a Jewish one. While Hermann's professional training as a doctor might have appealed to a bourgeois woman, such cultivation does not satisfy a Zionist who longs for signs of physical manliness, which she can test out for herself on the dance floor: "[H]er eyes kept hanging, adoringly, on Bäumke's splendid form. And that man was undeniably the lion of the evening."[65] The "queen" of the Zionist ball has chosen a blond, Christian man as her partner, a move that suggests that, even at Zionist events, German Jewish men must contend with threats to their masculinity.

While Salomea proclaims her commitment to Zionism, Krämer's narrative undercuts her seeming idealism. The ball scene suggests, in short, that Salomea is ideologically inconsistent. Hermann's mother previously claimed (when explaining why she thought Salomea's Zionist views would not prevent her from marrying Hermann) that young women often change their deeply held beliefs for love, a theory the ball scene tests. Hermann objects to the way Salomea mistreats her Jewish admirers and lets herself be governed by her desire for Bäumke. He resents the fact that a woman who viewed his ideological leanings as a barrier to their union quickly forgets any reservations about flirting with a man who is not even a member of the "race," and he speculates grimly that she will give up her ideals entirely to become Bäumke's wife or mistress, since: "A young girl . . . cannot always remain excited merely for a distant ideal."[66]

Salomea is first presented as an independent, intelligent woman who is committed to her political beliefs. She studies Hebrew and is active in the Zionist cause. She is, in short, the type of female character one might expect from an author who was politically engaged herself, although in feminism and pacifism, rather than Zionism.[67] Yet in the ball scene, Krämer suggests Salomea is more interested in men (or power over them) than in a political cause. It is not surprising that her "almost chic" name, Salomea, invokes the notorious princess Salome from the Gospels, who performed a seductive dance to convince her lustful stepfather King Herod of Judea to kill John the Baptist.[68]

While Salomea advocates for a Jewish nation and disparages Hermann for choosing to stay in Germany, her Zionism reenacts oft-repeated European cultural tropes. Scholars such as Michael Stanislawski demonstrate that founding

Zionist leaders were indelibly influenced by European ideas and draw connections between Zionist body culture (spurred by the ideal of the healthy, muscular "New Jew") and European nationalism.[69] Although social critics have recognized the ways in which central and eastern European Jews established an Ashkenazic elite in the yishuv and state of Israel, Krämer was more interested in how Zionists interacted with other German Jews. In her character Salomea, Krämer offers the example of a fictional female Zionist and questions the depth of her convictions. Salomea's behavior reveals her ideological inconsistency, since she does not allow her politics to disrupt her obvious attraction to Bäumke.[70] Salomea's actions lead Hermann to reevaluate his process of acculturation, and he soon pursues a non-Jewish partner of his own.

Salomea exercises her feminine power at the ball in ways that might not have been available to her in other settings. Zionist ideology stressed the pursuit of a martial, physical Jewish masculinity, which meant women such as Salomea had a more circumscribed role than in the contemporaneous activities of the political left.[71] Indeed, while Salomea puts her body on display at the pageant, it is Hermann who later gets to prove himself though his words at a Zionist meeting by giving a speech in defense of German Jewish identity. Salomea disappears from the story as soon as she is no longer a viable romantic prospect for Hermann, and it is unclear if she even attended his speech. At the ball, however, Salomea can be queen and decide with which of her admirers she will dance. She even tests out her attraction to Bäumke in corporeal yet socially sanctioned ways. Nonetheless, it seems unlikely she actually becomes his wife or lover. When Bäumke next appears, in a Bavarian country cottage, he is kissing another woman. His flirtation with Salomea was presumably of short duration and may have simply been confined to the one social event. In attending the ball, Hermann encounters Zionist and German non-Jewish threats to his self-esteem as a German Jewish man. By using the female right of refusal at the Zionist ball, Salomea undermines the traditional Jewish commitment to endogamy while also reifying the social status of a Christian German officer.

Despite what Krämer's novel might suggest, women did not necessarily risk their political convictions by attending balls. In her autobiography *Living My Life*, Jewish anarchist leader Emma Goldman describes attending her first ball in St. Petersburg at age fifteen. Her sister Helena had received two tickets to the modish German Club from her employer, and she invited Goldman. While, as we have seen in this chapter, Jews often struggled to acquire exclusive ball invitations, Goldman instead faced two different challenges that her sister helped her overcome: obtaining material for a proper dress and securing her father's approval. Goldman was elated by "the prospect of my first ball, the bliss of dancing in public."[72] Yet at the last minute, her father changed his mind. Not surprisingly for a future revolutionary, Goldman decided to defy him. She and Helena waited until their parents were asleep and snuck out of the house.

The ball lived up to Goldman's high expectations. Unlike many Jewish characters who attended non-Jewish balls, she did not face any social exclusion:

> I was asked for every dance, and I danced in frantic excitement and abandon. . . . "I will dance!" I declared; "I will dance myself to death!" My flesh felt hot, my heart beat violently as my cavalier swung me round the ball-room, holding me tightly. To dance to death—what more glorious end![73]

The sisters returned home at five in the morning, their parents none the wiser. Goldman describes attendance at a ball as an act of rebellion that lays the foundation for her future activism. She unwittingly refutes Krämer's questioning of women's political engagement in *Der Weg des jungen Hermann Kahn* by showing that dancing is an act of joy and passion that can inspire women to greater political commitments. Goldman is able to enjoy her popularity on the dance floor in a way that Franzos's Judith Trachtenberg could only imagine, since her dancing partners do not threaten her safety as a woman or as a Jew. Although Goldman acknowledges certain restrictions regarding tickets and clothing, she emphasizes the intergenerational conflict with her father, who tries to keep her home to punish her for a minor infraction.

In this sense, Goldman's depiction of her first ball emphasizes the type of family conflict that occurs more typically in the context of wedding dance scenes. As will be seen in the next chapter, weddings are sites where dancers face the most censure from communal authorities. While a political revolutionary such as Goldman considers it necessary to rebel against her father's rules, most fictional characters are unable to so fully disregard the expectations of their family and community. Their forays into transgressive dancing often lead to tragic conclusions.

CHAPTER 5

THE WEDDING

Celebratory Ritual and Social Enforcement

WHEN ABRAHAM HERSH ASHKENAZI hears that men and women are dancing together at his son's wedding, he acts immediately. In this scene from Israel Joshua Singer's *Di brider Ashkenazi* (*The Brothers Ashkenazi*), Abraham Hersh marches over to the couples dancing in the women's section and shouts at them: "Out, gentiles and reprobates! . . . This isn't a German [daytshe] wedding!"[1] Although both the bride and groom come from wealthy Hasidic families that are involved in the Łódź textile industry, the two sets of parents invite very different types of guests to the wedding. In fact, the differences between the guests simply underscore the mismatch between the groom, Talmud scholar Simha Meir, and the elegant bride Dinele, who is in fact in love with her future brother-in-law. The guests from the bride's side are members of the Łódź elite who are accustomed to mixed-sex partner dances. Abraham Hersh cannot bear the thought that they would shame his most honored guest, the Alexander Rebbe, by engaging in transgressive dancing. Furious, Abraham Hersh begins beating them with his fur hat and is joined by his more traditionally pious guests: "The aroused Hasidim extinguished the lamps and doused the waxed floors with pitchers of water to render them unfit for mixed dancing."[2] While the sophisticated guests from the bride's side could waltz at balls without fear of religiously motivated interruption, weddings are the site where traditional communal authorities exercised the greatest control over dancing. Indeed, when literary characters explicitly invoke the prohibition on mixed-sex dancing, it is most frequently in connection with wedding dancing.

In 1950, fourteen years after Singer published *Di brider Ashkenazi* in book form, his younger brother Isaac Bashevis Singer dedicated *Di familye Mushkat* (*The Family Moskat*) to Israel Joshua, who had died of a heart attack in 1944. As in his older brother's novel, Isaac Bashevis depicts chaotic wedding dancing at an arranged marriage between a pious Hasid and a dreamy young woman who, like Dinele in *Di brider Ashkenazi*, is in love with somebody else. As one fictional wedding guest recounts in a letter, "The Hasidim yelled that it was forbidden for men and women to dance together, but there was such a tumult that nobody paid any attention to them. Koppel the salesclerk came to the wedding without his wife, and I heard that he danced a waltz with Leah [the bride's aunt]."[3] The scandalized wedding guest continues her report by concluding that the wedding does not seem Jewish on account of the improper dancing: "Never in my life have I seen such an ill-starred wedding [*shvarts-khasene*, lit. black wedding]. It was (if you'll forgive the comparison) worse than among Russian ruffians [*yevonim*]."[4]

These two texts by celebrated Yiddish writers suggest that traditionally minded Jews identified mixed-sex dancing variously with well-to-do Germans (as in *Di brider Asheknazi*) or with lower-class Russians (as in *Di familiye Mushkat*). This style of dancing is viewed as foreign to Hasidic wedding customs and deemed worthy of censure, since it is associated with both high and low status Christians, who were often regarded as hostile to Jews. Even when elders are unaware or refuse to acknowledge that a bride or groom resents an arranged marriage, a scene of mixed-sex dancing is a way for an author to displace the bride or groom's emotional turmoil onto the bodies of defiant wedding guests. That is to say, both Singer brothers use transgressive dance scenes to underscore the distress of a bride who is unhappy with her marriage. While the wedding scene in *Di brider Ashkenazi* represents a challenge to communal order in the nineteenth century, the wedding scene in *Di familye Mushkat* shows the further entrenchment of modern sexual mores in the 1910s, even in a social milieu where marriages are still arranged. Both of these wedding scenes, like numerous others, demonstrate that the wedding was a site in which rebellious dancers were forced to contend with the normal social order.

Wedding Dancing, Ritual, and Social Expectations

A wedding is a ritual that demands communal witnessing and recognition; without external acknowledgment, the validity of a marriage could be called into question.[5] Shtetl weddings brought together all kinds of guests: city-dwellers returning to their hometowns, rebbes with their followers, curious local nobility, beggars who were fed as part of a ritual act of charity (and were entitled to a dance with the bride), and relatives from the two families who may or may not have gotten along with one another.[6] In fact, in the case of the broygez tants (dance of anger), wedding guests would even perform a ritualized quarrel and reconciliation.[7] Yet the broygez tants was typically performed by two women, often the new mothers-in-law.[8] In describing the dancing at her parents' 1866 wedding in the hamlet of Ploskin (now in Belarus), Miriam Shomer Zunser claims that other than "the prohibition of men dancing with women" there were no restrictions or set forms for the wedding dancing, and dancers could choose to dance on their own or with a same-sex partner.[9] In other words, the choice of partner was more strictly regulated than the choreography of the dance. Yet the literary texts I discuss in depth in this chapter describe married women publicly dancing at weddings with unmarried men.

Wedding attendees who engaged in transgressive dancing risked censure by community elders, who were more likely to find out about mixed-sex dancing at weddings than at other venues, since they were often already in attendance and able to monitor the proceedings. Even when rabbis did not personally attend a wedding celebration, they might still be called upon to put a halt to improper dancing.[10] Thus, as will be seen in Leopold von Sacher-Masoch's *Der Judenraphael* (The Raphael of the Jews) and Joseph Opatoshu's *A roman fun a ferd-ganef* (*Romance of a Horse Thief*), weddings frequently demonstrate the resilience of dominant social norms.

Wedding scenes are one of the most common occasions for dancing in Jewish literature. They are also one of the most paradoxical, since they combine an expectation of joy with ritualized sorrow. The freylekhs is a popular wedding dance whose name literally means "joyous one."[11] Jews are traditionally obligated to gladden a bride by dancing before her.[12] According to memoirist Pauline Wengeroff, pleasing a bride is the greatest commandment.[13] Yet, as we have seen, dancing *before* a bride does not mean dancing *with* a bride; the ritualized mitsve tants uses a handkerchief to separate men and women on the dance floor, while performing a dance that is at least officially for the bride's pleasure. Despite this emphasis on a bride's enjoyment, in the ritual of the *kale baveynen*, the badkhn literally makes the bride cry cathartic tears.[14] What is more, wedding ceremonies include reminders of sorrow and historical trauma.[15] Weddings invoke a broad range of emotions, which are compounded in situations in which the bridal couple does not share the community's sense of celebration.

Weddings are ostensibly happy occasions; yet for brides or grooms who feel ambivalent about the match, they are miserable experiences that prove communal authorities exercise control over even their most intimate personal relationships. Obligatory dancing simply increases this suffering. In Michał Waszyński's 1937 film *Der dibek* (*The Dybbuk*, adapted from S. An-sky's play by the same name), wealthy bride Leye imagines she is with her dead soulmate, Khonen, as she dances with a ghostly figure in a skull mask surrounded by a group of frenzied beggars. Despondent at being pushed to marry another man instead of Khonen, she invites her lover's spirit to possess her instead. The intensity of this dance scene, the most famous one in Yiddish cinema, keeps audiences focused on Leye's emotional turmoil.[16]

Most literary depictions of these unhappy dance scenes involve separate-sex dancing, because a society that imposed arranged marriages (rather than suggesting suitable partners) also typically maintained sex segregation on the dance floor.[17] Yet even the chaste mixed-sex interaction of the mitsve tants could cause renewed pain. Esther Singer Kreitman (sister of Israel Joshua Singer and Isaac Bashevis Singer) underscores her protagonist Dvoyre's unhappiness about her arranged marriage through a wedding dance she refers to as a "*sheydim-tants*" (dance of demons), an image Kreitman repeats in the novel's title, *Der sheydim-tants* (*The Dance of Demons*, 1936). Kreitman portrays a mitsve tants as a new torture for a young woman who questions her social milieu. When a spectator later asks her about the wedding dancing, she describes it as "the dance of the demons" and explains it is a ritual dance, almost breaking down in tears.[18] Dvoyre's adverse reaction to her wedding dancing underscores the way dance typically celebrates and affirms a marriage and stresses Dvoyre's unwillingness to participate in the marriage itself.

Forced wedding dancing could also foreshadow an unwelcome betrothal—and the compulsory physical intimacy it implied. While mixed-sex dancing was especially taboo in situations where dance partners were not considered appropriate spouses, in situations where mixed-sex dancing was more accepted, a young woman might be pressured into dancing with someone her parents viewed as a potential match. In her 1920 short serialized novel *Esther*, Clementine Krämer describes dancing at a Jewish wedding in a rural German village around 1910.[19] Young people arrange themselves in mixed-sex pairs to dance a schottisch, with the bridal couple at the head, a formation that honors the couple and the institution of marriage. Young Esther Stein performs her own fanciful dance around them—until an adult man, Liepmann Schuhrmann, comes out of the crowd and tries to force her to dance with him. Liepmann takes hold of the little girl's body and even attempts to kiss her. Where once she had full control over her own dance, now she is entirely at his disposal. Esther reacts with horror to this violation. Krämer underscores the extent of Liepmann's inappropriate behavior, since his dirty boots stain Esther's white dress, and it is impossible to remove the marks—a rather obvious metaphor for Liepmann's desire to deflower Esther. While it is unclear what contortions he makes to get mud from his boots on his unwilling dance partner's dress, this final indignation symbolizes how she carries the emotional toll of the encounter with her for years to come.

Krämer draws a direct connection between forced dancing and an unwanted arranged marriage, both of which deprive a woman of her ability to consent to physical contact. Esther's mother Fradel disapproves of the young girl's dancing, which identifies her as the kind of parent who will try to force her daughter into an unwelcome marriage. Unlike Esther's father, who encourages her dancing and asks if she would like to be a dance leader (*Vortänzerin*), Fradel dismisses her daughter's physical self-expression, saying she would prefer that Esther shift her mental energy "in the direction of cleaning and washing and darning stockings."[20] In other words, she would like Esther to practice domestic skills that are appropriate for a wife. Worse yet, Fradel undermines her daughter's effort to distance herself from Liepmann, since she blithely chats with him, an act that adds to Esther's discomfort: "Someone commented that it was an old custom to stick to the mother if you want to court the daughter. And Estherchen heard this from her father's knees. And understood. And shivered."[21] Even as a child, Esther is terrified of the possibility that Liepmann intends to follow up his assault on the dance floor with actual conjugal rights and the prospect that her mother could be complicit. She cannot think of the wedding without remembering the unpleasant incident. Her concerns are later proven correct, when, years later, her mother does pressure her to enter into an arranged marriage with Liepmann, something Esther is determined to avoid at all costs. Krämer uses the wedding dance scene to explain why her protagonist decides to leave her family and village and try her luck as a dancer in Munich, a career path that allows her public autonomy over her own dancing body.

Wedding dancing could also indicate inclusion in—or exclusion from—a family unit. In "Mishpahah" ("Family"), Lithuanian-born Hebrew writer Dvora Baron's lyrical story about infertility in a shtetl, childless couple Barukh and Dinah struggle with the knowledge that if they do not have children after ten years of marriage, then they must divorce so that Barukh can fulfill his religious obligation to have children. Baron repeatedly underscores the importance of the "chain of generations," which Barukh and Dinah are expected to preserve with offspring of their own.[22] As their ten-year anniversary approaches with no pregnancy in sight, Dinah is increasingly marginalized within the family. At a family wedding, eighteen-year-old Lieba drags Barukh from his chair into a circle of dancing women: "Whirling around and around him, she drew him into the circle of dancing girls, Liebas and Mushas of her own age, who formed a chain, their arms linked, spinning and changing places in a dance that made the onlookers dizzy."[23] Yet while the women take delight in Lieba's antics with Barukh, Dinah is excluded: "Now she was outside the chain, a link that had been wrenched from its place."[24] Dinah's unbearable situation becomes even more poignant when, in preparation for her anticipated divorce, Dinah teaches Lieba how to take care of her husband. Lieba does not merely separate Barukh from his wife at the wedding and dance with him; she seems (perhaps unwittingly) to be rehearsing for the role of second wife even though he is still married to Dinah. By pulling Barukh into the circle of nubile young women, Lieba publicly reenacts the communal pressures that threaten Barukh and Dinah's marriage.

As these examples suggest, authors were fascinated with the taboo of mixed-sex dancing, and they repeatedly invoked it in their descriptions of traditional Jewish weddings. Transgressive dancing was an irresistible way of presenting local color, exoticism, modernization, and evidence of social control. Not surprisingly, writers used this motif to enhance their ethnographic depictions. Sacher-Masoch depicts a cholera wedding (a practice sometimes referred to as a *"shvartse khasene,"* lit. black wedding) in his novella *Hasara Raba*, which is set in Galicia. In this eerie folk ritual, a young couple is married off in a cemetery in order to stop a cholera epidemic.[25] The cholera wedding reveals the sheer power community authorities hold over marriage arrangements and wedding festivities, since the couple is typically from the humblest of circumstances and encouraged—or compelled—to undergo this eerie ritual for the benefit of their neighbors.

Yet Sacher-Masoch decides that even the cholera wedding does not provide enough atmospheric interest on its own and decides to combine it with a fantasy of transgressive dancing. In his novella, penniless Chaike Wieselchen Konaw is married off in the cemetery to strapping but religiously lax Baruch Koreffle Rebhuhn, on the very same day Chaike's scholarly brother Jehuda gets married with full pomp to beautiful Penina Rosenstock, the daughter of the wealthiest man in town. Yet when Penina catches sight of her new working-class brother-in-law Baruch, she longs to dance with him: "She did not dance. She sneered as she saw the women dancing with the women and men dancing with men, following the Jewish custom. She thought about how lovely it would be to dance with Baruch."[26] Penina's wish for a transgressive dance with her handsome brother-in-law reveals her inconvenient sexual attraction to him. Sacher-Masoch thus criticizes the Jewish custom of arranged marriages, and even the traditional social prestige of scholars, since Penina desires a man who, unlike her new husband, is a paragon of male physicality. Penina's mixed-sex dancing fantasy introduces the reader to her complete disregard for the traditional Jewish value system. Yet, despite her rebellious desires, Penina obeys communal authorities with regard to the wedding ritual. Indeed, weddings are sometimes portrayed as the final and most complete triumph of communal authorities before young people decide to reject religious traditions.

Even when characters do not physically touch on the dance floor, wedding dancing could be an occasion for flirtation and fantasy. In Fradel Shtok's 1919 short story "Der shlayer" ("The Veil"), a sheltered young woman flirts with a charismatic flutist at her cousin's wedding. Because Manya's father abandoned the family, Manya's mother Zlate and her children are socially marginalized. The wedding is thus a rare opportunity for Manya to go to a festive event. Shtok does not describe the precise dance choreography in any detail, or even mention the other dancers (presumably a group of women). Instead, she focuses on the interactions of Manya and the unnamed flutist, implicitly allowing her protagonist to focus on a male outsider instead of an appropriate female dance partner. Manya does not touch the musician or formally dance with him, yet his musical accompaniment nonetheless guides her body around the dance floor: "When she danced the Lancers, she bowed politely to the flute player."[27] Their eye contact creates a greater sense of intimacy, and Manya interacts with him as if they were actually partnered on the dance floor. Shtok suggests that Manya and the flutist's exchanges—both intentional and unintentional—are a form of dance. Manya is exhilarated by her experience of the wedding, including the flirtation and sense of belonging to a community. Yet when she leaves the wedding celebration, Zlate fastens her absent husband's coat tightly around her daughter's neck, as if she were choking her with the burden of parental restrictions.

In Sacher-Masoch's *Der Judenraphael* and Opatoshu's *A roman fun a ferd-ganef*, young men publicly dance with women at weddings, with disastrous results. These dances are particularly transgressive because both Plutin, in *Der Judenraphael*, and Zanvl, in *A roman fun a ferd-ganef*, dance with partners whom they would not be allowed to marry. In one case, a Christian man dances with his Jewish inamorata at her wedding to another man. In the other case, a Jewish horse thief dances with a married woman, even though his sweetheart is watching. In both instances, mixed-sex wedding dancing helps show why these men are not socially permissible marriage partners for the women they love.

"Like the Montagues at the Capulets' Ball": *Der Judenraphael*

Internationally renowned during his lifetime for his middlebrow erotic fiction, Austrian writer Leopold von Sacher-Masoch (1836–1895) is best known today for a rather dubious honor. Sexologist Richard von Krafft-Ebing derived the term "masochism" from Sacher-Masoch's stories featuring

domineering women, who, in accordance with the author's particular pref-
erence, often wear fur.[28] Born to a noble family in Lemberg (today Lviv,
Ukraine) in close proximity to Hasidic Jewish communities, Sacher-Masoch
wrote several collections of stories about traditional Jewish life in Habsburg
Galicia. He was unusual for a writer of ghetto tales—because of the bla-
tant eroticism of his fiction and because, despite accusations to the contrary,
Sacher-Masoch did not have a Jewish background.[29] His liberal cosmopolitanism was characterized by feelings of affinity with Austro-Hungarian
minorities, including Jews.[30] Sacher-Masoch typically portrayed beautiful,
liberal-minded Jewish women sympathetically, at the same time he frequently took a harsher attitude toward male Hasidim.[31]

Sacher-Masoch's dance scenes fuse his interests in erotic, artistic, and
ethnographic themes, elements that have generally been addressed separately throughout his complicated reception history. For many years, scholars
emphasized Sacher-Masoch's distinctive brand of eroticism, which was
frequently described as a perversion.[32] Studies of his Jewish fiction tend
to discuss his ethnographic accuracy and use of sexual themes. More recent studies recognize Sacher-Masoch's deep commitment to the visual
arts and music.[33] Yet scholars tend to overlook Sacher-Masoch's spectacular
dance scenes. Set in works as varied as a musical novel, German court stories, a short story about a Podolian harvest festival, and tales of Jewish life,
Sacher-Masoch's dance scenes combine careful attention to local color with
sensational plot elements.[34]

By focusing on dance scenes in Sacher-Masoch's 1882 novella *Der Judenraphael*, I will show that this account of Jewish life in Galicia is artistically
more complex than has previously been recognized. The few scholarly assessments of the novella tend to focus on Sacher-Masoch's peculiar form
of philosemitism. Hannah Burdekin describes it as "a clear example of
Sacher-Masoch's strange mixture of occasional sympathy and a relish for
descriptions of human suffering."[35] While Sacher-Masoch typically depicts
Jewish cultural practice with deft (if at times questionable) ethnographic detail, the sensational dancing in *Der Judenraphael* reflects the melodramatic
qualities of the novel's star-crossed lovers themselves. The beautiful Jewess
Hadaßka and the Polish artist Plutin begin and end their tragic love affair in
the midst of highly stylized and deeply transgressive dance scenes. The two

pivotal scenes of communal dancing (a Purim ball and a wedding) reveal how Sacher-Masoch employs his knowledge of Jewish folkways for maximum exotic appeal while simultaneously using imagery drawn from western European high culture to elevate the stature of his Jewish heroine. Sacher-Masoch thus invokes a standard of artistic taste that appealed to a middlebrow readership. Such values would have generally seemed incomprehensible to the Jewish communal authorities whose decisions about Hadaßka's personal life are implicitly responsible for the novella's tragic ending.

Sacher-Masoch intended *Der Judenraphael* to be part of his six-part novella cycle, *Das Vermächtnis Kains* (The Heritage of Cain), which was never finished. *Der Judenraphael* was to be included in the final section, entitled *Der Tod* (Death).[36] This novella tells the ambivalent story of Plutin, an antisemitic Polish painter.[37] His combined hatred of and fascination with Jews leads him to create mean-spirited caricatures of local Jews, a practice that inspires them to call him by the nickname "der Judenraphael" (the Raphael of the Jews). Plutin and his artist friends also devise mean-spirited pranks that humiliate Jewish men. Plutin is unable to resist attending Jewish celebrations, however, and falls in love with a beautiful Jewish woman, Hadaßka, whom he meets at a Purim ball. She convinces Plutin to abandon his antisemitism, but he continues to torment Lebele Hirsch, the rather pathetic man Hadaßka's parents have chosen as her fiancé, now ostensibly out of jealousy rather than prejudice. Hadaßka is unwilling to convert and marry Plutin but would rather die than marry anyone else. She dies scandalously dancing in Plutin's arms on her wedding day, and Plutin retreats to the wilderness to follow her in death.

Two key dance scenes occur in *Der Judenraphael*. Their position in the novella brackets the romantic relationship central to the arc of the plot—the Purim celebration is where Plutin and Hadaßka meet, and the wedding dance is where she dies and his fate is sealed. These two episodes also divide the plot in two: The first dance scene, a frenzied dance party, bids farewell to Plutin's wild youth and ushers him into a romantic role; the second dance scene, which focuses on the physical connection between the two lovers, cements the bond of a couple that can only be united in death. The two dance settings, a Purim ball and a wedding, are common locations for dances in Jewish literature. Moreover, Sacher-Masoch exploits these locations for

maximum atmospheric effect, which is carnivalesque in the former and romantic in the latter. In each instance, Plutin crosses boundaries by attending
a Jewish ritual function under dubious pretenses and exploiting the social
environment to get closer to Hadaßka.

At the Purim ball, where Plutin's disguise makes him appear to be a
member of the rabbinic elite, the wild dancing and carousing of the Jewish guests provides the distraction necessary for him to pursue Hadaßka. At
the wedding, Plutin uses the threat of physical violence to flout the prohibition on mixed-sex dancing, which is particularly taboo since, in this case, it
involves dancing with another man's bride. Dance and mixed-sex sociability establish social relationships and define religious and gender boundaries.
Sacher-Masoch combines formulaic, sensational plot elements with canonical literary allusions to elevate the status of his Jewish heroine, suggesting
that her emotional empathy across religious lines makes her superior to more
close-minded traditional Jews and to Polish antisemites, even if he is unable
to envision a happy outcome for his fantasy of religious tolerance. Dance and
mixed-sex sociability establish social relationships, at the same time that they
demarcate religious and gender boundaries.

Der Judenraphael is a work of local color fiction, yet it repeatedly invokes
European high culture, even in the title. Sacher-Masoch does not explain
why Galician Jews choose to give their tormentor Plutin a nickname inspired
by the Italian High Renaissance painter Raphael, although a likely explana-
tion is that Raphael was famous for his skill as a draftsman, and he relied
heavily on drawings to plan his paintings. Sacher-Masoch, who was very
familiar with German Romanticism, may have also wanted to draw parallels
with an artist seen as a sensualist turned Christian painter.[38] Once Plutin
meets Hadaßka, however, he falls in love at first sight and transforms from
an antisemitic Raphael into a latter-day Rembrandt van Rijn, since like the
seventeenth-century Dutch painter, he creates sympathetic genre paintings
of Jews. At the same time, like the Romantic vision of Raphael as reformed
sensualist, Plutin's love for Hadaßka arguably not only strips him of his antisemitism, but it also makes him a better Christian, who displays a newfound
(yet problematic) love for his Jewish neighbors.[39]

While Sacher-Masoch evokes classical painting in his references to
the visual arts and deploys folk culture when discussing music, his dance

scenes in *Der Judenraphael* are much more highly contrived. The fanciful, highly dramatic nature of the two dance scenes reflects the impossibility of the boundary-crossing romantic plot. Sacher-Masoch alludes to three examples of high culture in the two dance scenes: the biblical Book of Esther, the play *Romeo and Juliet*, and the ballet *Giselle*. All three works emphasize boundary-crossing romance, disguised identities, and opportunities for dance. Sacher-Masoch's use of these canonical texts reconciles his liberal tendencies with a primarily aesthetic interest in Jewish culture. Dance is a focal point for the intersection of these interests, and the most public transgression against traditional Jewish social norms in the novella.

Sacher-Masoch's most explicit allusion to a canonical text in *Der Judenraphael* is the Book of Esther. Indeed, writers frequently invoke both the biblical Esther and the legendary Esterke, Jewish mistress of Polish King Casimir the Great (r. 1310–1370), when describing interethnic relationships between Jewish women and Christian men in Poland.[40] Hadaßka's name is even a diminutive form of Hadassah, the Hebrew name for Queen Esther. Plutin explicitly identifies Hadaßka as an exotic Esther figure while he is attending her father's Purim ball in the disguise of a Hasidic rebbe. Inspired by the scriptural account of Haman lying at Esther's feet, begging for his life from the cold, proud queen, Plutin flirts with Hadaßka, using a rather extraordinary pick-up line: "If you were Esther now . . . and there was a Haman here in Wrublowize, would you also let him hang?"[41] Still under the mistaken assumption that she is speaking to a rebbe, she tells him there is a Haman in her town: Plutin the painter who caricatures Jews.

Hadaßka's response to Plutin's outrageous flirtation is measured and sympathetic. She feels righteously angry about the cruel antics of the Judenraphael, yet she does not seek to punish him. Since she considers it impossible for an artist, endowed with a spark of divine creativity, to be truly evil, she would not condemn Plutin to hang. Instead, she would like to educate him so that he can better understand Jews. Adopting the language of universalism, Hadaßka explains that Jews, like every people, have good and bad sides. She speaks in a way designed to appeal to liberal readers—as well as to Plutin himself, whom she quickly convinces of her viewpoint.

While Hadaßka is not a sadistic character, Sacher-Masoch's interpretation of the biblical text portrays Esther as one of his despotic heroines. In his rendering, it is Esther, not her husband, the Persian King Ahasuerus, who decrees Haman's death. Furthermore, it is almost as if Esther were engaged in a sadomasochistic relationship with Haman that ultimately results in her condemning him to death. Haman's hanging is not merely punishment for attempted genocide, but instead a terrible token of a beautiful woman's cruelty. Sacher-Masoch further underscores this point later in the novella, when Plutin's friend Hlamton dresses up as Queen Esther for another Purim celebration. Hlamton callously torments Lebele Hirsch, who is under the mistaken impression that he is talking to a coquettish widow rather than to a slightly built man in drag. Sacher-Masoch's novella identifies the figure of Esther with female sadism, yet in order to portray the Jewish Esther figure Hadaßka sympathetically, Sacher-Masoch creates an effeminate, male, non-Jewish Esther who cruelly mistreats and sexually humiliates a hapless Jewish man.[42] The parallels between Hadaßka and Hlamton are even more striking since the two Esther figures switch partners—Plutin and Hlamton used to earn money singing folksongs together, with Hlamton disguised as a woman, and Lebele Hirsch later becomes Hadaßka's fiancé. The social configuration of these two Esthers and their male partners suggests a partner-swapping dance.

Hadaßka and Plutin do not dance at the Purim party, yet dance facilitates their interaction. Sacher-Masoch describes the Purim celebration where they meet as a Jewish carnival. Revelers dress up in fine clothes, sing folksongs, and dance the "Kosak" (kazatsky) and the "Kolomijka" (kolomyika, Yiddish: *kolomeyke*).[43] Lebele Hirsch dresses as King Solomon, in a manner suggestive of the stereotype of the effeminate oriental male, and he is waited on by a harem of beautiful Jewish women.[44] The women who do not attend to Solomon's immediate needs play flutes and tambourines or dance. This image is pure fantasy; it is difficult to imagine Polish Hasidic women dressing as harem women for Purim. Sacher-Masoch presents the Purim ball as a site where revelers can violate restrictions on contact between the sexes more easily than at weddings.

Sacher-Masoch creates a scene of colorful chaos at the Purim ball, full of costumes and mistaken identities. The atmosphere suggests Mikhail Bakhtin's concept of the carnivalesque, a topsy-turvy environment in which social rules are momentarily suspended.[45] The Purim celebration enables

Plutin and Hadaßka to meet in a way that prevents their prejudices from interfering with romance, since Hadaßka is initially unaware that Plutin is not
Jewish and that he is, worse yet, the notorious caricaturist. The wild frenzy of
the dancing, instigated by Solomon's harem, conveniently creates a distraction that enables Plutin and Hadaßka to talk privately together. Ordinary
social boundaries between the sexes and religious groups are temporarily ig-
nored in the context of the Purim celebration.

A costumed dance is thus a clever narrative ploy to enable an unlikely
couple to fall in love unintentionally, and Sacher-Masoch was certainly not
the first to create this plot twist. Early in the novella, Sacher-Masoch explicitly references William Shakespeare's tragedy *Romeo and Juliet*. "[L]ike
the Montagues at the Capulets' ball [Maskenfest],"[46] Plutin and his friends
arrive uninvited in Jewish homes to amuse themselves with Jewish beauties.
The comparison with the Capulet ball is also apt when Plutin and his friends
attend the Purim party disguised as five wise rebbes from Jerusalem. In the
same way Romeo, standing at the side of the dance floor, is astonished to
notice Juliet for the first time, Hadaßka appears to Plutin in the midst of
Purim revelry.[47]

This scene has many classic elements of Sacher-Masoch's prose. Frenzied
women chase traditional Jewish men, trying to kiss them. When Hadaßka
emerges, she wears a fur and appears frozen as a work of art, a motif that
also appears in Sacher-Masoch's most famous novella, *Venus im Pelz* (*Venus
in Furs*).[48] Her resemblance to a Rembrandt painting foreshadows Plutin's
conversion from Raphael to Rembrandt. At the same time, Plutin's reaction
to seeing Hadaßka parallels Romeo's speech after noticing Juliet. Romeo describes Juliet using comparisons between light and darkness, such as teaching
the torches to burn bright and a snowy dove among crows. Hadaßka, similarly, emerges from the darkness of her fur wrap like an angel coming out of
a dark night, which also reminds readers that she wears the preferred costume of Sacher-Masoch's demonic women. In Shakespeare's play, Romeo
asks himself, "Did my heart love until now?"[49] Plutin also asks himself a
rhetorical question, "Where have I already seen her?"[50] Plutin's immediate
feeling of kinship with a Jewish woman is just one way Sacher-Masoch seeks
to undermine anti-Jewish prejudice. Sacher-Masoch takes delight in exotic
images of Jews but portrays Hadaßka sympathetically.

The boundary-crossing romance and encounter at a costume party share structural similarities with *Romeo and Juliet*, yet the comparison would be unthinkable without the romantic deaths of the lovers. Like Juliet, Hadaßka refuses to be the bride of another man, promising to die before she will marry the husband selected by her parents. She agrees with Plutin that she was created for him, in order to love him. Yet Hadaßka is unwilling to convert or marry a non-Jew, and the only conversion Plutin considers is his decision to stop being an antisemite. Sacher-Masoch may have personally believed that, "intermarriage was a delightful way to irritate anti-Semites," as Barbara Hyams argues, yet his fictional Jewish women rarely marry their Christian lovers.[51] Unlike a writer such as Karl Emil Franzos, who depicted ill-starred romance to advocate for cultural and political change, Sacher-Masoch's artistic vision itself demanded a tragic end to the novella. Gilles Deleuze views delayed gratification as an important part of masochistic pleasure, and the impossibility of Plutin and Hadaßka's love affair is a form of infinitely delayed gratification.[52] Hadaßka's proclamation of loyalty to her family and faith are portrayed as positive traits, although her parents would probably argue that the true show of commitment to a Jewish community would involve building a Jewish family of her own and raising Jewish children, rather than dying artistically on her wedding day. Sacher-Masoch's resolution of this interethnic romance thus reflects his philosemitic fascination with Jewish women rather than a concern with Jewish communal continuity, a crucial distinction between Sacher-Masoch's ghetto fiction and that of Jewish writers such as Leopold Kompert.

Hadaßka's decision to die before marriage would, according to German and Slavic folk belief, turn her into a *willi*. These ghostly dancers are brides who die before their wedding day and gather by night at crossroads to compel male travelers to dance with them, until the unfortunate men die of exhaustion. Jewish-born German writer Heinrich Heine's description of willis was so popular when he published it in the 1830s that it was soon adapted into the French Romantic ballet *Giselle*.[53] Sacher-Masoch explicitly compares Hadaßka to a willi when she dances a couple dance with Plutin. Sacher-Masoch does not directly cite the ballet *Giselle*, and claimed not to have been influenced by Heine,[54] yet there are many parallels between the exotic sexuality of the beautiful Jewess (a figure Hadaßka embodies) and the otherworldly femininity of the romantic ballerina. In both the novella and the ballet, lovers are separated by social boundaries, a man courts his love interest disguised as someone from her social group, the main villain is a suitor who shares the heroine's background, and, most significantly, a beautiful young woman dies while dancing. Viewed in the context of the ballet, Hadaßka and Plutin perform a *pas de deux* when they dance together.[55] In fact, the two dance scenes in *Der Judenraphael* mimic the two-act structure of the ballet itself; the Purim bacchanalia corresponds with the earthly first act, the wedding dance with the otherworldly second act.[56]

The couple dance takes place on Hadaßka's wedding day, immediately following the marriage ceremony. It is at this moment that Plutin enters, brandishing a gun. In contrast to the traditional wedding dancing, "Men with men and women with women" that is already taking place, Plutin demands to dance with the bride.[57] Hadaßka complies, relieved that now she can die in her lover's arms. Her new husband Lebele Hirsch tries to interfere, shouting "We Jews don't permit a man to dance with a dame. I won't stand for my wife to jump around with the porets [landowner], the goy [non-Jew]!"[58] When Lebele Hirsch attempts to pull Hadaßka away from Plutin, the artist grabs him by the beard and pulls him to the ground. In a scene that would have seemed nightmarish to traditional Jews yet promised melodramatic entertainment to Sacher-Masoch's readers, Plutin physically abuses the Jewish bridegroom and gains the opportunity to dance intimately with the Jewish bride.

Sacher-Masoch depicts Plutin and Hadaßka's dance as highly dramatic and romantic. He does not specifically state the dance they perform, or whether a sheltered Jewish woman had any opportunity to learn European couple dancing (although conceivably she learned while attending school in Lemberg). Based on the conventions of national dances performed in Romantic ballets, one might expect a mazurka, since the setting is in Galicia.[59] On the other hand, the fact that the couple flies around the hall in close embrace suggests a more scandalous partner dance, such as a waltz or polka.

Earlier in the novella, Sacher-Masoch conveyed Esther's cruel potential while allowing Hadaßka to avoid fully identifying with it. Now Sacher-Masoch compares Hadaßka to the threatening figures of a willi and the angel of death. While normally both of these figures are fatal for their interlocutors, since willis dance men to death and the angel of death literally causes it, Hadaßka does not immediately endanger Plutin. Instead, she welcomes her own death. In this sense, she exemplifies Jean-Paul Sartre's characterization of the beautiful Jewess as a sexualized victim, even though she is brutalized, not by Cossacks as in Sartre's example, but by conflicted value systems that put her into an impossible position.[60] Hadaßka is self-sacrificing, even when Sacher-Masoch's aesthetic choices and typical preferences would initially suggest otherwise.

Plutin views death as an opportunity for artistic expression. During the course of the novel, he is eager to freeze Hadaßka in place, imagining her both as a painting and a sculpture. He even paints her as an angel in a genre painting. Plutin finds Hadaßka attractive, whether she is frozen, willing to die for him, or dead. In a moment that defies belief, he fails to notice when she dies in his arms. Plutin continues dancing with her, and then, once he becomes aware of her fate, eagerly awaits his own death.

Sacher-Masoch's *Der Judenraphael* is a middlebrow extravaganza. It is inspired as much by the sentimental narratives and romantic formulas that would allow a financially struggling writer to sell books as it is by literary ambition. Nonetheless, this novella is a more complex and ambivalent text than Sacher-Masoch's shorter works of regional fiction. While Sacher-Masoch concerned himself with ethnographic accuracy throughout his ghetto tales, his use of dance in *Der Judenraphael* reflects the artistic temperaments of the lovers themselves, which he marshals in support of his own philosemitic views. At once Esther, Juliet, and Giselle, Hadaßka is both a positive representation of Jewish femininity and a fitting counterpart for the artist Plutin. Sacher-Masoch identifies her with tragic heroines, prefiguring her own doomed romance and premature death.

In his dance depictions, Sacher-Masoch combines elements of popular exoticism, high culture, and liberal, philosemitic politics. He employs these elements to romanticize the beautiful Jewess Hadaßka, whose engagement with the dance floor displays her enlightened values, rather than the dangerous sexuality that characterizes so many of his female dancers. In this novella, as in his corpus as a whole, Sacher-Masoch uses dance to reflect physical desire in an aesthetically pleasing way that takes into account the cultural milieu of the dancers for maximum crowd-pleasing affect. Sacher-Masoch subverts Jewish social hierarchies by depicting an interethnic love affair and lampooning traditionally religious men yet is unable to imagine an ending where Hadaßka actively resists communal expectations by converting so she can marry her lover. In this middlebrow erotic novella, Sacher-Masoch does not truly question the expectation of female passivity or the supremacy of western European culture. As in the dance scenes, his goal is to entertain.

Since Hadaßka and Plutin are unable to enjoy a sexual union, their outrageous final dance is as close as they come to consummating their love affair. This dance scene is designed to excite readers, while nonetheless keeping threatening female sexuality in check. Minor characters, such as the members of King Solomon's harem who torment Jewish men, embody aggressive female sexuality, yet Hadaßka herself avoids the characteristics of Sacher-Masoch's demonic dancing women. Instead of forcing men to dance, she elicits sympathy for Jewish womanhood by martyring herself on the dance floor out of love for a Christian man. Just as Sacher-Masoch's depictions of Jewish dance favor sensational exoticism over ethnographic accuracy, the resolution of his star-crossed romantic plot emphasizes liberal and artistic ideals over the community values of his Galician characters. In contrast to Sacher-Masoch's particular attitude toward Jews, which causes him to portray a Jewish woman sympathetically while treating a Jewish man in a manner that is virtually indistinguishable from antisemitism, Opatoshu portrays a very different type of Jewish masculinity and presents both virginal and seductive Jewish women. Yet, in both novellas, the emotional climax is a wedding dance scene.

"Pas d'espagne!": *A roman fun a ferd-ganef*

In a review of Opatoshu's 1912 novella *A roman fun a ferd-ganef*, Yiddish writer Moyshe Nadir (pseudonym for Isaac Reiss) comments, somewhat disparagingly, on the author's writing style. He claims that Opatoshu repeats effective words multiple times, as if he were flirting with them: "[T]he word 'pas d'espagne,' for instance ('dancing a pas d'espagne') can be found five or six times in the book."[61] Nadir cites a Russian ballroom dance, the pas d'espagne, as an example of Opatoshu's use of foreign terms. Based on Nadir's description, one would think that Opatoshu mentioned the dance multiple times, when in fact it is referenced only once, as a command shouted

out to wedding musicians. This one, fateful pas d'espagne is performed during a pivotal wedding dance scene, which casts aftershocks throughout the
entire novella. A horse thief loses his chance to become respectable after he
slights his love interest by publicly dancing with a married woman. Nadir
overstates the number of times Opatoshu cites the name of the dance, but he
underestimates the critical importance of the pas d'espagne for the novella
and of social dance for Opatoshu's work as a whole.[62]

Born in the Stupsk Forest near Mława, a shtetl in Poland, Opatoshu
(1886–1954) immigrated to the United States in 1906 and became a member of the American Yiddish modernist group *Di Yunge* (the Young Ones).
Even in this experimental literary milieu, Opatoshu's work stands out for
the striking physicality he brought to Yiddish belles lettres. His grandson
describes him as a sensual man in both his literary work and bohemian
personal life: "[T]he treatment of sexuality and lust in Opatoshu's writings
was not an anomalous, wholly imaginative departure from his actual per-
sona. . . . Women of all generations have told me that they found [Joseph]
an extremely attractive figure—forceful, confident, lusty, flirty, but always ap-
preciative and respectful."[63] Unusually for a Yiddish writer, Opatoshu was
able to support himself through his literary work, including newspaper publications and speaking engagements around the world.[64] His most popular
works were translated into multiple languages, including German, and his
personal papers include newspaper clippings from public readings in Vienna.[65] In works set in such varied locations as nineteenth-century Poland,
early twentieth-century New York, ancient Judea, and medieval Germany,
Opatoshu explored themes and characters whose corporeality and position
on the margins of respectable society were more closely aligned with literary
naturalism than with European models of Jewish life.

Opatoshu first published *A roman fun a ferd-ganef* in *Shriftn* (Writings),
a publication of Di Yunge. *Shriftn* was targeted at an elite Yiddish-speaking
readership and published in editions of just 500 to 1,000 copies.[66] The novella
was reprinted in book form in 1917 and adapted into a film in 1971.[67] Even
in a modernist context, Opatoshu's novella was extraordinary. He combined
semi-autobiographical elements and a Russian Polish setting with an anti-
hero of a type that, according to Mikhail Krutikov, more closely resembles
American frontier heroes than "the quintessentially Old World Tevye and

Menakhem-Mendl," referring to two of Sholem Aleichem's most famous protagonists.[68]

Opatoshu's description of healthy, illiterate Jewish criminals differed markedly from the Yiddish literature of his time. Gennady Estraikh, Sabine Koller, and Krutikov express a similar assessment:

> Opatoshu's heroes represented a new type of Jewish character: young, active, wilful, and energetic, ready to break established social norms and cultural conventions, and sometimes even the law. His shtetl stories are free of nostalgia and sentimentality.[69]

Ruth Wisse states that *A roman fun a ferd-ganef* combines a fairly conventional love story with "a frankly lustful hero and a richer treatment of erotic desire than was customary in Yiddish prose."[70] Most critical assessments of the novella focus on the protagonist's robustness and criminality, without acknowledging disreputable female characters. Opatoshu's use of provocative dance scenes adapts American literary aesthetics for a work set in eastern Europe and enables him to describe women's participation in the culture of his dissolute Jewish underworld. The hero Zanvl is born to a family of Jewish criminals and engages in the family business, but his unhappy fate is truly sealed by his participation in mixed-sex dancing.

The pas d'espagne (Yiddish: *padespan*) is a ballroom dance with elements similar to a waltz. The name means Spanish step in French, and most sources describe it as a Russian dance, although a 1912 French dance manual says it was danced in France.[71] Despite this international appeal, the pas d'espagne appears much less frequently in dance manuals or literary fiction than the waltz, quadrille, or lancers. In fact, one of these rare mentions is in Opatoshu's first published work, his 1910 short story "Oyf yener zayt brik" (On the Other Side of the Bridge), where a married man dances a pas d'espagne with his pretty boarder shortly before they begin an affair.[72] Such a flirtatious connotation is hardly surprising, since the pas d'espagne involves two partners turning toward and away from each other, often swinging their arms in a stylized "Spanish" style. This motion of turning away is very important, since in Yiddish folk dance, eye contact between partners and facing each other is crucial. Most communication in traditional Ashkenazic partner dances happens with the eyes, rather than with direct touch. In fact, turning a back on a partner is a key component of the broygez tants, which demonstrates how turning one's back to a partner during a dance is a radical departure from the norms of Jewish social dancing. In the context of the novella, the pas d'espagne is more closely identified with Warsaw than with Spain, yet it cannot be fully separated from the practice of Hispanomania in European culture in general and Jewish culture in particular.

Spanish themes were incredibly popular in nineteenth-century European ballet and social dance.[73] The extraordinary career of "Spanish" dancer Lola Montez (born Eliza Gilbert, ca. 1820–1861) was only one example of this cultural phenomenon.[74] Dances such as the fandango and the bolero were celebrated for their exotic sensuality. In his 1828 dance manual *The Code of Terpsichore*, Italian dance theorist Carlo Blasis lists physical agitation, desire, gallantry, and impatience as some of the features of Spanish dances.[75] Eduard Reisinger says that "fire and flames" are characteristics of the fandango and of Spanish national character in his 1889 dance manual.[76] He also describes the bolero as fiery[77] and the fandango as dissolute,[78] lush, and indecent.[79] In a similar vein, Albert Czerwinski claims in 1862 that lively movements and gesticulations characterize Spanish dances.[80] He notes Moorish influence on Spanish dances[81] and observes that in the sixteenth century, some writers claimed that provocative dances such as the sarabande were invented by the devil.[82]

Polish-born American Jewish choreographer Nathan Vizonsky (1898–1968) contrasts the emotional energy of Spanish dance with eastern European Jewish folk dances, claiming in a 1930 Yiddish-language article "Vegn yidishn folks-tants" (About Jewish Folk Dance) that Jewish dance is not dominated by passion, but instead emphasizes gentle humor, biting satire, and deep tragedy.[83] Yet immigration, urbanization, and acculturation challenged the makeup of Jewish dance. Yiddish-speaking Jews who moved to cities such as New York embraced mixed-sex social dance as a leisure pursuit and token of Americanization that often marked a sharp contrast with the dance practices in their hometowns.

It is clear from Opatoshu's repeated descriptions of dance in a variety of contexts that he was interested in dance as a literary motif.[84] In setting a novella full of American-style physicality and naturalism in Poland, Opatoshu makes use of European local color in service of his aesthetic aims. He does so by including unscrupulous Jewish criminals (rather than American frontier

characters) and also in his use of erotically charged dance. Opatoshu's motivations for including the pas d'espagne probably resembled those that
inspired Russian dancers to adopt a Spanish-style dance in the first place:
cosmopolitanism, passion, and sexual tension. Opatoshu inserts these elements into his literature through his sensual descriptions of dance.

Opatoshu includes three dance scenes in his novella. Each of these scenes
prompts readers to ponder questions of propriety and impropriety, legal-
ity and illegality, boundary-crossing, transgression, liminality, and desire. The
first scene takes place in a tavern, the second at a wedding, and the third at a
brothel. Each scene illustrates Zanvl's inability to escape a life of crime and
draws clear distinctions between his underworld connections and his sweetheart's respectable Hasidic upbringing.[85] Both the tavern and the brothel are
explicitly coded as underworld sites, where Zanvl carouses with his nefarious
friends after engaging in illegal activity and where Jews and Christians mingle
to an extent unimaginable in more respectable locations. Yet dancing in these
venues does not have the same immediate and devastating consequences as the
pas d'espagne. The wedding dance scene is the moment in which Zanvl must
publicly confront his dilemma about choosing between a respectable path and
the life he has led, and it proves he is unable to withstand the temptation of
the underworld.[86] For Opatoshu, a naturalist writer, dance manifests the inner
drives that compel characters toward an inescapable outcome. While Zanvl
initially romances a respectable young woman and flirts with the idea of turning away from a criminal path, he is unable to resist the lure of the tavern, his
old friends, or a daring couple dance with his friend's seductive wife Beyle.

In a scene at his sister's wedding, Zanvl goes to the women's section so
that he can see his sweetheart Rachel, who promised to wear a white dress.
Opatoshu's use of color in this scene is almost cartoonishly overdetermined,
and the white dress underscores Rachel's virginal status and her hope of
becoming Zanvl's bride. Beyle, in contrast to Rachel, wears a colorful and
sophisticated ensemble that immediately identifies her as a sexually experienced woman from Warsaw. While Zanvl and Rachel do not openly interact
with each other, for fear of drawing attention to their secret relationship,
Beyle is forthright with Zanvl and immediately takes control of the situation,
demanding that the young man dance with her and choosing what their next
dance will be—a pas d'espagne:

"And now, Zanvl, [go in the circle] and we'll dance."

"But the women . . . they'll–" he stammered.

"Big deal! I'll tell them I'm one of your aunts, all right?" Beyle laughed and her black eyes sparkled.

Zanvl threw the musicians some money, took Beyle by the arm and made his way through the couples. Some of the older women looked askance, but it was a wedding, after all! Everyone watched Beyle soar, float lightly as a bird, barely touching the floor. Zanvl held her lightly, and with his head bent over he felt himself becoming drunk on the perfume of her bosom, floating in a magical dance in which Beyle's silk dress seemed to be hissing like a horde of snakes. Beyle shouted across to the musicians: [pas d'espagne]![87]

Beyle's dance with Zanvl is explicitly transgressive and seductive. Although they operate in a public space, Zanvl notices intimate details about Beyle: her bewitching scent, the way her dress sounds like snakes. Beyle presents an image that is strikingly sinister, exotic, and even phallic. Her identification with snakes reminds readers of the biblical story of Adam and Eve (Genesis 3), since a serpent tempted Eve to violate a divine prohibition and encourage Adam to join her in transgression. Opatoshu's description of Beyle's foreignness and eroticism prepares Zanvl for a seductive dance, even before Beyle announces to the musicians what they will perform.

The sexual tension becomes even more noticeable when the couple actually dances the pas d'espagne. The dance floor empties, and everyone watches as Beyle and Zanvl separate, approach each other, and finally embrace:

Nobody else danced. Beyle stood at one corner, Zanvl at the other. Beyle lifted her train with her right hand and lifted her patent leather shoes and black, transparent stockings from their place. She hummed quietly, preparing to dance, and the sky-blue shawl slid on her neck, dazzling the eyes with its color. She lifted one leg, brushed aside her short white petticoat, made a grand bow with her elastic body, provocatively raised her shoulder and moved towards Zanvl, moved towards him with her sparkling dark eyes. . . . Then they took hold of each other in close embrace.[88]

At Beyle's suggestion, the couple dances a racy pas d'espagne, alone on the dance floor. Wedding musicians were frequently paid per dance by the dancers, rather than the hosts of the event, and only those dancers who paid for a particular dance had the right to participate. Opatoshu exploits the scene for maximum dramatic and visual effect. He allows the anticipation to build, using the dance choreography: describing the characters separating, facing each other in preparation for the dance, approaching each other, and finally embracing. The fact that Beyle lifts her skirt is provocative and reminds readers of the earlier tavern dance scene in which the tavern maid Manke lifted her skirts while dancing with Beyle's husband in an attempt to capture Zanvl's attention. Opatoshu does not describe the specific dance steps, but he fully emphasizes the emotional and visual impact of the overall dance figure: separating, anticipating, and approaching.

This scene is emotionally riveting, yet it would be difficult to identify the dance as a pas d'espagne from Opatoshu's description alone. Since dance plays a largely symbolic role in the novella, Opatoshu does not focus on ethnographic detail. The elements of separating and approaching, while maintaining eye contact, are also features of more traditional Jewish dances. Opatoshu presents the pas d'espagne as daring and exotic at the same time that he has erased the most foreign elements of the choreography itself: the Spanish-styled hand gestures and partners who turn away from each other. His dance choreography, like Wisse's characterization of the romantic plot trajectory, is thus erotic without truly breaking with convention.

Opatoshu's use of eye contact and spectatorship in this scene enhances the theatricality of this moment and intensifies the emotional drama. Characters do not speak about their desires, but instead they communicate their feelings through an elaborate network of looking and reacting to what they see. Throughout the wedding scene, Opatoshu links characters through sight, as they gaze and are conscious of being observed. Beyle and Rachel perform their own advancing and retreating motions with their eyes as they silently fight over Zanvl; one could even say that their darting and more prolonged looks dance around each other. In this same way, Zanvl is passed between the two women, a consequence of his confusion and inability to act decisively. He looks at Beyle and flushes; he turns to Rachel and goes pale. Indeed, even his physical appearance is completely determined by these two women, each of whom knows precisely what she wants from him, in contrast to his own weak will. Like a mirror that simply reflects the woman he faces, Zanvl's blushes mimic Beyle's colorful attire while his pallor copies Rachel's white dress.

Zanvl's fellow criminals respect him for his strength and aggression as a horse thief, yet the young man loses his agency when confronted with the two rival women. The seductress Beyle pushes him into a female space and a feminine role by prevailing upon him to dance in a room full of women. She treats him like a naughty boy and chooses their dance. Even when they dance together, Opatoshu describes her physical presence in much more positive and self-controlled terms. Her dancing body is light, graceful, and seductive. Zanvl's motions are most notable for their awkwardness; confronted with his conflicted feelings and guilt, he repeatedly stands up and sits down but is ultimately unable to muster the courage to talk to and clarify matters with Rachel. Zanvl's inability to apologize to the woman he adores underscores his overall unsuitability to be the husband of such a respectable girl. In fact, he remains incapable of addressing her articulately for the duration of the novella, which chronicles the overall deterioration of Zanvl's moral character, social standing, and economic status.

The shape and form of the pas d'espagne choreography—which involves advancing and retreating, facing and turning away, and stylings with a foreign, cosmopolitan flare—is a useful organizing principle for the pivotal role of dance in Opatoshu's novella. Dance both adds to a disreputable ambiance and aids in seedy flirtation, although in the case of Opatoshu's particularly obvious wedding dance scene, it pushes the plot and character development forward while mirroring, in the very steps and figures, the struggles and interpersonal dynamic of the characters. Zanvl resists, yet cannot escape from, the allure of the underworld and his criminal associates, much in the same way he is unable to refuse Beyle's invitation to dance. The structure of the dance itself recapitulates Zanvl's struggle and failure to give up the life of crime into which he was born—especially since Opatoshu includes dance scenes in his descriptions of underworld settings. Zanvl pulls away yet ends up embracing both Beyle and the underworld she represents. In the review cited at the beginning of this section, Nadir's biggest compliment about Opatoshu is that he knows his scoundrels. Indeed, he knows them well enough to know that they should dance.

Traditional Judaism and the ideology of romantic love both posit weddings as joyous occasions. Nonetheless, literary wedding celebrations are often sites of surveillance and social control. Transgressive dancing can be quickly shut down when it takes place at weddings in full view of religious authorities. Yet dancers might also enjoy some of the communal aspects of wedding dancing, such as the expectation of gladdening the bride.

In literary texts, writers such as Sacher-Masoch and Opatoshu strive for a balance between criticism of communal social control, exciting local color details, allusions to European culture, and reliance on sexual themes. Mixed-sex dancing titillates audiences with explicitly transgressive physicality, while nonetheless showing a certain measure of restraint. Sacher-Masoch displaces his usual theme of sexual aggression from his heroine onto minor characters. Since Hlamton (dressed in drag as Esther) acts the part of a cruel Jewish women, and the women of King Solomon's harem display uninhibited sexuality, Sacher-Masoch is free to depict Hadaßka according to conventional bourgeois ideas of femininity, including a romantic demise at her own wedding. Similarly, Opatoshu forces his character Rachel to confront Zanvl's confused sexual desires at his sister's wedding, where he dances with Beyle. While Rachel would not have joined Zanvl in a tavern or brothel, the wedding scene is decisive precisely because Zanvl publicly shows his ties to the underworld in a nominally respectable site.

Yet wedding dancing is not necessarily so melodramatic, even though it has always involved engagement with social expectations. In Yiddish writer Kadya Molodovsky's undated, typewritten draft of her article "Trayne–di muter fun vilner gaon, Rabi Eliyahu" (Trayne–Mother of the Vilna Gaon, Rabbi Eliyahu), for a series of portraits of famous woman for the *Forverts* (Forward), Trayne dances at the wedding of a poor couple to give them joy.[89] This action demonstrates her concern for the feelings of even the most marginal members of society, a responsibility that is worth risking even her own physical well-being. Trayne's selfless act wins her the best possible boon for a pious Jewish woman: a son who will become a great rabbi (1720–1797).

Molodovsky wrote such portraits of famous women under a pseudonym, Rivke Zilberg, that she borrowed from the protagonist of her earlier novel

Fun Lublin biz Nyu-York: Togbukh fun Rivke Zilberg (*A Jewish Refugee in New York: Rivke Zilberg's Journal*)—a character who struggled with the pressure to marry. Molodovsky was a prolific writer in many genres, who set her work in Europe, the Middle East, and New York. In texts such as her piece about Trayne, she frequently portrays dance as a way of bringing communities together. Yet in *Fun Lublin biz Nyu-York*, as will be seen in the next chapter, Molodovsky uses dance to depict the dislocation of a new immigrant to America.

CHAPTER 6

THE DANCE HALL

Commercial Leisure Culture and American Sexual Mores

DANCES WERE AN EXTREMELY POPULAR form of entertainment for immigrants to New York around 1900, including eastern European Jews.[1] Whether in commercial dance halls or neighborhood associations, dancing academies or saloons, writers identified dance spaces with youthful revelry and American capitalism. Indeed, writers often do not make rigid distinctions between the specific locations, since all of these venues were part of the working-class dance culture loosely associated with dance halls.[2] American Jewish writers identify dancing with a cultural shift in personal relationships and private life as a result of the process of Americanization. This phenomenon is exacerbated by the fact that dancing does not simply remain in the dance halls, but instead enters the domestic sphere and is an important aspect of reunions for *landsmanshaftn* (hometown associations). The popularity of social dances did not end with the restrictive Immigration Act of 1924, but instead continued through World War II in a context in which war refugees might feel alienated from the materialism of the country that had reluctantly offered them a safe haven. Although dances promised romance and flirtation, they often also served as a reminder of the way American capitalist impulses complicated Jewish courtship and marriage patterns.

Literary texts emphasize the role of dance venues in creating a leisure culture that was inseparable from monetary concerns. Sara Smolinsky, the protagonist of Anzia Yezierska's 1925 novel *Bread Givers*, notes how her co-workers in the sweatshop and step-niece go to dances with beaux, but she does not specify the location.[3] When Sara finally goes out dancing with an admirer, she does not explicitly state if they visit a dance hall—instead focusing on how she relishes the opportunity to escape from her normal responsibilities, in the embrace of a man who can afford such pleasures:

> He took me into his open arms and off we went. . . . He glided over the floor,
> a thing of wings. . . . The joy of the dance thrust loose the shut-in prisoner in
> me. I was a bird that had leaped out of her cage. Wild gladness sang in my
> veins, swept me up, up, away from this earth.[4]

Sarah E. Chinn observes, "The space of dancing is the space of adolescent independence, of fun and heterosociality, of flirting, of asserting a specific kind of urban American identity."[5] Yet this pursuit of fun and independence was a complicated endeavor, since leisure pursuits cost money at a time when working-class immigrants struggled to save their meager resources.

Abraham Cahan's 1896 novella *Yekl: A Tale of the New York Ghetto* and Kadya Molodovsky's 1942 novel *Fun Lublin biz Nyu-York: Togbukh fun Rivke Zilberg* (*A Jewish Refugee in New York: Rivke Zilberg's Journal*) reveal how authors use dance to show how American leisure culture challenges the romantic expectations of immigrant protagonists. Despite the nearly fifty-year gap between Cahan's novella and Molodovsky's novel, and the markedly different historical contexts—Cahan depicting the great wave of eastern European Jewish immigration to the United States from 1881–1924 and Molodovsky writing about World War II—the fact that both authors develop the dance motif so strongly in their narratives reveals the pervasiveness of dancing in American Jewish culture. Dancing is, on the one hand, a way for characters to show they are no longer "greenhorns" (new immigrants), to practice American sociability, and to experience a thrilling break from the daily grind. At the same time, these authors and their contemporaries suggest that the dance floor offers dubious pleasures, which threaten to sever protagonists' ties with traditional Jewish values and the families they left behind in Europe.

Dance Hall Culture and American Jewish Literature

Dancing was a key way for immigrants to participate in American leisure culture, even though most dance spaces were divided along ethnic lines.[6] Historian Kathy Peiss recounts, "Of all the amusements that bedazzled the single working woman, dancing proved to be her greatest passion."[7] In stark contrast to the drudgery of factory labor, the "neighborhood hall, ballroom, or saloon" seemed designed to give a woman pleasure.[8] Jews and other groups encountered a variety of different opportunities for dancing—from the more supervised dances at weddings and neighborhood social clubs to the structured and generally alcohol-free environment of the dancing academies to the more permissive dance halls, which tended to be connected to saloons.[9] Peiss describes how the "gaily decorated hall, riveting beat of the orchestra, and whirl of dance partners created a magical world of pleasure and romance" for women who had already discarded their daytime attire for "their fanciest finery."[10] Historian Randy McBee describes how "[T]he dance craze that swept across the United States at the turn of the century offered men a unique opportunity to show off their athleticism and skill."[11] Yet at the same time, dance halls could be ambivalent spaces for men, since they allowed women the opportunity to challenge men over the use of public space, with the result that "all men found themselves occasionally being passed over for dances; their partners usually refused escorts home, and the women were generally better dancers than the men leading them."[12] Men were expected to entice women through their individuality and spontaneity on the dance floor, and by treating them to refreshments during the breaks, which could be both thrilling and anxiety inducing. For eastern European Jewish immigrants, many of whom had grown up in traditional villages where gender segregation and arranged marriages were the norm, these easy relations between the sexes were a heady mix.

Commenting on New York's immigrant dance halls, McBee notes that, "Apart from their parents, couples could dabble in romance and experiment with new types of heterosocial relationships, relationships that contrasted sharply with the idea that parents should arrange marriages or supervise courtships."[13] Outside the supervision of traditional community structures, Jewish youth were free to engage in mixed-sex dancing. Men treated women to soda and gave them pleasure by twirling them on the dance floor, instead of spending their time in the all-male study house. In contrast to traditional Jewish social norms, which emphasized homosocial behavior, the dance hall was deliberately heterosexual.[14] Social dances, by their nature, invite participants to consider their dance partners as individuals whose physical compatibility and adherence to social graces are a necessary prerequisite to a romance or successful marriage.

Young people flocked to dance halls in the early twentieth century, at the same time that moralists and social reformers cautioned against the dangers of unrefined behavior.[15] In his 1912 Yiddish-language etiquette manual, *Etikete* (Etiquette), Tashrak (pseudonym for Israel Joseph Zevin) warns women not to go to balls without a proper escort, dance more than three times with the same partner, sit in dark corners, or show an immodest degree of emotion, especially since balls are a site where "young blood is especially inclined to forget itself."[16] While Tashrak wrote his advice for a Yiddish-speaking audience, other writers took a harsher tone in describing the problems of tenement life for English-speaking readers. Reformer Belle Lindner Israels, who came from a Jewish background herself, warned, "You cannot dance night after night, held in the closest of sensual embraces, with every effort made in the style of dancing to appeal to the worst that is in you, and remain unshaken by it."[17] Similarly, in his essay "The Puzzle of the Underworld," published in *McClure's Magazine* in 1913, muckracker George Kibbe Turner identifies dance halls with sexual immorality, since they enable the "sex hunting of the boys" who seek the company of "'bad girls.'"[18] Turner explains, "The natural instinct of the man to test and tempt the woman is solidified in the dance-hall into what is, for all practical purposes, a perfect system."[19] While Turner does not refer explicitly to Jews in this piece, his 1909 essay "Daughters of the Poor" attacks Jews for their involvement in sex trafficking and claims that Lower East Side dance halls are the main place where (Jewish) women are recruited for prostitution (by Jewish men).[20] Turner identifies dancing with sexual activity, an association that also repeats throughout literary fiction. Jewish writers depicted the dance hall as a place where young immigrants made their first forays into heterosexual courtship.

In his semi-autobiographical 1917 novel *The Rise of David Levinsky*, Abraham Cahan explicitly contrasts European and American dance practice.

Dance conveys an American sexual ethos that marks a sharp departure from
European Jewish sensibilities, at least in Cahan's rendering. In David's hometown of Antomir, "Dancing with a girl, or even taking one out for a walk, was
out of the question."[21] He finds a very different situation in America, where
brazen flirtation is the order of the day. David's friend Max Margolis, a ped-
dler who frequents the dance halls, encourages the young greenhorn to learn
this skill: "A fellow like you ought to make a hit with women. Why don't you
learn to dance?"[22]

David finds the nonchalant sexuality in the dance halls shocking: "Here
were highly respectable young women who would let men encircle their
waists, each resting her arm on her partner's shoulder, and then go spinning
and hopping with him, with a frank relish of the physical excitement in
which they were joined."[23] David is fascinated by the sexual pleasure women
display on the dance floor, even though he is unwilling to take dancing lessons himself: "As this young woman went round and round her face bore
a faint smile of embarrassed satisfaction. I knew that it was a sex smile."[24]
David is highly attuned to the sensual promise of dancing and the connection between activities on the dance floor and those performed in the
bedroom. As he admits, "To watch the dancing couples became a passion
with me."[25] Nonetheless, even in this ostensibly permissive atmosphere,
codes of propriety remain. Upwardly mobile American society was governed, not by respect for the study of religious law, but instead by economic
prosperity and material success. David is soon kicked out of the dance hall
on account of his ragged clothing and sloppy appearance. In such works,
fictional characters view the dance floor as an aspirational space in which
they try to imitate the manners of genteel Americans, as modeled by other
Jewish immigrants.[26]

Dance scenes can reveal class and ethnic divides. In Joseph Opatoshu's
1922 short story "Shmelts-top" (Melting Pot), the staff of a night school
decides to organize a "ball" for their students, in the hopes of keeping them
away from dance halls and saloons.[27] The ball is an uncomfortable social
event for the Jewish protagonist, Miss Kaplan, who has been trying to avoid
the sexual interest of the Italian men whom she teaches English. Opatoshu
portrays their desiring gaze as frankly ravenous: "[F]orty pairs of famished
eyes devoured her."[28] At the ball, she is dismayed when an older colleague

instructs her to ask one of the Italians to dance, without regard for the young woman's discomfort. Although Miss Kaplan had hoped to be a mother or sister figure for her students, the dance highlights how her body is on display—Jessica Kirzane notes that Miss Kaplan is "thrust into a role as a potential love interest, for the sake of the cause of assimilation" for a group of men she finds intimidating and is unable to control.[29]

Social dance conventions allow Miss Kaplan's dance partner to take authority over her body and subvert the power dynamic that she has fought to maintain in the classroom. Her reluctant invitation to a student sounds like a command: "Mister Gabrielo Farello, come have a dance!"[30] Yet Gabrielo speaks "more with his hands than with his mouth," an indication of his greater comfort with physicality and a reminder of his imperfect English.[31] When he dances with Miss Kaplan, Gabrielo's ability to dance well does not disguise the way he overwhelms her physically: "[L]ight as a bird he moved along with her on tiptoe."[32] Their encounter on the dance floor emboldens Gabrielo to escalate his courtship of his unwilling teacher, yet another example of a character misreading momentary physical closeness on the dance floor as a sign of emotional intimacy or a prelude to greater physical liberties. While Miss Kaplan's act of asking a man to dance may appear to subvert gender hierarchies as a form of brash American womanhood, she experiences this moment as a loss of power.

Unwanted sexual advances were not the only threat to women's autonomy on the dance floor. Courtship itself represented the very real threat that women might lose their newfound financial independence or ties to the community after getting married, an issue Kadya Molodovsky addresses in her 1954 short story "A futerne mantl" ("A Fur Coat").[33] When Celia Belkin, a contentedly unmarried working woman, meets Jack Mandel at the annual Poritshe landsmanshaft ball, his controlling tendencies and obsession with money are obvious. In the middle of dancing with Celia, Jack asks her how much she paid for her blue satin dress.[34] Celia is taken aback by this question, especially since she delights in dressing up to meet her friends for this annual event. Celia gives in to the community pressure to let Jack court her and later marry her, but his stinginess poisons their relationship. When he tries to prevent her from spending her own money on a festive fur coat for the next year's ball, they get divorced. In this and other texts, landsmanshaft

balls reveal tensions between communal expectations and American capitalist ethos, especially in situations where men and women combine courtship
with economic concerns.

The landsmanshaft ball in Sholem Asch's 1946 novel *Ist river* (*East River*)
fulfills an important social function: "[F]or a girl to appear at the Lenchiz
annual ball with an escort [bokher] was tantamount to announcing an engagement."[35] When Rachel Greenstick goes to the annual ball with her beau
Irving Davidowsky, the entire neighborhood gets involved. Rachel's family
and friends go to great lengths to dress her up within the family's limited
means, and all around the block neighbors peer outside their tenements to
watch her and Irving head out for the event. On their way to the ball, Irving
tells Rachel about his plans to start his own business, and she says he should
write to her wealthy banker uncle. Yet it soon becomes apparent that Irving is
interested in his business as an end in itself, rather than as a way of financing
a life with Rachel. While the ball guests speculate about Rachel and Irving's
future together, and young men ask him for permission to dance with the
woman they view as his, Irving is more preoccupied with the thought of a
potential investor than he is focused on Rachel herself. As in Molodovsky's
"A futerne mantl," it is a dangerous sign for a relationship when an unmarried man is unable to stop thinking about accumulating money even when he
is at a ball. Ultimately, Irving ends up abandoning the Jewish woman everyone expects him to marry for an Irish Catholic neighbor, Mary McCarthy,
who was one of the people who helped Rachel prepare for the ball.

Asch's discussions of the Lenchiz ball emphasize the social expectations it encodes, rather than Irving's participation in courtship rituals. Asch
spends much more time narrating Rachel's preparations and her conversation with Irving about his career ambitions than portraying the ball itself.
Indeed, the most detailed description of dance in the novel occurs much
later, during Asch's lengthy account of "dance mania" during the Jazz Age,
when dance halls were ubiquitous and dancers were "crammed cheek to
cheek, bodies pressed together, men and women, young and old mixed together."[36] While the passionate Jazz Age dance halls might seem at first
glance to be far removed from the communal landsmanshaft ball, Asch
connects them in his novel since he uses his description of the dance fad—
—and its impact on women's fashion—to introduce Irving's success in the

garment industry.[37] Ironically, the business that Irving planned with Rachel at the landsmanshaft ball comes to fruition with Mary's help in the context of a fashion market driven by dance halls. Asch suggests that both the landsmanshaft ball and the dance hall are places that blur the boundaries between work, leisure, and romance. In this respect, his writing uses a similar strategy to that of Cahan in *Yekl*.

"A *Valtz* from the Land of *Valtzes!*": *Yekl*

Toward the beginning of *Yekl*, the protagonist Jake faces a dilemma. His coworker Fanny (one of his many female admirers) spots him at a dancing school, even though he had previously told her that he was going straight home after work. As in many points throughout the novella, Jake is unable to express his inner conflict through words. Unbeknownst to Fanny, he is in fact a married man who should be saving money for his wife's ship passage to America instead of spending his wages at the dancing school. Jake temporarily resolves his predicament through a show of masculine vigor that displays brute force rather than gallantry: Jake abandons his dance partner Mamie, pulls Fanny from her chair, declares "*lesh have a valtz* from the land of *valtzes!*" and proceeds to spin his new partner around until she stops protesting and melts into his arms in grateful bliss.[38] As noted in Tashrak's chapter on ballroom deportment in *Etikete*, Jake's decision to change dancing partners in the middle of a song is a serious breach of ballroom etiquette. His behavior is just as unrefined as his Yiddish-inflected speech.[39] Jake's multilingual exclamation reflects the cultural, linguistic, and emotional complexity of the novella as a whole, and it conveys the crucial significance of dance for the text's themes and narrative arc. Both thematically and structurally, Jake experiences America as "the land of *valtzes*."

Cahan arrived in the United States from the Russian empire in 1882 and became one of the leading proponents of Americanization among Yiddish-speaking immigrants. Bernard G. Richards comments, "Teacher, labor organizer, orator, editor, novelist, the most gifted and resourceful of Yiddish journalists—it is difficult to single out his chief achievement."[40] Cahan edited the influential daily *Forverts* (*Forward*) for nearly half a century and also wrote English-language social realist fiction about the lives of Jewish immigrants in New York. *Yekl* established Cahan's literary fame in English and won him recognition as an American social realist.[41] Yet even with the support of eminent realist writer William Dean Howells, it was a challenge for Cahan to find a publisher. Editors were not convinced that a novella describing poor Jews and a dancing school fulfilled their artistic visions.[42] While waiting to find an English-language publisher, Cahan serialized the novella in Yiddish in *Arbeter tsaytung* (Worker's Newspaper) from October 1895 to January 1896. He called this version *Yankl der yanki* (Yankl the Yankee), a title Howells had initially rejected for sounding like a vaudeville act.[43] Later in 1896, D. Appleton and Company agreed to publish the English novella, and Howells wrote a favorable review of *Yekl* in *The World*.[44] In stark contrast to the notion that an immigrant dancing school could not be properly artistic, Howells cites the episode in the dancing academy in his list of scenes that prove the excellence of Cahan's prose and the promise of his future work.[45] Although *Yekl* was not a commercial success, the novella later became a classic of American immigrant fiction.[46] In 1975, it was adapted into the acclaimed feature film *Hester Street*, which opens with the scene in Joe's dancing academy.[47]

Most *Yekl* scholarship focuses on Jake's performance of masculinity, his grotesquely incomplete process of Americanization, or Cahan's use of Yiddish-inflected English.[48] Cahan's portrayal of the dance floor raises all of these questions and more. Indeed, some scholars examine *Yekl* in the context of turn-of-the-century leisure culture, at times using the frameworks of spectacle, burlesque, and vaudeville to draw connections between Cahan's literary style and the activities of his characters.[49] Chinn considers *Yekl* a source of information about youth culture at dancing academies and notes, "[The] waltzing that takes place at Joe's is quite different from the formal round dance described in the dance manuals of the mid- and late-nineteenth century."[50] As Merle L. Bachman observes,

> [The] dance hall is a testing ground for American culture. It is a place where, even in a strictly Jewish context (for apparently there are no gentiles there) a sort of "mixing" takes place, of men and women (very much against Jewish tradition) and of languages (Yiddish, English, and dialects of both).[51]

Yet even though the scene in the dancing academy is difficult to overlook, scholars have paid little attention to the way Cahan uses dance to structure his novella as a whole.

Dance typifies the conflict between European and American value systems in *Yekl*, particularly as relates to family and marital bonds. Indeed, dancing plays a crucial role in the marital conflict at the center of the novella's plot. To start with, Jake's fondness for dancing prevents him from saving money to send steamship tickets to his family in Russia. Instead, he spends his money at Joe's dance school. In order to raise the necessary funds, he borrows twenty-five dollars from Mamie, who assumes he intends to turn their interactions on the dance floor into an actual courtship. Moreover, Jake's participation in dance hall culture socializes him as an American man and creates a greater cultural divide between himself and Gitl, the wife he left behind. Gitl is conscious of looking and acting very differently from the women who frequent the dancing school. When her rival Mamie makes a social call dressed in intimidating finery, Jake tells his wife that their caller must be on her way to a ball, a term that Gitl barely recognizes. Furthermore, Jake's participation on the dance floor suggests he is, in fact, a bachelor. He dances and flirts with young women, without breathing a word of the fact he is married.[52] Finally, Jake and Mamie plan to open a dance school of their own after Mamie pays for Jake's divorce and they get married. The activity that brought them together will, they hope, be their livelihood as husband and wife. In short, dance pushes along the plot arc as it forces Jake and Gitl apart.

Cahan depicts the dance floor as a boisterous, cramped, even grotesque site of spectacle. Dancers try to replace their European reserve with bourgeois American manners, yet ultimately reveal their own working-class reality. While his contemporary Emma Goldman decries oppressive working conditions that interfere with a dancer's stamina, Cahan instead emphasizes the absurdity of his characters' pretensions.[53] Cahan's characters burn with the desire to become fully American, yet they fail to achieve this cultural ambition. Dancers do not appear to be individuals but rather a "waltzing swarm," as if they were buzzing insects rather than actual human beings.[54] Jake views the dance academy as a site of escape, yet Cahan shows that it has permeable boundaries with the "New York Ghetto." His description anticipates Turner's complaint: "Even little children dance the grotesque steps upon the sidewalk."[55] Music spills out into the street, where children dance and young women longingly watch "young women like themselves" inside the dance school.[56] There is no true barrier between the dance hall and the crush of humanity on the street.[57] Even waltzing is insufficient to truly elevate the working-class immigrants to the status of genteel Americans.

Cahan portrays dance as a working-class entertainment that aspires to, but cannot fully represent, the refinement of an American ballroom. Dancers at Joe's dancing academy conduct themselves in a manner that lacks genteel expression and posture. They still wear their work clothes, and many of the couples "had the air of being engaged in hard toil rather than as if they were dancing for amusement."[58] Dancers do not obey the conventions of formal ballroom etiquette: They do not pay heed to any possible unintended messages that could be sent by dancing with a partner several times in a row, and they freely ignore both the music and the dance master if they would prefer to dance a waltz instead of a lancers. This lack of concern for general dance floor decorum is magnified by a disregard for traditional sexual mores.

In Cahan's novella, characters negotiate different forms of pleasure. Jake regards dancing as a form of currency, which he uses to keep both Mamie and a wealthy but shy businessman "satetzfiet" (satisfied).[59] Jake barters his and Mamie's physical services on the dance floor in exchange for favors. When one considers Jake's emphasis on physical satisfaction on the dance floor, this trade resembles a form of prostitution. In contrast to proper ballroom etiquette, which requires a gentleman to ask a lady for a dance, Jake asks Mamie to invite the businessman to dance, which comes close to asking her to proposition a potential dancing school patron. Although Cahan does not suggest that Mamie performs sexual favors as part of the exchange, Jake acts as her "pimp" for the potential financial benefit of Joe's dancing school. Indeed, moralists associated dance halls with vice and prostitution.[60] Later in the text, Mamie has no problem asking a man to reward her for services rendered on the dance floor, since she pesters Jake to treat her to soda after she dances with him. Cahan does not indicate the extent to which "treating" implies other flirtatious or sexual behavior, although Jake himself judges some of the "dancing-school girls" to have questionable morals based on "his own sinful experience."[61] Even more explicitly, when Jake asks Mamie to dance with the "ungainly novice," she negotiates a fee in advance for performing this service.[62] After crassly, or flirtatiously, haggling over their favors, Jake and Mamie come to an agreement. The price of her acquiescence to dancing with the businessman is a couple of waltzes with Jake.

Jake claims that he likes women "whulshale" (wholesale) instead of favoring any particular lady.[63] Yet in his eagerness to show the dancing-school girls a "sholid good time" without becoming emotionally invested in any of them, Jake acts the part of a gigolo.[64] His waltz with Mamie is full of sexual energy and female pleasure:

> They spun along with all-forgetful gusto; every little while he lifted her on his powerful arm and gave her a "mill," he yelping and she squeaking for sheer ecstasy, as he did so; and throughout the performance his face and his whole figure seemed to be exclaiming, "Dot'sh a kin' a man *I* am!"[65]

Jake boisterously leads Mamie in an exuberant waltz that abandons all pretensions of physical elegance or refined expression.[66] The choreography suggests the spieling or pivoting dance, a parody form of the waltz, which Peiss describes as "a dance out of control, its centrifugal tendencies unchecked by proper dance training or internalized restraint. Instead, the wild spinning of couples promoted a charged atmosphere of physical excitement, often accompanied by shouting and spinning."[67] Moreover, Jake appears to play the part of a "spieler," a young man who assists the dancing master and is, in Israels's words, "expected to keep everybody happy and everybody busy," even though Cahan does not suggest he was formally employed by Joe.[68]

Jake spins and lifts Mamie, exhibiting muscular power rather than grace or nimbleness. Both dancers make undignified sounds, out of physical exertion and pleasure, in an example of how Cahan connects dancing with sexual intercourse. Jake proudly displays his skill and ability to please women on the dance floor, which are vital to his sense of masculine identity, yet even these accomplishments fall short of his goal of truly acting like an American.

Bachman describes dance in *Yekl* as "a burlesque of the genteel qualities associated with waltzing and the kind of civil restraint that middle- and upper-class America would expect from people claiming to be 'real Americans.'"[69] While social dance etiquette was less strict than the rules of English grammar—especially given the popularity of more boisterous dances—Cahan draws a connection between dancing style and English language usage. Indeed, the message Jake conveys with his body language—"Dot'sh a kin' a man *I* am!"—is a mangled version of standard English speech.

Jake associates dancing with freedom. It is arguably the clearest embodiment of American opportunity in the novella and certainly Jake's greatest source of pleasure in his otherwise austere working-class life.[70] New immigrants are able to express themselves using their own bodies, without having mastered the English language. Although Cahan does not draw an explicit connection between the dancing academy and liberation from traditional Jewish restrictions on interactions between the sexes, he fully articulates the freedom of unmarried people to dance and flirt to their heart's content. At Joe's dancing academy, Jake experiences easy mixed-sex physicality of a kind that was impossible during his bachelor days in Europe. When Jake gives up dancing after Gitl's arrival in America, he finds he misses the women from the dance school, "whose society and attentions now more than ever seemed to him necessities of his life."[71] While once Jake was nostalgic for the wife he left behind in Europe, now he is tormented by the thought that the other dancers are laughing at him and deem him less of an American because he stays home with his family.

Jake first learns about romantic love in the United States, at the same time he learns English and how to dance. When he eventually decides to divorce Gitl and begin an American-style romance with Mamie, their relationship talk combines Old World economic considerations with ideas of romance that they learned at the dancing school. Jake finally decides to marry Mamie, rather than another dancing-school girl, because her savings—a sizable "marriage portion" of 340 dollars—will allow him to divorce his traditionally minded wife and start a new life, unencumbered by a woman he considers an embarrassing greenhorn.[72] In exchange, Mamie demands that Jake charm her with his sweet words and gallant behavior, practices that he has honed on the dance floor. Jules Chametzky observes that Cahan's characters

> attempt to handle unfamiliar emotions with their broken English and seem only touching and a little absurd. The old language did not deal with such concepts as "love" while the new one is grasped only in clichés; the result is a sense of their acting out forces they cannot comprehend.[73]

This rather formulaic romantic dialogue can in fact be understood as a continuation of the outlandish dance floor choreography.

Both characters play with the formulas and choreography of polite American behavior, skills of which they are very proud even though they are unable to perfectly execute the forms. After all, the dancing school where they practiced American manners was entirely populated by Jewish immigrants. Cahan incorporates references to dance throughout the scene, tying together the threads of romance and dance at several auspicious moments. As the climactic scene opens, Mamie rehearses a waltz step at the moment Jake arrives. Although Cahan does not directly state it, Mamie's actions both remind the reader of an activity she shares with Jake and, since she is an individual performing one half of a partner dance, underscores her present availability as a single person. When Jake starts to tell her about his feelings for her, she claims he did not care for her before Gitl arrived, "laboring to disguise the exultation which made her heart dance."[74] Mamie's ordinary behaviors are inseparable from her fondness for dancing, reminding the reader of her ability to charm Jake and the gulf that separates her from Gitl.

Jake and Mamie discuss marriage and opening a dancing school together, yet they suspect each other's motivations. Even in this supposedly romantic moment, Jake and Mamie dance around each other, without truly establishing a harmonious partnership. Yet they do agree to the match, and Jake begins "dancing" with his new partner. His metaphorical waltz with Gitl ends, and now Mamie takes the lead. As Cahan's narrative reveals, the kind of man who will disregard a partner in the middle of a dance is the sort of man who will divorce his first wife and remarry a woman he meets while dancing. In the novella's circular conclusion, Jake's second marriage leaves him feeling just as trapped as before, only now dance is no longer an escape from the realities of marital life. While Jake loses the illicit pleasure of the dance floor, Gitl's neighbor Mrs. Kavarsky implies Gitl should "dance for joy" to be rid of her good-for-nothing husband.[75]

In *Yekl*, dance is an important component of the social life and Americanization process for eastern European Jewish immigrants, as well as a useful metaphor for the circular plot arc and the relationships between the characters. Like dancers switching partners before the next dance set, life in the New World demands a new life partner. Both Jake and Gitl realize that their shared history cannot overcome the incompatibility of their values and life goals in America, and thus they divorce and take on new partners. Jake is caught in a circular system with the women he encounters, ending his marital "dance" with his first wife Gitl only to begin the next number with his new wife Mamie. Yet, unfortunately for Jake, he has little of Cahan's sympathy—he may be an excellent dancer, but as a husband he lacks commitment. Mamie may find bliss in his arms on the dance floor, however a blissful marriage is another proposition entirely. Indeed, Jake and Mamie's relationship reveals their failure to replace Old World practical matchmaking with a modern love marriage based on emotional compatibility: Both their dance partnership and their decision to marry are closely tied to economic exchange. Whereas Mamie and Jake's striving for American identity appears to be a recipe for marital dissatisfaction, Gitl's European values prepare her for a presumably happy second marriage.[76]

In *Yekl*, Cahan questions the success of a relationship begun on the dance floor at the same time that he artfully uses dance as the novella's organizing narrative structure. While Jake's personal life may not be a resounding success, Cahan's use of a circular plot structure is an effective strategy for addressing American leisure culture and the upheaval of immigration. Writing decades later from the perspective of a female protagonist, Molodovsky explicitly connects the circularity of the dance floor with the dizzying experience of being a new immigrant.

"Jumping Straight into Hell":
Fun Lublin biz Nyu-York

Unlike most other American Yiddish writers, Molodovsky (1894–1975) already had an established literary career in Warsaw when she was invited to come to New York in 1935.[77] Arguably the most famous woman writer in Yiddish, her work across multiple genres combines Jewish religious themes and a sometimes nostalgic portrayal of European Jewry with a modernist aesthetic and concern with women's position in Jewish society.[78] Indeed, her writings are often critical of American materialism, such as her first major prose work, *Fun Lublin biz Nyu-York*. The novel chronicles a war refugee's first ten months living in America, from December 1939 to October 1940, on New York's Lower East Side. Initially serialized in the *Morgn zshurnal* (Morning Journal), from May 30 to August 11, 1941,[79] *Fun Lublin biz Nyu-York* seems to have been well received and appeared in book form in 1942.[80] Over the course of the novel, Molodovsky uses the motif of dance to develop a nuanced and devastating critique of American Jewish culture.[81] Notably,

the fictional diarist, Rivke Zilberg, does not dance until the end of the novel.
Still in the year of mourning for her mother, who was killed in the German
assault on Lublin, Rivke refuses invitations to dance from several male admirers. Her instance on observing the year of mourning sets her apart from
her American environment and serves as the most stubborn symbol of her
European identity. In fact, she acquires a job, an English vocabulary, and an
Americanized name long before she first agrees to dance.

It is not until the penultimate journal entry, shortly after the announce-
ment of her engagement to a Jewish American man nicknamed Red,
that Rivke allows Red's father to dance with her and, finally, dances with
Red—something he has wanted to do for almost the entirety of the novel.
The order of this dance allows her to transition from a dance partner who
speaks Yiddish (even though he dances like an American) to dancing with
her American-born fiancé. Yet despite having this opportunity to practice,
Rivke's style still strikes Red as old-fashioned, a testament to her European upbringing. He tells her, "You have to learn how to dance the modern
dances."[82] Rivke has otherwise successfully integrated into American culture,
at the expense of her own identity, and the only thing remaining is for her to
alter her dance moves accordingly.

In an enthusiastic May 1941 review of the upcoming serial in the *Morgn
zshurnal,* critic Alexander Mukdoyni claims it had been a long time since
he had read "such a tastefully humorous, such a refreshingly funny and at
the same time such a deeply tragic description of the life of a greenhorn, of
a refugee girl who ran from hell in Europe right into the American paradise."[83] Although the extreme specificity of this comment arguably tempers
its praise, this statement captures how Molodovsky juxtaposes humor and
romance with pathos and frustration, oppositions that she frequently underscores in the novel through the motif of dance. While Mukdoyni considers
the journey from Lublin to New York to be a path from European hell into
American paradise, the protagonist sees something hellish about American
culture, particularly with regard to dance.[84]

Throughout the novel, dance helps contrast the blasé, carefree attitude of
American Jews with the horrors experienced by their counterparts in Europe.
Molodovsky rarely allows a character to participate in or watch dance without
a reminder of the suffering and uncertainty abroad. Rivke, especially, cannot

forget; even after her year of mourning has ended, her sensitivity toward the suffering of her relatives leads her to refuse to participate in dancing. She writes, "When people started dancing, I left. Even though it's past my mother's yortsayt (may she rest in peace), I couldn't dance because I kept seeing Janet before me."[85] It is cruelly ironic that Rivke envisions her niece Janet, since the young girl has gone blind from a wartime head injury. While Rivke's choice to abstain from dancing out of solidarity, rather than mourning practice, comes late in the novel, Molodovsky's narrative choices imply that dance represents a betrayal of those left behind in Europe. Indeed, Rivke never mentions having danced in Lublin, although she frequently compares her life in America with parallel, more intimate experiences in her hometown. Instead, her references to dance are usually tinged with feelings of alienation.

Early in the novel, Rivke experiences visceral trauma when she watches her American-born cousin Marvin practice dancing, in the style of legendary band leader Benny Goodman, accompanied by the radio.[86] His lighthearted antics remind her of her mother's death and the fact that she does not know what has happened to the rest of her family in Europe:

> Marvin has decided to learn how to dance like Benny Goodman. He turns on the radio and dances for hours on end. He changes channels and dances. Dances and changes channels. It gives me a headache. When he dances, all I can think about is that my mother was killed by a bomb, and I don't know what's happening with my brothers, although I'm sure they're not dancing now. I have no idea what's become of my father either. I'd go to the ends of the earth to avoid Marvin's dancing, but where can I go?[87]

Rivke narrates a poignant culture clash, which might remind readers that, while Poland has already been invaded by Germany, the United States does not enter the war until over a year after the diary ends. It is unclear from the description whether she reacts more to the sound of the radio—perhaps even a war report, which Marvin ignores—or to the obliviousness of Marvin's dancing while his European family experiences unknown horrors. Even if one accepts literary critic Shmuel Charney's (pseudonym: Shmuel Niger) claim that Rivke is self-absorbed and interprets this scene as her wish to languish in her suffering, it is clear that the act of dancing serves as a trigger for her to remember her family's distress.[88]

In his review, Charney observes that Molodovsky depicts almost all of the young people in her novel as vulgar, superficial, or immodest.[89] Such an attitude can be seen in situations where they break into joyous dance at the home of Rivke's aunt and uncle. In one instance, Rivke and the older Lubliners read with interest a newspaper report about the situation faced by Jews in occupied Poland yet are interrupted when Rivke's cousins and their friends come in to celebrate, with dancing, that Marvin's picture was printed in a different newspaper. Not only does the episode demonstrate the differences between the press items that interest Rivke and those that draw the attention of the other young people (including Red), it also crystallizes a romantic rivalry between Rivke and Red's ex-girlfriend Ruth:

> When Red came in, Ruth got all excited. She was beside herself. She started dancing with Marvin and then Eddie and then she called Red over to dance with her too. Red spun her around a couple of times and then sat down.[90]

Ruth uses the collective dancing as a ploy to dance with Red. As Rivke sees it, Ruth can barely disguise her ardent feelings for the man she almost married. Although Red clearly signals his disinterest, within the realm of politeness, by only half-heartedly dancing with her, the fact that he speaks to Ruth in English, a language Rivke does not understand, increases her sense of alienation. At the same time, Red's insistence that Ruth must be too tired to dance repeats the sort of condescending lack of empathy that complicates his relationship with Rivke.

When Red later learns that Italy has entered the war, he celebrates by dancing jubilantly. He assumes now that Rivke will stay in America and marry him, since there is no longer any question that she might leave for Palestine to join Layzer, the man she had planned to marry when she lived in Lublin. Red focuses solely upon how the news impacts his own happiness rather than any sense of empathy for Rivke or consideration of the larger consequences of Italy joining the war. In fact, the manner of his dancing, from one woman to another in succession, resembles Ruth's dance during Marvin's celebration. Rivke observes that, "He danced with Selma, with my aunt, and with Mrs. Shore."[91] The similarity between his style of dance and Ruth's previous choreography emphasizes the affinity of these two Americanized characters, in contrast to Rivke's sensitivity. In case this point had not been underscored enough, Rivke learns of her niece Janet's injury within the same paragraph.

Molodovsky most profoundly uses dance as a metaphor for the gulf between Red and Rivke when they go to the movies. Red's engagement with the dance on screen reminds Rivke of their differences: "In the movies, we saw a black man dancing very nicely, and I heard Red tapping his feet to the music. He knows the steps to that dance. I'll never know how to dance like that."[92] Rivke does not generally mind the movies, and she even imitates a seductive movie character to charm Red when they first meet. Instead, there is something particular about dance itself, and Red's willingness to move his body in time with the music, that leads her to assume he can perform the same dance and for her to associate it with going to hell: "Is that even called dancing? It's really leaping as though, God forbid, jumping straight into hell. Maybe that's what I'll learn to do instead."[93] This moment is one of several instances in the novel in which Rivke assumes the hierarchical racial views of her Americanized relatives—even though she is critical about American culture with regard to most other matters.[94] She clearly identifies the African American dancer, and Red, with a form of dancing she dismisses as primitive jumping, rather than as a skill worthy of respect and emulation.[95] Rivke's uncertainty about being able to keep up with American technique on the dance floor, in comparison with her beau, parallels her anxieties about her performance in the workforce. In both cases, she denigrates a skill she doubts she can master.

At times characters who seem intimidatingly, or traitorously, well adjusted to the American workforce appear to dance harmoniously with their environment as they labor. Their easy acclimation to the daily grind contrasts with the values and lived experience of the greenhorn protagonist. Rivke narrates this feeling of estrangement when she watches a more experienced employee demonstrate sewing a glove in the factory where Rivke has just started working:

> Whenever I try to see what's going on, Shirley works even more quickly. It's as if she's dancing with the machine: up with the elbows, and then down, left and right. Shirley is no longer Shirley. The machine is no longer a machine. It's all done so quickly that it's a blur and I'll never know how to do it.[96]

Rivke is overwhelmed by Shirley's expertise with the sewing machine. In contrast with Rivke's meticulous work at her last job, embroidering by hand, her colleague's labor is a race that blurs the boundaries between human and machine. It is as if Shirley engages in a dance with the sewing machine itself. The fast pace leaves Rivke feeling as if she will never be able to master the skill. Not for the first time, she wonders if she would be better off joining Layzer, in Palestine: "I'd be better off going to Palestine, carrying bricks and mortar with Layzer rather than sitting here dancing around with the machine."[97] Yet although Layzer understands her in a way that her American relations and admirers cannot, she seems unable to muster the drive to save up money for a ticket and never even notifies her family about Layzer's existence. Despite her insinuations that she is far less materialistic than her American contemporaries, Rivke realizes that she would have a difficult future doing menial labor in the Middle East with a fellow Yiddish-speaker. Instead of prioritizing joining Layzer, she learns to "dance" with the sewing machine.

Interestingly, Molodovsky presents Rivke's struggle to gain a foothold in America as a kind of dance. Rivke describes the circular structure of her attempt to find employment through her network of fellow Lubliners as a karahod, a circle dance. She first goes to her mother's friend, Mrs. Rubin, whose husband runs a glove factory. Mr. Rubin claims not to have any openings and suggests she get a letter from a Lubliner rabbi to recommend her to another prominent Lubliner, Mr. Shamut, the vice president of an organization for refugees. When Mr. Shamut finally suggests a solution to Rivke (after several visits to his office), it is that she seek a position in the factory of a Lubliner who has made his fortune in America—ironically the same Mr. Rubin who sent her on the circular path in the first place. Rivke compares the dizzying situation to a karahod composed of her various Lubliner interlocutors: "A karahod spun before my eyes: Rabbi Finkl, Mr. Shamut, Pinchas Hersh-with-the-pickle."[98] The description suggests that they dance around with each other as she watches. At the same time, one could argue that Rivke has "danced" with each Lubliner in turn, only to return to the reluctant Mr. Rubin in the end.[99] As seen by the fact that she refers to Mr. Rubin's ridiculous nickname from Lublin, "Pinchas Hersh-with-the-pickle," Rivke acknowledges the absurdity of the situation. Although the karahod is European and her "partners" are all Lubliners, Rivke's experience shows how alien she finds her experience in America and how she would prefer to process the political upheaval at home, and mourn her mother, without also navigating the foreign customs and bureaucracy. In fact, throughout the novel Rivke repeats the dizzying circular structure of the karahod to convey her sense of displacement.[100]

Molodovsky juxtaposes Rivke's general feeling of being caught in a bureaucratic karahod with two other episodes involving dance that serve to underscore her ambivalence about America. When Mr. Shamut describes Mr. Rubin to Rivke, he initially refers to the factory owner's Lubliner identity in a way that uses an unexpected form of mixed dance to convey familiarity and dominance. Mr. Shamut tells the story of Mr. Rubin as a boy, Pinchas Hersh, who was so enthralled by the idea of dancing a polka-mazurka with a girl that his sister caught him practicing the dance in the kitchen with a pickle.

> So there they were, waiting for the pickle. The meat was getting cold, and Shimon Dovid was hungry. And still no Pinchas Hersh and no pickle. So his sister, Tsipke, jumped up and went into the storeroom and saw . . . what do you think she saw? There was Pinchas Hersh, holding a pickle in his hand and dancing the polka-mazurka with it [lit. her]. At the very moment that Tsipke entered the room, Pinchas Hersh was most delicately holding the pickle and dancing around the barrel. Tsipke broadcast the story far and wide, describing how Pinchas Hersh danced the polka-mazurka with a pickle. Afterward, Chanke Mostovlianski wouldn't even look at him, and the whole town started calling him Pinchas-Hersh-with-the-pickle.[101]

As a result of his absurd mixed dance, Pinchas Hersh receives a nickname that he is unable to escape until he immigrates to the United States, makes his fortune, and becomes a boss known as Mr. Rubin. As a consequence of Pinchas Hersh's innocently ridiculous behavior, he is unable to achieve his original goal of dancing with Chanke Mostovlianksi.[102] Even though Rivke does not acknowledge any prior dancing experience of her own, Pinchas Hersh's desire to dance a polka-mazurka with a young woman points to the existence of partner dances in Lublin.

This rather silly story suggests the transformative power of American capital, since becoming a factory owner gives Mr. Rubin the respect he lacked as Pinchas Hersh. At the same time, one sees the way a dance, and being witnessed dancing in an awkward way, has the potential to cause shame and damage reputations. Even though Mr. Rubin has established himself, Mr. Shamut still indulges in the nostalgic recollection of this embarrassing story to Mr. Rubin's potential employee. By telling the story, Mr. Shamut provides a reminder of the Lubliner connections that led Rivke to seek his help and, moreover, disguises his inability to provide immediate assistance to her. Mr. Shamut's lack of concern for Mr. Rubin's reputation is a way of displaying, at a deeper level, that he has power over Mr. Rubin and can compel him to offer a pretty refugee a job.

Yet Mr. Shamut's story about Mr. Rubin is only one of Rivke's encounters with dance during her bureaucratic karahod. The second moment takes place at a family wedding, which occurs between the meeting with Mr. Shamut, in which he tells her the story and about the potential job, and her meeting with Mr. Rubin to find out if the job exists. The wedding makes explicit the other circular "dance" in which Rivke is involved, one implied by her male "partners"—her being courted by two American men and the tension with two female rivals. At the same time Rivke's cousin Selma dances with her brother Marvin at the wedding, Selma's boyfriend Eddy flirts with Rivke, claiming he likes her better than anyone. Rivke refuses to engage with him and also declines to dance, using the excuse of mourning for her mother. Instead of flirting with Eddy, she instead shares a drink with his friend Red, whom she meets at the wedding and later marries. Rivke's manner of flirtation with Red combines techniques she learned in America: the bravado of a movie actress and Eddy's English phrase "I like you more than anyone."[103] Although, for the moment, Rivke's refusal of Eddy and pursuit of Red give her power over these American men, ultimately she is unable to escape the process of Americanization that their courtship represents.

Molodovsky's narrative structure resembles the circle dance itself, with characters who appear in Rivke's bureaucratic karahod reappearing throughout the novel. Later on, at a Lubliner Purim ball, Rivke sees both Mr. Shamut and Mr. Rubin, and they awkwardly discuss whether she has a job yet. Red wants to dance with Rivke, but she demurs, and he dances with Selma instead. The combination of the European tradition of self-help with American capitalism becomes strikingly clear when the Lubliner men donate money to dance a karahod with women of their choice. One of the guests of honor, Mr. Edelshteyn, pays the extravagant sum of twenty-five dollars to dance with Rivke, an amount representing more than she earns in a month. Yet Rivke stands by her principles and refuses to dance. The incident underscores the belief in the novel that it is easier for a girl to get married in America than to find a job; men are more willing to pay to court or dance with women than to hire them as employees. While Rivke effortlessly charms admirers and aspiring dance partners with her Old World looks and manners, she must work harder to earn a living as an immigrant woman.

Ironically, Mr. Edelshteyn's public admiration of Rivke prevents her from seeking him out as a potential employer. Red jealously tells her not to ask him for a job, a view supported by the very relatives who initially pressured Rivke to focus on finding a job instead of going to school. It is precisely because Mr. Edelshteyn wanted to dance with her that asking him for work is unthinkable. Rivke's willingness to allow Red to limit her income foreshadows her final transformation. Rivke Zilberg, who enjoys the job at the glove factory that she worked hard to get and perform successfully, becomes Mrs. Ray Levitt, who sells sandwiches in the lunchroom owned by her husband's parents and (at least according to A. Golomb's prediction in his review) dreams of Layzer when she closes her eyes.[104] In her final entry, Rivke returns to the circular motif of the karahod when she notes, "Everything I am experiencing now has no beginning and no end."[105] Dashed around circular bureaucracies throughout the novel and dismayed by a sense that she will never belong, she still meditates on alternative realities. Most poignantly, she reflects upon the way Layzer preserves Rivke Zilberg in his imagination, even as she herself goes forward into a new existence, having capitulated to American materialist culture.

Rivke experiences courtship and marriage as a loss of her identity, akin to the process of assimilation into American culture. Molodovsky repeatedly traps Rivke between the escapism of swing and the nostalgia of the karahod, the two dances amplifying the cultural choices of two different generations of American Jews. While several characters in Molodovsky's novel criticize the prevailing notion that marriage is a young woman's only option for economic survival, Rivke is unable—and perhaps unwilling—to stand up to familial pressure and the forces of Americanization. As a refugee, Rivke has been spared her mother's fate of being buried under rubble, yet Molodovsky raises the provocative question that her life in the American paradise might, instead, be a form of jumping into hell.

In these literary works, dancing is a sign of Americanization and of shocking new forms of familiarity between the sexes. It can be a gateway to sexual
intimacy, a symptom of changing linguistic and religious practice, and a
preferred leisure activity. At their most profound, dance scenes reveal deep
concerns with American culture, particularly since dance lessons are inseparable from notions of commerce and class. Working-class dancers at the
turn of the twentieth century operate within their own notions of refinement and respectability, which allude to but cannot replicate the behaviors of
American gentility. Decades later, after World War I and the Roaring Twenties, young Jews in the 1940s feel more of a connection to the swing dance
style of Benny Goodman than to the European culture of their parents and
grandparents. Comfortable in their American identities, Rivke's peers have
the freedom to enjoy leisure activities without the pressure of proving they
are American—and Rivke, who has more contact with Americans than does
Gitl, faces a profound loss of identity when she sheds her greenhorn identity
and marries an American-born man.

Dance is an organizing principle in both *Yekl* and *Fun Lublin biz Nyu-
York* that emphasizes physicality and circularity. Furthermore, dance is closely
related to courtship norms, and thus also to notions of giving and taking
pleasure on the dance floor, something both protagonists struggle to negotiate. Jake's obsession with dancing and flirting at the dancing academy leads
to the collapse of his marriage and a hasty second marriage: He dances too
eagerly and ends up juggling the interest of more women than he can handle.
Cahan identifies dancing with American-style physicality, and he examines
the ways his immigrant characters struggle to fully conform to these seemingly more relaxed American social norms. At the same time that Cahan
suggests dancing is the best way of achieving an American-style romantic
relationship, he also casts doubt on the sorts of relationships formed on the
dance floor.

Rivke's negative attitude toward dancing is the surest sign of her sense
of dislocation in America. Dance represents American frivolity and suggests
a lack of concern for the suffering of European Jewry. Molodovsky decen-
ters the romance plot that is central to so many dance scenes, while at the

same time acknowledging Rivke's limited options for social mobility. While Cahan treats self-sacrificing Gitl as a more sympathetic figure than her rivals at the dance academy, Molodovsky's ambivalence toward courtship practices (such as dancing) ultimately leads readers to question a vapid American culture that ignores the Holocaust. In their works, both Cahan and Molodovsky take a critical approach toward American dance spaces. Rather than view dance as a romantic step on the way to companionate marriage, they find it impossible to separate it from the pervasive influence of American capitalism. In this sense, their circular plots take the trajectory of modern Jewish literature back where it started, by questioning the feasibility of companionate marriages. Neither passion nor common social circles nor hopes for financial security are enough to guarantee a successful marriage. Instead, they suggest, rather unromantically, that common values and background are a better way of ensuring future happiness.

Still, even though these authors use dance plots to represent changing values and culture, they also show that the racy appeal of the mixed-sex dance floor continues in this American context in literary texts across the first half of the twentieth century. Writers depict the tensions between memories of Europe, the reality of sweatshop labor, and aspirations toward American social mobility and inscribe these forces onto the bodies of their Jewish dancers. Many of these cultural dynamics shifted in the second half of the twentieth century—as social dancing became a less ubiquitous cultural practice, as Orthodox communities invested the taboo on mixed-sex dancing with different symbolism, and as most American Jews experienced an increasingly shallow relationship with Ashkenazic folkways. Yet despite these changes, mixed-sex dancing continues to resonate culturally up through today in works of popular culture that imagine new forms of agency for women.

"WHAT COMES FROM MEN
AND WOMEN DANCING"

IN 1964, Jerry Bock and Sheldon Harnick had a problem. As lyricist and composer, respectively, for the Broadway musical *Fiddler on the Roof*, in development at the time, they were busy creating what they called their "bête noire number 1."[1] This song would feature the appealing political firebrand Perchik and show why he was a radical choice of husband for a sheltered young woman from a traditional family. *Fiddler on the Roof* was adapted from Sholem Aleichem's collection of short stories about the impact of modernization on an eastern European Jewish family.[2] While Sholem Aleichem was renowned for his narration of vernacular speech, a Broadway musical demanded more spectacle and a greater dramatic focus on the two lovers. Perchik would need to demonstrate the challenge he represented to village traditions, but in a form that would enthrall the musical's audience.

Bock and Harnick labored to create a song that would strike the right balance, yet this undertaking proved to be quite a challenge. In her cultural history of the musical, Alisa Solomon reports that none of the dozen different attempts—including duets with Hodel—seemed to work:

> Perchik ended up sounding too propagandistic ("You'll hear a rumble and the earth will shake / And Romanovs will crumble and the chains will break") or too cornball ("A dairy farmer's daughter / And a cigarette maker's son / Met

in a tiny village / And there became as one"). Or too propagandistic *and* too cornball ("When we're free to be free / What a world that will be").[3]

Finally, after these multiple attempts, the artistic duo came up with an appropriate song, "a satisfying argument song in which Perchik schools Hodel in how he'd behave 'if I were a woman' ('I'd want to know why / I had to take orders / from men not a quarter as smart as I')."[4] While viewers today might bristle at Perchik's attempt to explain to Hodel how a woman should act, when the show was initially performed for audiences in Detroit, it received applause and a few laughs.[5] Yet much to Bock and Harnick's chagrin, director Jerome Robbins cut the number entirely. Even though the song worked, it took four and a half minutes in a musical that was already very long. As Robbins explained, "I think I can accomplish the same thing in thirty seconds of dance and it may even be stronger."[6] In staging this now-famous dance scene, Robbins repeated many of the same tropes that appeared in literary texts from the nineteenth and early twentieth centuries. *Fiddler on the Roof* went on to become a major cultural text for American Jewish identity and arguably the most famous example of Ashkenazic dance in popular culture overall.

In Act I, Scene 6 of *Fiddler on the Roof*, Hodel and Perchik argue about village customs. Perchik disparages communal norms that prevent boys and girls from touching or even looking at one another: "Do you know that in the city boys and girls can be affectionate without [the] permission of a matchmaker? They hold hands together, they even dance together—new dances—like this."[7] Perchik forcefully proves his point to Hodel: According to the stage directions he "seizes her and starts dancing," which leaves her "[s]tartled" and "[b]ewildered."[8] Yet as Perchik pulls Hodel through the choreography of a couple dance he learned in Kiev, the audience witnesses them falling in love. As they conclude, Perchik declares, "There. We've just changed an old custom."[9] Not surprisingly for a point that can be made in thirty seconds of dancing, *Fiddler on the Roof* is not subtle about the implications of mixed-sex dancing.

As far as the musical is concerned, Perchik's most significant radical act is his introduction of mixed-sex dancing to the shtetl of Anatevka. Perchik privately teaches Hodel to dance and then scandalizes the Jewish community by publicly dancing with her at her sister's wedding. What is more, Perchik inspires other couples—including Hodel's parents and the Anatevka rabbi—to attempt partner dances of their own, since he pushes the rabbi to admit that dancing is "not exactly forbidden."[10] Yet even if the rabbi (like so many historical rabbis discussed in Chapter 1) is unable to prevent mixed-sex dancing, another force of order steps in: As "the dance reaches a wild climax," the constable and his men enter with clubs and begin the pogrom that ends Act I.[11] While dancing does not explicitly *cause* the pogrom, it raises the emotional tenor of the scene in preparation for a devastating conclusion.

Even in the face of this violence, the Jewish inhabitants of Anatevka do not forget the dramatic change in social norms that mixed-sex dancing represents. When Perchik is later arrested for his political activities, they conclude, "[T]hat's what comes from men and women dancing."[12] In fact, even some theatergoers found the behavior Perchik incited to be too audacious. In his notoriously harsh review of *Fiddler on the Roof*, literary critic Irving Howe complains that the Yiddish press was only critical of the musical with regard to "such details as the dancing between a rabbi and a girl."[13] While Howe grudgingly accepts that a musical about traditional Jewish life depicts transgressive mixed-sex dancing, he views the rabbi's "hopping around with a girl" as Broadway excess.[14] *Fiddler on the Roof* is both more nostalgic and mainstream American than most of the other texts discussed in this book. It is not so surprising that it depicts dancing as an activity that thrusts an entire Jewish community into modernity, rather than simply several individuals who may not fully conform to communal standards.

Perchik's dance with Hodel is almost certainly the most famous example of (breaking) the Jewish taboo on mixed-sex dancing. Yet as we have seen, it is neither the first, nor the only, instance in which this motif was employed for the purposes of entertainment or fleshing out a narrative. Much like Robbins, nineteenth- and twentieth-century authors recognized the dramatic potential of mixing-sex dancing. Their literary works explore the parameters of Jewish social integration in dance classes, taverns, balls, weddings, and dance halls. Just as Robbins consciously chose dance to illustrate Perchik's character, his relationship to Hodel, and the forces of change he represents, so too did writers employ dance as an enjoyable form of social criticism. Their dance scenes in German, Yiddish, and other modern Jewish literatures perform a key dramatic function in plot arcs and character development. Robbins's decision to use dance to push his story forward represents a continuity in narrative technique, in keeping with the striking utility of dance for literary production.

As *Fiddler on the Roof* makes clear, the motif of mixed-sex dancing resonates in films and literary texts throughout the twentieth century and into the twenty-first century. Contemporary works about mixed-sex dancing differ wildly in terms of genre, setting, and the dance styles they depict, yet they also verge away from the nineteenth- and early twentieth-century works discussed elsewhere in this book. While dancing remains an entertaining way for authors to build their plots and characters, recent literary and film texts tend not to use dance scenes to warn about the dangers of transgressive dancing, even when they acknowledge the destabilizing potential of the dance floor.[15] At the same time that contemporary Orthodox communities have become more stringent about preventing mixed-sex dancing than they often were in the years following World War II,[16] literary texts that are written for non-Orthodox and non-Jewish audiences often treat dancing as a form of confident self-expression rather than as a way of courting disaster. Although these works may engage directly or indirectly with contemporary issues—including social, class, and ethnic divides—authors tend not to be as didactic as Karl Emil Franzos or Marcus Lehmann. Significantly, these works frequently feature strong female protagonists and have happy endings.

The classic 1987 romantic film *Dirty Dancing* shows the continued efficacy of the mixed-sex dancing trope in an American context several generations removed from the shtetl and the Lower East Side tenement, in a setting where Jews are the privileged majority. It suggests that transgressive dancing could still be a radical act in the 1960s, at a time when idealistic young people like protagonist Frances "Baby" Houseman were becoming civil rights activists and protesting the Vietnam War. Set at a Catskills resort in 1963, the film portrays an interethnic relationship between bourgeois Jewish resort guest Baby and working-class dance instructor Johnny Castle.[17] When the film begins, Baby's doting father brags that she is going to change the world, yet Baby has very little control over her own body. She performs awkwardly in a merengue class, and when the instructor tells the female students to each choose a male dancing partner, Baby is shown leading an elderly woman instead, seemingly incapable of claiming a space for herself as a heterosexual woman on the dance floor. Later that evening, she dances with the resort owner's obnoxious grandson, presumably at the suggestion of her parents.[18] Even though the young man brags about what a good catch he is, his bourgeois credentials do not make him a desirable dancing partner. He is neither skillful nor attentive and is unable to prevent another dancer from bumping into Baby on the crowded dance floor.

Johnny, in contrast, effortlessly clears a wide space for himself and his mambo partner in the center of the dance floor, which helps them avoid jostling and allows them to show off their skill in a place everyone can see.[19] It is only when Johnny starts teaching Baby to dance—including the importance of maintaining the boundaries of her "dance space," the immediate physical space around her—that she learns to relax, feel comfortable in her own body, and develop her sexual confidence. Johnny's most famous line from the movie—when he tells Baby's parents "Nobody puts Baby in the corner" before publicly dancing with her—is a claim that he is better able to respect her space and autonomy than is her family. His statement echoes the view of numerous literary texts that mixed-sex dancing was a way for women to experience pleasure and public recognition with male partners that would have been impossible within the social constraints imagined for them by their parents. While Baby's parents support her goals of a college education and joining the Peace Corps, they are initially unwilling to accept her relationship with a working-class and presumably non-Jewish man. The film suggests dancing is a challenge to even liberally minded bourgeois Jewish values because it breaks down ethnic and class barriers. Yet, ultimately it does so in a way that even Baby's parents can enjoy, since they and all the other resort guests end up joining in Baby and Johnny's dance finale.

While *Dirty Dancing* does not specifically invoke eastern Europe, other late twentieth-century and early twenty-first-century works negotiate the taboo of mixed-sex dancing in settings that, like Perchik's dance with Hodel, are familiar to readers of nineteenth- and early twentieth-century fiction. Rebecca Goldstein's 1995 novel *Mazel* employs numerous tropes of modern Yiddish literature to narrate a family saga about three generations of Jewish women. Significantly, most of the major characters are women, and almost all of the important relationships in the novel are between women. Perhaps for this reason, Goldstein portrays mixed-sex dancing ambivalently. Even when mixed-sex dances are joyous, they are frequently identified with disaster. The protagonist Sasha Saunders is a rabbi's daughter from a Polish shtetl who becomes a celebrated Yiddish theater actress in Warsaw in the 1930s. Her talent as an actress draws the attention of an aspiring medical student named Maurice who vows that if he passes the university entrance exams, he will claim a tango with Sasha. Immediately following this much-anticipated dance, the two become lovers: "She sang him 'The Gypsy's Tango' and he spun her and dipped her and whirled her around until she was dizzy and she collapsed against him laughing, naked and laughing, so that who but a *golem* would have needed champagne?"[20] While the exuberant love scene is touching, Goldstein still associates it with catastrophe: The next morning, Sasha and Maurice awaken to the news of the non-aggression pact between Nazi Germany and the Soviet Union.

Dance scenes animate a variety of cultural moments in the novel: Orthodox Jewish weddings in both the 1920s and 1990s, the "drunken dance" that is interwar Poland on the eve of World War II,[21] and the "May Dance" of the Columbia student revolt in the 1960s.[22] While Sasha gladly participates in radical cultural and political movements, her daughter and granddaughter do not get involved in these activities. Ironically, and much to Sasha's chagrin, her granddaughter Phoebe decides to marry a Modern Orthodox man and move to the suburbs. At Phoebe's wedding, men and women dance separately. Goldstein depicts this separate-sex dancing positively, since it cements the bond between the three generations of women in a family in which the male relatives are absent or almost incidental: "And Sasha and Chloe and Phoebe were all dancing together, their arms linked around one another's waists and their feet barely touching the billowing floor, as they swirled in the circles [of women] drawn within circles within circles."[23] Goldstein uses the prohibition on mixed-sex dancing to create a communal feminine space in which non-Orthodox Jews can negotiate their relationships with loved ones of the same sex who have become Orthodox. Yet unlike many of the writers discussed in this book, she does not use dance scenes to moralize about forbidden romantic relationships. Her ambivalence toward mixed-sex dancing reflects the way she centers her story around women, and she uses separate-sex dancing to prioritize an emotional relationship between grand-mother, daughter, and granddaughter.[24]

In late twentieth- and early twenty-first-century fiction, dancing is a token of female empowerment, rather than a warning about the dangers of interethnic romance. Kerry Greenwood's 1997 murder mystery *Raisins and Almonds: A Phryne Fisher Mystery*, set in 1920s Melbourne, offers a no-tably unproblematized relationship between Jewish and non-Jewish dance partners, simply because they, unlike most similar characters in nineteenth-century novels, do not expect their relationship to be a permanent one. The novel thus carries on the legacy of women writers such as Clementine Krämer and Kadya Molodovsky, who use dancing to focus on the emotional universe of their (female) characters rather than to build star-crossed roman-tic plots.[25]

Greenwood's irrepressible detective, Phryne Fisher, first met her dance partner Simon Abrahams at a public dance hall, where she was looking for an exotic lover. Simon's stereotypically Jewish "flavour" intrigues her: He is a relatively short, dark-eyed, olive-skinned virgin who gestures emphatically and is emotionally close to his family.[26] Simon and Phryne are the best danc-ers at the Foxtrot Competition run by the Jewish Young People's Society at the Braille Hall. Yet even being the best dancers does not win them the prize, since the judges prefer to award it to a couple where both dancers are mem-bers of the society. Phryne and other characters are very conscious of the fact that Simon is expected to marry a Jewish woman, although Phryne enjoys the transgressive nature of her relationship with her Jewish lover:

> Here . . . I am the exotic. I am the—what was the word? I am the *shiksa*, the foreigner, the non-Jew, and how nice they are being to me. I wonder how much trouble the poor boy is going to get into for taking me as a partner, and not one of the nice girls his mother wants him to marry? He really does dance like a dream.[27]

Part of Simon's appeal for Phryne is that, despite his infatuation with her, she knows that this is only a short-term arrangement because he will ul-timately marry a Jewish woman of whom his family approves. Phryne's frankness about the temporary nature of this relationship ironically helps her to befriend his mother, since Phryne explains she is only hoping to "borrow"

Simon, not marry him.[28] While Simon's emotional openness and lack of experience might be unconventional traits for an exotic lover, his dancing ability is a way for Greenwood to show his physical finesse in an environment that reveals the expectations of his social world.

Several recent fantasy novels use dance scenes to depict relationships between Jewish characters and magical creatures from other folk traditions. These dance scenes imbue works with local color and can even communicate a broader message about intercultural tolerance. In Helene Wecker's 2013 novel *The Golem and the Jinni*, which is set on the Lower East Side in 1899, the titular characters visit a dance hall with the Golem's friends from work, with the Golem passing as a human Jewish woman. Predictably, the evening's festivities have fateful consequences. The scene is initially magical, since it is the first time the female Golem and male Jinni, Ahmed, act in public as if they were courting. Yet events take a different, dramatic turn, and Wecker chooses the dance hall scene to violently reveal their supernatural identities to the Golem's unsuspecting co-workers: The Golem becomes enraged and Ahmed must use his powers to rein in her superhuman strength.[29] Wecker suggests a connection between the sexual energy of the dance floor and behavior that violates social norms, both because the Golem's first appearance with Ahmed at the dance hall ends in a violent incident and because the Golem goes on her rampage at the dance hall in order to punish a man who has impregnated her co-worker but refuses to marry her. Wecker's fantasy novel invokes the powerful force of mixed-sex dancing (and here mixed–supernatural creature dancing) that appeared as a plot catalyst in realist fiction from the nineteenth and early twentieth centuries. At the same time, the Golem's Jewish co-workers do not raise serious objections to her relationship with a man who is obviously not a member of their community, which conveys the idea that the Golem and the Jinni are kindred spirits who belong together despite coming from different magical traditions.

Naomi Novik's 2018 fantasy novel *Spinning Silver* similarly weaves together the Rumpelstiltskin story with various Jewish and Slavic folklore elements—and repeats these same cultural motifs in a notable dance scene.[30] Miryem Mandelstam, a Jewish moneylender's daughter in a fictional Lithuania, successfully takes over the family business and brags she can turn silver into gold. Her claim attracts the interest of the Staryk king (a magical creature similar to an elf), who takes her to his wintry kingdom to be his queen and enrich his coffers with gold. As part of a dramatic confrontation at the end of the novel, Miryem convinces the Staryk to accompany her to the mortal kingdom so she can dance at her cousin's wedding. Although men and women initially dance in separate circles, when Miryem joins the women's circle, the Staryk comes with her, and he magically turns the Jewish wedding dancing into an elfin dance circle. As one guest, a Christian peasant boy, describes, "Something strange happened when he started dancing. We were in two circles, but somehow after he joined the dancing there was only one circle, with all of us in it."[31] Not only do the two circles of men and women combine, older guests and children begin dancing, even if they are not actually physically agile or tall enough to participate. The Staryk magically transports the circle of dancers to a snowy forest clearing, and the dancers are "too busy dancing to be scared or cold" in a situation where the only thing that matters is that "we had decided to be there."[32]

Unlike the elfin dance circles of European legend, in which mortals participate at their peril, the Staryk king uses his powers to enhance the community feeling of this Jewish wedding. The dancers move toward and away from the bridal couple at the center of the circle, and a group of men lifts them in the air on their chairs, performing Jewish wedding dance choreography in a magical context: "Everything was dancing. The trees were dancing, too, their branches swaying, and their leaves made a noise like singing. . . . We all kept going, and none of us wanted to stop."[33] Although the Staryk initially took Miryem from her home against her will, his willingness to participate in, and even contribute to, the wedding dancing is a pivotal moment in his transformation into a sympathetic character with whom Miryem can actually envision having a relationship. In fact, the wedding dancing foreshadows Miryem's eventual marriage to the Staryk (performed according to Jewish ritual), since the dancing fuses Jewish and Staryk elements. Yet, much in the same way Novik avoids discussing whether Miryem's relatives object to mixed-sex dancing at the wedding, she also neglects to mention whether the Staryk converts to Judaism at the novel's end in order to marry Miryem or whether the rabbi who marries them has any objection to a Jewish woman marrying a Staryk lord. Just as the magical wedding dance effaces any physical impediments to dance, Novik's happy resolution to the novel acknowledges Jewish ritual distinction without delving into deeper religious differences that could interfere with a love match. Novik, like Wecker, draws on Jewish folklore in her novel but does not police the boundaries of Jewish culture or explore controversies regarding biological Jewish continuity.

Contemporary writers of Jewish historical fiction publish in a post-Holocaust world in which most readers are not presumed to be Jewish, and even Ashkenazic readers are several generations removed from the shtetl. While these audiences may be aware of the prohibition on mixed-sex dancing—in part due to the joke mentioned in the introduction—they are often less familiar with the social dance steps or with reading dance scenes as a text. Perhaps for this reason, these works tend not to be very detailed or ethnographic about dance choreography; Novik's description of Jewish wedding dancing includes chair lifts that are popular at contemporary American Jewish weddings—including Phoebe's wedding in *Mazel*—but receives little attention in studies of eastern European Jewish dance.[34] Late twentieth- and early twenty-first-century writers depict a Jewish cultural milieu that no longer exists. They do not need to punish characters for wayward dancing in order to warn readers about violating communal boundaries, since these boundaries have already been irrevocably violated, either through genocide or—not to equate the two—by forces such as changing cultural norms.

Instead, some writers take a more cheerfully nostalgic approach and actually deliver the utopian promise of the dance floor. They depict mixed-sex dancing as an exciting way to embark on a relationship that is transgressive without being truly dangerous, since they tend not to dwell on the stakes of marriage outside the Jewish community. While characters such as Baby, the Golem, and Miryem dance with non-Jews, their love interests demonstrate that they understand and share values with their Jewish partners and that this emotional compatibility transcends any religious or cultural divides. Ultimately, in these works, Jewish communities tend to accept unconventional matches; Hodel and Baby even convince their parents to participate in spectacular dance scenes. Most of these late twentieth- and early twenty-first-century narratives end happily, since contemporary authors tend not to be invested in reinforcing or criticizing nineteenth-century Jewish communal authorities. As depicted most clearly in *Dirty Dancing* and *Raisins and Almonds*, dance scenes are also a way for female characters to explore their own pleasure and sexuality—at times using dance as a form of foreplay for sexual relationships that are healthy, enjoyable, and—in contrast to works by Leopold von Sacher-Masoch and Leon Kobrin—do not lead to either dancer's death. While dance scenes continue to develop characters and entertain readers, these more recent scenes tend to foreground concerns such as cultural exchange and female agency, rather than Jewish continuity or the maintenance of group boundaries.

Mixed-sex dancing has long been a transgressive cultural practice and an important literary symbol. In texts from the long nineteenth century into the twentieth century, dance scenes often lead directly or indirectly to misfortune. What "comes from men and women dancing" in these earlier texts is rarely an unambiguous happy end, but rather suicide, divorce, and loneliness. Such consequences can be seen as punishment for wayward dancing—and they reveal the growing pains of the process of acculturation. To be clear, while mixed-sex dancing implicitly simulates intercourse and can be viewed as a form of foreplay, the authors I discuss in this book were most deeply concerned with the transgression of religious, class, and cultural boundaries due to the tremendous upheaval that went on in the process of modernization, urbanization, acculturation, and emancipation between the Enlightenment and World War II. Mixed-sex social dance was a key sign of this process, especially because it challenged traditional boundaries between the sexes.

More than simply signifying sexual deviance, mixed-sex dancing stands in for the behaviors Jewish communal leaders found objectionable. Starting around 1780, balls and dancing lessons became symbols of Jewish participation in European society. Literary dance scenes depict the different ways Jewish men and women achieved social mobility, especially since these new courtship practices challenged traditional matchmaking patterns. Dance scenes entertain readers and facilitate plot and character development. In these middlebrow literary texts, formulaic plot sequences often replicate dance choreography; characters find themselves trapped within dance squares or pushed along in a circle.

German, Yiddish, and other writers depict the dance floor as a contested space, which serves a valuable purpose in commenting upon Jewish acculturation and gender roles. These writers focus on the dance floor to demonstrate how mixed-sex leisure culture is an essential component of

Jewish modernity—and of entertaining their readers. Dance lessons were a way for young people to train their bodies according to aristocratic standards and also practice the more tender emotions. Where Yiddish writers were concerned with the sexual stakes of dancing lessons, German writers focused more on the shame felt by gawky or inelegant dancers, especially in mixed-sex dances or when Jews and Christians danced together. Writers depicted rural taverns as a space where boundaries between Jews and Christians were easily blurred. In this context, the children of Jewish tavernkeepers contended with a lack of formal Jewish education and the temptation of illicit dancing with their Christian neighbors. Aristocratic balls were an important site for courtship, which also meant they were spaces where Jewish characters negotiated insider and outsider status—regardless of whether balls were majority Christian or majority Jewish. Weddings brought together guests from different facets of eastern European Jewish society, including rabbis and other communal leaders. As a result, transgressive dancing was more quickly stopped at weddings than in other dance locations. Commercial dance halls in New York were venues where eastern European Jewish immigrants could spend their leisure time, in an environment that was influenced by capitalism and American sexual mores. The literary theme of dance is by no means unique to German Jewish and Yiddish literature, but, as we have seen, the trope of Jewish mixed-sex dancing charts the particularities of the Jewish "dance" with modern culture.

Appendix: List of Social and Folk Dances

bolero—Spanish dance in triple time performed by solo dancers or couples accompanied by castanets.

broygez tants—The angry dance. Performed at eastern Ashkenazic weddings, often by the two mothers-in-law. Pantomime quarrel, followed by a cathartic reconciliation: the *sholem tants* (dance of peace).

Charleston—Fast-paced, syncopated American social dance, involving swift kicks and knees rotating through inward and outward twisting motions. Originating as an African American solo dance form, it was particularly popular in the 1920s.

contradanse—Folk dance genre for several couples in a line or square. Eighteenth-century French variant of English country dance that spread to Germany by the nineteenth century. Involves the execution of a set sequence of figures.

fandango—Lively Spanish couple dance in 3/4 or 6/8 time in which dancers speed up and stop suddenly.

foxtrot—American ballroom dance combining short and fast steps that originated in the 1910s and achieved peak international popularity in the 1930s.

française—Type of quadrille, known as *quadrille française.*

freylekhs—Most popular eastern Ashkenazic (wedding) dance, whose name means "joyous one." Circle dance with variations: Dancers take one another's hands or shoulders; may develop into more than one circle (such as an inner and outer circle) or winding lines depending on the dancers' hold; one or more dancers (or couples) may dance inside the circle; dancers may form arches and go through them.

German cotillion—Playful nineteenth-century ballroom dance games performed according to set rules, often held after supper at balls. Also known as the German or the cotillion. Not to be confused with the *cotillon* (English: cotillion), an eighteenth-century French ballroom dance in square formation.

hopke—Another name for freylekhs.

hora—Romanian and Bessarabian circle dance form with slow and fast permutations that was part of the eastern Ashkenazic dance repertoire. Also name for archetypical Israeli circular folk dance, whose steps are more closely related to dances such as the Bessarabian *bulgarish* (Yiddish: *bulgar*).

kamarinskaia—Fast improvised Russian folk dance in 2/4 time that became widespread among Belarusians, Ukrainians, and other ethnic groups. Often involving flashy male solo figures, it was also performed in women's, couple, and group versions in a variety of contexts, including balls. In Yiddish, *kamarinske*.

karahod—Belarusian, Russian, and Ukrainian circle dance. Also used as a name for freylekhs.

kazatsky—Vigorous Russian and Ukrainian Cossack dance featuring squats and other virtuosic moves that became part of the eastern Ashkenazic dance repertoire. Also known as *kozak* or *kozachok*. In Yiddish, *kazatske*.

kolomyika—Fast-paced circle or couple dance from eastern Galicia that was part of the Ashkenazic dance repertoire in western Ukraine and southeast Poland. In Yiddish, *kolomeyke*.

kosher tants—Another name for the mitsve tants. Also refers to dance performed by women at eastern Ashkenazic weddings after the veiling of the bride.

lancers—Five-figure quadrille that was popular in the late nineteenth century. Often performed by women in traditional eastern Ashkenazic communities. Also called the lancers quadrille or *les lanciers*. In different spellings (including "liantsers"), it appears frequently in Yiddish literature.

mambo—Cuban ballroom dance from the 1940s that achieved widespread cross-cultural popularity as a competitive, acrobatic style in the 1950s, when it was a favorite dance at Jewish resorts in the Catskill Mountains.

mazurka—Polish national dance in triple meter that was danced in ballrooms across Europe beginning in the nineteenth century. The ballroom version is performed by a circle of couples, involving foot stomping and heel clicking.

merengue—Internationally popular Dominican dance for couples, characterized by a limping step with the weight always on one foot.

minuet—Slow, stately French ballroom dance in triple time that was popular across Europe in the eighteenth century.

mitsve tants—Dance that fulfills the Jewish commandment of gladdening the bride. Performed with separating handkerchief. Imbued with deep spiritual significance in Hasidic thought.

pas d'espagne—In Yiddish, *padespan*, a Russian ballroom dance in a Spanish style. Referred to as *pas d'espan* in the contemporary Yiddish dance community.

patsh tants—Ashkenazic circle dance that involves clapping hands and may involve switching partners.

polka—Lively Bohemian couple dance in 2/4 time. One of the most popular nineteenth-century ballroom dances.

polka-mazurka—Hybrid ballroom dance for couples that incorporates polka steps with the triple meter of the mazurka. Popular in the mid-nineteenth century.

polonaise—Polish national dance in triple meter involving dignified walking. Internationally popular, it is often used to open balls.

quadrille—French ballroom dance for four couples in a square, comprised of four to six contradanse figures. Fashionable internationally throughout the nineteenth century. In Yiddish, *kadril.*

sarabande—Dance with possible South American or Spanish and Arab origins that was considered risqué in sixteenth-century Spain. The slow, stately French version in triple meter was popular in the seventeenth and eighteenth centuries.

schottisch—German couple dance in 2/4 time that was popular in ballrooms internationally in the mid-nineteenth century. Also called *schottische.*

sher—Ashkenazic dance for four couples in a square formation. Figures can include joining hands in a circle; advancing and retreating as a couple; promenading; solo dancing in the center of the circle; spinning one's own partner or other dancers; a winding figure known as "threading the needle," and so on. Often danced by women in traditional Jewish communities. Although the second most popular eastern Ashkenazic wedding dance, it is mentioned only infrequently by name in Yiddish literature.

shimmy—Popular dance in 1910s and 20s with African American origins. Characterized by rapid, horizontal vibrating of the upper body.

spieling dance—Centrifugal parody waltz that was popular in New York dance halls around 1900. Also called pivoting dance.

swing—Term for lively, athletic African American–originated couple dances (such as the Lindy Hop) that developed alongside swing music in the 1920s–40s.

tango—Argentine couple dance in 2/4 time performed in close embrace that became internationally popular as a ballroom dance form in the 1910s.

waltz—Couple dance in triple time derived from the ländler, an Austrian and Bavarian folk dance. In this most characteristic nineteenth-century ballroom dance, couples turn while embracing, which was considered scandalous around 1800.

Notes

Book Epigraph

1. Unless otherwise noted, all translations are my own. My transliterations of Yiddish generally follow YIVO transcription, although I also rely on extant transliterations of titles, especially by the Yiddish Book Center and YIVO Institute for Jewish Research, for the convenience of the reader.

Bundism (Jewish socialism) was illegal at certain points in its history, although not in the independent Polish state, where Mordechai Gebirtig (born Bertig, 1877–1942) wrote his songs. The original Yiddish is closer to "Who cares?" For a literal translation of the entire song and transliterated Yiddish text, see Gebirtig, *Mordechai Gebirtig*, 111. See also Gebirtig, *Mayne lider*, 42–43. In this opening song verse, Gebirtig mentions Zionists, Bundists, and Agudas Yisroel (an Orthodox party), all of which were active in interwar Poland. For Gebirtig's attitudes toward dance, see Gross, "Mordechai Gebirtig," 113.

Introduction

1. For short analyses of this joke, see Friedman and Friedman, *God Laughed*, 2; Leveen, "Only When I Laugh," 38. For a literary reference to the joke, see Englander, "What We Talk About When We Talk About Anne Frank," 27.

2. At the conclusion of a 1932 piece in the Bundist journal *Yugnt-veker* (Awakener of Youth) about adolescent sexual life (which advocated abstinence), Dr. A. Goldshmid declares that, in organizational life, young people should protect themselves from any sexual excitement, including dancing, "especially the bourgeois forms, which are practiced today even in proletarian organizations." A. Goldshmid, "Dos seksuele lebn

fun der yugnt," *Yugnt-veker* 11, no. 17 (August 15, 1932): 9. For further discussion, see Jacobs, *Bundist Counterculture in Interwar Poland*, 21. In a 1948 Yiddish-language story, Burshtyn describes a passionate tango, "which dramatized free love and eroticism." See Burshtyn, "Der masken bal fun der fardorbenhayt," 41. For a discussion of sex in American Yiddish literature, see Hellerstein, "The Art of Sex in Yiddish Poems"; Lambert, *Unclean Lips*, 141–174.

3. See sources such as Arcangeli, "Dance Under Trial," esp. 143; Pennino-Baskerville, "Terpsichore Reviled," esp. 492; Salhi, "Introduction: The Paradigm of Performing Islam Beyond the Political Rhetoric," 8; Wagner, *Adversaries of the Dance*, 388. For a discussion of Puritan Increase Mather's condemnation of "gynecandrical" ("mixed" or "promiscuous") dancing in a 1684 morality tract, see Wiggins, *Sport in America*, 12.

4. For Adventist, Baptist, Mormon, and Muslim versions, see sources such as "It Could Lead to Dancing—Adventists and Sex," *The Other Adventist Home* (April 20, 2018): http://www.theotheradventisthome.com/2018/04/it-could-lead-to-dancing-adventists-and.html; Mark Oppenheimer, "The First Dance," *New York Times Magazine* (January 28, 2007): https://www.nytimes.com/2007/01/28/magazine/28dancing.t.html; u/paula_sutton, "Dancing," *reddit*: https://www.reddit.com/r/Jokes/comments/15ik99/dancing/. In an email correspondence from April 2019, Faith Jones recalled that she heard a Mormon version of the joke in Vancouver in the 1970s. For Mormon attitudes toward mixed-sex dancing, see Hicks, *Mormonism and Music*, 74–86. For a play about queer inclusion within the Mennonite church that follows a queer dancer in a Mennonite context and references the punchline in the title, see Wideman, *This Will Lead to Dancing* (Toronto: Theatre of the Beat, 2017). Johnny Wideman graciously answered my questions about the play.

5. Other than a few passing references to works of world literature that help contextualize my discussion of the social importance of dance, the literary texts I discuss depict Jewish engagement in mixed-sex social dancing. Most of the writers were also Jewish themselves, although Austrian nobleman Leopold von Sacher-Masoch is a notable exception. As a shorthand, I sometimes refer to the texts in my corpus as Jewish literature, especially since most works were written by a Jewish author and/or intended for a Jewish audience.

6. Heshy Fried, "'It Could Lead to Mixed Dancing' Is Antiquated and Needs to Be Replaced," *Frum Satire* (August 20, 2013): http://www.frumsatire.net/2013/08/20/it-could-lead-to-mixed-dancing/. Although Fried claims the phrase is outdated, he still considers it the most effective way to lampoon religious taboos.

7. Scholars who study this era do not all begin their periodization in the same year, especially since these shifts happened at different times across Europe, moving generally from west to east. Two of the defining historical incidents that are often used to denote the start of the period of emancipation are Austrian Emperor Joseph II's Edict of Tolerance (*Toleranzedikt*, 1781–1782) and the decision by the French National Assembly to grant citizenship to Jews (1790–1791). See Katz, *Out of the Ghetto*, 30. My

starting date in the late eighteenth century roughly corresponds with the start of the *Haskalah* (Jewish Enlightenment) in the German states and Habsburg empire. Katz starts his study in 1770, perhaps in part so that his examination of a century of Jewish emancipation ends with the unification of Germany. He notes, too, the activities of Moses Mendelssohn's intellectual circle in Berlin during the 1770s and 80s (see ibid., 50), although acknowledging on p. 59 that Mendelssohn did not become "the outspoken interpreter of Jewish expectations" until the 1780s. In Kaplan's edited volume about German Jewish daily life from 1618–1945, Lowenstein's section on the era of emancipation spans 1780–1870; see Kaplan, "Introduction," in *Jewish Daily Life in Germany*, 7. Most texts I discuss were written between the mid-nineteenth century and the first few decades of the twentieth century.

8. For instance, see Lesser, *A Jewish Youth in Dresden*, 113.

9. Margolis, "A Tempest in Three Teapots."

10. When anticipating the possibility that she might never marry, Lewald identifies dancing with youthful courtship and associates not dancing with aging. See Lewald, *Meine Lebensgeschichte*, vol. 2, 204, 300. For English, see Lewald, *The Education of Fanny Lewald*, 182, 194.

11. Maimon, *Salomon Maimons Lebensgeschichte*, vol. 2, 276–279. For English, see Maimon, *The Autobiography of Solomon Maimon*, 240–243.

12. Auerbach, *Bräutigamsbriefe von Berthold Auerbach*, 33.

13. As Isaac Bashevis Singer noted, "Nomberg learned to dance the modern dances—the tango, the shimmy, the foxtrot, the Charleston. He danced often at the Writers' Association House." Singer, "Memoirs and Episodes from the Writers' Association House in Warsaw," 9e. For more about Nomberg and other Yiddish cultural figures dancing at Tłomackie 13, see Segalovitsh, *Tłomatske 13*, 170–173, 179.

14. For more about the changing role of gender in modern Jewish literature and culture, see Baader, *Gender, Judaism, and Bourgeois Culture in Germany*; Boyarin, *Unheroic Conduct*; Naimark-Goldberg, *Jewish Women in Enlightenment Berlin*; Seidman, *The Marriage Plot*. For recent studies of Jewish space, see Cohen, *Place in Modern Jewish Culture and Society*; Ernst and Lamprecht, *Jewish Spaces*; Lipphardt, Brauch, and Nocke, *Jewish Topographies*. For a study of Jewish space that focuses on literary texts, see Mann, *Space and Place in Jewish Studies*. One exception is the rise of gender segregation in Israeli society; see Weiss, "A Beach of Their Own."

15. Recent scholarship in Jewish Studies has explored different types of space where social mixing occurred. For instance, see Cypess and Sinkoff, *Sara Levy's World*; Dynner, *Yankel's Tavern*; Hertz, *Jewish High Society in Old Regime Berlin*; Pinsker, *A Rich Brew*; Zadoff, *Next Year in Marienbad*. For a literary account juxtaposing traditionally pious young men who "were ashamed to look a woman in the face" with mixed-sex leisure culture on a beach, including "almost naked couples" who "danced barefoot in the hot sand," see Grade, *The Yeshiva*, 381. For Yiddish, see Grade, *Tsemakh atlas*, 400.

16. Rakovsky, *My Life as a Radical Jewish Woman*, 27. For Yiddish, see Rakovsky, *Zikhroynes fun a yidisher revolutsionerin*, 21. Similarly, Ruth Katz (a rabbi's daughter who was born in 1913 in Russian Poland in the town of Wizajny) notes that her father was unusually permissive in allowing young men and women to talk, dance, and sing together on Friday nights in a room in their house. See Kramer and Masur, "Ruth Katz," 144.

17. In *Ha-ne'ehavim veha-ne'imim, oder, Der shvartser yungermantshik* (*The Beloved and Pleasing, or, The Dark Young Man*), Jacob Dinezon's bestselling 1877 Yiddish novel of bourgeois Russian Jewish life in the 1840s, mixed-sex dancing is explicitly identified with ideas of fashion and romance from outside the Jewish community. As one character laments,

> The Christians have their custom of letting the groom choose his bride without a matchmaker, but at least we don't do that, thank God! And to think my own dear daughter almost introduced this fashion into our household. Soon they'll want to allow men and women to dance together at weddings the way Christians do. *Nu*, Master of the Universe, can anything good come of this?

Dinezon, The *Dark Young Man*, 198. For Yiddish, see Dinezon, *Ha-ne'ehavim veha-ne'imim*, 247.

18. Wurst, *Fabricating Pleasure*, esp. xvii–xviii.

19. Bourgeois Jews might even view attendance at balls as a duty. See Kaplan, *The Making of the Jewish Middle Class*, 132.

20. Attendance at spas also often involved balls; see Naimark, *Jewish Women in Enlightenment Berlin*, 167. Bourdieu identifies the middlebrow with minor works of major arts and major works of minor arts, and he associates it with the bourgeoisie. See Bourdieu, *Distinction*, 16. For the importance of nineteenth-century German Jewish middlebrow literature, see Hess, *Middlebrow Literature and the Making of German-Jewish Identity*.

21. Turner, *From Ritual to Theatre*, 37. For a useful discussion of the concept of play, see Huizinga, *Homo Ludens*, 7–13. Characteristics of play include voluntary participation, separation from "real" life (including through dressing up), taking place within a designated space, applying one's own sense of order and rules, and an element of tension.

22. For more about the German cotillion, see Aldrich, *From the Ballroom to Hell*, 17–18. For an instance of Jews performing the (German) cotillion, see Poliakova, *A Jewish Woman of Distinction*, 176–177.

23. Geertz, "Deep Play," 70, 79, 83–84. Geertz compares the emotional investment in a high-stakes Balinese cockfight to canonical literary texts like *Crime and Punishment* (see ibid., 79). In contrast to Geertz's emphasis on pride, rage, and masculinity, the texts I discuss invoke emotional responses from readers that are closely connected to heterosexual courtship and Jewish emancipation, including titillation, empathy, and indignation.

24. For criticism and eroticization of sex segregation in modern Jewish literature, see Seidman, *The Marriage Plot*, 253–293.

25. For more about romantic love in modern Jewish literature, see Garloff, *Mixed Feelings*; Lezzi, *"Liebe ist meine Religion!"*; Seidman, *The Marriage Plot*. For changes in Jewish attitudes toward romantic love, see Biale, *Eros and the Jews*; Boyarin, *Unheroic Conduct*; Kaplan, "'Based on Love.'" For a discussion of Jewish attitudes toward romantic love in imperial Germany, see Kaplan, "As Germans and as Jews in Imperial Germany," in *Jewish Daily Life in Germany*, 195. Christian Bailey's forthcoming study of love between Jews and other Germans also promises to illuminate this topic.

26. Watt, *The Rise of the Novel*, 18.

27. For studies of dance and literary modernism, see Brandstetter, *Poetics of Dance*; Jones, *Literature, Modernism, and Dance*; Kolb, *Performing Femininity*; Ruprecht, *Gestural Imaginaries*.

28. Seidman, *The Marriage Plot*, 59; Watt, *The Rise of the Novel*, 136.

29. Jewish mixed-sex dancing was not a uniquely Ashkenazic phenomenon. See Goldberg, *Jewish Passages*, 242–243; for Jewish ball attendance in late Ottoman Izmir, see Danon, *The Jews of Ottoman Izmir*, 96–113.

30. I include Leopold Kompert (a Bohemian-born Jewish writer who published German-language regional fiction in Vienna and incorporated Yiddish terms into his work) among the German writers, even though he lived in the Habsburg empire and not in the German empire or what is now Germany. This kind of general linguistic designation becomes more complicated in the case of Abraham Cahan, who wrote in both Yiddish and English. I describe him as an American Jewish or Yiddish writer due to his influential Yiddish literary and journalistic career, to his concerns as an immigrant writer that make it difficult to completely separate his Yiddish and English works, and to the fact that even his English-language novel *Yekl* was first published in a Yiddish version (and later adapted into a film with largely Yiddish dialogue).

31. These scenes tend to involve men who dress in drag. For instance, Kolmar, *Die jüdische Mutter*, 137–138. For English, see Kolmar, *A Jewish Mother from Berlin*, 103–104.

32. See, for instance, Shtok, "Der shlayer," in *Gezamelte dertseylungen*, 111. For an English translation of this story, see Schtok's "The Veil" in Forman et al., *Found Treasures*, 103.

33. See Kompert, *Die Kinder des Randars*, 68.

34. See Opatoshu, *A roman fun a ferd-ganef*, 70. For English, see Opatoshu, *Romance of a Horse Thief*, 182.

35. For further discussion, see Chapter 3.

36. The "structure" of a dance refers to whether the dance is fast or slow, whether it is for one or four couples, whether it involves close contact or approaching and retreating, and so forth.

37. For more about this genre, see studies such as Fuchs and Krobb, *Ghetto Writing*; Glasenapp and Horch, *Ghettoliteratur*; Hess, *Middlebrow Literature and the Making of German-Jewish Identity*, 72–110.

38. For more about this genre, see Roskies, *A Bridge of Longing*, 17. For more about shtetlekh in the Yiddish literary imagination, see Katz, *The Shtetl*; Miron, *The Image of the Shtetl*. For more about the shtetl, see Shandler, *Shtetl*; Zborowski and Herzog, *Life Is with People*.

39. Ruprecht, *Dances of the Self*, xiii.

40. Ferber, *A Dictionary of Literary Symbols*, 52.

41. A Jewish woman, who goes to a dance, meets a Christian writer and falls in love with him. When he insists on her baptism, she says she would rather drown. Song text in Erk, "98d. Die Judentochter," *Deutscher Liederhort*, vol. 1, 353–354. Bohlman and Holzapfel cite several German and two Yiddish variations; see Bohlman and Holzapfel, *The Folk Songs of Ashkenaz*, 15–23.

42. See Turner, *From Ritual to Theatre*, 47.

43. For instance, see Engelhardt, *Dancing Out of Line*; Wilson, *Literature and Dance in Nineteenth-Century Britain*.

44. Prior to my own scholarship, these studies typically did not acknowledge the Jewishness of authors who wrote about dance or of fictional Jewish social dancers. For a discussion of Heinrich Heine's writings on dance, see Ruprecht, *Dances of the Self*, 97–136; for dance in George Eliot's *Daniel Deronda*, see Engelhardt, *Dancing Out of Line*, 108, and Wilson, *Literature and Dance in Nineteenth-Century Britain*, 71.

45. For social histories that discuss bourgeois (German) Jewish dance, see Kaplan, *The Making of the Jewish Middle Class*, 132; Wobick-Segev, *Homes Away from Home*, 32–37, 63–66, 133–140. For more ethnographic and folkloric studies of Yiddish dance (songs), see Cahan, "Tsum oyfkum fun yidishn tantslid"; Feldman, "Bulgareasca, Bulgarish, Bulgar"; Feldman, *Klezmer*, 163–202; Friedland, "'Tantsn Is Lebn'"; Rubin, "Dancing Songs." A rare example of a text about Jewish dance aesthetics is Vizonsky, "Vegn yidishn folks-tants." Karen Goodman includes a translation and analysis in her unpublished talk, "Thinking About Nathan Vizonsky, Thinking About Yiddish Dance" (paper presented at the annual meeting for the Association for Jewish Studies, Boston, 2010). I thank her for sharing both texts with me.

46. Gollance, "Gesture, Repertoire, and Emotion."

47. I use the term "liminal" due to its currency in scholarship. The overall range of dance scenes I discuss (containing both ritual forms, such as weddings, and leisure culture, such as balls) resists easy classification into Turner's categories of "liminal" and "liminoid," especially due to the important social function of dance in Hasidic communities. See Turner, *From Ritual to Theatre*, 53.

48. Works that offer theoretical insights into leisure culture spaces but do not directly address the dance floor include: Foucault, "Of Other Spaces"; Habermas, *The*

Structural Transformation of the Public Sphere, 9–10; Lefebvre, *The Production of Space*, 310. Pinsker has applied Soja's concept of the "thirdspace" to Jewish café culture (a leisure space that sometimes included dancing); see Pinsker, *A Rich Brew*, 9–10. Tuan discusses how dancing can change the way people relate to space, because they are freed "from the demands of purposeful goal-directed life" but does not elaborate on the dance floor itself; see Tuan, *Space and Place*, 129.

49. While dynamic social dance scenes continue to exist, there is less of an assumption that mastering a standard set of ballroom or folk dances is obligatory for courtship or (elite) class status. At the same time, contemporary social dance often offers new opportunities for solo dance, flexible gender roles, and a broader array of dance styles. Studies that discuss shifts in social dance culture after World War II include: Bosse, "Whiteness and the Performance of Race in American Ballroom Dance"; Lawrence, "Disco and the Queering of the Dance Floor"; Malnig, *Ballroom, Boogie, Shimmy Sham, Shake*; Walkowitz, "The Cultural Turn and a New Social History."

50. See Huizinga, *Homo Ludens*, esp. 10.

51. My thinking on this topic is informed by Lefebvre's writing about the creation of social space through human behaviors, bodies, and actions. See Lefebvre, *The Production of Space*, 26–46.

52. La Roche, *Geschichte des Fräuleins von Sternheim*, 186. For English, see La Roche, *The History of Lady Sophia Sternheim*, 103. For more about masquerade balls in literature, see Castle, *Masquerade and Civilization*.

53. Valéry, "Philosophy of the Dance," 70–71.

54. For more about the mitsve tants, or dance that fulfills the commandment of gladdening the bride, see Chapter 1. Although performed in a sex-segregated context, this dance tests the limits of the prohibition on mixed-sex dancing.

55. Such as divorce, as in Cahan's *Yekl*.

56. For a study of interethnic romance in American Jewish literature that addresses some of the same American Yiddish writers as this book, see Kirzane, "The Melting Plot."

Chapter 1

1. G. Kuper [I. J. Singer], "Ofitsirn tantsn mit yidishe meydlekh af a yidishn bal un in shtetl iz khoyshekh," *Forverts* (May 7, 1930): 6. The translation of the title comes from Norich, *The Homeless Imagination in the Fiction of Israel Joshua Singer*, 124.

2. For more about the "evil inclination" in Jewish religious thought, see Jacobs, "Yetzer Ha-Tov and Yetzer Ha-Ra," in *A Concise Companion to the Jewish Religion*, 308–310. Singer's personified yetser hore is an example of the evil inclination as another name for Satan, although the feuilleton maintains the association between the yetser hore and sexual desire. For Jewish writings on Satan, see Pintel-Ginsberg, "Satan."

3. For a study that notes the importance of charity balls for Jewish philanthropy, see Rabin, *Jews on the Frontier*, 40.

4. See Friedhaber, "The Bride and Her Guests," 225–233. Rabbi A. Neuwirth's contention that mixed-sex dancing was unthinkable before the modern era is questionable, since it presumes that previous generations of Jews consistently followed the instructions of their religious leaders. See A. Neuwirth, "Tanzen," *Der Israelit: Ein Centralorgan für das orthodoxe Judentum* 64, no. 28 (July 12, 1923): 1–2, and A. Neuwirth, "Tanzen," *Der Israelit: Ein Centralorgan für das orthodoxe Judentum* 64, no. 29 (July 19, 1923): 3–5.

5. Consider Cecil Roth's citation of a 1791 Yiddish-language pamphlet from London, which "deplored contemporary laxity in unmeasured terms. Parents allowed their children to go bareheaded; men and women came together in dancing academies, where they embraced one another without shame; they dressed like lords and ladies, and could not be distinguished from Gentiles." Engaging in mixed-sex dancing is associated with other activities that blur the boundaries between Jews and Christians. See Roth, *The Great Synagogue*, 141.

6. See Kaplan, *The Making of the Jewish Middle Class*, 85–116; Seidman, *The Marriage Plot*. For broader context, see Coontz, *Marriage, a History*. I use the term "companionate marriage" to refer to marriages that are based on the emotional and sexual compatibility of the spouses, rather than economic concerns or family relationships.

7. For more about the development and popularity of the waltz, especially in Vienna, see Knowles, *The Wicked Waltz and Other Scandalous Dances*, 25–30. See also Aldrich, *From the Ballroom to Hell*, 18–20. Hess draws a connection between the French Revolution and the "waltz revolution" that superseded the minuet; see Hess, *Der Walzer*, 115.

8. Hess also notes, "The waltz gives every couple independence and a freedom of action that was until that point unknown"; see Hess, *Der Walzer*, 124–125.

9. Quoted in A. Neuwirth, "Tanzen," *Der Israelit: Ein Centralorgan für das orthodoxe Judentum* 64, no. 29 (July 19, 1923): 4; see also Carlebach, *Sittenreinheit*, 17.

10. Löw, *Beiträge zur Jüdischen Alterthumskunde*, 322–323. For more about Löw, who was born in Moravia, see Miller, *Rabbis and Revolution*, 5.

11. While most scholars identify the Haskalah with the Enlightenment, Litvak argues that this movement should be considered a form of eastern European Romanticism. See Litvak, *Haskalah*, 24–25.

12. Biale, *Eros and the Jews*, 161.

13. [Hirsch], "Religion Allied to Progress," in *Judaism Eternal*, 224. For German, see [Hirsch], *Die Religion im Bunde mit dem Fortschritt*, 3.

14. Katz, *Jewish Emancipation and Self-Emancipation*, 3.

15. Ibid., 5.

16. Freytag, *Soll und Haben*, 144. For a discussion of Freytag's use of antisemitic stereotypes in this novel, see Mellman, "Detoured Reading.'"

17. While authors may have been inspired by European marriage plots, Biale and Seidman observe that social mobility through marriage tended to be more of an option for traditional Jewish men, since poor but intellectually gifted scholars were able to marry wealthy brides. Biale, *Eros and the Jews*, 63; Seidman, *The Marriage Plot*, 150.

18. Although this book focuses on literary texts, mixed-sex dancing appears as a sign of acculturation in films such as *Das alte Gesetz* (*The Ancient Law*, 1923), *Ost und West* (*East and West*, 1923), and *Tkies-kaf* (*The Vow*, 1937).

19. A Jew's choice to convert to Christianity in order to marry someone he or she met at a dance might best be described through the rubric of assimilation, whereas a Purim ball at a Jewish social club could be categorized as dissimulation. For a critical discussion of the term assimilation, see Sorkin, "Emancipation and Assimilation." For an example of a text that advocates using acculturation as it is less ideological than assimilation, see Meyer and Brenner, *German-Jewish History in Modern Times*, 2–3. For a discussion of dissimulation in relation to assimilation and acculturation, see Skolnik, *Jewish Pasts, German Fictions*, 5–7.

20. A. Neuwirth, "Tanzen," *Der Israelit: Ein Centralorgan für das orthodoxe Judentum* 64, no. 28 (July 12, 1923): 1.

21. Berman, "Hasidic Dance," 94–95.

22. See ibid., 95; also, A. Neuwirth, "Tanzen," *Der Israelit: Ein Centralorgan für das orthodoxe Judentum* 64, no. 28 (July 12, 1923): 1. For a discussion of dancing and gender segregation at late twentieth-century Chabad Lubavitch celebrations of this ritual, see Gellerman, "Rehearsing for Ultimate Joy Among the Lubavitcher Hasidim."

23. Berman, "Hasidic Dance," 95. According to an anonymous eleventh-century rabbinic ruling, "It is forbidden for men and women to intermingle [at a wedding] whether at the meal, at the dancing, or at any other part [of the celebration]. The women must be by themselves, and the men by themselves . . . for at a happy occasion especially the sensual passions are aroused." Quoted from *Sefer haPardes*, no. 149, in Agus, *Urban Civilization in Pre-Crusade Europe*, 728–729. Neuwirth apparently attributes this passage to the renowned commentator Rashi; see A. Neuwirth, "Tanzen," *Der Israelit: Ein Centralorgan für das orthodoxe Judentum* 64, no. 28 (July 12, 1923): 2.

24. See also Friedhaber, "The Bride and Her Guests," 225.

25. Zunz, *Zur Geschichte und Literatur*, 171.

26. Responsa 66. For English, see Ellinson, *Women and the Mitzvot*, 65.

27. Friedhaber, "The Bride and Her Guests," 227.

28. Sparti, "Jewish Dancing-Masters and 'Jewish Dance' in Renaissance Italy," 237, 240. Sparti notes that Guglielmo Ebreo of Pesaro was the "foremost choreographer, composer, theorist, dancer, and dancing-master of the fifteenth century." See ibid., 235. For an earlier account of this subject that refers to early modern Jewish (mixed-sex) dancing more broadly, see Baron, *The Jewish Community*, 315–316.

29. Sparti, "Jewish Dancing-Masters and 'Jewish Dance' in Renaissance Italy," 246.

30. Binyamin Ze'ev ben Matityahu, *Binyamin Ze'ev*, para. 304, p. 439a–b.

31. See "169. Responsa Binyamin Zeev, #303," 205.

32. *Kanah hokhmah kanah binah*, 204.

33. Albert Wolf, "Fahrende Leute bei den Juden," *Mitteilungen zur jüdischen Volkskunde* 27, no. 3 (1908): 90.

34. Ibid., 90–91.

35. Ibid., 91; Albert Wolf, "Fahrende Leute bei den Juden," *Mittheilungen zur jüdischen Volkskunde* 28, no. 11 (1908): 152–153.

36. Iggers, *Die Juden in Böhmen und Mähren*, 59. For English, see Iggers, *The Jews of Bohemia and Moravia*, 62. See also Salmen, ". . . *denn die Fiedel macht das Fest*," 31–32.

37. Quoted in Schmitges, "Yiddish Dance Songs," 153, footnote 19.

38. Ibid., 153. See also M. Grunwald, "Die Statuten der 'Hamburg-Altonaer Gemeinde' von 1726," *Mittheilungen der Gesellschaft für jüdische Volkskunde* 11, no. 1 (1903): 13.

39. Bodenschatz, *Kirchliche Verfassung der heutigen Juden sonderlich derer in Deutschland*, 128.

40. Kagan, "Be'ur halakhah," in *Mishnah Berurah*, para. 339, p. 186.

41. Most discussions of tantshoyzer are found in older scholarship, which compounds the confusion. For references to tantshoyzer, especially in connection with the taboo on mixed-sex dancing, see Abrahams, *Jewish Life in the Middle Ages*, 380–381; Baron, *The Jewish Community*, 315–316; Kriwaczek, *Yiddish Civilisation*, 137–138; Wolf, "Fahrende Leute bei den Juden," *Mitteilungen zur jüdischen Volkskunde* 27, no. 3 (1908): 90.

42. Feldman, *Klezmer*, 177–178.

43. Friedhaber, "The Bride and Her Guests," 226. See also Brayer, *The Jewish Woman in Rabbinic Literature*, 145.

44. Friedhaber, "The Bride and Her Guests," 226–227.

45. Ibid., 228–229. For an early modern description, see Bodenschatz, *Kirchliche Verfassung*, 127–128. For an analysis of Bodenschatz and an English translation, see Schmitges, "Yiddish Dance Songs," 154–155. For an Israeli perspective, see Mazor and Taube, "A Hassidic Ritual Dance." See also Ginzberg, *The Music of the Mitsve Tants in the Court of the Hasidic Rebbes*, xi–xviii.

46. For more about the spiritual role of dance in Hasidic thought, see Biale, *Hasidism*, 218–220.

47. Unger, *A Fire Burns in Kotsk*, 74. For Yiddish, see Unger, *Pshiskhe un Kotsk*, 95.

48. Some sources are listed in Friedhaber, "The Bride and Her Guests," 230–232.

49. According to Soviet ethnomusicologist Moyshe Beregovski in a 1937 essay, "[F]or the most part, the descriptions of weddings [in belles lettres and in memoirs] date from the nineteenth century, and at that time men did not participate in couple dances. . . . [C]ouple dances were done by women (or girls) alone." See Beregovski, *Old Jewish Folk Music*, 533.

50. Feldman, *Klezmer*, 207–208.

51. [Lifshitz], "R. Yedidiye Vayls kamf kegn maskaradn un tents in Karlsrue," 452–453.

52. For more about Lipschitz, including his attempt to fight the "plague of dance and entertainment" (*tants- un farvaylung-mageyfe*) in Warsaw, see Shatzky, *Geshikhte fun yidn in Varshe*, 297.

53. Frenk, "Di milkhome kegn der '*hefkeyrus*' in amolikn Varshe," 103.

54. Ibid., 106.

55. For more about Jewish communal authorities in Poland, see Bartal, *The Jews of Eastern Europe*, 84–85.

56. Mendele Moykher-Sforim, "Omar Mendele Moykher-Sforim," 274. For an alternative English translation, see Mendele Mocher Sforim, "Of Bygone Days," 272.

57. Elon, *The Pity of It All*, 209. For German, see Heid and Schopes, *Juden in Deutschland*, 13.

58. Lewald, *The Education of Fanny Lewald*, 172. For German, see Lewald, *Meine Lebensgeschichte*, vol. 2, 156.

59. Herz, "Memoirs of a Jewish Girlhood," 314. For German, see Herz, *Henriette Herz*, 19.

60. Herz, *Henriette Herz*, 25. For English, see Herz, "Memoirs of a Jewish Girlhood," 319.

61. Schnitzler, *Tagebuch*, 14–16. In his diary entry from February 2, 1880, Schnitzler (ibid., 26) wrote:

> Saturday morning. I came home from the Sophiensaal at five in the morning. Fanny was there with her mother—and naturally we stuck together the whole time to the old woman's great annoyance. Fanny danced 3 quadrilles, the first with me, the second with Sam R. facing me, the third with me. Quite pretty conversations during the Tour des mains, balancé, and other nice figures: specifically, that we would have really liked to kiss one another, that we loved each other so much—all sorts of things that, granted, are not entirely new but always pleasant to hear. How lovely it was to go hand-in-hand and promenade during the quadrille, something we eagerly cultivated, arm in arm. It took a great deal of effort not to forget my surroundings, imagine myself in the Quai Park, and "fall right upon her neck" as I put it.

62. Meiring, *Die Christlich-Jüdische Mischehe in Deutschland*, 111–112. Meiring thanks her informant but does not provide a location for the diary manuscript.

63. Ibid., 112.

64. For instance, when reporting on an interview she conducted, Meiring observes: "What did Ruth P. care about the religious affiliation of the dancing partner she met in the Hamburg Curio-Haus at an artists' festival in 1928? They were immediately on familiar terms, a 'must' in those days, and Ruth enjoyed being idolized by her new admirer

and being 'fully monopolized.'" Ruth marries him, despite her father's disapproval. See ibid., 118.

65. Sacher-Masoch, "How Slobe Gets Her Sister Married," in *Jewish Life: Tales from Nineteenth-Century Europe*, 83. For German, see Sacher-Masoch, "Wie Slobe ihre Schwester verheiratet," in *Jüdisches Leben in Wort und Bild*, 104.

66. Franzos, *Esterka Regina*, in *Die Juden von Barnow*, 189. This is my translation. For an alternative English version, see Franzos, *Esterka Regina*, in *The Jews of Barnow*, 202. For further analysis of this dance scene, see Gollance, "Harmonious Instability," 170–177.

67. Clementine Krämer, "Der Weg des jungen Hermann Kahn," *Allgemeine Zeitung des Judentums* 82, no. 5 (February 1, 1918): 60.

68. Kolmar, *Die jüdische Mutter*, 137–138. For English, see Kolmar, *A Jewish Mother from Berlin*, 103–104. For a discussion of this scene, see Seelig, *Strangers in Berlin*, 152. Kolmar's novel was completed in 1931 and first published posthumously. See ibid., 132.

69. Seidman, *The Marriage Plot*, 183–184.

70. According to Jacob Baltzan's (1872–1939) memoirs from the town of Leova, Moldova (near Bessarabia), he was the first boy to dance with girls at a family wedding, which was initially quite scandalous. Yet after the first transgression (the account does not state the date, but it seems likely to have been in the late 1880s or early 1890s), it does not take long for mixed-sex dancing to become an accepted behavior. See Jacob Baltzan, "Our House in Leova," *JewishGen:* http://www.jewishgen.org/Yizkor/leova/leo0oo.html. Etta Freilich Wandrei describes the limitations on mixed-sex dancing and mingling between Jews and Christians in her oral history testimony about her life in Vishni Bystry (today Ukraine) prior to 1939. Wandrei bristled against such restrictions in her "very strict Orthodox village" where even "Jewish girls couldn't dance with the Jewish boys." She sought out a new religious Zionist group in the community: "I joined them to dance and sing with boys." See Etta Freilich Wandrei, "Notes from Yale University Archives Interview with Etta Freilich Wandrei," *JewishGen:* http://kehilalinks.jewishgen.org/verkhnyaya_bystra/memoir2.html. See also Etta W. Holocaust Testimony (HVT-1482) at the Fortunoff Video Archives for Holocaust Testimonies, Yale University Library.

71. Singer, *Of a World That Is No More*, 133. For Yiddish, see Singer, *Fun a velt vos iz nishto mer*, 138.

72. Singer, *Of a World That Is No More*, 169. For Yiddish, see Singer, *Fun a velt vos iz nishto mer*, 177.

73. Cahan, *Bleter fun mayn lebn*, 252. For English, see Cahan, *The Education of Abraham Cahan*, 100. This translation only mentions the quadrille. For a discussion of this scene, which includes some of my own translations, see Gollance, "'A *Valtz* from the Land of *Valtzes*!'" 398–399.

74. Cahan, *Bleter fun mayn lebn*, 253. Translation is my own. For another version, see Cahan, *The Education of Abraham Cahan*, 100.

75. Mintz, "The Ruined Wedding (On Account of an Agreement Between the Rabbi of Khmelnik and the Musicians)," in Kugelmass and Boyarin, *From a Ruined Garden*, 148. For Yiddish, see Mints, "Mayne zikhroynes," 213. For a literary account of a musician being warned that a rabbi had forbidden playing for mixed-sex dancing but then not noticing when men join women in dancing, see Halitvack [Edward Raphael Lipsett], "Blume's Wedding—A Sketch," *The Reform Advocate* 4 (September 14, 1907): 122. This Chicago weekly was edited by prominent Reform Rabbi Emil G. Hirsch.

76. Mintz, "The Ruined Wedding," in Kugelmass and Boyarin, *From a Ruined Garden*, 149. See also Mints, "Mayne zikhroynes," 214. "Real sport" is *kavalier* in the Yiddish, a term that is also used sometimes for a male dance partner.

77. Mintz refers to the dance as a "kutner" or "larsey." I have been unable to find any other information about these dances in my own research or in conversation with other Yiddish dance scholars, although one possibility is that "larsey" is a misattribution of the lancers.

78. Perle, *Everyday Jews*, 95. For Yiddish, see Perle, *Yidn fun a gants yor*, 134.

79. Opatoshu, "A khasene," in *Gezamlte verk*, vol. 9, 112.

80. For an example of a Polish nobleman dancing with Jewish men at a Jewish wedding in a memoir, see Kotik, *Journey to a Nineteenth-Century Shtetl*, 276. For Yiddish, see Kotik, *Mayne zikhroynes*, 196.

81. Singer, *The Manor*, 81. Although no translator is credited on the title page, the book's front matter lists Joseph Singer and Elaine Gottlieb as translators. The family epic was originally serialized from 1953–1955. For Yiddish, see Itzik Bashevis, "Der hoyf," *Forverts*, section 2 (February 22, 1953): 5. In the original they dance a polka-mazurka, and Singer notes that Helena asks Miriam Lieba to dance and that she dances the role of the "kavalier." See also Nowak, "The Technique of Mazurka Dances in the Gentry-Bourgeois and Peasant Environments."

82. Singer, *The Manor*, 104. See Bashevis, "Der hoyf," *Forverts*, section 2 (March 8, 1953): 3.

83. Seidman, *The Marriage Plot*, 16. For another perspective on this issue, see Grossman, "The Yiddish-German Connection."

84. Examples include Hess, *Middlebrow Literature and the Making of German-Jewish Identity*; Skolnik, *Jewish Pasts, German Fictions*; Wallach, *Passing Illusions*.

Chapter 2

1. For a discussion of Kuh's biography and poetic output, see Kayserling, *Der Dichter Ephraim Kuh*; Rhotert, "Ephraim Moses Kuh."

2. Auerbach, *Dichter und Kaufmann*, vol. 2, 78. For an English translation of the ball scene (which leaves out this line), see Auerbach, *Poet and Merchant*, 326–331.

3. Franzos, *Die braune Rosa*, in *Junge Liebe*, 30.

4. Meiring, *Die Christlich-Jüdische Mischehe in Deutschland*, 112.

5. Eleanor Alexander, "Lecture given at the Goethe Institut San Francisco," unpublished manuscript, n.d. [2001?], Leo Baeck Institute Archives, LBI Berlin Collection, LBIJMB MM III 3, p. 16.

6. Although this chapter focuses on how European Jews learned how to dance, Klapper makes a similar point about bourgeois American Jews; see Klapper, *Jewish Girls Coming of Age in America*, 197–202.

7. Kaplan, *The Making of the Jewish Middle Class*, 132.

8. Ibid. For original, see Olly Schwarz, "Lebens-Erinnerungen 1870–1959," unpublished manuscript, 1959, Chicago, Leo Baeck Institute Archives, LBI Memoir Collection, ME 590, p. 15.

9. Mann, *Tonio Kröger*, 32.

10. Singer, *The Brothers Ashkenazi*, 165. For Yiddish, see Singer, *Di brider Ashkenazi*, 229. The novel was first serialized in the *Forverts* in 1934–1935.

11. Singer, *The Brothers Ashkenazi*, 194. For Yiddish, see Singer, *Di brider Ashkenazi*, 272.

12. Freytag, *Soll und Haben*, 132, 138–139, 181–182.

13. Kaplan, *The Making of the Jewish Middle Class*, 132.

14. Wechsberg, *The Vienna I Knew*, 18.

15. For an account of a Jewish teenager's participation in dance lessons in early 1940s Hungary, see Laszlo, *Footnote to History*, 116–118. Laszlo notes that these classes did not simply teach the foxtrot, tango, and waltz; another important skill was "learning how a gentleman should behave with ladies on and off the dance floor." See ibid., 116.

16. For women's dance repertoire, see Gollance, "Gesture, Repertoire, and Emotion," 108–112.

17. For women's acculturation patterns, see Hertz, *Jewish High Society in Old Regime Berlin*; Parush, *Reading Jewish Women*.

18. Sparti, "Jewish Dancing-Masters and 'Jewish Dance' in Renaissance Italy," 235–250.

19. These dance masters could have their own schools or be itinerant, they include: Abraham Tachau from Prague who appeared at the 1679 Leipzig trade fair, Lazarus May in Emden around 1750, an unknown Jewish dance master in Jever in 1827, and Franz Gartner from 1851 in Koblenz; see Salmen, ". . . *denn die Fiedel macht das Fest*," 76; Mannheim tax records from 1735 mention the dance master "Jud Elckan," who in 1746 received permission to hold a dance school on Sundays and holidays after church services, in exchange for payment of thirty florins to the hospital; see Salmen, *Der Tanzmeister*, 95. In 1753 neighbors complained that, in Mannheim, Christians and Jews committed "acts of wantonness from afternoon until late at night, even during Lent" on the dance floor of the widow of the dance master Leser Elkan; see Berthold Rosenthal, "Oberrabbiner Michael Scheuer als Kritiker seiner Zeit," *Zeitschrift für die Geschichte der Juden in Deutschland* 3, no. 1 (1931): 73.

20. For instance, an antisemitic Viennese caricature from 1842 depicts a hook-nosed dancing master who greedily eats a piece of cake; see Salmen, *Der Tanzmeister*, 315.

21. "Schulfeste," in *Programm der Realschule der israelitischen Gemeinde Philanthropin*, 54. The Tanzschule Feretty (Feretty Dance School) was later advertised in a Frankfurt Jewish community paper; see *Frankfurter Israelitisches Gemeindeblatt: Amtliches Organ der Israelitischen Gemeinde* 8, no. 2/3 (October/November 1929): 95.

22. "Geschäftliche Mitteilungen," *Frankfurter Israelitisches Gemeindeblatt: Amtliches Organ der Israelitischen Gemeinde* 11, no. 8 (April 1933): 202; "Purimveranstaltung," *Frankfurter Israelitisches Gemeindeblatt: Amtliches Organ der Israelitischen Gemeinde* 9, no. 7 (March 1931): 230; "Tanzabend," *Frankfurter Israelitisches Gemeindeblatt: Amtliches Organ der Israelitischen Gemeinde* 12, no. 5 (January 1934): 201.

23. For instance, see Vhaytman, "Oyf a tants-farshtelung," in *Gute zitn un shehne manyern*, 124–127.

24. See Czerwinski, *Geschichte der Tanzkunst bei den cultivirten Völkern von den ersten Anfängen bis auf die gegenwärtige Zeit*, 14–15; Junk, *Handbuch des Tanzes*, 121–122.

25. For instance, Max Daniel's father Sally Daniel (b. 1854) led the contradanse and the polonaise in Bublitz (today Bobolice, Poland). See "Max Daniel," in Richarz, *Jewish Life in Germany*, 222. For German, see Max Daniel, "Meine Familiengeschichte," unpublished manuscript, [n.d.], [San Francisco], Leo Baeck Institute Archives, LBI Memoir Collection, ME 814, p. 6. Henriette Hirsch recalls how her parents attended charity balls in Berlin, where they led the polonaise and participated in the contradanse and Quadrille à la Cour. See Wobick-Segev, *Homes Away from Home*, 33–34. For German, see Henriette Hirsch, "Erinnerungen an meine Jugend," unpublished manuscript, 1953, Ramat Gan, Israel, Leo Baeck Institute Archives, LBI Memoir Collection, ME 304, pp. 9–10. Interestingly, Hirsch initially comments that "of course" her father (Hirsch Hildesheimer, who was professor of history at the Orthodox rabbinical seminary in Berlin that was founded by his father, Esriel Hildesheimer) did not dance, at least not "round dances" (p. 9). Her use of the term "round dances" refers to ballroom dances, such as waltzes and polkas, where couples move in circles around the dance floor, rather than circular folk dances.

26. For instance, Beregovski, *Old Jewish Folk Music*, 533; Feldman, *Klezmer*, 207–213.

27. For instance, Raffael in Baum's "Der Knabe und die Tänzerin" in *Schloßtheater: Erzählungen*, 95.

28. For instance, Jemima Löw in Raabe's *Holunderblüte*, in *Erzählungen*, 105–108.

29. For instance, Maier in Leopold Kompert's *Die Jahrzeit*. See Kompert, *Die Jahrzeit*, in *Geschichten einer Gasse*, vol. 1, 26–27.

30. Compare villainous Reb Yoysefkhe and virtuous Markus in Aaron Halle Wolfssohn's *Laykhtzin un fremelay* (*Silliness and Sanctimony*). For Reb Yoysefkhe's willingness

to pretend he likes enlightened pursuits, see Wolfssohn, *Silliness and Sanctimony*, 95. For Yiddish, see Erik, *Di komedyes fun der Berlin oyfklerung*, 141.

31. For instance, Yankl in Kobrin's *Yankl Boyle*. See Kobrin, "Yankl Boyle," in *Gezamelte shriftn*, 22.

32. See Knowles, *The Wicked Waltz*, 3–14.

33. Engelhardt, *Dancing Out of Line*, 6, 20, 71.

34. Rocco, *Der Umgang in und mit der Gesellschaft*, 155.

35. *Conversations-Lexikon für alle Stände*, 412.

36. Laenger, *Erinnerungs-Buch*, 119.

37. Inspired by Heinrich Heine's writings about the Germanic folk beliefs, the ballet tells of a German peasant woman who dies before her wedding day. She is reborn as a *willi*, a ghostly dancer who forces men to dance to death. For an analysis of *Giselle* in terms of gender and class politics, see Banes, *Dancing Women*, 23–35.

38. *Die Gefahren des Tanzes*, 102.

39. Lewald, *The Education of Fanny Lewald*, 110–111. For German, see Lewald, *Meine Lebensgeschichte*, vol. 1, 289–290.

40. Although a dancing Jewish woman's fragile health is an important concern in Raabe's *Holunderblüte*, her heart condition is caused by the poor living conditions in the Prague ghetto rather than by strenuous dancing.

41. The germanophone canon includes many momentous dance scenes in works as varied in style and period as Sophie von La Roche's *Geschichte des Fräuleins von Sternheim* (*The History of Lady Sophia Sternheim*), Georg Büchner's *Woyzeck*, Adalbert Stifter's *Brigitta*, Arthur Schnitzler's *Traumnovelle* (*Dream Story*), and Christa Wolf's *Der geteilte Himmel* (*Divided Heaven*). While many of these texts explore themes of desire and betrayal, some also delve into questions of class or political differences in a way that relates more closely to the texts I discuss in this study than to the etiquette recommendations of dance manuals.

42. Voss, *Der Tanz und seine Geschichte*, 13.

43. See Wesner, *Gesellschaftliche Tanzkunst*, 29.

44. See Gilman, "*You, Too, Could Walk Like a Gentile*. Jews and Posture."

45. See Gilman, "The Jewish Foot," in *The Jew's Body*, 38–59; Mosse, *Confronting the Nation*; Wildmann, "Jewish Gymnasts and Their Corporeal Utopias in Imperial Germany."

46. Hertz, *Jewish High Society in Old Regime Berlin*, 13.

47. For a discussion of Jewish attitudes toward etiquette during the Haskalah, see Zaban, "'Folded White Napkins.'"

48. Dancing could be connected with other physical activities. In his memoirs, Austrian Jewish writer Stefan Zweig notes that, when he was thirteen, he bought books with the money his parents gave him for dance lessons: "At eighteen I could not yet swim, dance, or play tennis; and today I still can neither ride a wheel [bicycle] nor

drive a car, and in all sports any ten-year-old could put me to shame." See Zweig, *The World of Yesterday*, 58. For German, see Zweig, *Die Welt von Gestern: Erinnerungen eines Europäers*, 53.

49. For more about Sephardim in the German Jewish imagination, see Efron, *German Jewry and the Allure of the Sephardic*; Skolnik, *Jewish Pasts, German Fictions*.

50. Baum, "Der Knabe und die Tänzerin," in *Schloßtheater: Erzählungen*, 95. For further discussion of this story, see George, *The Naked Truth*, 190–192.

51. See Baader, *Gender, Judaism, and Bourgeois Culture in Germany*; Hertz, *Jewish High Society in Old Regime Berlin*; Parush, *Reading Jewish Women*.

52. See Hess, *Middlebrow Literature and the Making of German-Jewish Identity*, 111–156; Seidman, *The Marriage Plot*. In German literary texts such as Fanny Lewald's *Jenny* (1843) and Georg Hermann's *Jettchen Gebert* (1906), a bourgeois Jewish woman's (in)ability to marry a man of her choosing is decisive for her happiness and one of the main ways she can take control of her future.

53. In traditional Ashkenazic society, however, promising male scholars could achieve social mobility by marrying wealthy brides. See Biale, *Eros and the Jews*, 63; Seidman, *The Marriage Plot*, 150. Compare to a young woman's social mobility through work and education in works set in America such as Yezierska, *Bread Givers*.

54. See Parush, *Reading Jewish Women*, esp. 38–56. For the German context around 1800, see Hertz, *Jewish High Society in Old Regime Berlin*, 147. For the role of this gulf in conversions, see Endelman, "Gender and Conversion Revisited."

55. For a more in-depth analysis of this archetype, see studies such as Valman, *The Jewess in Nineteenth-Century British Literary Culture*; Krobb, *Die schöne Jüdin*. Analyses of the beautiful Jewess often note the relationship with orientalism; see, for instance, Brunotte, "The *Beautiful Jewess* as Borderline Figure in Europe's Internal Colonialism." Schwadron discusses a more assertive and comic Jewess figure in twentieth- and twenty-first-century America, see Schwadron, *The Case of the Sexy Jewess*.

56. For analysis of *Wally die Zweiflerin*, see Lezzi, "*Liebe ist meine Religion!*" 326–333. For discussion of *Die Jüdin von Toledo*, see Helfer, *The Word Unheard*, 143–169.

57. Eliot, *Daniel Deronda*, 607.

58. For more about orientalism, see Said, *Orientalism*. For a response from a German Jewish Studies perspective, see Brunotte, Ludewig, and Stähler, "Orientalism, Gender, and the Jews."

59. For discussion of the play as a cultural phenomenon, see Hess, *Deborah and Her Sisters*.

60. For more about how male Yiddish writers depicted female characters in their work, see studies such as Adler, *Women of the Shtetl*; Klepfisz, "Queens of Contradiction: A Feminist Introduction to Yiddish Women Writers," in Forman et al., *Found Treasures*, 38–40; Krutikov, *Yiddish Fiction and the Crisis of Modernity*, 164–170.

61. Raabe, *Holunderblüte*, in *Erzählungen*, 103. Raabe has been criticized for his use

of antisemitic stereotypes, particularly in his 1864 novel *Der Hungerpastor* (*The Hunger Pastor*); see Klüger, "Die Säkularisierung des Judenhasses am Beispiel von Wilhelm Raabes 'Der Hungerpastor.'" *Holunderblüte* was first serialized in the Stuttgart illustrated weekly *Über Land und Meer. Allgemeine Illustrirte Zeitung* (Over Land and Sea. General Illustrated Newspaper) in 1863.

62. When the medical student tells her he loves her, she denies the truth of his claim, and indeed he has already admitted to the readers that he does not love her, even if love is the closest word for his feelings. Jemima's conviction is in a sense convenient for the narrator: When he leaves Prague (her father urges him to do so for his own health) and comes back to find that she has died, he can have a clear conscience that Jemima's death is the fault of her poor social circumstances rather than an emotional failure on his part.

63. [Bekerman], *Der tants klas*, 5. He writes under the pseudonym Sh. B.

64. Chagall, *Burning Lights*, 112–113. For Yiddish, see Chagall, *Brenendike likht*, 104–107. She would not have been allowed to participate in this dancing as an adult, since in her community it was only performed by men.

65. Reyzen, "Di vos tantsn nit," 659–660.

66. For one example, see Cahan, *Bleter fun mayn lebn*, vol. 1, 252. For English, see Cahan, *The Education of Abraham Cahan*, 100; Gollance, "*A Valtz* from the Land of *Valtzes!*" 398–399.

67. Freeze, *Jewish Marriage and Divorce in Imperial Russia*, 46.

68. Kompert, *Die Jahrzeit*, 24. For analysis of the dance scenes in this story, see Gollance, "Harmonious Instability," 121–129.

69. Kotik, *Journey to a Nineteenth-Century Shtetl*, 289–290. For Yiddish, see Kotik, *Mayne zikhroynes*, vol. 1, 211.

70. Shtern, *Heyder un besmedresh*, 65–67. See also Roskies and Roskies, *The Shtetl Book*, 218.

71. Shtern, *Heyder un besmedresh*, 65–67.

72. Wengeroff, *Memoirs of a Grandmother*, vol. 1, 211. For German, see Wengeroff, *Memoiren einer Grossmutter*, vol. 1, 174. Shulamit Magnus translates "Kavaliere" as young men.

73. For instance, Zinaida Poliakova, daughter of a wealthy Russian Jewish banker and railway mogul, mentions dancing lessons in several diary entries from 1875. See Poliakova, *A Jewish Woman of Distinction*, 171, 174, 175.

74. Shtok, "A Dance." For Yiddish, see Shtok, "A tants," in *Gezamelte dertseylungen*, 19.

75. Dropkin, "A Dancer," in Forman et al., *Found Treasures*, 195. For Yiddish, see Dropkin, *In heysn vint*, 206.

76. Dropkin, "A Dancer," 195. For Yiddish, see Dropkin, *In heysn vint*, 206.

77. Grade, "It Has Begun," in *My Mother's Sabbath Days*, 231. For Yiddish, see Grade, "Es hot zikh ongehoybn," in *Der mames shabosim*, 276.

78. Kaplan, "As Germans and as Jews in Imperial Germany," in *Jewish Daily Life in Germany*, 255. For a literary example, see Singer, *The Brothers Ashkenazi*, 52. For Yiddish, see Singer, *Di brider Ashkenazi*, 70.

79. It costs two rubles a month for three dancing lessons a week and three rubles a month for five lessons a week.

80. [Bekerman], *Der tants klas*, 4.

81. For instance, the dance master has decided that he will only admit students who come from a suitable background: Seamstresses are not allowed to participate, even if they pay ten gulden a month, "because he wanted to conduct his business" with customers from a higher social class. Ibid., 7.

82. Ibid., 5.

83. Seidman, *The Marriage Plot*, 93.

84. Yakhnuk, *Yakhnuk's tants-klassin*, 13.

85. Mishnah Gittin 9:10; Bavli Gittin 90a. Thanks to Federico Dal Bo for this interpretation, which is particularly useful in the context of Yakhnuk's other comments about dance classes leading to sexual impropriety.

86. Yakhnuk, *Yakhnuk's tants-klassin*, 12.

87. For a discussion of how the pressures of assimilation led German Jews to feel shame and embarrassment, see Bauman, *Modernity and Ambivalence*, 128–132.

88. Kaplan, "As Germans and as Jews in Imperial Germany," in *Jewish Daily Life in Germany*, 255.

89. Ibid. See "Philipp Lowenfeld," in Richarz, *Jewish Life in Germany*, 235. Margarete Sallis (b. 1893) also notes that the dancing lessons she attended in Frankfurt involved elite Jewish and Christian families from the "upper ten thousand." See Margarete Sallis, "Meine beiden Vierzig Jahre," unpublished manuscript, 1975, Natanya, Leo Baeck Institute Archives, LBI Memoir Collection, ME 550, p. 22. Adolf Riesenfeld (b. 1884) recollects that his exposure to young women was limited to the social milieu of his dancing lessons. See Adolf Riesenfeld, "[Lebenserinnerungen] 1915–1917, 1927, 1940–1975," vol. 1: 1915–1941, unpublished manuscript, Leo Baeck Institute Archives, LBI Memoir Collection ME 787, entry from February 12, 1941.

90. Orfali adds, "A group of 10 to 12 couples took instructions together at a respected dancing school like the Krebs Institute in Nuernberg. Young men between 18 and 20 years of age asked young girls between the ages of 16 and 17 to be their partners, usually upon suggestions by their mothers." Orfali, *A Jewish Girl in the Weimar Republic*, 17.

91. Herz, "Memoirs of a Jewish Girlhood," 304. For German, see Herz, *Henriette Herz*, 8. A century after Herz, Emil Rocco comments critically on the popularity of French *professeur de danse* (dance professors) who teach children as young as three. See Rocco, *Der Umgang in und mit der Gesellschaft*, 5.

92. Lewald, *The Education of Fanny Lewald*, 107. For German, see Fanny Lewald, *Meine Lebensgeschichte*, vol. 1, 281–282.

93. Tableaux vivants (living pictures) was a nineteenth-century party game where guests posed as well-known works of art. The tableaux vivants scene in Lewald's *Jenny* arguably serves some of the same functions as dance scenes in other literary texts. For analysis of literary tableaux vivants, see McIsaac, "Rethinking Tableaux Vivants and Triviality"; Wittler, "Good to Think."

94. Lesser, *A Jewish Youth in Dresden*, 70.

95. Kaplan, *The Making of the Jewish Middle Class*, 132. For original German, see Adolf Riesenfeld, "[Lebenserinnerungen] 1915–1917, 1927, 1940–1975," vol. 1: 1915–1941, unpublished manuscript, Leo Baeck Institute Archives, LBI Memoir Collection ME 787, entry from November 2, 1917. Riesenfeld describes his feelings of excitement and shyness when the young women join the class—yet he overcomes his bashfulness sufficiently to ask one of his dancing partners (and, during the break, her mother) for permission to escort her home. For further discussion of Riesenfeld's choice of dance school, see Kaplan, "As Germans and as Jews in Imperial Germany," in *Jewish Daily Life in Germany*, 255. For original, see Adolf Riesenfeld, "[Lebenserinnerungen] 1915–1917, 1927, 1940–1975," vol. 1: 1915–1941, unpublished manuscript, Leo Baeck Institute Archives, LBI Memoir Collection ME 787, entry from February 12, 1941.

96. Orfali, *A Jewish Girl in the Weimar Republic*, 17–18.

97. See Franzos, *Judith Trachtenberg*, 8–9. For English, see Franzos, *Judith Trachtenberg: A Novel*, 4–5. For further discussion of dance lessons in *Judith Trachtenberg*, including my translation of this scene, see Gollance, "'Spaß mit der schönen Jüdin'," 70–71.

98. Mosenthal, "Schlemilchen," in *Erzählungen aus dem jüdischen Familienleben*, 25. Translation is my own. For an English translation that was originally published in 1907, see Mosenthal, "Schlemilchen," in *Stories of Jewish Home Life*, 50–51. The story was originally serialized in 1877 in *Über Land und Meer*.

99. For more about this novel, see Hess, "Fictions of a German-Jewish Public."

100. Jacobowski, *Werther der Jude*, 33. See also, ibid. 29. For a discussion of this stereotype, see Wallach, *Passing Illusions*, 102–110.

101. Jacobowski, *Werther der Jude*, 34.

102. Ibid.

103. Auerbach, *Poet and Merchant*, 62. The dream foretells the young man's death. For German, see Auerbach, *Dichter und Kaufmann*, vol. 1, 80–81.

104. For instance, tragic characters Judith Trachtenberg (*Judith Trachtenberg*) and Leo Wolff (*Werther der Jude*) later attend social dances that add to their conflicted feelings about their social positions.

105. Orfali, *A Jewish Girl in the Weimar Republic*, 149–150.

106. Ibid., 149.

Chapter 3

1. Abramowicz, *Profiles of a Lost World*, 65. For Yiddish, see Abramowicz, *Farshvundene geshtaltn*, 438.

2. Abramowicz, *Profiles of a Lost World*, 65. The translation describes the dance as a polka, but the Yiddish text calls it a hopke. For Yiddish, see Abramowicz, *Farshvundene geshtaltn*, 438. The derogatory term "*shikse*" for a non-Jewish woman is much stronger than the word choice of "Christian" in the published translation.

3. Abramowicz, *Profiles of a Lost World*, 65. For Yiddish, see Abramowicz, *Farshvundene geshtaltn*, 438.

4. It can be difficult to draw sharp distinctions between inns and taverns; see Kalik, *Movable Inn*, 164. For more about rural inns, see ibid., 165–168. Kalik notes that studies of rural eastern European Jews have been dominated by studies of tavernkeeping; see ibid., 219.

5. For discussions of rabbinic separations with regard to food, wine, and sexual matters respectively, see Kraemer, *Jewish Eating and Identity Through the Ages*; Fram, *Ideals Face Reality*, 95–105; Boyarin, *Carnal Israel*, 5–7.

6. Dynner, *Men of Silk*, 224–225. Gottlober was himself the son-in-law of a Jewish tavernkeeper in Chernikhov (Ukraine). See Ribak, "Getting Drunk, Dancing, and Beating Each Other Up," 205.

7. Jews viewed Christian peasants as "strong, coarse, drunk, illiterate, dumb, volatile, and sexually promiscuous"; see ibid., 203.

8. At the time of the partitions of Poland–Lithuania (1772–1795), approximately 85 percent of taverns were leased by Jews, and about 37 percent of Jews were tavernkeepers or their family members. Jews remained highly involved in the liquor trade despite efforts to ban Jews from rural tavernkeeping. See Dynner, *Yankel's Tavern*, 10, 15–16, 52–56, 81. For the economic history of the liquor trade in Poland, see ibid., 25–26. For information about how Jews negotiated restrictions on tavernkeeping, see Mahler, *Hasidism and the Jewish Enlightenment*, 21, 177–179. See also Kalik, *Movable Inn*, 26–29, for more about the social dynamics of Jewish-run taverns.

9. In nineteenth-century Polish (folk) literature, Jewish tavernkeepers are often (but not always) portrayed as devilish, crooked, nocturnal characters; see, for instance, Opalski, *The Jewish Tavern-Keeper and His Tavern*, 16–20. Unlike the Jewish literature discussed here, Opalski notes that Jewish tavernkeepers in Polish literature tended not to have families (ibid., 30). Nonetheless, the most famous Jewish tavernkeeper in Polish literature is almost certainly Jankiel from Adam Mickiewicz's 1834 epic poem, *Pan Tadeusz*. As reflects the revolutionary moment in which it was written, Jankiel loves Poland and raises his children accordingly. He is also a skilled *tsimbl* (hammered dulcimer) player, who accompanies the gentry in their joyful polonaise that ends the narrative. See the bilingual edition: Mickiewicz, *Pan Tadeusz*, 560–575.

10. See, for instance, Cahan, *The Education of Abraham Cahan*, 13. For Yiddish, see

Cahan, *Bleter fun mayn lebn*, 35–36. For traveler's reports of tavern interiors, see Dynner, *Yankel's Tavern*, 21–22.

11. Abramowicz notes that rural Jews, especially innkeepers, were concerned about their children converting; see Abramowicz, *Profiles of a Lost World*, 65–66. For Yiddish, see Abramowicz, *Farshvundene geshtaltn*, 439–440. See also Dynner, *Yankel's Tavern*, 69. For occasions for peasant dancing, see ibid., 29. Hasidic Rebbe Menachem Mendel of Rymanów (d. 1815) complained that Jewish tavernkeepers "could neither pray in a prayer quorum nor immerse themselves in ritual baths. Worse, they were violating the Sabbath, and their children were mingling with gentiles and 'slipping into coarseness [*gashmiyut*].'" Ibid., 69.

12. Ibid. 1, 3–4; Opalski, *The Jewish Tavern-Keeper*, esp. 9. Sholem Aleichem writes that his siblings were embarrassed when their parents became tavernkeepers; see Sholem Aleichem, *From the Fair*, 68. For Yiddish, see Sholem Aleichem, *Fun'm yarid*, 199. For more about Sholem Aleichem's writing about taverns, see Mahalel, "*Nit dos dorf, nit di kretshme.*" Maimon describes how his grandfather, a leaseholder on the estates of Prince Radzivil, was falsely accused of ritual murder by the local priest after he stopped accepting his credit in the tavern. See *The Autobiography of Solomon Maimon*, 8–9. For German, see *Salomon Maimons Lebensgeschichte*, 19–22. Kaufmann's ghetto tale, *Der böhmische Dorfjude* (The Bohemian Village Jew) is an example of German-language Jewish regional fiction that influenced Kompert; see Kaufmann, *Der böhmische Dorfjude*. Opalski also notes the negative role of the tavern as an educational institution in Polish writer Eliza Orzeskowa's 1874 novel *Eli Makower*, which was first published in the mid-1870s: "The worst traits of Eli, the main character of this novel, are the fruits of his 'education in the tavern.'" See Opalski, *The Jewish Tavern-Keeper*, 60. For a description from the 1880s of a rough tavern crowd, including beggars, who horrify the Jewish tavernkeepers, see An-sky, "In the Tavern." For information about Russian versions and a Yiddish translation of this story, see ibid., 209. For discussion of this story in connection with An-sky's own biography, see Safran, *Wandering Soul*, 12–13.

13. Schainker, *Confessions of the Shtetl*, 87.

14. Dynner, *Yankel's Tavern*, 32.

15. Asch, *Salvation*, 177, 180–184. For Yiddish, see Asch, *Der tilim-yid*, 299, 305–311.

16. For more about arendators, see Rosman, *The Lords' Jews*, 106–142.

17. Ibid., 114. See also Dynner, *Yankel's Tavern*, 17–18.

18. Rosman, *The Lords' Jews*, 114.

19. Trunk, *Poylin: My Life*, 34. For Yiddish, Trunk, *Poylin: Zikhroynes*, 57.

20. Trunk, *Poylin: My Life*, 34. For Yiddish, Trunk, *Poylin: Zikhroynes*, 57.

21. Bergner, *On Long Winter Nights . . .*, 53. For Yiddish, see Bergner, *In di lange vinternekht*, 33. Bergner's son was the Yiddish writer Melech Ravitch (pseudonym for Zekharye-Khone Bergner).

22. Roth, *The Radetzky March*, 78. For German, see Roth, *Radetzkymarsch*, 95.

23. Singer, *The Brothers Ashkenazi*, 192. For Yiddish, see Singer, *Di brider Ashkenazi*, 269.

24. Singer, *The Brothers Ashkenazi*, 194. For Yiddish, see Singer, *Di brider Ashkenazi*, 272.

25. Shtok, "Mandeln" in *Gezamelte dertseylungen*, 139, 143. For analysis, see Gollance, "A Dance"; Pratt, "Fradel Schtok," 88.

26. For rabbinic condemnations on Jewish tavernkeepers, including some that blame them for the 1648 Chmielnicki massacres, see Dynner, *Yankel's Tavern*, 65–66.

27. Sacher-Masoch, *Der Judenraphael*, 69.

28. Pinski, *Yankl der Shmid*, in *Dramen*, 20. For a translation of this play, see Nahma Sandrow's volume, *Yiddish Plays for Reading and Performance*. I thank her for sharing information about her book, which was still in production when I was completing this manuscript.

29. Pinski, *Yankl der Shmid*, in *Dramen*, 103–104. The marriage is threatened when Yankl drinks in celebration of his son's circumcision and ends up flirting and dancing with women. See Gollance, "Harmonious Instability," 229–233.

30. Opatoshu, *Romance of a Horse Thief*, 170. For Yiddish, see Opatoshu, *A roman fun a ferd-ganef*, 48.

31. Opatoshu, *Romance of a Horse Thief*, 171. For Yiddish, see Opatoshu, *A roman fun a ferd-ganef*, 48.

32. Opatoshu, *Romance of a Horse Thief*, 171. For Yiddish, see Opatoshu, *A roman fun a ferd-ganef*, 48.

33. Trunk, *Poylin: My Life*, 73. For Yiddish, see Trunk, *Poylin: Zikhroynes*, 116.

34. Trunk, *Poylin: My Life*, 75–76. For Yiddish, see Trunk, *Poylin: Zikhroynes*, 119.

35. For gender differences in Jewish education, see Parush, *Reading Jewish Women*, 59, 64–67. For an example from Polish modernist literature of a Jewish tavernkeeper's daughter who is charmed by music and peasant dancing, see Wypiański, *The Wedding*, 37–38. For Polish, see Wypiański, *Wesele*, 38–40.

36. This literary theme is corroborated by the high rate of conversion among the children of Polish tavernkeepers. See Dynner, *Yankel's Tavern*, 19, 69–70.

37. Peretz, "Downcast Eyes," 232. Morgentaler's decision to translate "kretshme" as "tavern" rather than "inn" shows that she is emphasizing the tavern portion of the inn. For Yiddish, see Peretz, "Aropgelozte oygn," in *Ale verk fun Y. L. Peretz*, 119–120.

38. For other examples of a tavern- or innkeeper's daughter fantasizing about a non-Jewish man, see Shmeruk, "Jews and Poles in Yiddish Literature," 181.

39. Peretz, "Downcast Eyes," 237. For Yiddish, see Peretz, "Aropgelozte oygn," in *Ale verk fun Y. L. Peretz*, 125.

40. Peretz, "Downcast Eyes," 237. For Yiddish, see Peretz, "Aropgelozte oygn," in *Ale verk fun Y. L. Peretz*, 125.

41. Kompert, *Die Kinder des Randars*, 86.

42. For instance, see Hess, *Middlebrow Literature and the Making of German-Jewish Identity*, 85; Wittemann, *Draußen vor dem Ghetto*, 280.

43. For more information on Bohemian arendators, see Winkelbauer, "Leopold Kompert und die böhmischen Landjuden," in Horch and Denkler, *Conditio Judaica: Judentum, Antisemitismus und deutschsprachige Literatur*, 190. In 1724, there were 328 Jewish arendators, and Winkelbauer suspects this figure did not change much until the middle of the nineteenth century when Jews began entering the liberal professions. Ibid., 192.

44. For more about the Jewish acculturation process in Bohemia, see Kieval, *Languages of Community*, 65.

45. See the introduction of this book for more about this genre.

46. Hess, *Middlebrow Literature and the Making of German-Jewish Identity*, 72.

47. See, for instance, Leuenberger, "'Wo ist des Juden Vaterland'—Jerusalem im Werk Leopold Komperts," in *Schrift-Raum Jerusalem*, 31–68; Wittemann, *Draußen vor dem Ghetto*, 277–286.

48. Palacky, *Geschichte von Böhmen*, 189.

49. Waldau, *Böhmische Nationaltänze*, 8.

50. Jolizza, *Die Schule des Tanzes*, 280–281.

51. Mendel Wilna describes the dancing at his own wedding as a kind of torture, since he would rather rebuild Jerusalem than establish a family: "There they danced around my wife and did thousands of follies. Suddenly she disappeared with the 'old women.' Then they came back, and danced around me and laughed and shrieked. They physically dragged me away, I resisted them, but they laughed about it, you can't imagine the laughter." Kompert, *Die Kinder des Randars*, 78–79.

52. Ibid., 28.

53. Ibid. I use Kompert's transliteration of this Yiddish word.

54. Ibid., 68.

55. Ibid.

56. Peleg, "Heroic Conduct," 33.

57. Stanislawski, *Zionism and the Fin de Siècle*, 94.

58. Kompert, *Die Kinder des Randars*, 119.

59. Ibid., 103.

60. Hess, *Middlebrow Literature and the Making of German-Jewish Identity*, 87.

61. Kompert, *Die Kinder des Randars*, 43–44.

62. Kobrin, "Yankl Boyle," in *Gezamelte shriftn*, 39, 43, 46. Kobrin refers more specifically to the Kriat Shema (Yiddish: *krishme*), sometimes called the Bedtime Shema.

63. Although less studied than tavernkeeping, fishing was also a common Jewish profession, especially since Jewish arendators leased lakes and oversaw groups of Jewish and non-Jewish fishermen. For more about Jewish fishermen in Lithuania, see Abramowicz, *Profiles of a Lost World*, 52–58. For Yiddish, see Abramowicz, *Farshvundene geshtaltn*, 417–427.

64. According to ethnomusicologist Dmitri Zisl Slepovich in a personal communication, igrishches are ritual games, typically for young people who want to find a marriage

partner, with roots in pre-Christian religion. For more information, the entry in a Belarusian ethnographic encyclopedia is helpful, especially the opening description: "A folk gathering with dance-/game- and theatricalized performance. It has its beginnings in universal celebrations of pagan ritual, and has deep roots in East Slavic folklore." The theatricalized performance involves dance, verbal play, and karahod (circle dance) games. Activities include stylized walking, mock weddings, mock funerals, and other games. I am grateful to Michael Alpert for his translation of this entry. See Z. [Zinaida] N. Mazheika, "Ihryshcha," in *Etnahrafija Bielarusi,* eds. I. P. Shamjakin et al. (Minsk: "Belaruskaja Saveckaja Encyklapedyja" imia Petrusja Broŭki, 1989), 218–219 (quote is from p. 218).

65. Kobrin, "Yankl Boyle," in *Gezamelte shriftn,* 38.

66. Sandrow, *Vagabond Stars,* 172–173.

67. Ibid., 172.

68. Ibid. Like some other scholars, Sandrow classifies this text as a novel.

69. "Leon Kobrin, Noted Jewish Writer, Dies at 73 Author of Many Plays, Novels," *JTA* (April 2, 1946): https://www.jta.org/1946/04/02/archive/leon-kobrin-noted-jewish-writer-dies-at-73-author-of-many-plays-novels

70. Sandrow, *Vagabond Stars,* 173. For an English translation of the play, see Kobrin, "Yankel Boyla," in *Epic and Folk Plays of the Yiddish Theatre,* 101–139. While Kobrin's novella narrates Natasha's appreciation of Yankl's dancing and only alludes to their experience as dance partners, in the play they actually dance together, at the urging of a crowd. Yet as soon as they finish, Yankl is chastised for forgetting his dying father. Indeed, in the play, Yankl's romantic interest in Natasha defies his father's wish that he marry his cousin Khayke. See Kobrin, *Yankl Boyle,* 50.

71. For more about Kobrin and a brief excerpt of the play in English, see Sandrow, *Vagabond Stars,* 172–175.

72. YIVO Institute for Jewish Research, Leon Kobrin Papers, RG 376, Folder 7.

73. See Hoberman, *Bridge of Light,* 266. He quotes Mukdoyni's *Teyater* as found in Howe and Bibo, *How We Lived,* 261–262. On p. 262 in the Howe and Bibo volume, Mukdoyni notes that in peacetime "[the molodyets] sang and danced and laughed."

74. For a discussion of dancing and early Zionism, see Chapter 4.

75. In the novella he drowns himself; in the play he hangs himself.

76. Kobrin, *Yankl Boyle,* 13.

77. Ibid., 14.

78. Ibid., 15.

79. For more about the generation gap around 1900 between immigrants to the United States and their children, see Chinn, *Inventing Modern Adolescence,* 77–102.

80. Kobrin, *Yankl Boyle,* 17, 18.

81. Ibid., 20.

82. Ibid. Yankl appears to dance *prisyadka,* in the style of the kazatsky (i.e., Cossack) squat dance.

83. Maes, *A History of Russian Music*, 28. For an example of a kamarinskaia performance in a Yiddish theatrical performance, see Berkovitsh, *Hundert yor yidish teater in Rumenye*, 31. I thank Michael Alpert for his translation of A. L. Varlamaj, "Kamarynskaja," in *Etnahrafija Biełarusi*, eds. I. P. Shamjakin et al. (Minsk: "Belaruskaja Saveckaja Encyklapedyja" imia Petrusja Broŭki, 1989), 238.

84. Dostoyevsky, *The Village of Stepanchikovo and Its Inhabitants*, 103–104. For Russian, see Dostoevsky, "Selo Stepanchikovo i ego obitateli," 76–77.

85. For a comparison with the solo dance style of traditional Jewish men, see Feldman, *Klezmer*, 182–183.

86. Kobrin, *Yankl Boyle*, 22.

87. Ibid., 19.

88. Ibid.

89. It is interesting to note that Kobrin never describes Nokhem's tavern. In contrast to the boisterous scene during Rachel's death in *Die Kinder des Randars*, Kobrin notes that the tavern is empty when Nokhem is on his deathbed. Ibid., 21.

90. Ibid., 42.

91. For more about Yiddish literary portrayals of lower-class non-Jews in both Europe and the United States, see Ribak, "Getting Drunk, Dancing, and Beating Each Other Up," 203–224.

92. Kobrin, *Yankl Boyle*, 22–23.

93. Ibid., 40.

94. While Kompert explains why Moritz is sent to Gymnasium, Kobrin does not detail why Yankl does not seem to have the option of following in his profession as a tavernkeeper. Perhaps his uncle preferred to take over a profitable lease, and certainly Yankl's decision to become a fisherman opens up several plot threads for Kobrin, yet there were also social and legal reasons for young Jews to move away from tavernkeeping in the late nineteenth century. See Dynner, *Yankel's Tavern*, 153–174. For comparison, in Roth's *Radetzkymarsch* a Jewish tavernkeeper in Habsburg Galicia is forced to pass on the ancestral tavern to his daughters and sons-in-law because his male descendants have pursued positions as officers, clerks, and intellectuals, see Roth, *The Radetzky March*, 78. For German, see Roth, *Radetzkymarsch*, 96.

Chapter 4

1. Baron, *Die Judenfrage auf dem Wiener Kongreß*, 125–126.

2. Regina Neisser, "Fanny von Arnstein: Zur 100. Wiederkehr ihres Todestages (8. Juni, 1818)," *Im deutschen Reich: Zeitschrift des Centralvereins Deutscher Staatsbürger Jüdischen Glaubens* 24, no. 6 (June 1918): 255.

3. Spiel, *Fanny von Arnstein*, 287. For German, see La Garde-Chambonas, *Gemälde des Wiener Kongresses*, vol. 1, 350.

4. McCagg, *A History of Habsburg Jews*, 63.

5. La Garde-Chambonas, *Gemälde des Wiener Kongresses*, vol. 2, 255.

6. See Baron, *Die Judenfrage auf dem Wiener Kongreß*, 50–54; Graetz, *Geschichte der Juden von den ältesten Zeiten bis auf die Gegenwart*, 327; Kohler, "Jewish Rights at the Congresses of Vienna," 36; 45–47.

7. For a discussion of this play in the context of eighteenth-century German culture, see Delphine Bechtel, "Reb Henoch, oder: Woß tut me damit?—Hybride Sprache, Zwittergestalten: Kulturen im Kontakt in einer jüdischen Komödie der Aufklärungszeit," in Euchel, *Reb Henoch*, 19–44, esp. 28.

8. Bourgeois Jews might even view attendance at balls as a duty. See Kaplan, *The Making of the Jewish Middle Class*, 132.

9. Lewald, *The Education of Fanny Lewald*, 94. For German, see Lewald, *Meine Lebensgeschichte*, vol. 1, 254.

10. Edgeworth, *Harrington*, 168. Edgeworth wrote *Harrington* in large part as a corrective for her previous negative depictions of Jews. For more about her epistolary friendship with Rachel Mordechai, which led her to rethink her Jewish characters, see MacDonald, *The Education of the Heart*.

11. [Meyer], *Zwei Schwestern*, 161. For more about Meyer and her work, see Hess, *Middlebrow Literature and the Making of German-Jewish Identity*, 139–154; Lezzi, *"Liebe is meine Religion!"* 136–155, esp. 144–145 for a discussion of the ball scene.

12. [Meyer], *Zwei Schwestern*, 165. She refers to Tantalus from Greek mythology, a Lydian king who is condemned to stand in a pool of water under a fruit tree for eternity; the water recedes from him when he tries to drink from it, and the fruit escapes his grasp when he tries to eat.

13. Goldschmidt, *A Jew*, 150. For Danish, see Goldschmidt, *En Jøde*, 141. For more about Goldschmidt, see Gurley, *Meïr Aaron Goldschmidt and the Poetics of Jewish Fiction*.

14. At the ball, Bendixen meets Thora, a Christian woman, and they fall in love. Yet even in Thora's socially liberal family, Bendixen feels out of place and is sensitive to what he perceives as anti-Jewish slights, which lead him to break off the engagement. He proves himself in the military yet ultimately returns to the Jewish community of his youth to become a stereotypical Jewish financier. The ball scene thus represents the pinnacle of Bendixen's aspirations in Danish society.

15. *Elvire* was published anonymously between March 25, 1868, and June 3, 1868. Lehmann later anthologized the story and claimed authorship in his ca. 1893 collection *Gesammelte Erzählungen für das jüdische Haus* (Collected Stories for the Jewish Home). Although I usually refer to the book editions of works that were initially serialized, I refer to the edition of *Elvire* in *Der Israelit* because it follows a clearer page numbering system and is easily accessible through a digital edition. See also Lezzi, "Secularism and Neo-Orthodoxy." For a rather hagiographic biography by Lehmann's son, see Lehmann, *Dr. Markus Lehmann*. For more about *Der Israelit*, see Hess, *Middlebrow Literature and the Making of German-Jewish Identity*, 159–160.

16. For a discussion of Lehmann's rabbi narrators that mentions *Elvire*, see Hess, *Middlebrow Literature and the Making of the German-Jewish Identity*, 177–181.

17. [Lehmann], *Elvire, Der Israelit* 9, no. 14–15 (April 1, 1868): 239.

18. Ibid.

19. Ibid.

20. Ibid.

21. Reisinger, *Die Tanzkunst und die Tänze*, 53.

22. *Judith Trachtenberg* was serialized between 1889 and 1890 in *Deutsche Dichtung* (German Literature), the journal Franzos edited in Berlin and published in book form in 1891. Eli Rosenblatt drew my attention to a serialized version of *Judith Trachtenberg* in the Dutch colonial newspaper *Java-Bode* (between April 4 and July 9, 1891) in Batavia, Dutch East Indies (today Jakarta, Indonesia). The novel was translated into English in the same year and was also translated into Danish (1890) and French (2003). A Yiddish translation was published as *Der graf un di yidin* (The Count and the Jewess) in two editions, in 1895 and 1904. In 1920, Henrik Galeen made a film version, which has been lost. George Roland, a New York-based editor who refashioned extant films as talkies, appears to have re-released much of Galeen's footage with a frame narrative as *Yidishe tokhter* (*A Daughter of Her People*, 1932). For more about these film versions, see Hoberman, *Bridge of Light*, 60, 182–184, 188–189.

23. Steiner, *Karl Emil Franzos*, 29.

24. Ernst, "'Ach! Was wißt ihr Gebildeten in den großen Städten . . .':—Zum Motiv des Lesens in 'Ghettogeschichten' von Karl Emil Franzos," in *Karl Emil Franzos*, 78; Gabriele von Glasenapp, "'Nur die Liebe macht Selig, der Glaube aber blind.'—Zur Inszenierung interreligiöser Liebesbeziehungen im Werk von Karl Emil Franzos," in Ernst, *Karl Emil Franzos*, 59.

25. Steiner, *Karl Emil Franzos*, 47. For more about Franzos's concerns about Austrian antisemitism, see Margarita Pazi, "Karl Emil Franzos' Assimilationsvorstellung und Assimilationserfahrung," in Horch and Denkler, *Conditio Judaica*, 229.

26. Franzos, *Judith Trachtenberg: Erzählung*, 9. I have opted to use my own translations. For an alternative English translation of the relevant dance scenes, see Franzos, *Judith Trachtenberg: A Novel*, 4–23.

27. Franzos, *Judith Trachtenberg: Erzählung*, 21–22.

28. Ibid., 26.

29. Ibid.

30. Ibid., 27.

31. Ludewig, "Fiktionale Authentizität und poetischer Realismus," 150.

32. Lesser, *A Jewish Youth in Dresden*, 113.

33. Zangwill, *The Children of the Ghetto: A Study of a Peculiar People*, in *Selected Works of Israel Zangwill*, 128. He cites *Midrash Tanchuma, Naso* 1.

34. Ibid., 141.

35. While Jewish leaders and laypeople from across the denominational spectrum have wrestled with issues related to women's agency in marriage rituals, nineteenth- and early twentieth-century Jewish fiction and film sometimes treated the idea of a woman getting married without her consent as a culturally specific plot twist. For more about Jewish marriage, see Labovitz, *Marriage and Metaphor*.

36. Zangwill, *The Children of the Ghetto*, 140.

37. For more about this novel, see Valman, "Amy Levy and the Literary Representation of the Jewess," esp. 93 for a reference to the ballroom; Valman, *The Jewess in Nineteenth-Century British Literary Culture*, 173–205; Rochelson, "Jews, Gender, and Genre in Late-Victorian England," esp. 321 where Rochelson describes Judith and Reuben's meeting at the ball as the climactic scene in the novel.

38. Levy, *Reuben Sachs*, 146.

39. Ibid., 153.

40. Ibid., 166.

41. Ibid., 148.

42. [Amy Levy], "Middle-Class Jewish Women of To-Day. By a Jewess," *Jewish Chronicle* (September 17, 1886): 7.

43. Levy, *Reuben Sachs*, 169.

44. Singer, *The Family Moskat*, 485. The novel was first serialized in the *Forverts* from 1945 to 1948. For Yiddish, see Singer, *Di familye Mushkat*, vol. 2, 596–597.

45. Singer, *The Family Moskat*, 491. Singer, *Di familye Mushkat*, vol. 2, 604.

46. For biographical information, see Werner J. Cahnman, "The Life of Clementine Kraemer," unpublished manuscript, 1963, Clementine Kraemer Collection, Leo Baeck Institute, AR 2402, Folder 47.

47. For recent scholarship on Krämer, see Loentz, "The Literary Double Life of Clementine Krämer"; Loentz, "'The Most Famous Jewish Pacifist Was Jesus of Nazareth . . .'"; Wallach, *Passing Illusions*, 117–121. For a specific discussion of her work on dance, see Gollance, "Harmonious Instability," 276–283.

48. Clementine Krämer, "Der Weg des jungen Hermann Kahn," *Allgemeine Zeitung des Judentums* 82, no. 10 (March 8, 1918): 119. The novel was serialized from February 1 to April 19, 1918.

49. For instance, Yiddish writer David Ignatoff describes a New York Zionist ball in his novel *In keslgrub* (In Whirlpool). See Ignatoff, *In keslgrub*, 121–125.

50. Wobick-Segev, *Homes Away from Home*, 134–138.

51. Shoham, *Carnival in Tel Aviv*, 12.

52. Spiegel, *Embodying Hebrew Culture*, 99. As Spiegel points out, all three prizewinners had trained in Europe; see ibid., 104.

53. Ibid., 1. For more about this Romanian and Moldovan folk dance, see Yaakov Mazor, "Hora," *Jewish Music Research Center*: https://www.jewish-music.huji.ac.il/content/hora

54. The biblical story is recounted in I Kings 10:1–10, 13. For more about the Queen of Sheba as a dancer, see Heschel, "Lilith," 18; Silberman, "The Queen of Sheba in Judaic Tradition," 84.

55. Clementine Krämer, "Der Weg des jungen Hermann Kahn," *Allgemeine Zeitung des Judentums* 82, no. 11 (March 15, 1918): 130.

56. Ibid.

57. Schnitzer, *Höfische Maskeraden*, 2–3.

58. Clementine Krämer, "Der Weg des jungen Hermann Kahn," *Allgemeine Zeitung des Judentums* 82, no. 11 (March 15, 1918): 130.

59. Ibid.

60. Ibid.

61. Clementine Krämer, "Der Weg des jungen Hermann Kahn," *Allgemeine Zeitung des Judentums* 82, no. 12 (March 22, 1918): 142.

62. Clementine Krämer, "Der Weg des jungen Hermann Kahn," *Allgemeine Zeitung des Judentums* 82, no. 11 (March 15, 1918): 130.

63. Clementine Krämer, "Der Weg des jungen Hermann Kahn," *Allgemeine Zeitung des Judentums* 82, no. 12 (March 22, 1918): 142.

64. Ibid.

65. Ibid.

66. Ibid.

67. For Krämer's political activities, see Loentz, "'The Most Famous Jewish Pacifist Was Jesus of Nazareth,'" 126–127.

68. Krämer explains that Salomea was named for her grandfather Salomon (Solomon) according to the traditional Ashkenazic custom of honoring a deceased relative, but she suggests that her name could be identified with the Salome dance craze of the turn of the century, even though she was born in Galicia. See Clementine Krämer, "Der Weg des jungen Hermann Kahn," *Allgemeine Zeitung des Judentums* 82, no. 10 (March 8, 1918): 118. For more about how Salome was represented by Jewish authors, see Gollance, "Delilah's Dance."

69. Stanislawski, in *Zionism and the Fin de Siècle* (p. 93), notes that for Zionist leaders Theodor Herzl and Max Nordau,

> [A]t least as insidious as the ghetto Jew was the bourgeois Jew, represented as a fat (and effeminate) cigar-smoking capitalist with a carefully coiffed wife (or mistress) on his arm or as a deracinated German- or Austrian-Jewish student, intellectual, lawyer, or journalist at home in the coffee house and lecture hall but cut off entirely from nature, from military life, from "real" manhood.

70. For a discussion of early Zionist attitudes toward race and mixed marriages, see Dafna Hirsch, "Zionist Eugenics, Mixed Marriage, and the Creation of a 'New Jewish Type.'"

71. For more about women and the Zionist movement, see Berkowitz, *Zionist Culture and West European Jewry Before the First World War*, 92–94; Rose, *Jewish Women in Fin de Siècle Vienna*, 109–140. Allison Rose (ibid., 121) notes:

> The Zionist movement concentrated on distancing itself from perceived traditional gender relationships of the East European shtetl, in which the physically weak (yet at the same time privileged, due to his access to Jewish learning) Jewish man was dominated by his strong-willed and worldly wife. In contrast, Zionism criticized the bourgeois Jewish woman for not working for the Zionist movement, as well as for failing to attend to the Jewish religious and cultural needs of the family. In this sense, Zionists idealized the domestic attributes of the traditional Jewish woman.

For Jewish women's engagement with leftist politics, see Shepherd, *A Price Below Rubies*, and esp. 176–179 for a comparison with women's participation in the Zionist movement. Elissa Bemporad's forthcoming biography of Bundist activist Ester Frumkin also promises to illuminate this issue.

72. Goldman, *Living My Life*, 18.

73. Ibid., 19.

Chapter 5

1. Singer, *The Brothers Ashkenazi*, 78. For Yiddish, see Singer, *Di brider Ashkenazi*, 104. For more about the "*daytsh*"—a term that could be used for non-Jewish Germans, acculturated German Jews (yekes), or westernized eastern European Jews—see Schumacher-Brunhes, "The Figure of the Daytsh in Yiddish Literature." Singer typically uses the term "daytsh" in the novel to refer to the large non-Jewish German population of Łódź.

2. Singer, *The Brothers Ashkenazi*, 78. For Yiddish, see Singer, *Di brider Ashkenazi*, 104.

3. Singer, *Di familye Mushkat*, vol. 1, 272. Translation is my own. For a published English translation, see Singer, *The Family Moskat*, 216–217. The novel was first serialized in the *Forverts* from 1945 to 1948.

4. Singer, *Di familye Mushkat*, vol. 1, 272. Translation is my own. For a published translation, see Singer, *The Family Moskat*, 217. This version renders "*shvarts-khasene*" as "madhouse" and "*yevonim*" (lit. Greeks; word refers to Russian or Ukrainian soldiers or policemen or ruffians) as "peasants."

5. For more about Ashkenazic weddings and wedding dances, see Friedland, ""Tantsn Is Lebn," 76–80; Kirshenblatt-Gimblett, "Weddings"; Seid, "Wedding Dances."

6. Although set in a German village rather than a shtetl, Arie Löb Rozenthal's 1822 Yiddish comedy *Die Hochzeit zu Grobsdorf* (The Wedding in Grobsdorf) addresses issues of gender, age, and ethnic mixing on the dance floor in connection with a

wedding. This play has received scholarly attention as an example of Western Yiddish. See Lowenstein, "The Complicated Language Situation of German Jewry." 31. I thank Lea Schäfer for sharing her draft of a forthcoming play edition.

7. For a description of a broygez tants, see Yom-Tov Levinsky, "The Angry Dance," in Kugelmass and Boyarin, *From a Ruined Garden*, 125–126. For Yiddish, see Levinsky "Der broygez tants." For analysis, see Gollance, "Gesture, Repertoire, and Emotion," 113–114.

8. Although most ethnographic accounts describe the broygez tants as a dance performed by women, Vizonsky notes a variation for a man and a woman; see Vizonsky, *Ten Jewish Folk Dances*, 21–24.

9. Zunser, *Yesterday*, 91. Zunser was a playwright and journalist. Her father, Nokhem Meyer Shaykevitch, also known as Shomer, was perhaps the most famous writer of Yiddish melodramas.

10. As discussed in Chapter 1, when the Singer brothers' grandfather stopped the "*shatnez-tents*" (mixed dance).

11. See Feldman, *Klezmer*, 74–75, for a description of freylekhs forms and variations. For names of regional variants, see Gollance, "Gesture, Repertoire, and Emotion," 108–109.

12. For more about wedding entertainment, see Lifschutz, "Merrymakers at a Jewish Wedding."

13. Wengeroff, *Memoirs of a Grandmother*, vol. 2, 71. For German, see Wengeroff, *Memoiren einer Grossmutter*, 180.

14. Feldman, *Klezmer*, 148.

15. See Safran, "Dancing with Death and Salvaging Jewish Culture" for discussion of Ashkenazic folk practices that juxtapose weddings (and wedding dancing) with death. For a discussion of whether the ritual of breaking of a glass at weddings is a sign of mourning for Jerusalem, see Goldberg, *Jewish Passages*, 148–158. For a discussion of Jewish legal opinions about music at wedding celebrations after the destruction of the Second Temple, see Kahn, "Music in Halachic Perspective."

16. For further discussion of this scene and the film *Der dibek*, see Alpert, "*Freylekhs* on Film," 133–134; Hoberman, *Bridge of Light*, 279–284; Meir, *Stepchildren of the Shtetl*, 192–195; as well as my forthcoming article on choreographer Judith Berg in the edited volume *Women on the Yiddish Stage*.

17. For instance, Kompert, *Die Kinder des Randars*, 78–79; Kompert, *Die Schweigerin*, vol. 4, 47; Sholem Aleichem, *The Nightingale*, 194; for Yiddish, see Sholem Aleichem, *Yosele Solovey*, in *Ale verk fun Sholem Aleykhem*, vol. 2, 191–192; Isaac Bashevis Singer, "The Black Wedding," in *Collected Stories*, 180–182; for Yiddis, see Isaac Bashevis Singer, "Di shvarts-khasene," in *Gimpl tam: Un andere dertseylungen*, 309. Here, as in *Di familye Mushkat*, Singer uses the term "black wedding" for a misbegotten wedding (rather than referring to the practice of marrying off marginal people in a cemetery

in order to combat cholera epidemics). For a discussion of how nineteenth-century authors and memoirists depicted arranged marriages as traumatic for young men and women, especially in contrast to romantic narratives, see Seidman, *The Marriage Plot*, 71–82.

18. Kreitman, *The Dance of the Demons*, 211. For Yiddish, see Kreitman, *Der sheydim-tants*, 243.

19. The novel was serialized as *Esther* in the *Allgemeine Zeitung des Judentums* from April to June 1920 and as *Die Tänzerin* (The Dancer) in the *Israelitisches Familienblatt* (Israelite Family Paper) from September to November 1920. For more about the novel, see Wallach, *Passing Illusions*, 118–121, esp. 118 for its publication history.

20. Clementine Krämer, "Esther," *Allgemeine Zeitung des Judentums* 84, no. 15 (April 8, 1920): 166.

21. Ibid.

22. Baron, "Family," 58. For Hebrew, see Baron, "Mishpahah," 11.

23. Baron, "Family," 83. For Hebrew, Baron, "Mishpahah," 30.

24. Baron, "Family," 84. For Hebrew, Baron, "Mishpahah," 31.

25. For more about cholera weddings, see Meir, *Stepchildren of the Shtetl*, esp. 89–116.

26. Sacher-Masoch, *Hasara Raba*, 24. Translation is my own. For a published English translation, see Leopold von Sacher-Masoch, "Hasara Raba," 41.

27. Schtok, "The Veil," in Forman et al., *Found Treasures*, 103. For Yiddish, see Shtok, "Der shlayer," in *Gezamelte dertseylungen*, 111.

28. Biale, "Masochism and Philosemitism," 312; Hyams, "The Whip and the Lamp," 68; Spinner, "Anecdotal Evidence," 66. Spinner takes a more critical stance toward Sacher-Masoch's portrayal of Jews and Jewish folkways; see ibid., 69–70. Burdekin also questions whether his work should be characterized as philosemitic; see Burdekin, *The Ambivalent Author*, 148.

29. See Maria Kłańska, "'. . . echt jüdische Geister: Der Geist der Liebe und der Geist der Familie.' Leopold von Sacher-Masoch und die Juden," in Kobelt-Groch and Salewski, *Leopold von Sacher-Masoch*, 197; Wodenegg, *Das Bild der Juden Osteuropas*, 32;

30. Milojević, *Die Poesie des Dilettantismus*, 219.

31. See Burdekin, *The Ambivalent Author*, 166–168.

32. For instance, Koschorke, *Leopold von Sacher-Masoch*.

33. Cybenko, "'Jetzt heißt es auftreten, eine neue Szene beginnt,'" 221; MacLeod, "Still Alive."

34. Sacher-Masoch texts with dance scenes include "Die Bachantinnen von Bonne humeur," in *Deutsche Hofgeschichten*, 42–50; "Chreubini und Théroigne," in *Im Reich der Töne*, 113–130; "Das Erntefest," in *Österreichische Erzählungen des 19. Jahrhunderts*, 292–310.

35. Burdekin, *The Ambivalent Author*, 164.

36. Sacher-Masoch's most famous work, *Venus im Pelz* (*Venus in Furs*) appeared in the first section, *Die Liebe* (Love), published in 1870, and *Hasara Raba* in the second volume, *Das Eigentum* (Property), which appeared in 1874.

37. Plutin's name may derive from Pluto, the Roman god of wealth and the underworld. Thanks to the participants in the November 2016 "Slavics Without Borders" colloquium at Yale University for suggesting this etymology.

38. For more on the tension between Raphael's eroticism and German Romanticism, see MacLeod, *Fugitive Objects*, 84–94.

39. For a discussion of the thorny connections between the artist, the masochist, and the male Jew, see Hans Otto Horch, "Der Außenseiter als 'Judenraphael.' Zu den Judengeschichten Leopolds von Sacher-Masoch," in *Conditio Judaica*, vol. 2, 277–278.

40. For literary examples, see Franzos, *Esterka Regina*, in *The Jews of Barnow*, 177. For German, see Franzos, *Esterka Regina*, in *Die Juden von Barnow*, 170; Peretz, "Downcast Eyes," 234; for Yiddish, see Peretz, "Aropgelozte oygn," in *Ale verk fun Y. L. Peretz*, 121. For more about the Esterka legend, see Shmeruk, *The Esterke Story in Yiddish and Polish Literature*. For more examples from German literature, see Krobb, *Die schöne Jüdin*.

41. Sacher-Masoch, *Der Judenraphael*, 94.

42. For more about cross-dressing, see Garber, *Vested Interests*, esp. 224–233, for ideas of Jewish effeminacy; see ibid., 304–352, for ethnic drag focusing on European attitudes toward Middle Eastern culture.

43. Sacher-Masoch, *Der Judenraphael*, 88. For more about Jewish kazatsky performance, see Gollance, "Gesture, Repertoire, and Emotion," 106–107.

44. For more about gender in orientalist discourse, see Brunotte, Ludewig, and Stähler, "Orientalism, Gender, and the Jews"; Said, *Orientalism*, for instance, 207–208.

45. Bakhtin, *Rabelais and His World*, 10.

46. Sacher-Masoch, *Der Judenraphael*, 72.

47. Ibid., 90.

48. See MacLeod, "Still Alive," 648.

49. [Shakespeare], *The Tragedy of Romeo and Juliet*, 1066.

50. Sacher-Masoch, *Der Judenraphael*, 90.

51. Hyams, "The Whip and the Lamp," 71.

52. Deleuze, "Coldness and Cruelty," in *Masochism*, 71.

53. For this description, see Heine, "Elementargeister." For libretto, see Justament, *Giselle, ou Les Wilis*.

54. Sacher-Masoch, *Souvenirs*, 64.

55. The *pas de deux* is a couple dance and a characteristic form of classical ballet that emerged in the nineteenth century. It represents the love of the two romantic leads.

56. For comparison of the two acts, see Banes, *Dancing Women*, 25.

57. Sacher-Masoch, *Der Judenraphael*, 139.

58. Ibid.

59. Garafola, "Introduction," in *Rethinking the Sylph*, 6. Sholem Asch uses a similar motif in his 1916 play *Unzer gloybn* (Our Faith), where the Jewish bride's Polish lover disguises himself as a Jewish man so that he can dance her out of an open door during a Jewish dance (presumably a mitsve tants) accompanied by a mazurka melody. See Asch, "Unzer gloybn: A folks-shtik in fir aktn," in *Dramatishe shriftn*, vol. 2, 61–62 (the page numbering in this volume is inconsistent). Fittingly, the bride's name is Esterke. I thank Caraid O'Brien for sharing her draft translation.

60. Sartre, *Anti-Semite and Jew*, 48–49.

61. Moyshe Nadir, "Bukh-eyn-bukh-oys: 'A roman fun a ferd-ganef un andere dert-seylungen,' fun Y. Opatoshu," *Der groyser kundes* [n.d.]: 10. Joseph Opatoshu Papers, YIVO Institute for Jewish Research, RG 436, Folder 400.

62. In fact, in the one English translation of the novella, the name of the dance has been replaced with a more familiar polka. While this decision avoids a footnote—an important consideration for the volume in which the translation was published—replacing a pas d'espagne with a polka complicates a close reading of the dance's structure.

63. Dan Opatoshu, "In New York Velder: Yosef/Joseph Opatoshu—Constructing a Multinational, 20th Century, (Very) Modern Yiddish Identity," in Koller et al., *Joseph Opatoshu*, 25.

64. Ibid., 26.

65. Joseph Opatoshu Papers, YIVO Institute for Jewish Research, RG 436, Folder 404.

66. Wisse, *A Little Love in Big Manhattan*, 41.

67. Although written by Opatoshu's son David and featuring a star-studded cast, including Yul Brynner, Abraham Polonsky's adventure film *Romance of a Horsethief* only loosely followed the plot of the Yiddish novella and contained no dancing. For more about physicality in the film, see Erens, *The Jew in American Cinema*, 313–314.

68. Krutikov, *Yiddish Fiction and the Crisis of Modernity*, 66.

69. Estraikh, Koller, and Krutikov, "Joseph Opatoshu's Search for *Yidishkayt*," in Koller et al., *Joseph Opatoshu*, 2.

70. Wisse, *A Little Love in Big Manhattan*, 51–52.

71. See Bottallo, *Guide du bon danseur*, 114. Helen Winkler includes Dick Crum's translation of the section on the pas d'espagne in her unpublished Yiddish dance handbook for the Edmonton International Folk Dancers; see Helen Winkler, "Yiddish Dance Workshop: Dances of the Jews of Eastern Europe" (workshop handbook, February 8, 2003), 30.

72. Opatoshu, "Oyf yener zayt brik," in *Gezamlte verk*, vol. 1, 119. First published in the second issue of Di Yunge's anthology *Literatur*, the story immediately won Opatoshu reknown.

73. Jeschke, "Hispanomania in Dance Theory and Choreography."

74. Montez was a performer and celebrity, and the controversial mistress of King

Ludwig I of Bavaria. See Jeschke, "Lola Montez and Spanish Dance in the 19th Century."

75. Ibid., 44.

76. Reisinger, *Die Tanzkunst und die Tänze*, 37.

77. Ibid., 198.

78. Ibid.

79. Ibid., 205.

80. Czerwinski, *Geschichte der Tanzkunst bei den kultivierten Völkern*, 59.

81. Ibid., 64.

82. Ibid., 64–65. He claims that the bolero is "a nobler, more modest and decent dance than the fandango." Ibid., 86.

83. Vizonsky, "Vegn yidishn folks-tants," 29.

84. See Gollance, "Harmonious Instability," 236.

85. Zanvl's enjoyment of the tavern sets in motion a series of events that lead to his meeting with his friend Gradul's wife Beyle and their scandalous dance at the wedding. His visit to the brothel is part of an episode that seals his criminal fate and leads to Beyle's widowhood (after her husband is fatally shot on a smuggling venture) and then to their forbidden sexual relationship. As a childless widow, according to Jewish law Beyle must either ritually divorce or formally marry her late husband's brother before becoming involved with another man. Opatoshu makes this point explicit in his Yiddish text.

86. For a discussion of the tavern scene, see Chapter 3.

87. Opatoshu, *Romance of a Horse Thief*, 180, with my more literal translations of dance terms in brackets. For Yiddish, see Opatoshu, *A roman fun a ferd-ganef*, 67.

88. Ibid.

89. Kadia Molodowsky Papers, YIVO Institute for Jewish Research, RG 703, Folder 70. The provenance of Molodovsky's account is unclear. While her name is spelled various ways, I have used the spelling from the published English translation of *Fun Lublin biz Nyu-York* (Kadya Molodovsky) for my analysis and the spelling from the Yiddish Book Center's Spielberg Digital Yiddish Library (Kadia Molodowsky) for citations from the original Yiddish.

Chapter 6

1. Between Tsar Alexander II's assassination in 1881 (and the subsequent pogroms) and 1924, two and a half million Jews from Russia, Poland, the Austro-Hungarian empire, and Romania immigrated to the United States. "Close to 85 percent of them came to New York City, and approximately 75 percent of those settled initially on the Lower East Side." See Polland and Soyer, *Emerging Metropolis*, 111.

2. While studies of American commercial leisure culture tend to emphasize dance halls, they also acknowledge a network of varied dance locations. McBee describes "a dance hall culture that, while fractured along class, ethnic, and gender lines . . . still

bound the different palaces, neighborhood halls, academies, and taxi-dance halls together." See McBee, *Dance Hall Days*, 53. See also Chinn, *Inventing Modern Adolescence*,
104, 107.

3. Yezierska, *Bread Givers*, 156, 177, 180.

4. Ibid., 193.

5. Chinn, *Inventing Modern Adolescence*, 103–104.

6. McBee draws a greater distinction between the courtship patterns of the 1880s
and 90s (when couples tended to marry quickly) and those of the first three decades
of the twentieth century (when young people engaged in a peer culture in dance halls)
than between the practices of different ethnic groups, although he acknowledges that
dance spaces (such as neighborhood clubs, weddings, or dance academies) were often
segregated by ethnic group. See McBee, *Dance Hall Days*, 14–15, 53, 82. Nonetheless,
scholars have noted some different cultural practices between different ethnic groups,
such as Italian families tending to be stricter with their children than Jewish families
(such as insisting upon chaperonage). See Ewen, *Immigrant Women in the Land of Dollars*, 209; McBee, *Dance Halls Days*, 29.

7. Peiss, *Cheap Amusements*, 88.

8. Ibid.

9. For more about different dance spaces, see McBee, *Dance Hall Days*, 53–59.
For dances organized by landsmanshaftn, see Soyer, *Jewish Immigrant Associations and
American Identity in New York*, 104–106. For a (negative) contemporary description of
dance academies, see Israels, "Dance-Hall Reform (1909)."

10. Peiss, *Cheap Amusements*, 88.

11. McBee, *Dance Hall Days*, 6.

12. Ibid., 10. See also ibid., 116–117. Even more bourgeois Jews shared these
concerns about male participation in dancing. An 1897 column in the first English-
language Jewish women's magazine complained about the rapid changes in popular
dance styles:

> At a recent dancing function the gyrations were as novel to me as if I had just arrived
> from the backwoods of Borneo. And others were apparently in the same predica-
> ment, for the walls were lined with seemingly eligible men and youths, and many a
> charming girl was obliged to take a feminine partner in preference to having none.

See "Partners for the Dance," *The American Jewess* 4, no. 6 (1897): 287.

13. McBee, *Dance Hall Days*, 3.

14. McBee notes tensions between all-male spaces (such as saloons or barbershops)
and homosocial leisure practices at dance halls (such as men congregating outside or
women waiting together for the next dance), on the one hand, and heterosocial courtship practices at dance halls, on the other, but it is worth noting that Jake in *Yekl* does
not engage in these activities. See McBee, *Dance Hall Days*, 42–45, 128–130.

15. For two opposing viewpoints, see Bowen, *Our Most Popular Recreation Controlled*

by the Liquor Interests, and William Inglis, "Is Modern Dancing Indecent?" *Harper's Weekly* 57 (May 17, 1913): 11–12.

16. Tashrak, "At a Ball." For Yiddish, see Tashrak, *Etikete*, 92.

17. Israels, "Dance-Hall Reform (1909)," 119.

18. George Kibbe Turner, "The Puzzle of the Underworld," *McClure's Magazine* 41, no. 3 (July 1913): 108. This piece is not overtly antisemitic like some of Turner's other writings, but it does describe dances with African American origins in perjorative terms.

19. Ibid.

20. Writing about the experience of Jewish women in "these places," which are "plastered across their front with the weird Oriental hieroglyphics of Yiddish posters," Turner says:

> She cannot yet talk the language, but rigid social custom demands that she be able to dance. . . . A strident two-piece orchestra blasts big, soul-satisfying pieces of noise out of the surrounding atmosphere, and finally a delightful young Jewish-American man, with plastered hair, a pasty face, and most finished and ingratiating manners, desires to teach her to dance. Her education in American life has begun. . . . These lonely and poverty-stricken girls, ignorant and dazed by the strange conditions of an unknown country, are very easily secured by promise of marriage, or even partnership.

George Kibbe Turner, "Daughters of the Poor: A Plain Story of the Development of New York City as a Leading Centre of the White Slave Trade of the World Under Tammany Hall," *McClure's Magazine* 34 (November 1909): 55–56. For more about Turner, see Soderland, *Sex Trafficking, Scandal, and the Transformation of Journalism*, 98–123.

21. Cahan, *The Rise of David Levinsky*, 42. For more about dance in Cahan's novel, see Gollance, "'*A Valtz* from the Land of *Valtzes!*'" 406–13. A shorter version of the novel was serialized in *McClure's Magazine* in 1913.

22. Cahan, *The Rise of David Levinsky*, 116.

23. Ibid., 140.

24. Ibid.

25. Ibid.

26. Cahan and his contemporaries questioned how successfully Jewish immigrants could master a new sort of physical deportment. When commenting upon influence of nationality on motion, Dodworth notes,

> The Jewish people furnish a remarkable example of this persistency of race distinctions in motion; for, although mingling with all nations, they retain their peculiarities. . . . The dancing of each nation, when moving to the same waltz, is generally marked by peculiarities that are not due so much to any difference of physical form as to early habit."

See Dodworth, *Dancing and Its Relations to Education and Social Life*, 12–13.

27. Jewish communal organizations also offered social dances "to make sure that dancing took place among well-matched adolescents in a suitable environment rather than more heterogeneous, less-supervised neighborhood dance halls." See Klapper, *Jewish Girls Coming of Age in America*, 200–201.

28. Opatoshu, "Shmelts-top," in *Gezamlte verk*, vol. 8, 140. The title of this short story is an explicit reference to Israel Zangwill's *The Melting Pot*, a play about assimilation. For more about this story, see Kirzane, "The Melting Plot," 249–251. See also p. 121 for the attitudes of Jewish immigrants toward Italian immigrants. For concerns about racial mixing through dance and male "tango pirates," who were often Italian or Jewish, see Melnick, *A Right to Sing the Blues*, 33–35.

29. Kirzane, "The Melting Plot," 250.

30. Opatoshu, "Shmelts-top," in *Gezamlte verk*, vol. 8, 142.

31. Ibid.

32. Ibid.

33. For more about working women's participation in consumer culture, see Enstad, *Ladies of Labor, Girls of Adventure*.

34. See Molodowsky, "A Fur Coat," in *A House with Seven Windows*, 26. For Yiddish, see Molodowsky, "A futerne mantl," in *A shtub mit zibn fenster*, 9.

35. Asch, *East River*, 153. For Yiddish, see Asch, *Ist river*, 182.

36. Asch, *Ist river*, 280. Translation is my own. For an alternative English translation, see Asch, *East River*, 230.

37. Asch, *East River*, 231–232. See also Asch, *Ist river*, 281–283.

38. Cahan, *Yekl*, 22. The quote refers to a Yiddish idiom for describing a bona fide example of something.

39. Tashrak, *Etikete*, 91. While "cutting in" was an accepted part of certain social dance milieux, especially those with many more male than female dancers, it was only appropriate when following certain rules, which does not seem to be the case for Jake and Mamie.

40. Bernard G. Richards, "Introduction: Abraham Cahan Cast in a New Role," in Cahan, *Yekl*, iv.

41. Dexter Marshall, "The Life of A. Cahan, Novelist: How a Russian-Hebrew Nihilist Came to Write of New York's Cosmopolitan East Side," *Boston Sunday Post* (September 27, 1896), reprinted in Kirk and Kirk, "Abraham Cahan and William Dean Howells," 44.

42. According to John S. Phillips, associate editor of *McClure's*, "Art should concern itself with beautiful things. A dancing school on the poor East Side, ignorant people, a man who isn't true to his wife. What do these have to do with Art?" Quoted in Kirk and Kirk, "Abraham Cahan and William Dean Howells," 44.

43. Taubenfeld wonders if the name "Yankl" may have also been too close to the

word "Yankee" for the comfort of American readers such as Howells. See Taubenfeld, "*Only an 'L,'*" 161.

44. Kirk and Kirk, "Abraham Cahan and William Dean Howells," 37.

45. Ibid.

46. Lipsky, *The Rise of Abraham Cahan*, 69.

47. For more about the film, see Erens, *The Jew in American Cinema*, 325–327; Hammerman, *Silver Screen, Hasidic Jews*, 104–131.

48. For examples of such scholarship, see Bachman, *Recovering "Yiddishland,"* 43–79; Motley, "'Dot'sh a' Kin' a man I am!'"; Taubenfeld, "'*Only an 'L,'*'"; Wirth-Nesher, "'Shpeaking Plain' and Writing Foreign." For more about the burly, physically dominant type of masculinity that Jake—and his white, middle-class, northern contemporaries—hold dear, see Rotundo, *American Manhood*, 222–246. For more about American Jewish masculinity, see Igra, *Wives Without Husbands*, 43–62; Imhoff, *Masculinity and the Making of American Judaism*; Mora, "From Jewish Boys to American Men"; Prell, *Fighting to Become Americans*, 21–57.

49. See Bachman, *Recovering "Yiddishland,"* 43–79; Haenni, "Visual and Theatrical Culture, Tenement Fiction, and the Immigrant Subject in Abraham Cahan's *Yekl*."

50. Chinn, *Inventing Modern Adolescence*, 110–111. See ibid., 107–113, for Chinn's analysis of *Yekl*.

51. Bachman, *Recovering "Yiddishland,"* 64.

52. Women could also abandon their romantic partners for the dance floor: In her 1918 autobiography, Rose Gollup Cohen (1880–1925) describes neglecting her fiancé to flirt and dance with other men at her engagement party; see Cohen, *Out of the Shadow*, 216. On p. 135 she also describes young people dancing mixed-sex Russian folk dances to the accompaniment of dance songs on Saturday afternoons in someone's home (presumably a tenement apartment).

53. Goldman describes her bitter disappointment as a new immigrant when a beau who had spent four years working in a garment factory "lacked spirit and fire" when dancing because the strength had been sapped out of him by the sewing machine. See Goldman, *Living My Life*, 19.

54. Cahan, *Yekl*, 63.

55. George Kibbe Turner, "The Puzzle of the Underworld," *McClure's Magazine* 41, no. 3 (July 1913): 108.

56. Cahan, *Yekl*, 15.

57. At the turn of the last century, the Lower East Side had one of the highest population densities on earth. See Dwork, "Health Conditions of Immigrant Jews on the Lower East Side of New York," 5–7.

58. Cahan, *Yekl*, 15–16.

59. Ibid., 18.

60. Peiss, *Cheap Amusements*, 98. See also Israels, "Dance-Hall Reform (1909)," 121,

George Kibbe Turner, "Daughters of the Poor: A Plain Story of the Development of New York City as a Leading Centre of the White Slave Trade of the World Under Tammany Hall," *McClure's Magazine* 34 (November 1909): 45–61.

61. Cahan, *Yekl*, 32. Peiss notes that treating could involve an implied exchange of monetary expenditures for sexual services: "Engaging in treating ultimately involved a negotiation between the desire for social participation and adherence to cultural sanctions that strongly discouraged premarital sexual intimacy." Peiss, *Cheap Amusements*, 109.

62. Cahan, *Yekl*, 20.

63. Ibid., 25.

64. Ibid., 20.

65. Ibid.

66. His behavior seems to typify the kind of vulgar dancing that popular exhibition dancers Vernon and Irene Castle warn against in their 1914 dance manual as they insist that proper dance etiquette requires "a man to stand far enough from his partner to allow freedom of movement; he should not hug or clutch her during the dance. His arms should encircle her lightly, and he should barely rest his hand against her back, touching her only with his finger-tips and wrist." See Castle and Castle, *Modern Dancing*, 135.

67. Peiss, *Cheap Amusements*, 101. Interestingly, Cahan tends to refer to versions of the waltz or lancers, rather than more risqué animal dances. For a discussion of waltzing and spieling, see Tonko, *Dancing Class*, 23–25.

68. Israels, "Dance-Hall Reform (1909)," 120. See also Chinn, *Inventing Modern Adolescence*; 110; McBee, *Dance Hall Days*, 72–73.

69. Bachman, *Recovering "Yiddishland,"* 66.

70. Jake's explicit envy of the bachelors at the dancing school parallels the way contemporary condemnations of family deserters portrayed the immigrant husbands who "spent their wages on their own pleasures" and mistook American liberty for the license to abandon their families. See Igra, *Wives Without Husbands*, 51, 53.

71. Cahan, *Yekl*, 44.

72. Ibid., 80.

73. Chametzky, "Regional Literature and Ethnic Realities," 392.

74. Cahan, *Yekl*, 76.

75. Ibid., 88.

76. Gitl last appears at the divorce proceedings, so readers never see her marry her suitor Mr. Bernstein.

77. Braun, "Kadya Molodowsky," 189.

78. Klepfisz makes this claim about Molodovsky's fame, saying that she is "anthologized and discussed in English more frequently than any other woman poet writing in Yiddish." Klepfisz, "Di Mames, Dos Loshn/The Mothers, the Language," 34. While

scholars and translators have drawn attention to other Yiddish women writers in subsequent decades, Molodovsky's stature has, if anything, grown due to new translations of her prose work.

79. Anita Norich, "Introduction," in Molodovsky, *A Jewish Refugee in New York*, vii–viii. For more about the novel's publication in the context of Molodovsky's other writing from this period, see Hellerstein, "Finding Her Yiddish Voice," 67. The novel is discussed on pp. 51–55.

80. As far as Alexander Mukdoyni was aware, the serialized novel was a great hit with readers. See Dr. Mukdoyni, "Vi a grine grint zikh oys," *Morgn zshurnal* (May 20, 1942), in section "Bikher un shrayber." Clipping found in the Kadia Molodowsky Papers, YIVO Institute for Jewish Research, RG 703, Folder 162.

81. For more about the novel's publication history, see Norich, "Introduction," in Molodovsky, *A Jewish Refugee in New York*, vii. Newman notes that *Fun Lublin biz Nyu-York* was broadcast in 1943 as a radio play on WEVD, a Yiddish radio station, and adapted in 1953 into a play manuscript, *A hoyz oyf grend strit* (A House on Grand Street). Surprisingly, Newman refers to *Fun Lublin biz Nyu-York* as a novella; her discussion of *Fun Lublin biz Nyu-York* does not address Rivke's ambivalence toward American Jewish culture. See Newman, *Kadya Molodowsky*, 112, 323. For the play manuscript, see the Kadia Molodowsky Papers, YIVO Institute for Jewish Research, RG 703, Folders 83–84. For more about Molodowsky's feelings about her own immigration to the United States, see Hellerstein, "Introduction," in *Paper Bridges,* 37–38.

82. Molodovsky, *A Jewish Refugee in New York*, 171. For Yiddish, see Molodowsky, *Fun Lublin biz Nyu-York*, 276.

83. Dr. Mukdoyni, "Fun Lublin biz Nyu-York," *Morgn zshurnal*. Undated clipping [May 29, 1941] found in Kadia Molodowsky Papers, YIVO Institute for Jewish Research, RG 703, Folder 162. The review appeared the day before the first installment of the novel was printed and was presumably designed to encourage readers to pay attention to it.

84. Molodovsky, *A Jewish Refugee in New York*, 135. For Yiddish, see Molodowsky, *Fun Lublin biz Nyu-York*, 219.

85. Molodovsky, *A Jewish Refugee in New York*, 168. For Yiddish, see Molodowsky, *Fun Lublin biz Nyu-York*, 271.

86. "King of Swing" Benny Goodman, a first-generation Jewish American clarinetist and bandleader, was a key figure in what Dinerstein describes as the "whitefacing of swing," which made a popular African American style of dance seem less threatening and more respectable to white Americans. See Dinerstein, *Swinging the Machine*, 278.

87. Molodowsky, *A Jewish Refugee in New York*, 8. For Yiddish, see Molodowsky, *Fun Lublin biz Nyu-York*, 15.

88. Sh. Niger [Shmuel Charney], "Fun Lublin biz Nyu-York," *Der tog* (May 16, 1942): 4. Clipping in Kadia Molodowsky Papers, YIVO Institute for Jewish Research,

RG 703, Folder 162. For more about the recent scholarly move away from using Charney's pseudonym, see Bromberg, "We Need to Talk About Shmuel Charney."

89. Sh. Niger [Shmuel Charney], "Fun Lublin biz Nyu-York," *Der tog* (May 16, 1942): 15.

90. Molodovsky, *A Jewish Refugee in New York*, 89. For Yiddish, see Molodowsky, *Fun Lublin biz Nyu-York*, 144.

91. Molodovsky, *A Jewish Refugee in New York*, 132. For Yiddish, see Molodowsky, *Fun Lublin biz Nyu-York*, 213.

92. Molodovsky, *A Jewish Refugee in New York*, 135. For Yiddish, see Molodowsky, *Fun Lublin biz Nyu-York*, 219.

93. Molodovsky, *A Jewish Refugee in New York*, 135. For Yiddish, see Molodowsky, *Fun Lublin biz Nyu-York*, 219.

94. She accepts unquestioningly that African American women will perform low-status domestic labor that she considers demeaning; when her aunt dismisses a woman that a neighbor refers to as "di shvartse ayere" ([y]our colored girl) to save money and expects Rivke to clean for the family instead, she feels affronted. See Molodovsky, *A Jewish Refugee in New York*, 7. For Yiddish, see Molodowsky, *Fun Lublin biz Nyu-York*, 14.

95. For more about race and tap dancing in America, see Dinerstein, *Swinging the Machine*, 221–249; Pugh, *America Dancing*, 29–83; for a discussion of the views eastern European Jewish immigrants held about Blacks between 1881 and 1920, see Ribak, *Gentile New York*, esp. 127–133.

96. Molodovsky, *A Jewish Refugee in New York*, 123. For Yiddish, see Molodowsky, *Fun Lublin biz Nyu-York*, 199.

97. Molodovsky, *A Jewish Refugee in New York*, 123. For Yiddish, see Molodowsky, *Fun Lublin biz Nyu-York*, 199.

98. Ibid., 39. Translation is my own, since Norich does not mention the karahod. See Molodovsky, *A Jewish Refugee in New York*, 24.

99. The term "karahod" refers to the circular shape of the dance, including a dance comprised of a circle of couples.

100. The symbolism of circular structures is repeated in Rivke's last entry, where she comments upon the circular structure of her life. See Molodovsky, *A Jewish Refugee in New York*, 171. For Yiddish, see Molodowsky, *Fun Lublin biz Nyu-York*, 277.

101. Molodovsky, *A Jewish Refugee in New York*, 23–24. For Yiddish, see Molodowsky, *Fun Lublin biz Nyu-York*, 39.

102. Perhaps her discomfort with his unusual behavior is amplified because pickle in Yiddish, *zoyere ugerke*, is feminine, which means Pinchas Hersh dances in the pantry with another "her."

103. Molodowsky, *A Jewish Refugee in New York*, 26. For Yiddish, see Molodowsky, *Fun Lublin biz Nyu-York*, 42–43.

104. A. Golomb, "Shtiler, a mentsh iz untergegangn (vegn Kadie Molodovskis roman 'Fun Lublin biz Nyu-York')," *Afn shvel* 13–14 (May–June 1942): 10.

105. Molodovsky, *A Jewish Refugee in New York*, 171. For Yiddish, see Molodowsky, *Fun Lublin biz Nyu-York*, 277.

Epilogue

1. Solomon, *Wonder of Wonders*, 194.

2. For a discussion of different adaptations of *Tevye der milkhiger* (*Tevye the Dairy-man*), see Wolitz, "The Americanization of Tevye or Boarding the Jewish 'Mayflower,'" 514–536.

3. Solomon, *Wonder of Wonders*, 194.

4. Ibid.

5. Ibid., 195.

6. Ibid.

7. Stein, Bock, and Harnick, *Fiddler on the Roof*, 53.

8. Ibid., 53–54.

9. Ibid., 53.

10. Ibid., 83.

11. Ibid., 84.

12. Ibid., 102

13. Irving Howe, "Tevye on Broadway," *Commentary* (November 1964): https://www.commentarymagazine.com/articles/irving-howe/tevye-on-broadway/

14. Ibid.

15. For instance, the third episode of the 2020 Netflix miniseries *Unorthodox*—about a woman named Esty who leaves her Satmar Hasidic community for a secular life in Berlin—features a scene of mixed-sex dancing in a Berlin club. The episode includes several wrenching flashbacks of Esty's painful sexual experiences with her Satmar husband, which contrast starkly with the dancing in the club that leads directly to Esty's first pleasurable sexual encounter, with a non-Jewish man. The club scene is presented as a positive moment in Esty's character arc, even though she is spotted at the club by her husband's cousin and drama ensues.

16. In the early 1960s, rabbis in Manchester, England, tried to forbid mixed-sex dances in synagogues and were sharply rebuked in the Jewish press; see Mississippi Fred MacDowell, "The Great Mixed Dancing Controversy of 1960–61," *On the Mainline* blog, (June 20, 2011): http://onthemainline.blogspot.com/2011/06/great-mixed-dancing-controversy-of-1960.html. In a more recent ruling, Rabbi Isaac Jacob Weiss warns against girls going to dancing schools, where they wear inappropriate clothing and perform mixed-sex dancing. These activities could lead to mixed-sex dancing in even more dubious locations and, at the very least, the wasting of seed and masturbation. He claims that parents who send their children to dancing schools are worse than

the ancients who burned their children alive for idolatrous purposes. See Weiss, *She'elot u-teshuvot minhat Yitshak*, para. 109, 188–189.

17. Johnny's last name may be borrowed from early twentieth-century ballroom dancers Vernon and Irene Castle.

18. For analysis of the class, race, and sexual implications of dancing in this film, see Dyer, "White Enough."

19. The 2019 documentary *Mamboniks* explores Jewish participation in the 1950s mambo craze.

20. Goldstein, *Mazel*, 313. In Jewish folklore, a golem is a clay or mud creature that is magically brought to life.

21. Ibid., 307.

22. Ibid., 345.

23. Ibid., 356–357.

24. For more about how literary dance scenes show emotional connections between women, see Gollance, "Gesture, Repertoire, and Emotion."

25. For further discussion of this motif in Krämer's *Esther*, see Gollance, "Harmonious Instability," 276–277.

26. Greenwood, *Raisins and Almonds*, 3.

27. Ibid., 4.

28. Ibid., 66.

29. Wecker, *The Golem and the Jinni*, 294–304.

30. In Miryem's cynical retelling of the Rumpelstiltskin story at the beginning of novel, she mentions the miller's daughter dancing with the prince, which Miryem views as additional proof of her message that it is impossible to change the status quo. Yet the wedding dance scene later in the novel suggests that, in fact, it is possible for a lower status woman to marry a higher status man and gain his respect. See Novik, *Spinning Silver*, 3.

31. Ibid., 341.

32. Ibid.

33. Ibid., 342.

34. For the description of the chair lifts, see ibid., 341–342. A character tells musicians to play the hora, which may be a way of signaling a Jewish circle dance to readers who are familiar with Israeli dance (see ibid., 339–340). Faster horas of the sort described in the novel, with clapping and stomping, have their origins in Romania and Moldova. For more about the hora, see Chapter 4.

Bibliography

Libraries and Archives

Dance Library of Israel (Tel Aviv)

Derra de Moroda Dance Archives (Salzburg)

Deutsches Tanzarchiv Köln (Cologne)

Jüdisches Museum Wien Bibliothek (Vienna)

Leo Baeck Institute (New York)

National Library of Israel (Jerusalem)

New York Public Library (New York)

Österreichische Nationalbibliothek (Vienna)

Wienbibliothek im Rathaus (Vienna)

Yiddish Book Center (Amherst, MA)

YIVO Institute for Jewish Research (New York)

Unpublished Papers

Leo Baeck Institute Archives, LBI Berlin Collection

Leo Baeck Institute Archives, LBI Memoir Collection

Leon Kobrin Papers, YIVO Institute for Jewish Research, RG 376

Clementine Kraemer Collection, Leo Baeck Institute, AR 2402

Kadia Molodowsky Papers, YIVO Institute for Jewish Research, RG 703

Joseph Opatoshu Papers, YIVO Institute for Jewish Research, RG 436

Periodicals

Afn shvel (New York)

Allgemeine Zeitung des Judentums (Berlin)

Commentary (New York)

Der groyse kundes (New York)

Der Israelit (Frankfurt am Main)

Forverts (New York)

Frankfurter Israelitisches Gemeindeblatt (Frankfurt am Main)

Harper's Weekly (New York)

Im deutschen Reich (Berlin)

Jewish Chronicle (London)

McClure's Magazine (New York)

Mitteilungen zur jüdischen Volkskunde (Vienna)

Mittheilungen der Gesellschaft für jüdische Volkskunde (Hamburg)

The American Jewess (New York)

The Reform Advocate (Chicago)

Yugnt-veker (Warsaw)

Zeitschrift für die Geschichte der Juden in Deutschland (Berlin)

Published Primary Sources

"169. Responsa Binyamin Zeev, #303." In *Controversy and Dialogue in the Jewish
    Tradition: A Reader* (pp. 205–208). Edited by Hanina Ben-Menachem, Neil S.
    Hecht, and Shai Wosner. London: Routledge, 2005.

Abramowicz, Hirsz. *Farshvundene geshtaltn, zikhroynes un siluetn.* Buenos Aires:
    Tsentral-farband fun poylishe yidn in Argentine, 1958.

——. *Profiles of a Lost World: Memoirs of East European Jewish Life Before World
    War II.* Translated by Eva Zeitlin Dobkin. Detroit: Wayne State University
    Press, 1999.

Ansky, S. "In the Tavern." Translated by Robert Szulkin. In *The Dybbuk and Other
    Writings* (pp. 53–70). Edited by David G. Roskies. New Haven: Yale University
    Press, 2002.

Asch, Sholem. *Dramatishe shriftn.* Vol. 2: *Natsionale dramen.* New York: Sholem Ash
    komite, 1922.

——. *Der tilim-yid.* Warsaw: Kultur-lige, 1937.

——. *East River: A Novel.* Translated by A. H. Gross. New York: G. F. Putnam's
    Sons, 1946.

——. *Ist river.* New York: Elias Laub, 1946.

———. *Salvation.* Translated by Willa and Edwin Muir. New York: G. P. Putnam's Sons, 1951.

Auerbach, Berthold. *Dichter und Kaufmann: Ein Lebensgemälde.* 2 vols. Stuttgart: Adolph Krabbe, 1840.

———. *Poet and Merchant: A Picture of Life from the Times of Moses Mendelssohn.* Translated by Charles T. Brooks. New York: Henry Holt, 1877.

———. *Bräutigamsbriefe von Berthold Auerbach.* Edited by Anton Bettelheim. Berlin: Rudolph Masse, 1910.

Baron, Dvora. "Mishpahah." In *Parshiyot: sipurim mekubatsim* (pp. 11–35). Jerusalem: Mosad Bialik, 1968.

———. "Family." In *"The First Day" and Other Stories* (pp. 58–89). Edited by Chana Kronfeld and Naomi Seidman. Translated by Naomi Seidman with Chana Kronfeld. Berkeley: University of California Press, 2001.

Baum, Vicki. *Schloßtheater: Erzählungen.* Munich: Wilhelm Heyne Verlag, 1985.

[Bekerman, Shimen]. *Der tants klas: A zeltener roman vos di lezer velin zayn hekhst tsu friden* Vilna: L. L. Mats, 1914.

Bergner, Hinde. *In di lange vinternekht. . . . Mishpokhe-zikhroynes fun a shtetl in Galizie, 1870–1900.* Montreal: M. Ravitch, 1946.

———. *On Long Winter Nights . . . : Memoirs of a Jewish Family in a Galician Township (1870–1900).* Translated by Justin Daniel Cammy. Cambridge, MA: Harvard University Press, 2005.

Binyamin Ze'ev ben Matityahu. *Binyamin Ze'ev.* Venice: D. Bomberg, 1538.

Bodenschatz, Johann Christoph Georg. *Kirchliche Verfassung der heutigen Juden sonderlich derer in Deutschland.* Vol. 2. Frankfurt am Main: Georg Otto, 1749.

Bottallo, Barthélemy G. *Guide du bon danseur, par le professeur B.–G. Bottallo.* Paris: Imp. Jouve & cie, 1912.

Bowen, Louise de Koven. *Our Most Popular Recreation Controlled by the Liquor Interests: A Study of Public Dance Halls.* Chicago: Juvenile Protective Association of Chicago, 1911.

Burshtyn, Samuel. *"Der masken bal fun der fardorbenhayt."* In *Der masken bal fun der fardorbenhayt: Dertseylungen, dikhtungen, eseyen* (pp. 40–44). New York: Shoulson Press, 1949.

Cahan, Abraham. *Bleter fun mayn lebn.* Vol. 1. New York: "Forverts" Association, 1926.

———. *The Rise of David Levinsky.* New York: Harper Torchbooks, 1960.

———. *The Education of Abraham Cahan.* Translated by Leon Stein, Abraham P. Conan, and Lynn Davison. Philadelphia: Jewish Publication Society of America, 1969.

———. *Yekl and the Imported Bridegroom and Other Stories of the New York Ghetto.* New York: Dover Publications, 1970.

Carlebach, Salomon. *Sittenreinheit: Ein Mahnwort an Israels Söhne und Töchter, Väter und Mütter,* 2nd ed. Berlin: Verlag Hausfreund, 1919.

Castle, [Mr. Vernon], and [Mrs. Irene] Castle. *Modern Dancing*. New York: World Syndicate (n.d.) [1914].

Chagall, Bella. *Brenendike likht*. New York: Folks-farlag, 1945.

———. *Burning Lights*. Translated by Norbert Guterman. New York: Schocken Books, 1946.

Cohen, Rose. *Out of the Shadow: A Russian Jewish Girlhood on the Lower East Side*. Ithaca, NY: Cornell University Press, 1995.

Conversations-Lexikon für alle Stände: Eine Encyklopedie der vorzüglichsten Lehren, Vorschriften und Mittel zur Erhaltung des Lebens und der Gesundheit der Menschen und der nutzbaren Thiere, sowie zur Conservirung aller für die Bedürfnisse, die Bequemlichkeit und das Vergnügen der Menschen bestimmten Einrichtungen, Produkte und Waaren. Leipzig und Stuttgart: J. Scheible's Verlags-Expedition, 1834.

Czerwinski, Albert. *Geschichte der Tanzkunst bei den cultivirten Völkern von den ersten Anfängen bis auf die gegenwärtige Zeit*. Leipzig: J. J. Weber, 1862.

Die Gefahren des Tanzes, dargestellt in einigen Erzählungen, und der Jugend zur Beherzigung un Warnung gewidmet von einem ihrer Freund. 2nd ed. Augsburg: Joseph Wolffischen Verlagsbuchhundlung, 1832.

Dinezon, Jacob. *Ha-ne'ehavim veha-ne'imim, oder, Der shvartser yungermantshik*. Warsaw: Farlag "akhiseyfer," 1928.

———. *The Dark Young Man*. Translated by Tina Lunson. Adapted and edited by Scott Hilton Davis. Raleigh, NC: Jewish Storyteller Press, 2019.

Dodworth, Allen. *Dancing and Its Relations to Education and Social Life*. New York: Harper & Brothers, 1900.

Dostoyevsky, Fyodor. *The Village of Stepanchikovo and Its Inhabitants: From the Notes of an Unknown*. Translated by Ignat Avsey. Ithaca, NY: Cornell University Press, 1987.

———. *"Selo Stepanchikovo i ego obitateli. Iz zapisok neizvestnogo."* In *Sobranie sochinenii v piatnadtsati tomakh* (vol. 3, pp. 5–204). Leningrad: Nauka, 1988.

Dropkin, Celia. *In heysn vint*. New York: Brider Shulsinger, 1959.

Edgeworth, Maria. *Harrington*. Edited by Susan Manly. Peterborough, ON: Broadview, 2004.

Eliot, George. *Daniel Deronda*. Ware: Wordsworth Classics, 1996.

Englander, Nathan. "What We Talk About When We Talk About Anne Frank." In *What We Talk About When We Talk About Anne Frank* (pp. 3–32). New York: Alfred A. Knopf, 2012.

Erik, Max, ed. *Di komedyes fun der berliner oyfklerung*. Kiev: Melukhe-farlag, 1933.

Euchel, Isaac. *Reb Henoch, oder: Woß tut me damit*. Edited by Marion Aptroot and Roland Gruschka. Hamburg: Helmut Buske Verlag, 2006.

Forman, Frieda, et al., ed. *Found Treasures: Stories by Yiddish Women Writers*. Toronto: Second Story Press, 1994.

Franzos, Karl Emil. *The Jews of Barnow.* Translated by M. M. MacDowall. Edinburgh: W. Blackwood and Sons, 1882.

——. *Junge Liebe.* Breslau: Eduard Trewendt, 1884.

——. *Judith Trachtenberg: A Novel.* Translated by Mrs. L. P. and C. T. Lewis. New York: Harper & Bros., 1891.

——. *Die Juden von Barnow: Geschichten.* Stuttgart: J. G. Cotta'sche Buchhandlung Nachfolger, 1920.

——. *Judith Trachtenberg: Erzählung.* Berlin: Verlag der Nation, 1987.

Freytag, Gustav. *Soll und Haben: Roman in sechs Büchern.* Berlin: Verlag von Th. Knaur Nachs (n.d.).

Gebirtig, Mordechai. *Mayne lider.* New York: Arbeter-ring bay dem arbeter-ring bildungs-komitet, 1948.

Goldman, Emma. *Living My Life.* Vol. 1. New York: Dover Publications, 1970.

Goldschmidt, Meir. *En Jøde: Roman.* Copenhagen: Gyldendalske Boghandel, 1929.

——. *A Jew.* Translated by Kenneth H. Ober. New York: Garland Publishing, 1990.

Goldstein, Rebecca. *Mazel.* New York: Penguin Books, 1995.

Grade, Chaim. *Der mames shabosim.* Chicago: L. M. Stein, 1955.

——. *Tsemakh atlas: Di yeshive.* Vol. 2. New York: Bikher-farlag, 1968.

——. *The Yeshiva.* Vol. 2. Translated by Curt Leviant. Indianapolis: Bobbs-Merrill Company, 1977.

——. *My Mother's Sabbath Days: A Memoir.* Translated by Channa Kleinerman Goldstein and Inna Hecker Grade. Lanham, MD: Rowman & Littlefield Publishers, 2004.

Greenwood, Kerry. *Raisins and Almonds: A Phryne Fisher Mystery.* Scottsdale: Poisoned Pen Press, 2007.

Heine, Heinrich. "Elementargeister." In *Schriften 1831–1837* (pp. 654–655). Edited by Karl Pörnbacher. Vol. 5 of *Sämtliche Schriften in zwölf Bänden.* Edited by Klaus Briegleb. Frankfurt am Main: Ullstein Werkausgaben, 1981.

Herz, Henriette de Lemos. *Henriette Herz: Ihr Leben in Erinnerungen, Briefen und Zeugnissen.* Edited by Rainer Schmitz. Frankfurt am Main: Insel Verlag, 1984.

——. "Henriette Herz: Memoirs of a Jewish Girlhood." In *Bitter Healing: German Women Writers from 1700–1830, An Anthology* (pp. 297–331). Edited by Jeannine Blackwell and Susanne Zantop. Translated by Marjanne Goozé with Jeannine Blackwell. Lincoln: University of Nebraska Press, 1990.

[Hirsch, Samson Raphael]. *Die Religion im Bunde mit dem Fortschritt, von einem Schwarzen.* Frankfurt am Main: Druck von Reinhold Baist, 1854.

——. *Judaism Eternal: Selected Essays from the Writings of Rabbi Samson Raphael Hirsch.* Edited and translated by I. Grunfeld. Vol. 2. London: Soncino Press, 1956.

Iggers, Wilma Abeles, ed. *Die Juden in Böhmen und Mähren: Ein historisches Lesebuch.* Munich: C. H. Beck, 1986.

——. *The Jews of Bohemia and Moravia: A Historical Reader.* Translated by Wilma
    Abeles Iggers, Káča Poláčková-Henley, and Kathrine Talbot. Detroit: Wayne
    State University Press, 1992.
Ignatoff, David. *In keslgrub: Roman.* [New York?]: Farlag amerike, 1919.
Israels, Belle Lindner. "Dance-Hall Reform (1909)." In *I See America Dancing:
    Selected Readings, 1685–2000* (pp. 120–121). Edited by Maureen Needham. Ur-
    bana: University of Illinois Press, 2002.
Jacobowski, Ludwig. *Werther der Jude,* 6th ed. Berlin: Verlag Berlin-Wien (n.d.).
Jolizza, W. K. von. *Die Schule des Tanzes: Leichtfaßliche Anleitung zur Selbstlernung
    moderner und alter Gesellschaftstänze.* Vienna: A. Hartleben (n.d.) [1907].
Junk, Victor. *Handbuch des Tanzes.* Stuttgart: Ernst Klett Verlag, 1930.
Justament, Henri. *Giselle ou Les Wilis: Ballet fantastique en deux actes.* Edited by
    Franz-Manuel Peter. Hildesheim: Georg Olms Verlag, 2008.
Kagan, Israel Meir. *Mishnah Berurah.* Vol. 2. Warsaw: Shriftgesser, 1891.
Kanah hokhmah kanah binah. Edited by Shmuel Diamont. Kraków: Yosef Fisher, 1894.
Kaufmann, Jakob. *Der böhmische Dorfjude.* In *Jeschurun: Taschenbuch für Schilderungen
    und Anklänge aus dem Leben der Juden* (pp. 59–94). Edited by Carl Maien and
    Siegmund Frankenberg. Leipzig: L. Fort, 1841.
Kobrin, Leon, *Gezamelte shriftn.* New York: Hebrew Publishing Company, 1910.
——. *Yankl Boyle: A fisher drame.* New York: Odeon Theatre, 1913.
——. "Yankel Boyla." In *Epic and Folk Plays of the Yiddish Theatre* (pp. 101–139).
    Edited and translated by David S. Lifson. Rutherford, NJ: Fairleigh Dickinson
    University Press, 1975.
Kolmar, Gertrud. *A Jewish Mother from Berlin: A Novel; Susanna: A Novel.* Translated
    by Brigitte M. Goldstein. New York: Holmes & Meier, 1997.
——. *Die jüdische Mutter.* Göttingen: Wallstein Verlag, 1999.
Kompert, Leopold. *Geschichten einer Gasse.* Vol. 1. Berlin: Louis Gerschel, 1865.
——. *Leopold Komperts sämtliche Werke in zehn Bände.* Vol. 4: *Neue Geschichten aus dem
    Ghetto.* Leipzig: Max Hesse (n.d.) [1906].
——. *Die Kinder des Randars.* Vol. 9 of *Edition Mnemosyne.* Edited by Primus-Heinz
    Kucher. Klagenfurt: Alekto Verlag, 1998.
Kotik, Yekhezkel. *Mayne zikhroynes.* Vol. 1. Berlin: Klal-farlag, 1922.
——. *Journey to a Nineteenth-Century Shtetl: The Memoirs of Yekhezkel Kotik.* Edited
    and translated by David Assaf. Detroit: Wayne State University Press, 2002.
Kreitman, Esther. *Der sheydim-tants.* Warsaw: H. Bzshoza, 1936.
——. *The Dance of the Demons.* Translated by Maurice Carr. New York: Feminist Press
    at the City University of New York, 2004.
Kugelmass, Jack, and Jonathan Boyarin, eds. and trans. *From a Ruined Garden: The
    Memorial Books of Polish Jewry,* 2nd ed. Bloomington: Indiana University Press,
    1998.

La Garde-Chambonas, Auguste Louis Charles, Comte de. *Gemälde des Wiener Kongresses, 1814–1815: Erinnerungen, Feste, Sittenschilderungen, Anekdoten.* Edited by Gustav Gugitz. 2 vols. Munich: Georg Müller, 1912.

Laenger, L. *Erinnerungs-Buch: Zum Nutzen und Vergnügen für meine Schüler und Schülerinnen. Nebst einem Anhange der neuesten gesellschaftlichen Tänze für gebildete Stände.* Hildburghausen: s.n., 1820.

La Roche, Sophie von. *The History of Lady Sophia Sternheim.* Edited by James Lynn. New York: New York University Press, 1992.

——. *Geschichte des Fräuleins von Sternheim.* Edited by Barbara Becker-Cantarino. Stuttgart: Philipp Reclam, 2006.

Laszlo, Andrew. *Footnote to History.* Lanham, MD: University Press of America, 2002.

Lesser, Louis. *A Jewish Youth in Dresden: The Diary of Louis Lesser, 1833–1837.* Edited by Christopher R. Friedrichs. Bethesda: University Press of Maryland, 2011.

Levinsky, Yom-Tov. "Der broygez tants." In *Sefer Zembrov/Zembrove* (pp. 393–394). Edited by Yom-Tov Levinsky. Tel Aviv: ha-Irgunim shel yots'e ha-ir be-'Artsot ha-Berit, Argentinah ve-Yisra'el, 1963.

Levy, Amy. *Reuben Sachs.* London: Macmillan and Co., 1888.

Lewald, Fanny. *Meine Lebensgeschichte.* 2 vols. Berlin: Otto Janke, 1871.

——. *The Education of Fanny Lewald: An Autobiography.* Edited and translated by Hanna Ballin Lewis. Albany: State University of New York Press, 1992.

Löw, Leopold. *Beiträge zur Jüdischen Alterthumskunde.* Vol. 2: *Die Lebensalter in der jüdischen Literatur.* Szegedin: Sigmund Burgers Witwe, 1875.

Maimon, Salomon. *Salomon Maimons Lebensgeschichte: Von ihm selbst geschrieben und herausgegeben von K. P. Moritz. In zwei Theilen.* 2 vols. Berlin: Friedrich Vieweg dem ältern, 1792–1793.

——. *The Autobiography of Solomon Maimon.* Edited by Yitzhak Y. Melamed and Abraham P. Socher. Translated by Paul Reitter. Princeton: Princeton University Press, 2018.

Mann, Thomas. *Tonio Kröger.* Berlin: S. Fischer Verlag (n.d.) [1914].

Mendele Moykher-Sforim [Sholem Yankev Abramovitsh]. "Omar Mendele Moykher-Sforim: Hagdome tsu 'Shloyme Reb Khayims,' geshribn arum 1901." In *Dos Mendele-bukh* (pp. 259–275). Edited by Nachman Mayzel. New York: YKUF, 1959.

——. "Of Bygone Days." Translated by Raymond Scheindlin. In *A Shtetl and Other Yiddish Novellas* (pp. 249–372). Edited by Ruth R. Wisse. Detroit: Wayne State University Press, 1986.

[Meyer, Rahel]. *Zwei Schwestern: Ein Roman.* Vol. 1. Berlin: Verlag von Veit und Comp, 1853.

Mickiewicz, Adam. *Pan Tadeusz.* Translated by Kenneth R. Mackenzie. New York: Hippocrene Books, 1992.

Mints, Moyshe Leyzer. "Mayne zikhroynes." In *Pinkes Khmielnik: Yizker-bukh nokh der horev-gevorene yidisher kehile* (pp. 189–214). Edited by Efrayim Shedletski. Tel Aviv: Irgun yotse'e Hmyelnik beYisrael, 1960.

Molodovsky, Kadya. *Fun Lublin biz Nyu-York: Togbukh fun Rivke Zilberg.* New York: Papirene brik, 1942.

——. *A shtub mit zibn fenster.* New York: Matones, 1957.

——. *A House with Seven Windows: Short Stories.* Translated by Leah Schoolnik. Syracuse, NY: Syracuse University Press, 2006.

——. *A Jewish Refugee in New York: Rivke Zilberg's Journal.* Translated by Anita Norich. Bloomington: Indiana University Press, 2009.

Mosenthal, Salomon Hermann. *Stories of Jewish Home Life.* Freeport, NY: Books for Libraries Press, 1971.

——. *Erzählungen aus dem jüdischen Familienleben.* Edited by Ruth Klüger. Göttingen: Wallstein Verlag, 2001.

Novik, Naomi. *Spinning Silver.* New York: Del Rey, 2018.

Opatoshu, Joseph. *A roman fun a ferd-ganef un andere dertseylungen.* New York: Literarisher farlag, 1917.

——. *Gezamlte verk.* Vol. 1. Vilna: B. Kletskin, 1928.

——. *Gezamlte verk.* Vol. 8. Vilna: B. Kletskin, 1928.

——. *Gezamlte verk.* Vol. 9. Vilna: B. Kletskin, 1928.

——. *Romance of a Horse Thief.* Translated by David G. Roskies. In *A Shtetl and Other Yiddish Novellas* (pp. 141–211). Edited by Ruth R. Wisse. Detroit: Wayne State University Press, 1986.

Orfali, Stephanie. *A Jewish Girl in the Weimar Republic.* Berkeley: Ronin Publishing, 1987.

Pinski, Dovid. *Dramen.* Warsaw: J. Lidski, 1909.

Peretz, I. L. *Ale verk fun Y. L. Peretz.* Vol. 5: *Folkstimlekhe geshikhtn.* New York: "CYCO" bikher farlag, 1947.

——. "Downcast Eyes." Translated by Goldie Morgentaler. In *The I. L. Peretz Reader* (pp. 230–242). Edited by Ruth R. Wisse. New Haven: Yale University Press, 2002.

Perle, Yehoshue. *Yidn fun a gants yor.* Warsaw: H. Bzshoza, 1936.

——. *Everyday Jews: Scenes from a Vanished Life.* Edited by David G. Roskies. Translated by Maier Deshell and Margaret Birstein. New Haven: Yale University Press, 2007.

Poliakova, Zinaida. *A Jewish Woman of Distinction: The Life and Diaries of Zinaida Poliakova.* Edited by ChaeRan Y. Freeze. Translated by Gregory Freeze. Waltham, MA: Brandeis University Press, 2019.

Programm der Realschule der israelitischen Gemeinde Philanthropin (Realschule und höhere Mädchenschule) zu Frankfurt A. M. Frankfurt am Main: Kumpf & Reis, 1902.

Raabe, Wilhelm. *Erzählungen.* Vol. 9 of *Wilhelm Raabe Sämtliche Werke,* Part I, 2nd ed. Edited by Karl Hoppe, Hans Oppermann, and Hans Plischke. Göttingen: Vandenhoeck & Ruprecht, 1974.

Rakovsky, Puah. *Zikhroynes fun a yidisher revolutsionerin.* Buenos Aires: Tsentral farband fun poylishe yidn in Argentine, 1954.

——. *My Life as a Radical Jewish Woman: Memoirs of a Zionist Feminist in Poland.* Edited by Paula E. Hyman. Translated by Barbara Harshav with Paula E. Hyman. Bloomington: Indiana University Press, 2002.

Reisinger, Eduard. *Die Tanzkunst und die Tänze.* Vienna: C. Daberkow, 1889.

Reyzen, Avrom. "Di vos tantsn nit." *Di tsukunft* 17, no. 10 (October 1912): 659–660.

Richarz, Monika, ed. *Jewish Life in Germany: Memoirs from Three Centuries.* Translated by Stella P. Rosenfeld and Sidney Rosenfeld. Bloomington: Indiana University Press, 1991.

Rocco, Emil. *Der Umgang in und mit der Gesellschaft: Ein Handbuch des guten Tons.* Halle a. d. Saale: Otto Hendel (n.d.) [ca. 1891].

Roth, Joseph. *Radetzkymarsch: Roman.* Munich: Deutscher Taschenbuch Verlag, 1989.

——. *The Radetzky March.* Translated by Joachim Neugroschel. New York: Alfred A. Knopf, 1996.

Sacher-Masoch, Leopold von. *Hasara Raba.* Leipzig: E. L. Morgenstern, 1882.

——. *Deutsche Hofgeschichten: Geschichten aus der Zopfzeit.* Leipzig-Rendnitz: Oswald Schmidt, 1887.

——. *Im Reich der Töne: Musikalische Novellen.* Mannheim: J. Bensheimer, 1891.

——. *Jüdisches Leben in Wort und Bild.* Mannheim: J. Bensheimer, 1891.

——. *Souvenirs: Autobiographische Prosa.* Translated by Susanne Farin. Munich: Belleville, 1985.

——. *Österreichische Erzählungen des 19. Jahrhunderts.* Edited by Alois Brandstetter. Salzburg: Residenz Verlag, 1986.

——. *Der Judenraphael: Geschichten aus Galizien.* Vienna: Böhlau, 1989.

——. "Hasara Raba." In *A Light for Others and other Jewish Tales from Galicia* (pp. 28–148). Translated by Adolf Opel. Riverside, CA: Ariadne Press, 1994.

——. *Jewish Life: Tales from Nineteenth-Century Europe.* Translated by Virginia L. Lewis. Riverside, CA: Ariadne Press, 2002.

Sartre, Jean-Paul. *Anti-Semite and Jew.* Translated by George J. Becker. New York: Schocken Books, 1965.

Schnitzler, Arthur. *Tagebuch, 1879–1892.* Vol. 4 of *Schnitzler-Tagebuch.* Edited by Peter Michael Braunwarth et al. Vienna: Verlag der Österreichischen Akademie der Wissenschaften, 1987.

Segalovitsh, Zusman. *Tlomatske 13: Fun farbrentn nekhtn.* Buenos Aires: Tsentralfarband fun poylishe yidn in Argentine, 1946.

[Shakespeare, William]. *The Tragedy of Romeo and Juliet.* In *The Riverside Shakespeare* (vol. 2, pp. 1055–1099). Edited by G. Blakemore Evans. Boston: Houghton Mifflin Company, 1974.

Sholem Aleichem. *Fun'm yarid: Lebnsbashraybungen.* New York: Ferlag "Varhayt," 1916.

———. *Ale verk fun Sholem Aleykhem.* Vol. 2. Buenos Aires: Ikuf, 1952.

———. *From the Fair.* Translated by Curt Leviant. New York: Viking, 1985.

———. *The Nightingale: Or, the Saga of Yosele Solovey the Cantor.* Translated by Aliza Shevrin. New York: G. P. Putnam's Sons, 1985.

Shtok, Fradel. *Gezamelte dertseylungen.* New York: Farlag "Nay tsayt," 1919.

———. "A Dance." Translated by Sonia Gollance. *In geveb: A Journal of Yiddish Studies* (December 2017): https://ingeveb.org/texts-and-translations/a-dance

Singer, Isaac Bashevis. *Gimpl tam: Un andere dertseylungen.* New York: Tsiko, 1963.

———. *The Family Moskat.* Translated by A. H. Gross. London: Secker & Warburg, 1966.

———. *The Manor.* New York: Farrar, Straus and Giroux, 1967.

———. *Di familye Mushkat.* 2 vols. Tel Aviv: Farlag I. L. Peretz, 1977.

———. "Memoirs and Episodes from the Writers' Association House in Warsaw: Memoirs of Isaac Bashevis Singer, Apprentice Journalist." *Qesher* 10 (November 1991): 4e–11e.

———. *Collected Stories: Gimpel the Fool to The Letter Writer.* Edited by Ilan Stavans. New York: Literary Classics of the United States, 2004.

Singer, Israel Joshua. *Fun a velt vos iz nishto mer.* New York: Farlag Matones, 1946.

———. *Di brider Ashkenazi.* New York: Farlag Matones, 1951.

———. *Of a World That Is No More.* Translated by Joseph Singer. London: Faber and Faber, 1970.

———. *The Brothers Ashkenazi.* Translated by Joseph Singer. New York: Other Press, 2010.

Stein, Joseph, Jerry Bock, and Sheldon Harnick. *Fiddler on the Roof.* New York: Crown Publishers, 1964.

Tashrak [Y. Y. Zevin]. *Etikete: A veg vayzer fun laytishe oyfirung, heflikhkayt un sheyne manieren far mener un froyen.* New York: Hebrew Publishing Company, 1912.

———. "At a Ball." Translated by Sonia Gollance. National Yiddish Book Center: http://www.yiddishbookcenter.org/language-literature-culture/yiddish-translation/ball

Trunk, Y. Y. *Poylin: Zikhroynes un bilder.* Vol. 1. New York: Farlag Medem-klub, 1944.

———. *Poylin: My Life Within Jewish Life in Poland, Sketches and Images.* Translated by Anna Clarke. Toronto: University of Toronto Press, 2007.

Unger, Menashe Unger. *Pshiskhe un Kotsk.* Buenos Aires: Tsentral-farband fun poylishe yidn in Argentine, 1949.

———. *A Fire Burns in Kotsk: A Tale of Hasidim in the Kingdom of Poland*. Translated by Jonathan Boyarin. Detroit: Wayne State University Press, 2015.

Vhaytman, G. *Gute zitn un shehne manyern*. Warsaw: Farlag Unzer lebn (n.d.) [ca. 1920].

Voss, Rudolph. *Der Tanz und seine Geschichte: Eine kulturhistorisch-choreographische Studie*. Berlin: O. Seehagen, 1869.

Waldau, Alfred. *Böhmische Nationaltänze: Culturstudie*. Vol. 1. Prague: Hermann Dominikus, 1859.

Wechsberg, Joseph. *The Vienna I Knew: Memories of a European Childhood*. Garden City, NY: Doubleday & Company, 1979.

Wecker, Helene. *The Golem and the Jinni*. New York: Harper Perennial, 2014.

Weiss, Isaac Jacob. *She'elot u-teshuvot minhat Yitshak*. Vol. 3. Jerusalem: Minhat Yitshak, 1993.

Wengeroff, Pauline. *Memoiren einer Grossmutter: Bilder aus der Kulturgeschichte der Juden Russlands im 19. Jahrhundert*. Vol. 1. Berlin: Verlag von M. Poppelauer, 1908.

———. *Memoirs of a Grandmother: Scenes from the Cultural History of the Jews of Russia in the Nineteenth Century*. Translated by Shulamit S. Magnus. 2 vols. Stanford: Stanford University Press, 2010–2014.

Wesner, [Frank]. *Gesellschaftliche Tanzkunst*. Leipzig: Verlag Junst und Wiss. (n.d.) [1890].

Wolfssohn, Aaron Halle. *Silliness and Sanctimony*. In *Landmark Yiddish Plays: A Critical Anthology* (pp. 81–111). Edited and translated by Joel Berkowitz and Jeremy Dauber. Albany: State University of New York Press, 2006.

Wypiański, Stanisław. *Wesele: Dramat w 3 Aktach*. Kraków: Altenberg, 1903.

———. *The Wedding*. Translated by Noel Clark. London: Oberon Books, 2012.

Yakhnuk, [Khayim-Avrom] Leybovitsh. *Yakhnuk's tants-klassin, oder di frehlikhe yugend: A kritishe ertsehlung fun yudishen lebin*. Grayevo [Grajewo]: Avrom-Mordkhe Pyurko, 1905.

Yezierska, Anzia. *Bread Givers: A Novel*. Garden City, NY: Doubleday, Page & Company, 1925.

Zangwill, [Israel]. *Selected Works of Israel Zangwill*. Philadelphia: Jewish Publication Society of America, 1938.

Zunser, Miriam Shomer. *Yesterday: A Memoir of a Russian Jewish Family*. New York: Harper & Row (n.d.) [ca. 1939].

Zunz, Leopold. *Zur Geschichte und Literatur*. Vol. 1. Berlin: Veit und Comp, 1845.

Zweig, Stefan. *The World of Yesterday: An Autobiography*. Lincoln: University of Nebraska Press, 1964.

———. *Die Welt von Gestern: Erinnerungen eines Europäers*. Frankfurt am Main: Fischer Taschenbuch Verlag, 1974.

Secondary Sources

Abrahams, Israel. *Jewish Life in the Middle Ages*. Philadelphia: Jewish Publication Society, 2010.

Adler, Ruth. *Women of the Shtetl—Through the Eyes of Y. L. Peretz*. Rutherford, NJ: Fairleigh Dickinson University Press, 1980.

Agus, Irvin A. *Urban Civilization in Pre-Crusade Europe: A Study of Organized Town-Life in Northwestern Europe During the Tenth and Eleventh Centuries Based on the Responsa Literature*. Vol. 2. Leiden: E. J. Brill, 1965.

Aldrich, Elizabeth. *From the Ballroom to Hell: Grace and Folly in Nineteenth-Century Dance*. Evanston, IL: Northwestern University Press, 1991.

Alpert, Michael. "*Freylekhs* on Film: The Portrayal of Jewish Traditional Dance in Yiddish Cinema." In *When Joseph Met Molly: A Reader in Yiddish Film* (pp. 131–135). Edited by Sylvia Plaskin. Nottingham: Five Leaves Publications in association with the European Jewish Publication Society, 1999.

Arcangeli, Alessandro. "Dance Under Trial: The Moral Debate 1200–1600." *Dance Research* 12, no. 2 (1994): 127–155.

Baader, Benjamin Maria. *Gender, Judaism, and Bourgeois Culture in Germany, 1800–1870*. Bloomington: Indiana University Press, 2006.

Bachman, Merle L. *Recovering "Yiddishland": Threshold Moments in American Literature*. Syracuse, NY: Syracuse University Press, 2008.

Bakhtin, Mikhail. *Rabelais and His World*. Translated by Helene Iswolsky. Bloomington: Indiana University Press, 1984.

Banes, Sally. *Dancing Women: Female Bodies on Stage*. London: Routledge, 1998.

Baron, Salo. *Die Judenfrage auf dem Wiener Kongreß*. Vienna: R. Löwit Verlag, 1920.

——. *The Jewish Community: The History and Structure to the American Revolution*. Vol. 2. Westport, CT: Greenwood Press (n.d.) [1972].

Bartal, Israel. *The Jews of Eastern Europe, 1772–1881*. Translated by Chaya Naor. Philadelphia: University of Pennsylvania Press, 2002.

Bauman, Zygmunt. *Modernity and Ambivalence*. Ithaca, NY: Cornell University Press, 1991.

Beregovski, Moshe. *Old Jewish Folk Music: The Collections and Writings of Moshe Beregovski*. Edited and translated by Mark Slobin. Syracuse, NY: Syracuse University Press, 2000.

Berkovitsh, Israel. *Hundert yor yidish teater in Rumenye, 1876–1976*. Bucharest: Kriterion, 1976.

Berkowitz, Michael. *Zionist Culture and West European Jewry Before the First World War*. Cambridge: Cambridge University Press, 1993.

Berman, Feigue. "Hasidic Dance: An Historical and Theological Analysis." PhD dissertation. New York University, 1999.

Biale, David. "Masochism and Philosemitism: The Strange Case of Leopold
    von Sacher-Masoch." *Journal of Contemporary History* 17, no. 2 (1982): 305–323.
——. *Eros and the Jews: From Biblical Israel to Contemporary America*. New York: Basic
    Books, 1992.
Biale, David, et al. *Hasidism: A New History*. Princeton: Princeton University Press,
    2018.
Bohlman, Philip V., and Otto Holzapfel, eds. *The Folk Songs of Ashkenaz*. Vol. 6.
    Middleton, WI: A. R. Editions, 2001.
Bosse, Joanna. "Whiteness and the Performance of Race in American Ballroom
    Dance." *Journal of American Folklore* 120, no. 475 (2007): 19–47.
Bourdieu, Pierre. *Distinction: A Social Critique of the Judgement of Taste*. Translated by
    Richard Nice. Cambridge, MA: Harvard University Press, 1984.
Boyarin, Daniel. *Carnal Israel: Reading Sex in Talmudic Culture*. Berkeley: University
    of California Press, 1993.
——. *Unheroic Conduct: The Rise of Heterosexuality and the Invention of the Jewish Man*.
    Berkeley: University of California Press, 1997.
Brandstetter, Gabriele. *Poetics of Dance: Body, Image, and Space in the Historical
    Avant-Gardes*. Translated by Elena Polzer and Mark Franko. New York: Oxford
    University Press, 2015.
Braun, Alisa. "Kadya Molodowsky (Kadye Molodovski) (10 May 1894—23
    March 1975)." In *Dictionary of Literary Biography*. Vol. 333: *Writers in Yiddish*
    (pp. 188–194). Edited by Joseph Sherman. Detroit: Gale, 2007.
Brayer, Menachem M. *The Jewish Woman in Rabbinic Literature: A Psychosocial Per-
    spective*. Vol. 1. Hoboken: Ktav Publishing House, 1986.
Bromberg, Eli. "We Need to Talk About Shmuel Charney." *In geveb: A Jour-
    nal of Yiddish Studies* (October 2019). https://ingeveb.org/articles/
    we-need-to-talk-about-shmuel-charney
Brunotte, Ulrike. "The *Beautiful Jewess* as Borderline Figure in Europe's Internal
    Colonialism: Some Remarks on the Intertwining of Orientalism and Antisemi-
    tism." *ReOrient* 4, no. 2 (2019): 166–180.
Brunotte, Ulrike, Anna-Dorothea Ludewig, and Azel Stähler. "Orientalism, Gender,
    and the Jews: Literary and Artistic Transformations of European Discourses."
    In *Orientalism, Gender, and the Jews. Literary and Artistic Transformations of
    European National Discourses* (pp. 1–16). Edited by Ulrike Brunotte, Anna-
    Dorothea Ludewig, and Axel Stähler. Berlin: De Gruyter, 2015.
Burdekin, Hannah. *The Ambivalent Author: Five German Writers and Their Jewish
    Characters, 1848–1914*. Oxford: Peter Lang, 2002.
Cahan, Y. L. "Tsum oyfkum fun yidishn tantslid: A folkslid-studie." *YIVO bleter:
    Khodesh-shrift fun yidishn visnshaftlekhn institut* 1, no. 1 (January 1931): 28–39.

Castle, Terry. *Masquerade and Civilization: The Carnivalesque in Eighteenth-Century English Culture and Fiction*. Stanford: Stanford University Press, 1986.

Chametzky, Jules. "Regional Literature and Ethnic Realities." *The Antioch Review* 31, no. 3 (Autumn 1971): 385–396.

Chinn, Sarah E. *Inventing Modern Adolescence: The Children of Immigrants in Turn-of-the-Century America*. New Brunswick, NJ: Rutgers University Press, 2009.

Cohen, Richard I., ed. *Place in Modern Jewish Culture and Society*. New York: Oxford University Press, 2018.

Coontz, Stephanie. *Marriage, a History: From Obedience to Intimacy, or How Love Conquered Marriage*. New York: Viking, 2005.

Cybenko, Larissa. "'Jetzt heißt es auftreten, eine neue Szene beginnt': Leopold von Sacher-Masoch und die Welt des Theaters." In *Leopold von Sacher-Masoch: Ein Wegbereiter des 20. Jahrhunderts* (pp. 221–244). Edited by Marion Kobelt-Groch and Michael Salewski. Hildesheim: Georg Ulms Verlag, 2010.

Cypess, Rebecca, and Nancy Sinkoff, eds. *Sara Levy's World: Gender, Judaism, and the Bach Tradition in Enlightenment Berlin*. Rochester, NY: University of Rochester Press, 2018.

Danon, Dina. *The Jews of Ottoman Izmir: A Modern History*. Stanford: Stanford University Press, 2020.

Deleuze, Gilles. *Masochism*. New York: Zone Books, 1989.

Dinerstein, Joel. *Swinging the Machine: Modernity, Technology, and African American Culture Between the World Wars*. Amherst: University of Massachusetts Press, 2003.

Dwork, Deborah. "Health Conditions of Immigrant Jews on the Lower East Side of New York: 1880–1914." *Medical History* 25, no. 1 (1981): 1–40.

Dyer, Richard. "White Enough." In *The Time of Our Lives: Dirty Dancing and Popular Culture* (pp. 73–85). Edited by Yannis Tzioumakis and Siân Lincoln. Detroit: Wayne State University Press, 2013.

Dynner, Glenn. *Men of Silk: The Hasidic Conquest of Polish Jewish Society*. New York: Oxford University Press, 2006.

——. *Yankel's Tavern: Jews, Liquor, and Life in the Kingdom of Poland*. Oxford: Oxford University Press, 2013.

Efron, John M. *German Jewry and the Allure of the Sephardic*. Princeton: Princeton University Press, 2016.

Ellinson, Getsel. *Women and the Mitzvot*. Vol. 2: *The Modest Way*. Translated by Raphael Blumberg. [Jerusalem]: Eliner Library, 1992.

Elon, Amos. *The Pity of It All: A History of Jews in Germany, 1743–1933*. New York: Metropolitan Books, 2002.

Endelman, Todd M. "Gender and Conversion Revisited." In *Gender and Jewish*

History (pp. 170–186). Edited by Marion A. Kaplan and Deborah Dash Moore. Bloomington: University of Indiana Press, 2011.

Engelhardt, Molly. *Dancing Out of Line: Ballrooms, Ballets, and Mobility in Victorian Fiction and Culture*. Athens: Ohio University Press, 2009.

Enstad, Nan. *Ladies of Labor, Girls of Adventure: Working Women, Popular Culture, and Labor Politics at the Turn of the Twentieth Century*. New York: Columbia University Press, 1999.

Erens, Patricia. *The Jew in American Cinema*. Bloomington: University of Indiana Press, 1984.

Erk, Ludwig. *Deutscher Liederhort*. Vol. 1. Hildesheim: Georg Olms Verlag, 1972.

Ernst, Petra, ed. *Karl Emil Franzos: Schriftsteller zwischen den Kulturen*. Innsbruck: Studienverlag, 2007.

Ernst, Petra, and Gerald Lamprecht, eds. *Jewish Spaces: Die Kategorie "Raum" im Kontext kultureller Identitäten*. Innsbruck: StudenVerlag, 2010.

Ewen, Elizabeth. *Immigrant Women in the Land of Dollars: Life and Culture on the Lower East Side, 1890–1925*. New York: Monthly Review Press, 1985.

Feldman, Walter Zev. "Bulgareasca, Bulgarish, Bulgar: The Transformation of a Klezmer Dance Genre." *Ethnomusicology* 38, no. 1 (1994): 1–35.

——. *Klezmer: Music, History, and Memory*. Oxford: Oxford University Press, 2016.

Ferber, Michael, ed. *A Dictionary of Literary Symbols*, 2nd ed. Cambridge: Cambridge University Press, 2007.

Foucault, Michel. "Of Other Spaces." Translated by Jay Miskowiec. *Diacritics* 16, no. 1 (Spring 1986): 22–27.

Fram, Edward. *Ideals Face Reality: Jewish Law and Life in Poland, 1550–1655*. Cincinnati: Hebrew Union College Press, 1997.

Freeze, ChaeRan Y. *Jewish Marriage and Divorce in Imperial Russia*. Hanover, NH: University Press of New England for Brandeis University, 2002.

Frenk, A. N. "Di milkhome kegn der '*hefkeyrus*' in amolikn Varshe: A kapitl geshikhte fun dem inerlekhn yidishn lebn in Varshe in der ershter helft fun 19-stn yorhundert." In *Almanakh tsum 10-yorikn yubileum fun "Moment"* (pp. 95–114). Warsaw: Der moment, 1921.

Friedhaber, Zvi. "The Bride and Her Guests: The Dance with the Separating Kerchief." In *Seeing Israeli and Jewish Dance (pp. 225–233)*. Edited by Judith Brin Ingber and translated by Judith Brin Ingber with Rabbi Moshe Silberschien. Detroit: Wayne State University Press, 2011.

Friedland, LeeEllen. "'Tantsn Is Lebn': Dancing in Eastern European Jewish Culture." *Dance Research Journal* 17 (1985): 76–80.

Friedman, Hershey H., and Linda Weiser Friedman. *God Laughed: Sources of Jewish Humor*. New Brunswick, NJ: Transaction Publishers, 2014.

Fuchs, Anne, and Florian Krobb, eds. *Ghetto Writing: Traditional and Eastern Jewry in German-Jewish Literature from Heine to Hilsenrath*. Columbia, SC: Camden House, 1999.

Garafola, Lynn, ed. *Rethinking the Sylph: New Perspectives on the Romantic Ballet*. Hanover, NH: University Press of New England for Wesleyan University, 1997.

Garber, Marjorie. *Vested Interests: Cross-Dressing and Cultural Anxiety*. New York: Routledge, 2012.

Garloff, Katja. *Mixed Feelings: Tropes of Love in German Jewish Culture*. Ithaca, NY: Cornell University Press and Cornell University Library, 2016.

Gebirtig, Mordechai. *Mordechai Gebirtig: His Poetic and Musical Legacy*. Edited by Gertrude Schneider. Westport, CT: Praeger, 2000.

Geertz, Clifford. "Deep Play: Notes on the Balinese Cockfight." *Daedelus* 134, no. 4 (Fall 2005): 56–86.

Gellerman, Jill. "Rehearsing for Ultimate Joy Among the Lubavitcher Hasidim: Simchas Bais Hasho'eva in Crown Heights." In *Seeing Israeli and Jewish Dance* (pp. 285–312). Edited by Judith Brin Ingber. Detroit: Wayne State University Press, 2011.

George, Alys X. *The Naked Truth: Viennese Modernism and the Body*. Chicago: University of Chicago Press, 2020.

Gilman, Sander L. *The Jew's Body*. New York: Routledge, 1991.

——. *"You, Too, Could Walk Like a Gentile.* Jews and Posture." In *Wegweiser und Grenzgänger: Studien zur deutsch-jüdischen Kultur- und Literaturgeschichte* (pp. 17–30). Edited by Stefan Vogt, Hans Otto Horch, Vivian Liska, and Malgorzata A. Maksymiak. Vienna: Böhlau Verlag, 2018.

Ginzberg, Binyomin. *The Music of the Mitsve Tants in the Court of the Hasidic Rebbes: 159 Hasidic Dance Melodies*. Bergenfield, NJ: JewishMusician.com Press, 2020.

Glasenapp, Gabriele von, and Hans Otto Horch. *Ghettoliteratur: Eine Dokumentation zur deutsch-jüdischen Literaturgeschichte des 19. und frühen 20. Jahrhunderts*. Tübingen: Niemeyer, 2005.

Goldberg, Harvey E. *Jewish Passages: Cycles of Jewish Life*. Berkeley: University of California Press, 2003.

Gollance, Sonia. "'Spaß mit der schönen Jüdin'. Mixed Space and Dancing in Karl Emil Franzos's *Judith Trachtenberg*." *Austrian Studies* 24 (2016): 65–78.

——. "A Dance: Fradel Shtok Reconsidered." *In geveb: A Journal of Yiddish Studies* (December 2017): https://ingeveb.org/articles/a-dance-fradel-shtok-reconsidered

——. "Delilah's Dance: Salomania and German-Jewish Orientalism." In *Bewegungsfreiheit: Tanz als kulturelle Manifestation (1900–1950)* (pp. 159–177). Edited by Rita Rieger. Bielefeld: transcript, 2017.

——. "Harmonious Instability: (Mixed) Dancing and Partner Choice in German-Jewish and Yiddish Literature." PhD dissertation, University of Pennsylvania, 2017.

——. "*A Valtz* from the Land of *Valtzes!*': Dance as a Form of Americanization in Abraham Cahan's Fiction." *Dance Chronicle* 41, no. 3 (2018): 393–417.

——. "Gesture, Repertoire, and Emotion: Yiddish Dance Practice in German and Yiddish Literature," *Jewish Social Studies: History, Culture, Society* 25, no. 1 (Fall 2019): 102–127.

Graetz, Heinrich. *Geschichte der Juden von den ältesten Zeiten bis auf die Gegenwart.* Vol. 11: *Beginn der Mendelssohn'schen Zeit (1750) bis in die neueste Zeit (1848).* Leipzig: Oskar Leiner, 1870.

Gross, Natan. "Mordechai Gebirtig: The Folk Song and the Cabaret Song." Translated by Gwido Zlatkes. *Polin: Studies in Polish Jewry* 16 (2012): 107–117.

Grossman, Jeffrey A. "The Yiddish-German Connection." *Poetics Today* 36, no. 1–2 (June 2015): 59–110.

Gurley, David Gantt. *Meïr Aaron Goldschmidt and the Poetics of Jewish Fiction.* Syracuse, NY: Syracuse University Press, 2016.

Habermas, Jürgen. *The Structural Transformation of the Public Sphere: An Inquiry into a Category of Bourgeois Society.* Translated by Thomas Burger with Frederick Lawrence. Cambridge: Polity Press, 2015.

Haenni, Sabine. "Visual and Theatrical Culture, Tenement Fiction, and the Immigrant Subject in Abraham Cahan's *Yekl.*" *American Literature* 71, no. 3 (September 1999): 493–527.

Hammerman, Shaina. *Silver Screen, Hasidic Jews: The Story of an Image.* Bloomington: Indiana University Press, 2018.

Heid, Ludger, and Julius H. Schopes, ed. *Juden in Deutschland: Von der Aufklärung bis zur Gegenwart.* Munich: Piper, 1994.

Helfer, Martha B. *The Word Unheard: Legacies of Anti-Semitism in German Literature and Culture.* Evanston, IL: Northwestern University Press, 2011.

Hellerstein, Kathryn, ed. and trans. *Paper Bridges: Selected Poems of Kadya Molodowsky.* Detroit: Wayne State University Press, 1999.

——. "Finding Her Yiddish Voice: Kadya Molodowsky in America." *Revue d'Etudes Anglophones* 12 (Spring 2002): 48–68.

——. "The Art of Sex in Yiddish Poems: Celia Dropkin and Her Contemporaries." In *Modern Jewish Literatures: Intersections and Boundaries* (pp. 189–212). Edited by Sheila E. Jelen, Michael P. Kramer, and Scott Lerner. Philadelphia: University of Pennsylvania Press, 2010.

Hertz, Deborah. *Jewish High Society in Old Regime Berlin.* Syracuse, NY: Syracuse University Press, 2005.

Heschel, Susannah. "Lilith." In *Encyclopaedia Judaica* (2nd ed., vol. 13, pp. 18–19). Edited by Fred Skolnik. Farmington Hills, MI: Thomson Gale, 2007.

Hess, Jonathan M. "Fictions of a German-Jewish Public: Ludwig Jacobowski's *Werther the Jew* and Its Readers." *Jewish Social Studies* 11, no. 2 (2005): 202–230.

——. *Middlebrow Literature and the Making of German-Jewish Identity.* Stanford: Stanford University Press, 2010.

——. *Deborah and Her Sisters: How One Nineteenth-Century Melodrama and a Host of Celebrated Actresses Put Judaism on the World Stage.* Philadelphia: University of Pennsylvania Press, 2018.

Hess, Remi. *Der Walzer: Geschichte eines Skandals.* Translated by Antoinette Gittinger. Hamburg: Europäische Verlagsanstalt, 1996.

Hicks, Michael. *Mormonism and Music: A History.* Urbana: University of Illinois Press, 2003.

Hirsch, Dafna. "Zionist Eugenics, Mixed Marriage, and the Creation of a 'New Jewish Type.'" *Journal of the Royal Anthropological Institute* 15, no. 3 (2009): 592–609.

Hoberman, J. *Bridge of Light: Yiddish Film Between Two Worlds.* New York: Museum of Modern Art, 1991.

Horch, Hans Otto, and Horst Denkler, eds. *Conditio Judaica: Judentum, Antisemitismus und deutschsprachige Literatur vom 18. Jahrhundert bis zum Ersten Weltkrieg.* Vol. 2. Tübingen: Niemeyer, 1989.

Howe, Irving, and Kenneth Bibo. *How We Lived: A Documentary History of Immigrant Jews in America, 1880–1930.* New York: Marek, 1979.

Huizinga, Johan. *Homo Ludens: A Study of the Play-Element in Culture.* Boston: Beacon Press, 1955.

Hyams, Barbara. "The Whip and the Lamp: Leopold von Sacher-Masoch, the Woman Question, and the Jewish Question." *Women in German Yearbook* 13 (1997): 67–79.

Igra, Anna R. *Wives Without Husbands: Marriage, Desertion, and Welfare in New York, 1900–1935.* Chapel Hill: University of North Carolina Press, 2007.

Imhoff, Sarah. *Masculinity and the Making of American Judaism.* Bloomington: Indiana University Press, 2017.

Ingber, Judith Brin, ed. *Seeing Israeli and Jewish Dance.* Detroit: Wayne State University Press, 2011.

Jacobs, Jack. *Bundist Counterculture in Interwar Poland.* Syracuse, NY: Syracuse University Press, 2009.

Jacobs, Louis. *A Concise Companion to the Jewish Religion.* Oxford: Oxford University Press, 2009.

Jeschke, Claudia. "Hispanomania in Dance Theory and Choreography." In *Les Choses espagnoles: Research into the Hispanomania of 19th Century Dance* (pp. 37–57). Edited by Claudia Jeschke, Gabi Vettermann, and Nicole Haitzinger. Munich: epodium, 2009.

——. "Lola Montez and Spanish Dance in the 19th Century." In *New German Dance Studies* (pp. 31–44). Edited by Susan Manning and Lucia Ruprecht. Urbana: University of Illinois Press, 2017.

Jones, Susan. *Literature, Modernism, and Dance*. Oxford: Oxford University Press, 2013.

Kahn, Aharon. "Music in Halachic Perspective." *Journal of Halacha and Contemporary Society* 14 (1987): 7–46.

Kalik, Judith. *Movable Inn: The Rural Jewish Population of Minsk Guberniya in 1793–1914*. Warsaw: De Gruyter, 2018.

Kaplan, Marion A. *The Making of the Jewish Middle Class: Women, Family, and Identity in Imperial Germany*. Oxford: Oxford University Press, 1991.

———. "'Based on Love': The Courtship of Hendele and Jochanan (1803–1804)." In *Jüdische Welten: Juden in Deutschland vom 18. Jahrhundert bis in die Gegenwart* (pp. 86–107). Edited by Marion Kaplan and Beate Meyer. Göttingen: Wallstein Verlag, 2005.

———, ed. *Jewish Daily Life in Germany, 1618–1945*. Oxford: Oxford University Press, 2005.

Katz, Jacob. *Out of the Ghetto: The Social Background of Jewish Emancipation, 1770–1870*. Cambridge, MA: Harvard University Press, 1973.

———. *Jewish Emancipation and Self-Emancipation*. Philadelphia: Jewish Publication Society, 1986.

Katz, Steven T., ed. *The Shtetl: New Evaluations*. New York: New York University Press, 2007.

Kayserling, M. *Der Dichter Ephraim Kuh: Ein Beitrag zur Geschichte der deutschen Literatur*. Berlin: Julius Springer, 1864.

Kieval, Hillel J. *Languages of Community: The Jewish Experience in the Czech Lands*. Berkeley: University of California Press, 2000.

Kirk, Robert, and Clara M. Kirk. "Abraham Cahan and William Dean Howells: The Story of a Friendship." *American Jewish Historical Quarterly* 52 (September 1962): 27–55.

Kirshenblatt-Gimblett, Barbara. "Weddings." In *YIVO Encyclopedia of Jews in Eastern Europe, 2007–09*. Vol. 2. Edited by Gershon Hundert. New Haven: Yale University Press, 2008.

Kirzane, Jessica. "The Melting Plot: Interethnic Romance in Jewish American Fiction in the Early Twentieth Century." PhD dissertation, Columbia University, 2017.

Klapper, Melissa R. *Jewish Girls Coming of Age in America, 1860–1920*. New York: New York University Press, 2005.

Klepfisz, Irena. "Di Mames, Dos Loshn/The Mothers, the Language: Feminism, Yidishkayt, and the Politics of Memory." *Bridges* 4 (Winter–Summer 1994/5754): 12–47.

Klüger, Ruth. "Die Säkularisierung des Judenhasses am Beispiel von Wilhelm Raabes 'Der Hungerpastor.'" In *Literarischer Antisemitismus nach Auschwitz* (pp. 103–110). Edited by Klaus-Michael Bogdal, Klaus Holz, and Matthias N. Lorenz. Stuttgart: J. B. Metzler, 2007.

Knowles, Mark. *The Wicked Waltz and Other Scandalous Dances: Outrage at Couple Dancing in the 19th and Early 20th Centuries*. Jefferson, NC: McFarland & Company, 2009.

Kobelt-Groch, Marion, and Michael Salewski, eds. *Leopold von Sacher-Masoch: Ein Wegbereiter des 20. Jahrhunderts*. Hildesheim: Georg Ulms Verlag, 2010.

Kohler, Max J. "Jewish Rights at the Congresses of Vienna (1814–1815), and Aix-La-Chapelle." *Publications of the American Jewish Historical Society* 26 (1918): 33–125.

Kolb, Alexandra. *Performing Femininity: Dance and Literature in German Modernism*. Oxford: Peter Lang, 2009.

Koller, Sabine, Gennady Estraikh, and Mikhail Krutikov, eds. *Joseph Opatoshu: A Yiddish Writer Between Europe and America*. London: Legenda, 2013.

Koschorke, Albrecht. *Leopold von Sacher-Masoch: Die Inszenierung einer Perversion*. Munich: Piper, 1968.

Kraemer, David. *Jewish Eating and Identity Through the Ages*. New York: Routledge, 2007.

Kramer, Sydelle, and Jenny Masur, eds. *Jewish Grandmothers*. Boston: Beacon Press, 1976.

Kriwaczek, Paul. *Yiddish Civilisation: The Rise and Fall of a Forgotten Nation*. New York: Alfred A. Knopf, 2005.

Krobb, Florian. *Die schöne Jüdin: Jüdische Frauengestalten in der deutschsprachigen Erzählliteratur vom 17. Jahrhundert bis zum Ersten Weltkrieg*. Tübingen: Niemeyer, 1993.

Krutikov, Mikhail. *Yiddish Fiction and the Crisis of Modernity, 1905–1914*. Stanford: Stanford University Press, 2001.

Labovitz, Gail. *Marriage and Metaphor: Constructions of Gender in Rabbinic Literature*. Lanham, MD: Lexington Books, 2009.

Lambert, Josh. *Unclean Lips: Jews, Obscenity, and American Culture*. New York: New York University Press, 2013.

Lawrence, Tim. "Disco and the Queering of the Dance Floor." *Cultural Studies* 25, no. 2 (2011): 230–243.

Lefebvre, Henri. *The Production of Space*. Translated by Donald Nicholson-Smith. Malden, MA: Blackwell Publishing, 1991.

Lehmann, Jon. *Dr. Markus Lehmann*. Frankfurt am Main: J. Kauffmann, 1910.

Leuenberger, Stefanie. *Schrift-Raum Jerusalem: Identitätsdiskurse im Werk deutsch-jüdischer Autoren*. Cologne: Böhlau, 2007.

Leveen, Lois. "Only When I Laugh: Textual Dynamics of Ethnic Humor." *MELUS* 21, no. 4 (Winter 1996): 29–55.

Lezzi, Eva. *"Liebe ist meine Religion!": Eros und Ehe zwischen Juden und Christen in der Literatur des 19. Jahrhunderts*. Göttingen: Wallstein Verlag, 2013.

——. "Secularism and Neo-Orthodoxy: Conflicting Strategies in Modern Orthodox Fiction." In *Secularism in Question: Jews and Judaism in Modern Times*
(pp. 208–232). Edited by Ari Joskowicz and Ethan B. Katz. Philadelphia: University of Pennsylvania Press, 2015.

Lifschutz, Ezekiel. "Merrymakers at a Jewish Wedding." *YIVO Annual Jewish Social
Science* 7 (1952): 43–83.

[Lifshitz], Y. "R. Yedidiye Vayls kamf kegn maskaradn un tents in Karlsrue." In
Arkhiv far der geshikte fun yidishn teater un drame (vol. 1, pp. 452–453). Edited by
Jacob Shatzky. Vilna: Yidisher visnshaftlekher institut, 1930.

Lipphardt, Anna, Julia Brauch, and Alexandtra Nocke, eds. *Jewish Topographies: Visions of Space, Traditions of Place.* Burlington, VT: Ashgate, 2008.

Lipsky, Seth. *The Rise of Abraham Cahan.* New York: Schocken Books, 2013.

Litvak, Olga. *Haskalah: The Romantic Movement in Judaism.* New Brunswick, NJ:
Rutgers University Press, 2012.

Loentz, Elizabeth. "'The Most Famous Jewish Pacifist Was Jesus of Nazareth . . .':
German-Jewish Pacifist Clementine Krämer's Stories of War and Visions for
Peace." *Women in German Yearbook: Feminist Studies in German Literature and
Culture* 23 (2007): 126–55.

——. "The Literary Double Life of Clementine Krämer: German-Jewish Activist
and Bavarian 'Heimat' and Dialect Writer." In *Nexus: Essays in German Jewish
Studies* (pp. 1109–1136). Edited by William Collins Donahue and Martha B.
Helfer. Rochester, NY: Camden House, 2011.

Lowenstein, Steven. "The Complicated Language Situation of German Jewry,
1760–1914." *Studia Rosenthaliana* 36 (2002–2003): 3–31.

Ludewig, Anna-Dorothea. "Fiktionale Authentizität und poetischer Realismus. Die
literarische Annexion und Rezeption Galiziens am Beispiel der Ghettogeschichten von Karl Emil Franzos und Leopold von Sacher-Masoch." In *Galizien
im Diskurs: Inklusion, Exklusion, Repräsentation* (pp. 137–155). Edited by Paul
Giersch, Florian Krobb, and Franziska Schößler. Studien zu Fremdheit und
Armut von der Antike bis zur Gegenwart 17. Frankfurt am Main: Peter Lang,
2012.

MacDonald, Edgar E., ed. *The Education of the Heart: The Correspondence of Rachel
Mordecai Lazarus and Maria Edgeworth.* Chapel Hill: University of North
Carolina Press, 1977.

MacLeod, Catriona. "Still Alive: Tableau Vivant and Narrative Suspension in
Sacher-Masoch's *Venus im Pelz.*" *Deutsche Vierteljahrsschrift für Literaturwissen-
schaft und Geistesgeschichte* 80, no. 4 (2006): 640–665.

——. *Fugitive Objects: Sculpture and Literature in the German Nineteenth Century.*
Evanston, IL: Northwestern University Press, 2014.

Maes, Francis. *A History of Russian Music: From Kamarinskaya to Babi Yar.*

Translated by Arnold J. Pomerans and Erica Pomerans. Berkeley: University of California Press, 2006.

Mahalel, Adi. "*Nit dos dorf, nit di kretshme*: Speaking About Jewish Taverns in the Works of Sholem Aleichem." *In geveb: A Journal of Yiddish Studies* (June 2020): https://ingeveb.org/articles/speaking-about-jewish-taverns-sholem-aleichem

Mahler, Raphael. *Hasidism and the Jewish Enlightenment: Their Confrontation in Galicia and Poland in the First Half of the Nineteenth Century.* Translated by Eugene Orenstein, Aaron Klein, and Jenny Machlowitz Klein. Philadelphia: Jewish Publication Society of America, 1985.

Malnig, Julie, ed. *Ballroom, Boogie, Shimmy Sham, Shake: A Social and Popular Dance Reader.* Urbana: University of Illinois Press, 2009.

Mann, Barbara E. *Space and Place in Jewish Studies.* New Brunswick, NJ: Rutgers University Press, 2012.

Margolis, Rebecca E. "A Tempest in Three Teapots: Yom Kippur Balls in London, New York, and Montreal." *Canadian Jewish Studies* 9 (2001): 38–84.

Mazor, Yaakov, and Moshe Taube. "A Hassidic Ritual Dance: The Mitsve Tants in Jerusalemite Weddings." *Yuval* 6 (1994): 164–224.

McBee, Randy. *Dance Hall Days: Intimacy and Leisure Among Working-Class Immigrants in the United States.* New York: New York University Press, 2000.

McCagg, William O., Jr. *A History of Habsburg Jews, 1670–1918.* Bloomington: Indiana University Press, 1989.

McIsaac, Peter M. "Rethinking Tableaux Vivants and Triviality in the Writings of Johann Wolfgang von Goethe, Johanna Schopenhauer, and Fanny Lewald." *Monatshefte* 99, no. 2 (2007): 152–176.

Meir, Natan M. *Stepchildren of the Shtetl: The Jewish Destitute, Disabled, and Demented of Eastern Europe.* Stanford: Stanford University Press, 2020.

Meiring, Kerstin. *Die Christlich-Jüdische Mischehe in Deutschland, 1840–1933.* Hamburg: Dölling und Galitz Verlag, 1998.

Mellman, Katja. "'Detoured Reading': Understanding Literature Through the Eyes of Its Contemporaries (A Case Study on Anti-Semitism in Gustav Freytag's *Soll und Haben*)." In *Distant Readings: Topologies of German Culture in the Long Nineteenth Century* (pp. 301–331). Edited by Matt Erlin and Lynn Tatlock. Rochester, NY: Camden House, 2014.

Melnick, Jeffrey. *A Right to Sing the Blues: African Americans, Jews, and American Popular Song.* Cambridge, MA: Harvard University Press, 1999.

Meyer, Michael A., and Michael Brenner, eds. *German-Jewish History in Modern Times.* Vol. 2: *Emancipation and Acculturation, 1780–1871.* New York: Columbia University Press, 1997.

Miller, Michael Laurence. *Rabbis and Revolution: The Jews of Moravia in the Age of Emancipation.* Stanford: Stanford University Press, 2011.

Milojević, Svetlana. *Die Poesie des Dilettantismus: Zur Rezeption und Wirkung Leopold von Sacher-Masochs.* Frankfurt am Main: Peter Lang, 1998.

Miron, Dan. *The Image of the Shtetl and Other Studies of Modern Jewish Literary Imagination.* Syracuse, NY: Syracuse University Press, 2000.

Mora, Miriam Eve. "From Jewish Boys to American Men: Jewish American Masculinity in the Twentieth Century." PhD dissertation, Wayne State University, 2019.

Mosse, George L. *Confronting the Nation: Jewish and Western Nationalism.* Hanover, NH: University Press of New England for Brandeis University, 1993.

Motley, Clay. "'Dot'sh a' Kin' a man I am!': Abraham Cahan, Masculinity, and Jewish Assimilation in Nineteenth-Century America." *Studies in American Jewish Literature* 30 (2011): 3–15.

Naimark-Goldberg, Natalie. *Jewish Women in Enlightenment Berlin.* Oxford: Littman Library of Jewish Civilization, 2013.

Newman, Zelda. *Kadya Molodowsky: The Life of a Yiddish Woman Writer.* London: Academica Press, 2018.

Norich, Anita. *The Homeless Imagination in the Fiction of Israel Joshua Singer.* Bloomington: Indiana University Press, 1991.

Nowak, Tomasz. "The Technique of Mazurka Dances in the Gentry-Bourgeois and Peasant Environments." In *Between National Identity and a Community of Cultures* (pp. 1–19). Edited by Kamila Stępień-Kutera. Warsaw: Fryderyk Chopin Institute, 2016.

Opalski, Magdalena. *The Jewish Tavern-Keeper and His Tavern in Nineteenth-Century Polish Literature.* Jerusalem: Zalman Shazar Center, 1986.

Palacky, Franz [František Palacký]. *Geschichte von Böhmen*, 3rd ed. Vol. 1. Prague: Gottliebe Haase Söhne, 1864.

Parush, Iris. *Reading Jewish Women: Marginality and Modernization in Nineteenth-Century Eastern European Jewish Society.* Translated by Saadya Sternberg. Waltham, MA: Brandeis University Press, 2004.

Peiss, Kathy. *Cheap Amusements: Working Women and Leisure in New York City, 1880 to 1920.* Philadelphia: Temple University Press, 1986.

Peleg, Yaron. "Heroic Conduct: Homoeroticism and the Creation of Modern, Jewish Masculinities." *Jewish Social Studies* 13, no. 1 (Autumn 2006): 31–58.

Pennino-Baskerville, Mary. "Terpsichore Reviled: Antidance Tracts in Elizabethan England." *Sixteenth Century Journal* 22, no. 3 (1991): 475–494.

Pinsker, Shachar. *A Rich Brew: How Cafés Created Modern Jewish Culture.* New York: New York University Press, 2018.

Pintel-Ginsberg, Idit. "Satan." In *Encyclopedia of Jewish Folklore and Traditions.* Edited by Haya Bar-Itzhak and Raphael Patai. London: Routledge, 2013: http://proxy.lib.ohio-state.edu/login?url=https://search.credoreference.com/content/entry/sharpejft/satan/o?institutionId=4358

Polland, Annie, and Daniel Soyer. *City of Promises: A History of the Jews of New York.*
    Vol 2: *Emerging Metropolis: New York Jews in the Age of Immigration, 1840–1920.*
    Edited by Deborah Dash Moore. New York: New York University Press, 2012.
Pratt, Norma Fain. "Fradel Schtok: Memory and Storytelling in the Early Twenti-
    eth Century." In *Di Froyen: Women and Yiddish, Tribute to the Past, Directions for
    the Future* (pp. 85–88). New York: National Council of Jewish Women, 1997.
Prell, Riv-Ellen. *Fighting to Become Americans: Assimilation and the Trouble Between
    Jewish Women and Jewish Men.* Boston: Beacon Press, 1999.
Pugh, Megan. *America Dancing: From the Cakewalk to the Moonwalk.* New Haven:
    Yale University Press, 2015.
Rabin, Shari. *Jews on the Frontier: Religion and Mobility in Nineteenth-Century
    America.* New York: New York University Press, 2017.
Rhotert, Hans. "Ephraim Moses Kuh." PhD dissertation, Ludwig Maximilian Uni-
    versity Munich, 1927.
Ribak, Gil. *Gentile New York: The Images of Non-Jews Among Jewish Immigrants.* New
    Brunswick, NJ: Rutgers University Press, 2012.
——. "Getting Drunk, Dancing, and Beating Each Other Up: The Images of the
    Gentile Poor and Narratives of Jewish Difference Among the Yiddish Intel-
    ligentsia, 1881–1914." In *Wealth and Poverty in Jewish Tradition* (pp. 203–224).
    Edited by Leonard J. Greenspoon. West Lafayette, IN: Purdue University
    Press, 2015.
Rochelson, Meri-Jane. "Jews, Gender, and Genre in Late-Victorian England: Amy
    Levy's *Reuben Sachs.*" *Women's Studies* 25 (1996): 311–328.
Rose, Allison. *Jewish Women in Fin de Siècle Vienna.* Austin: University of Texas
    Press, 2008.
Roskies, David, G. *A Bridge of Longing: The Lost Art of Yiddish Storytelling.* Cam-
    bridge, MA: Harvard University Press, 1995.
Roskies Diane K., and David G. Roskies. *The Shtetl Book: An Introduction to East
    European Jewish Life and Lore.* [New York]: Ktav Publishing House, 1979.
Rosman, M. J. *The Lords' Jews: Magnate-Jewish Relations in the Polish-Lithuanian
    Commonwealth During the Eighteenth Century.* Cambridge, MA: Harvard Uni-
    versity Press, 1990.
Roth, Cecil. *The Great Synagogue, London 1690–1940.* London: Edward Goldston,
    1950.
Rotundo, E. Anthony. *American Manhood: Transformations in Masculinity from the
    Revolution to the Modern Era.* New York: Basic Books, 1993.
Rubin, Ruth. "Dancing Songs." In *Voices of a People: The Story of Yiddish Folksong*
    (pp. 182–198). New York: Thomas Yoseloff, 1963.
Ruprecht, Lucia. *Dances of the Self in Heinrich von Kleist, E. T.A. Hoffmann, and
    Heinrich Heine.* Burlington, VT: Ashgate, 2006.

——. *Gestural Imaginaries: Dance and Cultural Theory in the Early Twentieth Century.* New York: Oxford University Press, 2019.

Safran, Gabriella. "Dancing with Death and Salvaging Jewish Culture in Austeria and the Dybbuk." *Slavic Review* 59, no. 4 (Winter 2000): 768–769.

——. *Wandering Soul: The Dybbuk's Creator, S. An-sky.* Cambridge, MA: Harvard University Press, 2010.

Said, Edward. *Orientalism.* New York: Random House, 2014.

Salhi, Kamal. "Introduction: The Paradigm of Performing Islam Beyond the Political Rhetoric." In *Music, Culture and Identity in the Muslim World: Performance, Politics and Piety* (pp. 1–14). Edited by Kamal Salhi. London: Routledge, 2014.

Salmen, Walter. ". . . *denn die Fiedel macht das Fest": Jüdische Musikanten und Tänzer vom 13. bis 20. Jahrhundert.* Innsbruck: Edition Helbing, 1991.

——. *Der Tanzmeister: Geschichte und Profile eines Berufes vom 14. bis zum 19. Jahrhundert.* Hildesheim: Georg Olms Verlag, 1997.

Sandrow, Nahma. *Vagabond Stars: A World History of Yiddish Theater,* 2nd ed. Syracuse, NY: Syracuse University Press, 1996.

Schainker, Ellie R. *Confessions of the Shtetl: Converts from Judaism in Imperial Russia, 1817–1906.* Stanford: Stanford University Press, 2017.

Schmitges, Andreas. "Yiddish Dance Songs: The Repertoire and Its Meaning for Yiddish Dance Research." In *Einbahnstraße oder "die heilige Brücke"?: Jüdische Musik und die europäische Musikkultur* (pp. 147–186). Edited by Antonia Klokova and Jascha Nemtsov. Wiesbaden: Harrassowitz Verlag, 2016.

Schnitzer, Claudia. *Höfische Maskeraden: Funktion und Ausstattung von Verkleidungsdivertissements an deutschen Höfen der Frühen Neuzeit.* Tübingen: M. Niemeyer, 1999.

Schumacher-Brunhes, Marie. "The Figure of the Daytsh in Yiddish Literature." In *Jews and Germans in Eastern Europe: Shared and Comparative Histories* (pp. 72–87). Edited by Tobias Grill. Berlin: De Gruyter Oldenbourg, 2018.

Schwadron, Hannah. *The Case of the Sexy Jewess: Dance, Gender, & Jewish Joke-Work in U.S. Pop Culture.* Kettering: Oxford University Press, 2018.

Seelig, Rachel. *Strangers in Berlin: Modern Jewish Literature Between East and West, 1919–1933.* Ann Arbor: University of Michigan Press, 2016.

Seid, Martha. "Wedding Dances." In *The Chasidic Dance* (pp. 13–15). Edited by Fred Berk. [New York]: Union of American Hebrew Congregations, 1975.

Seidman, Naomi. *The Marriage Plot: Or, How Jews Fell in Love with Love and with Literature.* Stanford: Stanford University Press, 2016.

Shamjakin, I. P., et al., eds. *Etnahrafija Bielarusi.* Minsk: "Belaruskaja Saveckaja Encyklapedyja" imia Petrusja Broŭki, 1989.

Shandler, Jeffrey. *Shtetl: A Vernacular Intellectual History.* New Brunswick, NJ: Rutgers University Press, 2014.

Shatzky, Jacob. *Geshikhte fun yidn in Varshe.* Vol. 1: *Fun di onheybn bizn oyfshtand fun 1831.* New York: Bibliotek fun YIVO, 1947.

Shepherd, Naomi. *A Price Below Rubies: Jewish Women as Rebels and Radicals.* Cambridge, MA: Harvard University Press, 1998.

Shmeruk, Chone. *The Esterke Story in Yiddish and Polish Literature: A Case Study in the Mutual Relations of Two Cultural Traditions.* Jerusalem: Zalman Shazar Center, 1985.

——. "Jews and Poles in Yiddish Literature in Poland Between the Two World Wars." *Polin: A Journal of Polish-Jewish Studies* 1 (1986): 176–195.

Shoham, Hizky. *Carnival in Tel Aviv: Purim and the Celebration of Urban Zionism.* Boston: Academic Studies Press, 2014.

Shtern, Yekhiel. *Heyder un besmedresh.* New York: Bibliotek fun YIVO, 1950.

Silberman, Lou H. "The Queen of Sheba in Judaic Tradition." In *Solomon and Sheba* (pp. 65–84). Edited by James B. Pritchard. London: Phaidon, 1974.

Skolnik, Jonathan. *Jewish Pasts, German Fictions: History, Memory, and Minority Culture in Germany, 1824–1955.* Stanford: Stanford University Press, 2014.

Soderland, Gretchen. *Sex Trafficking, Scandal, and the Transformation of Journalism, 1885–1917.* Chicago: University of Chicago Press, 2013.

Solomon, Alisa. *Wonder of Wonders: A Cultural History of Fiddler on the Roof.* New York: Metropolitan Books, 2013.

Sorkin, David. "Emancipation and Assimilation: Two Concepts and Their Application to German-Jewish History." *Leo Baeck Institute Year Book* 35 (1990): 17–33.

Soyer, Daniel. *Jewish Immigrant Associations and American Identity in New York, 1880–1939.* Cambridge, MA: Harvard University Press, 1997.

Sparti, Barbara. "Jewish Dancing-Masters and 'Jewish Dance' in Renaissance Italy: Guglielmo Ebreo and Beyond." In *Seeing Israeli and Jewish Dance* (pp. 235–250). Edited by Judith Brin Ingber. Detroit: Wayne State University Press, 2011.

Spiegel, Nina S. *Embodying Hebrew Culture: Aesthetics, Athletics, and Dance in the Jewish Community of Mandate Palestine.* Detroit: Wayne State University Press, 2011.

Spiel, Hilde. *Fanny von Arnstein: A Daughter of the Enlightenment, 1758–1818.* Translated by Christine Shuttleworth. Berg: New York, 1991.

Spinner, Samuel. "Anecdotal Evidence: Local Color and Ethnography in the 'Shtetl' Stories of Leopold von Sacher-Masoch." *Studia Rosenthaliana* 41 (2009): 65–79.

Stanislawski, Michael. *Zionism and the Fin de Siècle: Cosmopolitanism and Nationalism from Nordau to Jabotinsky.* Berkeley: University of California Press, 2001.

Steiner, Carl. *Karl Emil Franzos, 1848–1904: Emancipator and Assimilationist.* New York: Peter Lang, 1990.

Taubenfeld, Aviva. "*Only an 'L':* Linguistic Borders and the Immigrant Author in Abraham Cahan's *Yekl* and *Yankel der Yankee.*" In *Multilingual*

America: Transnationalism, Ethnicity, and the Languages of American Literature (pp. 144–165). Edited by Werner Sollors. New York: New York University Press, 1998.

Tonko, Linda J. *Dancing Class: Gender, Ethnicity, and Social Divides in American Dance, 1890–1920.* Bloomington: Indiana University Press, 1999.

Tuan, Yi-Fu. *Space and Place: The Perspective of Experience.* Minneapolis: University of Minnesota Press, 2005.

Turner, Victor. *From Ritual to Theatre: The Human Seriousness of Play.* New York: Performing Arts Journal Publications (n.d.) [1982].

Valéry, Paul. "Philosophy of the Dance." *Salmagundi,* no. 33/34 (1976): 65–75: www.jstor.org/stable/40546919

Valman, Nadia. *The Jewess in Nineteenth-Century British Literary Culture.* Cambridge: Cambridge University Press, 2007.

——. "Amy Levy and the Literary Representation of the Jewess." In *Amy Levy: Critical Essays* (pp. 90–109). Edited by Naomi Hetherington and Nadia Valman. Athens: Ohio University Press, 2010.

Vizonsky, Nathan. "Vegn yidishn folks-tants." *Shikage* 1 (1930): 28–29.

——. *Ten Jewish Folk Dances: A Manual for Teachers and Leaders.* Chicago: American Hebrew Theatrical League, 1942.

Wagner, Ann. *Adversaries of the Dance: From the Puritans to the Present.* Urbana: University of Illinois Press, 1997.

Walkowitz, Daniel J. "The Cultural Turn and a New Social History: Folk Dance and the Renovation of Class in Social History." *Journal of Social History* 39, no. 3 (2006): 781–802.

Wallach, Kerry. *Passing Illusions: Jewish Visibility in Weimar Germany.* Ann Arbor: University of Michigan Press, 2017.

Watt, Ian. *The Rise of the Novel: Studies in Defoe, Richardson and Fielding.* London: Chatto & Windus, 1957.

Weiss, Shayna. "A Beach of Their Own: The Creation of the Gender-Segregated Beach in Tel Aviv." *Journal of Israeli History: Politics, Society, Culture* 35, no. 1 (2016): 39–56.

Wiggins, David K., ed. *Sport in America.* Vol. 2: *From Colonial Leisure to Celebrity Figures and Globalization.* Champaign, IL: Human Kinetics, 2010.

Wildmann, Daniel. "Jewish Gymnasts and Their Corporeal Utopias in Imperial Germany." In *Emancipation Through Muscles: Jews and Sports in Europe* (pp. 27–43). Edited by Michael Brenner and Gideon Reuveni. Lincoln: University of Nebraska Press, 2006.

Wilson, Cheryl A. *Literature and Dance in Nineteenth-Century Britain: From Jane Austen to the New Woman.* Cambridge: Cambridge University Press, 2009.

Wirth-Nesher, Hana. "'Shpeaking Plain' and Writing Foreign: Abraham Cahan's *Yekl.*" *Poetics Today* 22, no. 1 (Spring 2001): 41–63.

Wisse, Ruth R. *A Little Love in Big Manhattan.* Cambridge, MA: Harvard University Press, 1988.

Wittemann, M. Theresia. *Draußen vor dem Ghetto: Leopold Kompert und die "Schilderung jüdischen Volkslebens" in Böhmen und Mähren.* Tübingen: Niemeyer, 1998.

Wittler, Kathrin. "Good to Think: (Re)conceptualizing German-Jewish Orientalism." In *Orientalism, Gender, and the Jews. Literary and Artistic Transformations of European National Discourses* (pp. 63–81). Edited by Ulrike Brunotte, Anna-Dorothea Ludewig, and Axel Stähler. Berlin: De Gruyter, 2015.

Wobick-Segev, Sarah. *Homes Away from Home: Jewish Belonging in Twentieth-Century Paris, Berlin, and St. Petersburg.* Stanford: Stanford University Press, 2018.

Wodenegg, Andrea. *Das Bild der Juden Osteuropas: Ein Beitrag zur komparatistischen Imagologie an Textbeispielen von Karl Emil Franzos und Leopold von Sacher-Masoch.* Frankfurt am Main: Peter Lang, 1987.

Wolitz, Seth L. "The Americanization of Tevye or Boarding the Jewish 'Mayflower.'" *American Quarterly* 40, no. 4 (1988): 514–536.

Wurst, Karin. *Fabricating Pleasure: Fashion, Entertainment, and Cultural Consumption in Germany, 1780—1830.* Detroit: Wayne State University Press. 2005.

Zaban, Yahil. "'Folded White Napkins': The Etiquette Discourse in Haskalah Literature." *Prooftexts: A Journal of Jewish Literary History* 35, no. 2–3 (Spring–Fall 2015): 291–312.

Zadoff, Miriam. *Next Year in Marienbad: The Lost Worlds of Jewish Spa Culture.* Translated by William Templer. Philadelphia: University of Pennsylvania Press, 2013.

Zborowski, Mark, and Elizabeth Herzog. *Life Is with People: The Culture of the Shtetl.* New York: Schocken Books, 1995.

Index

224n1, 229n70; leisure culture, 148–151, 156, 171. *See also* American dances; American Yiddish writers; New York
Unorthodox, 232n15
Unzer gloybn (Our Faith; Asch), 223n59
Urban spaces, 3, 32–33, 34–36, 121. *See also* New York

Valéry, Paul, 13
Venus im Pelz (*Venus in Furs*; Sacher-Masoch), 134
Das Vermächtnis Kains (The Heritage of Cain; Sacher-Masoch), 130
Vienna: balls, 3, 29, 93–94, 109 (fig.), 199n61; cartoons, 109 (fig.), 203n20; characters from, 32; regulations on Jewish dance in, 24
Vilna: radical Jewish youth, 3, 34–35; Vilna Gaon, 146
Visual arts, 129, 131, 134, 137
Vizonsky, Nathan, 141, 194n45
Voss, Rudolph, 50

Waldau, Albert, 76
Waltz, 2–3, 13, 17, 26, 34, 36, 47–48, 70, 93–94, 108–109, 115, 122, 136, 140, 156–159, 161, 196nn7–8, 202n15, 203n25, 226n26
Wandrei, Etta Freilich, 200n70
Warsaw: idea of in literature, 35, 57, 141–142, 178; Jewish balls, 3, 112; Jewish community, 27; Jewish writers in, 3, 4 (fig.), 162. *See also* Poland
Waszyński, Michał, *Der dibek* (*The Dybbuk*), 124
Weber, Max, 5
Wechsberg, Joseph, 44
Wecker, Helen, *The Golem and the Jinni*, 180, 182
Wedding dancing: with bride, 22, 25–26, 29, 130–131, 136–137; broygez tants, 123, 140–141, 220n8; in eastern Europe, 25, 34, 35, 123, 200n70; in fantasy novels, 181; folk dances,

67, 71–72; forbidden partners, 128; forced, 124–125; government regulations, 24; learning to dance, 55, 56; mitsve tants, 23, 25, 124, 223n59; mixed-sex, in fiction, 30–32, 36–37, 121–122, 125–127, 139, 142–144, 169; mixed-sex dancing stopped by rabbis, 3, 34, 184; musicians, 35, 36, 128, 143–144; peasant dancing, 71–72, 77, 78–79; pleasing bride as objective, 14, 22, 123–124, 146; religious prohibition of mixed-sex dancing, 22, 30–32, 123, 197n23; separate-sex, 30, 31 (fig.), 37–38, 56, 123, 124, 178–179, 197n23, 198n49
Weddings: emotions, 123–124; government regulations, 24; guests, 123, 184; Orthodox, 178–179; rituals, 123, 124, 127; "shvartse khasene" (cholera wedding), 127. *See also* Marriage
Der Weg des jungen Hermann Kahn (The Path of Young Hermann Kahn; Krämer), 32, 95, 113–118, 119, 217n48, 218n68
Weil, Yedidia, 26
Weiss, Isaac Jacob, 232–233n16
Wengeroff, Pauline, 56, 123–124
Werther der Jude (Werther the Jew; Jacobowski), 63
Wesner, Franz, 50
"Wie Slobe ihre Schwester verheiratet" ("How Slobe Gets Her Sister Married"; Sacher-Masoch), 30, 31 (fig.)
Willis, 135–137, 204n37
Winckelmann, Johann, 80
Women: African American, 231n94; agency, 6, 52, 102, 106, 113, 118, 125–126, 169; bodies, 47, 48, 49, 52; dance lessons for girls, 45, 55–56, 60, 202n6; dance repertoire for, 26, 45, 198n49; dance masters, 46, 202n19; dancing skills, 56, 62–63; education, 5, 53, 56,

60, 81, 101; gender roles for Jewish, 5, 6, 43, 44–45, 53, 59–60, 102, 125, 219n71; health risks of dancing, 48; literary stereotypes of Jewish, 47, 49, 53–55, 63, 96, 107, 137; social mobility, 49, 52; social positions, 52, 94, 106, 111; tavern workers, 69, 70–71, 81, 144; Zionist movement and, 5, 113, 115–118, 200n70, 219n71. *See also* Gender relations; Separate-sex dancing
World War II refugees, 148, 162–170

Yakhnuk, Khayim-Avrom, *Tants-klassin, oder di frehlikhe yugend: A kritishe ertsehlung fun yudishen lebin* (Dance Classes, or Happy Youth: A Critical Tale of Jewish Life), 59–60
Yankl Boyle (Kobrin), 66, 73, 83–91, 92, 88 (fig.), 214n94
Yankl der Shmid (Yankl the Blacksmith; Pinski), 54, 70
Yekl: A Tale of the New York Ghetto (Cahan), 149, 155–162, 171–172, 193n30, 195n55
Yezierska, Anzia, *Bread Givers*, 148–149, 205n53
Yiddish literature: audiences, 17, 39, 40; as category, 7–8; compared to German Jewish literature, 7, 38–40; dance lessons, 55, 56–60; female characters, 54; male characters, 47, 85–86, 140; marriage plots, 52, 58–59; mixed-sex dancing in, 7, 16–17, 33–36, 39, 40, 54; shtetl tales, 9; tavernkeepers, 68–69, 71–73; tavernkeepers' chil-

dren, 72–73, 83–91; wedding scenes, 36–37, 121–122, 124, 128, 142–145, 219–220n6, 223n59. *See also* American Yiddish writers
Yiddish theater: dance scenes, 85–86; cartoon, 88 (fig.); *Yankl der Shmid* (Yankl the Blacksmith; Pinski), 54, 70; *Yankl Boyle* (Kobrin), 84–86, 91; *Reb Henoch, oder: Woß tut me damit* (Reb Henoch, or, What Can Be Done with It?; Euchel), 94; *Der dibek* (*The Dybbuk*; An-sky), 124; *Die Hochzeit zu Grobsdorf* (The Wedding in Grobsdorf; Rozenthal), 219–220n6; *Unzer gloybn* (Our Faith; Asch), 223n59; *A hoyz oyf grend strit* (A House on Grand Street; Molodovsky), 230n81
Yidn fun a gants yor (*Everyday Jews*; Perle), 35–36
Di Yunge (the Young Ones), 139

Zangwill, Israel, *Children of the Ghetto: A Study of a Peculiar People*, 108–110; *The Melting Pot*, 227n28
Zilberg, Rivke, *see* Molodovsky, Kadya
Zionists: balls, 9, 113–118; Maccabees as models, 80; masculinity, 50, 85–86; New Jew, 50, 85; women, 5, 113, 115–118, 200n70, 219n71
Zunser, Miriam Shomer, 123, 220n9
Zunz, Leopold, 22
Zwei Schwestern (Two Sisters; Meyer), 96
Zweig, Stefan, 204–205n48

Stanford Studies in Jewish History and Culture
David Biale and Sarah Abrevaya Stein, Editors

This series features novel approaches to examining the Jewish past in the form of innovative work that brings the field into productive dialogue with the newest scholarly concepts and methods. Open to a range of disiplinary and interdisciplinary approaches from history to cultural studies, this series publishes exceptional scholarship balanced by an accessible tone, illustrating histories of difference and addressing issues of current urgency. Books in this list push the boundaries of Jewish Studies and speak compellingly to a wide audience of scholars and students.

For a complete listing of titles in this series, visit the Stanford University Press website, www.sup.org.